Practical Programming
for
Strength Training

3rd Edition

Practical Programming
for Strength Training

Mark Rippetoe & Andy Baker
with Stef Bradford

 The Aasgaard Company
Wichita Falls, Texas

Indexing & Proof – Mary Boudreau Conover
Layout & Proof – Stef Bradford

24 23 22   9 10 11 12

ISBN-13: 978-0-9825227-5-2 (paper)
ISBN-13: 978-0-9825227-6-9 (electronic)
ISBN-10: 0-98252275-4 (paper)
ISBN-10: 0-98252276-2 (electronic)

Printed in the United States of America
KC Book Manufacturing, North Kansas City, MO

The Aasgaard Company
3118 Buchanan St, Wichita Falls, TX 76308, USA
www.aasgaardco.com
www.startingstrength.com

Contents

Preface to the Third Edition

Every time a new edition of *Practical Programming* is released, greater clarity is the objective. The idea that novices, intermediates, and advanced lifters require different programming was essentially heresy when I submitted it to the *Strength and Conditioning Journal* ten years ago. The piece was rejected by two separate groups of reviewers who insisted that undulating periodization applied to everyone, and that by claiming it did not apply to novices I demonstrated a complete lack of understanding of the Organizing Principles of Science. Some progress has been made since then, and I hope this edition further clarifies the idea that human adaptation follows the same trajectory that all progressive phenomena display on the way to their limit. The book has sold more than 90,000 copies and helped more people get stronger than anything else in print except *Starting Strength: Basic Barbell Training*.

The first two editions were intended as basic diagrams for designing the reader's own programs – an outline of the basic principles of stress/recovery/adaptation. The book was designed as a template for the development of programs based on the way people of different levels of training advancement respond to stress. As it turns out, people want details – more examples of the specific programs in use for lots of different lifters – so here they are.

Stef Bradford PhD is actually the brains and talent behind the upgrade of this material. You'd think far less of my abilities if you knew how big a part of what I do is actually her idea. Our little secret, okay?

As for the detailed programs we've added, Andy Baker is as good at writing them as anybody I know, especially including me. When we decided to flesh out the book, he was my first choice. He has a feel for the numbers and for realistic progressions, and most of these detailed examples are his babies. If you can get him to help you with your training, you should.

Matt Reynolds was my other first choice. Another exceptionally talented programming consultant, Matt is busy with several projects but took the time to provide us with an advanced program in Chapter 8. If Andy's busy, call Matt. Or start with Matt if you want to.

Jordan Feigenbaum MD and Jonathon Sullivan MD PhD reviewed several parts of the manuscript for us. Jordan made dozens of valuable suggestions that improved the accuracy and clarity of the first five chapters, and Sully is an exceptionally intelligent and experienced resource for the nuances of human interaction with life and its complications. I count on both of these guys when I'm in over my head.

The experience we've acquired over the last 4 years has been facilitated by several important members of the staff of our seminar program. Tom Campitelli (also our staff photographer), Michael Wolf, Steve Hill, Jordan Feigenbaum, Matt Reynolds, Paul Horn, and several others just getting started have created the best possible business environment, where we all learn from each other. Without them, this new edition would not have been possible.

As usual, Mary Conover stopped what she was doing and prepared the index, making this book a much more valuable resource that it would otherwise have been.

My thanks also to you, the readers of our books and participants on the boards. Your valuable feedback has spurred the development of this edition of *PPST*.

—Rip

Wichita Falls, Texas
November 2013

1
Introduction

Welcome to the third edition of Practical Programming for Strength Training. This edition will take a slightly different approach to introducing the concept of strength training by first detailing what it is *not*. Three terms are often used to describe what may or may not happen in the gym: "Physical Activity," "Exercise," and "Training." This book is concerned with the last of these three, so we'd better define the first two now, so that Training will be definable separately and at length later.

Physical activity is what The American Heart Association wants you to get some of each week. "Physical activity is anything that makes you move your body and burn calories" is the quote from their website regarding what they consider to be necessary for continued physical existence. Essentially, not sitting or lying down is physical activity. We are not particularly concerned with this, because even elderly people can take a more productive approach to their physical existence than mere movement for an arbitrarily recommended period of time.

Physical fitness is a related concept. Defined by Kilgore and Rippetoe in 2006 in the *Journal of Exercise Physiology Online* [9(1):1–10]:

> *Possession of adequate levels of strength, endurance, and mobility to provide for successful participation in occupational effort, recreational pursuits, familial obligation, and that is consistent with a functional phenotypic expression of the human genotype.*

This definition is certainly an improvement upon previous attempts to quantify the concept, in that it is both a framework that remains relevant throughout a lifespan, and a definition based on evolutionary reasoning, i.e. why it is necessary to be fit from a genetic standpoint. The optimum expression of the human genotype is, by this definition, a fit human, and this is satisfying at many levels.

We, however, refuse to stop at this level, because we are athletes. We seek to optimize the expression of "physical fitness" through means more productive than merely not sitting down, because we are competitive – perhaps just with ourselves, but competitive nonetheless. We seek to escalate our physical capacities by means that the AHA would possibly deem excessive, and would certainly not regard as necessary for their purposes, which consist primarily of not dying from a cardiac event.

To this end, "Exercise" and "Training" are separate concepts worthy of definition and examination. The terms are often used interchangeably, and this is incorrect. The term "workout" is used in both exercise and training to denote a scheduled event that produces a physical stress (we don't usually refer to pushing the car when it runs out of gas as a "workout," although it may produce the same stress). Exercise and Training both utilize workouts, but the concepts are profoundly different.

Exercise is physical activity performed for the effect it produces *today* – right now. Each workout is performed for the purpose of producing a stress that satisfies the immediate needs of the exerciser: burning some calories, getting hot, sweaty, and out of breath, pumping up the biceps, stretching – basically just punching the physical clock. Exercise is physical activity done for its own sake, either during the workout or immediately after it's through. Exercise may well involve doing exactly the same thing every time you do it, as long as it accomplishes the task of making you feel like to want to feel *today*.

But athletes have a definite **performance** goal in mind – a point in time when their abilities will be displayed in a competitive venue, judged according to the rules of the sport, and compared against the performances of other athletes. The *performance* is the athlete's objective, the event that makes preparation both necessary and desirable. Mere exercising cannot effectively prepare an athlete for a performance, because improvement requires planning.

This improvement is dependent upon two separate processes with which the athlete must engage – Training and Practice. First, **training** is physical activity performed for purposes of satisfying a long-term performance goal, and is therefore about the *process* instead of the *constituent workouts of* the process. The *training* process results in metabolic and architectural changes that, over a period of time, yields a specific type of *accumulated physiological adaptation* the athlete must have for an improved performance. The physiological adaptation can be endurance, strength, or a combination of the two. One of the most important aspects of effective training is that this accumulated physiological adaptation can be *quantified* – measured with an objective metric and compared to the pre-adapted baseline and evaluated for effectiveness and efficiency. Quantification of these adaptations is an inherent part of any training program, with subsequent workouts assigned on the basis of the objective results of previous workouts.

The basis of training is the stress/recovery/adaptation cycle, the basic biology that underpins all organisms' relationship to their environments. If the training stress of a series of workouts does not increase progressively, either in exposure to the weight being lifted, the distance being covered, or the time spent under the stress load, then adaptation cannot take place, the activity cannot yield a quantifiable physiological adaptation, and the program is not *training*.

The second process is **practice**, the repetitive execution of movement patterns used in a performance that are dependent on *accuracy*, the ability to execute a movement pattern as close to the ideal model of the movement as possible, and *precision*, the ability to execute repeated attempts at the movement pattern with as little deviation between each attempt as possible. Practice yields *skill*, necessary for all sports in which accuracy and precision are components of the performance. Throwing a baseball at the catcher's mitt is a *skill* that must be practiced, many thousands of times over many years. Accuracy in this context would be hitting the point on the mitt the catcher wants the ball, and precision is doing this 35 times in an inning.

Training and practice differ in obvious ways. *Training* seeks to improve physical parameters that are not dependent on the specific movement patterns in which they will be applied. The endurance adaptation necessary for the successful performance of a 10K can also be applied to a 3-mile run, or, to some extent, to a century ride. The strength adaptation produced by a progressive barbell strength program is applicable in every circumstance in which force production is a factor, independent of the specific nature of any one performance. A 500-pound deadlifter/200-pound overhead presser can clean more than a 200-pound deadlifter/75-pound presser, he can hit you harder on the field, and he can throw both the shot and the baseball harder, and for more repetitions.

Skill is exquisitely dependent on the specific nature of the performance being practiced for. A MLB-regulation Rawlings baseball weighs between 5 and 5.25 ounces (141.75–148.83 g) and is between 9.00 and 9.25 inches in circumference. A bat is no more than 2.75 inches (70 mm) in diameter and no more than 42 inches (1.100 m) long, the weight thus being dependent on its composition. Pitching practice therefore means thousands of reps with a regulation baseball of this weight and size, and batting practice is the same. Throwing a heavy ball or swinging a heavy bat in "training" is a different mechanical task from a *performance*. Taken to excess, it screws up performance, because it is not *practice* – it is not specific to the performance. And in fact, when it is used it is applied sparingly for short periods of time at limited volumes, *in a misguided attempt to substitute for strength training*. It is not heavy enough to make you stronger, it cannot be programmed in a way that constitutes training, and it is not sufficiently identical to any performance in sports to constitute practice.

Most people are not competitive athletes, do not see themselves as competitive athletes, and have no definable objective other than losing some weight and being "in shape," which is similar to being physically fit without all the discussion of phenotypes and genetics. So most people are perfectly satisfied with exercising. The fitness industry knows this, and is more than willing to accommodate them. Machine-based workouts that lack the balance and systemic loading components of barbell training are primarily used for exercise. So are randomized programs like P90X, CrossFit, or anything available on DVD that promises to keep you and your muscles "confused." Modern health clubs are designed exclusively for exercising, training being far less profitable. The standard industry model is 55% of the floor space devoted to "cardio" equipment, on which repetitive motions of various types can be performed while watching television. The remaining 45% of the floor space is dominated by exercise machines designed primarily for the convenience of the gym staff – they are easy to use, easy to teach the use of, and easy to vacuum around.

Many clubs have no free weights other than dumbbells, and have no intention of teaching you to do exercises that require them. They are sales organizations, not exercise facilities, and if the people who buy the memberships don't come to the gym more than 3 times, that's just fine. Their business model is predicated on the ability to hire college students who are majoring in PE (exercise physiology, biomechanics, or whatever the department calls it at your school) for a little over minimum wage – kids who lack any experience in teaching barbell movements and who have not read this book. The business model is dependent on a fast turnover on the exercise floor, especially during peak usage times, and – as the floor plan suggests – the primary use of cardio equipment by the members, those of whom actually use the club. The idea is that the members will come in and play around on the machines for 20 minutes, climb on an exercise bike or treadmill for 30 minutes while they watch TV, hit the showers, and get the hell out of there. The staff's job is to make this happen efficiently. Exercise is therefore facilitated, while training is almost impossible.

At this point in time, the industry is in the process of changing rapidly, and hopefully for the better. The standard industry model of 55% "cardio" and 45% machines is giving way to "Functional Training" facilities that emphasize more intense exercise using barbell movements, whole-body calisthenic-type exercises, and running combined into strenuous workouts that actually accomplish the goal of providing sufficient stress to cause an adaptation. This is in stark contrast to the even-faster-growing planetary "fitness" franchises that quite literally *prohibit* exercise of sufficient intensity to make any difference, or certainly anything hard enough to cause you to make any noise. The down-side to many functional training facilities is the poorly-prepared staff, composed largely of highly-motivated young people who lack the experience and the expertise to ensure that correct technique keeps their members from getting injured. But as hard as a WOD at a CrossFit "box" might be, it still isn't training.

Training takes time, instruction, and dedication to the goal you're training for. It requires planning, input from people familiar with the process and what it takes to accomplish the process, and a willingness to grasp the fact that each workout is of value primarily for its place in the line of events that generates the final accomplishment.

This does not mean that each workout is not an enjoyable event, or that each small improvement that marks the successful workout does not satisfy the trainee's desire for the feeling of accomplishment that all athletes want. It does mean that for the person who trains, each piece of the puzzle fits into a larger picture that most people who merely exercise never see assembled, and probably don't even know about.

Strength Training

The topic of this book is training, not exercise, and in particular *strength training*. Successful athletes in all sports must train, and training for distance running is certainly approached with the same philosophy we employ to get strong: start where the athlete is today, and plan for improvement from there. We utilize primarily anaerobic resistance exercises, they utilize primarily aerobic endurance exercises. But training means the same thing for both of us – we don't wander into the weight room and play with the barbells any more than they wander onto the track and skip around until they get bored. Training means planning, and planning requires an understanding of what we're going to attempt to change about the athlete's physical capacity.

Strength training is a program that increases the athlete's ability to produce muscular force against an external resistance. It properly follows a logical progression, starting from the athlete's current strength level and moving in the direction of increased strength. Such a progression requires that two things happen.

First, a correct assessment of the athlete's current strength level is necessary if we are to make plans to increase it from there. This assessment can and properly should occur during the coaching of the lifts the athlete will be using in the program, since the lifts must be correctly instructed and perfected anyway. As the lifts are learned, weight can be added, since we must *learn* to lift heavier weights if we are to get stronger. Dedicating a separate assessment event at the inception of the program wastes time, and, more importantly, fails to recognize that the testing event itself constitutes a stress that causes adaptation. If the test is sufficiently intense to accurately assess current physical capacity, the resultant adaptation to the stress of the test changes the capacity of the test subject, thus rendering the data inaccurate for any time point subsequent to the test. It is much more efficient to use the first instruction day for the lifts to both teach the material *and* assess the capacity of the trainee. Since the program starts at this point and goes up from there for virtually all novice trainees, the second workout will build on the stopping point of the first workout, and the purposes of both instruction and assessment will have been served.

Second, a program must be constructed that most efficiently serves the purpose of creating a strength increase for the athlete. As we shall see, this entails the application of some basic training principles that are derived from the concept of stress/recovery/adaptation, and a correct assessment of where the athlete is with respect to his potential for physical adaptation.

Stress is an event that produces a significant change in the environment of an organism, sufficient to disrupt the physiological state that exists within an organism in equilibrium with its current environmental conditions. Stress can be a hard workout, a sunburn, a bear mauling, or 3 months of bed rest. **Adaptation** to the stress event is the organism's modification of its physiology to compensate for the new environmental conditions as it **recovers** from the stress (if it can – a suntan is easy, bears can be a problem). Adaptation to the stress is the organism's way of surviving in an environment that subjects organisms to a variety of changing conditions. Indeed, the ability to adapt to stress is one of the hallmarks of life.

The stress in our scenario is produced by the careful use of the barbell, which can create the conditions under which the adaptation is an increased ability to produce force with our muscles. But like any other organism subjected to repeated stress, the prior stresses produce an accumulation of adaptations that fundamentally change the organism. You are obviously not the same physical creature now that you were when you were born, and this is the result of both normal growth and the stresses to which you have been subjected during that time.

In our training scenario, this physical stress history has a bearing on what type of stress we can continue to apply, because your current state of adaptation constitutes a portion of your ultimate potential to adapt to stress. Each individual has a limit to his ability to adapt to stress, both acute stress in an immediate sense and chronic stress over the course of time. This limit is determined by genetic endowment as well as the physical circumstances in which the athlete exists, and ultimately controls the potential of the individual for athletic performance. In fact, all human potential is limited by processes that function this way, and that is why exceptional people in every field of endeavor are not the norm. These concepts are summarized in Figure 1-1.

The extent of an individual's approach to this limit determines how much potential improvement remains to be developed. An untrained 17-year-old kid and an advanced 38-year-old competitive lifter are opposite ends of a spectrum of the exploitation of physical potential. The kid has not developed any of his potential strength, and the advanced lifter is already very strong, having devoted 20 years to trying to get stronger. The kid has essentially all of his potential in front of him, while the lifter has developed essentially all of his potential to the best of his ability. The kid gets stronger quite easily and quite quickly, while the already-strong lifter works a complicated program for months at a time to develop just a tiny bit more strength, since he's already very strong. It's easier to get stronger if you're not already very strong. In fact, the kid gets stronger every workout than the advanced lifter does every six months. Depending on your perspective, this is either tragic or marvelous.

The spectrum of human performance is an example of the Principle of Diminishing Returns, commonly observable in countless examples from nature and human experience. Approaching the speed of light, learning to play the piano, and building a faster car are examples of things that start off easy and eventually become so difficult and expensive in terms of energy, time, or money that approaching their limit is essentially impossible. And were it not the case that human performance displays this same progression – easy at first, difficult at last – no one would ever have put 200 pounds on his squat in a year, and world records would always be broken at every competition.

And as blatantly obvious as this is, the norm in exercise programming is to ignore it. We are taught to test a novice for his 1-rep maximum capacity on the various exercises to be used, none of which he really knows how to do, none of which he can do correctly, and therefore none of which he can perform well enough that a test for max effort would actually mean anything. Then, bad data in hand, the Fitness Professional gives him a program that is more suitable for our advanced lifter, a program that has our novice working at submaximum loads most of the time, and adding weight on a predetermined, sometimes *monthly* schedule. This, instead of a schedule that accurately reflects his actual capacity for rapid adaptation, given that he hasn't ever rapidly adapted before and is therefore capable of doing so.

Worse even than this, progress over time may not be addressed in any meaningful way at all. If the topic is addressed, the advice is to wait until the weight you're lifting for 8–12 reps and 4–5 sets gets easy, and then go up a little. No attempt is made to actually *drive* progress, but if it happens to occur, that's probably okay, as long as you don't hurt yourself.

This is the norm, the conventional wisdom of exercise prescription. Some version of it is accepted as correct and proper by all the certifying bodies that deal with exercise prescription – the ACSM, NSCA, IDEA, ACE, AFAA, NETA, ASFA (Don't Pay Unless You Pass!), the YMCA, and The Cooper Clinic – because it is *evidence-based*, meaning that's what the peer-reviewed exercise science literature says you should do.

But exercise is not training, so our approach to the problem of planning to make people stronger is markedly different from that of the organizations primarily concerned with preparing personal trainers and exercise class instructors.

A Theoretical Approach

Our approach to training takes into consideration the fact that every individual trainee must be programmed with respect to where they are along the curves illustrated in Figure 1-1. In this book, the terms "novice," "intermediate," and "advanced," describe the trainee with respect to the time it takes for recovery from a homeostatic disruption induced by training. *These terms are not used to describe a trainee's strength or absolute athletic ability.* These terms may in fact be applied differently to athletes in different sports, but our use of the terms here is specific to the model illustrated in Figure 1-1.

Because a novice has never trained with weights before in a way programmed to produce a regular incremental strength increase, he lifts weights that are light relative to his ultimate physical potential for strength and power development. This may be the case despite the fact that he's had a gym membership for years, attending faithfully every week but failing to *train*. Essentially, the novice can recover from a single training session in a period of 48 to 72 hours. He can train "heavy" on Monday and be ready to go "heavy" again on Wednesday. These trainees are quite far away from their physical potential, and therefore lack the strength and the neural efficiency to generate a stress heavy enough to impede rapid recovery. For them, "heavy" is not really heavy. At the same time that strength and power are improving, recovery ability is improving too. Recovery processes are as trainable as any other physical parameter, and this is an extremely significant factor in training progress. But it is important to remember that recovery processes can always be exceeded by an inappropriate and excessive application of training stress. Recovery must occur before progress can be made.

Simply put, a **novice**, as we use the term here, *is a trainee for whom the stress applied during a single workout and the recovery from that single stress is sufficient to cause an adaptation by the next workout.* This allows the novice to add weight to his work sets every workout throughout the duration of the novice phase, thus accumulating a rapid increase in strength over a relatively short period of time. The novice phase is the period in the athlete's training history where the most rapid improvement in strength and ability can take place, if it is managed correctly by someone who understands the process and its potential.

The end of the novice phase is marked by a performance plateau, typically occurring sometime between the third and ninth month of training, with variations due to individual differences in genetic endowment and the correct management of the environmental factors that affect recovery. Programming for the novice is essentially the linear progression model that is defined specifically for weight training in our book *Starting Strength: Basic Barbell Training, 3rd Edition* (Aasgaard, 2011).

It is important to understand that the novice is adapted to inactivity (as it relates to weight training) and therefore can make progress even with training programs that are not specific to the task of increasing strength on the basic barbell exercises. For example, doing sets of 20 reps would also increase a

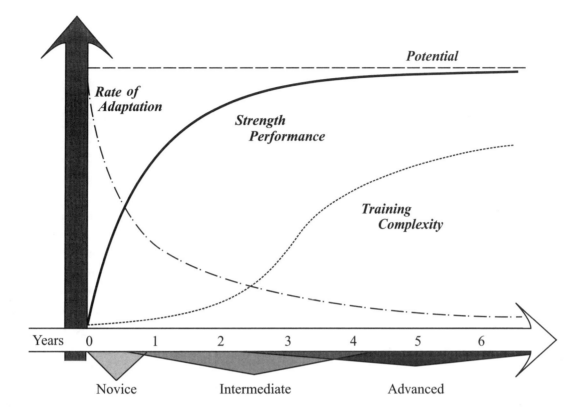

Figure 1-1. The generalized relationship between performance improvement and training complexity relative to time. Note that the rate of adaptation to training slows over a training career.

novice's absolute strength for a one-repetition lift. A previously sedentary beginner can even improve his 1RM (one-repetition maximum) squat by riding a bike. This would not be the case with intermediate or advanced trainees, where progress in strength, power, or mass is absolutely linked to appropriate application of specific training programs.

Novices accomplish two things with every workout: they "test" their strength with a new, higher workload, and the test loads the body to become stronger for the next workout. The act of moving 10 more pounds for the prescribed sets and reps both confirms that the previous workout was a success at improving the novice's strength, and causes his body to adapt and become stronger for the next workout. For the vast majority of lifters, this novice phase, when properly managed, will see the most rapid and productive gains in strength of an entire career under the bar.

The novice phase draws to a close when the easy gains have been made, and it becomes increasingly difficult to continue making progress from one workout to the next. Smaller jumps in weight will have been utilized and exhausted, and progress stalls despite every effort at managing recovery.

The **intermediate** lifter has a different set of problems to solve. As the intermediate lifter begins to handle training loads closer to his physical potential, his recovery ability is affected differently by the stress. Recovery requires a longer period of time – a period that normally encompasses the time during which multiple workouts will occur. From a practical standpoint, this time frame is most efficiently managed using a weekly schedule. Essentially, the intermediate lifter has developed the ability to apply a stress to the system that requires a longer period of time for recovery, while at the same time the stress *required* for a disruption of homeostasis has begun to exceed the capacity for recovery within that period of time it previously took, 48–72 hours. To allow for both sufficient stress and sufficient recovery, then, the training load must be varied over a longer period of time, and the week makes a convenient period in which to organize training. The actual time required may be shorter than a week at first – perhaps 5 days – and may grow to 8–9 days towards the end of the intermediate stages of training. The critical factor is the distribution of the increased workload, which allows enough stress to be applied in a pattern that facilitates recovery. The key to successful training in this stage of development is to balance these two important and opposing phenomena – the increased need for stress and the corresponding requisite increase in recovery time. The simple weekly organization of training loads facilitates recovery following one or more heavier training bouts within a single period of loading, and works well within the social framework of the calendar.

Intermediate trainees benefit from exposure to more exercises than novices. These athletes are developing their skills with new movement patterns, and as this happens they are developing their ability to *acquire* new skills. It is during this period that trainees actually become athletes, choosing a sport and making decisions that affect the rest of their competitive careers. These decisions are more effectively made if they are based on a broad exposure to a wide variety of training and competition options.

The end of the intermediate phase of training is marked by a performance plateau following a series of progressively more difficult weekly training organizations. This can occur in as little as two years or in as many as four or more, depending on individual tolerances and adherence to year-round progressive training. It is likely that 75% or more of all trainees will not require programming complexity beyond the intermediate level – remember, the amount of weight lifted or years of training do not classify a trainee. Virtually all strength training for athletes not competing in the barbell sports can be accomplished with this model. These athletes will not exclusively train in the weight room; they will focus much of their training on their primary competitive sport. This effectively extends the duration of this stage in the trainee's development to the extent that even very accomplished athletes will probably never exhaust the benefits of intermediate-level strength programming.

Advanced trainees in the barbell sports work relatively close to their ultimate physical potentials. This small subset of the training population is comprised almost exclusively of competitors in the sports of powerlifting and Olympic weightlifting, since this level of time and dedication cannot generally be demonstrated by casual trainees. The work tolerance of the advanced lifter is quite high, given that the ability of an athlete to recover from training is itself trainable. However, the training loads that the advanced athlete must handle in order to produce an adaptation are also quite high, since the adaptations that brought the athlete to the advanced stage have already occurred. This level of training volume and intensity is very taxing and requires longer periods of recovery than do intermediate training loads. Both the loading and the recovery parameters must be applied in more complex and variable ways and over longer periods of time. When combined, the loading and recovery periods required for successful progress range in duration from a month to several months. For example, we may apply a single week of very heavy training to induce a homeostatic disruption. That week of training may require three or more weeks of work at lighter loadings for complete recovery and adaptation to occur. The average slope of the improvement curve here is very shallow (Figure 1-1), closely approaching maximum physical potential at a very slow rate, and rather large amounts of training effort will be expended for rather small amounts of improvement. For this reason too, the number of exercises advanced trainees use is typically lower than for intermediates; they do not require exposure to new movement patterns and stress types, since they have already specialized and adapted to those that are specific to their particular sport.

Complex manipulation of training parameters is appropriate for use with advanced lifters. The majority of trainees will never attain the level of development that makes advanced periodization necessary, since most trainees voluntarily terminate their competitive careers before the advanced stage is reached.

An **elite** athlete is one who performs at an "elite" level by the standards of the sport in which he competes. By this definition, the "elite" designation could actually be applied to an intermediate lifter performing at the national/international level. There occasionally exist a few athletes so talented and genetically endowed that this situation occurs, and we have all seen freaks of this nature rise rapidly within a sport, seemingly without even paying the dues that most of his peers have paid. The elite athlete is usually in a special subset of the advanced category. Elite athletes are the genetically gifted few who also happen to be motivated to achieve success despite the enormous physical and social costs. They have stayed in their sport by virtue of their success, and have dedicated themselves to training at this level because their training investment has been returned.

Previous training has brought the athlete very close to his ultimate performance potential, and additional progress requires much greater program complexity to scratch out any small improvements that might still remain unrealized. These athletes must be exposed to training programs that are very complex – highly variable in terms of stress, although probably simple in terms of exercise selection – forcing the already adapted athlete closer to the ultimate level of performance. At this point the program may be considered in terms of several months, a year, or even an Olympic quadrennium. Any approach to the training of an athlete of this caliber is a highly individualized matter and is beyond the scope of this text. Far fewer than 0.1% of all trainees regardless of training history will ever reach this level.

Unlike beginners or intermediates, advanced trainees need large amounts of intense work to disrupt homeostasis and force adaptation. This means that the stress required for progress will creep nearer and nearer the maximum tolerable workload the body can produce and then recover from. An advanced athlete who is doing ten sets of squats and making progress may not make any progress with nine sets and may *"overtrain"* by doing eleven. The window for progress is extremely small.

But if workload is not increased, then neither performance nor recovery processes will improve, since no disruption of homeostasis is forcing them to do so. The manner in which increases in training load are applied is determined by the level of training advancement, as illustrated in Figure 1-1. The ability of a novice to adapt to training differs enough from that of the intermediate and advanced trainee that it is imperative that each level of training advancement be programmed according to the physiological parameters that characterize each stage of development. The most effective way to waste a lot of time in the weight room is to program a novice with an advanced lifter's routine.

Problems?

If this is so blatantly obvious, why do the certifying organizations not recognize this pattern and adjust their dogma accordingly? Could it be that the academic institutions in charge of the conventional wisdom about exercise have not studied this blatantly obvious pattern, and therefore it has not been published in the peer-reviewed journals that are the keepers of the conventional wisdom?

Let's frame the question in a better way: Why do four-year colleges and universities, whose job it is to graduate students with bachelor's degrees in PE and who at the same time must support a faculty of masters degree candidates and PhD professors, fail to study a phenomenon that necessarily takes place over a time frame of many years within a highly motivated group of competitive athletes that will not be accessible to The Department for use as study subjects and who will not alter their training to suit the needs of a study that compares different training methods over time?

The answer is obvious: They can't. Studies that might effectively investigate and compare actual training methods for athletes cannot be designed and conducted within the limitations of the university system of study. The Department has access to undergraduate students to serve as test subjects, virtually all of whom would be considered novices and would show the Novice Effect in response to any training protocol, i.e. everything works, more or less. They also have access to populations of elderly people who have time to be study subjects. They do not usually have access to competitive athletes who can alter their training for a study designed by someone unfamiliar with their sport and its training requirements. Semesters last about three months. Publications requirements are annual. Masters degree candidates are in the The Department for 2–3 years. They must publish to complete, or publish at the whim of The Chairman, whose job it is to appear productive to The Administration. The people in charge of study design and methodology would necessarily have been personally exposed to properly-designed training programs before they could possibly be equipped to ask the right questions. Such people are in very short supply within PE departments, as odd as that seems. People in PE departments are trying to either graduate, acquire tenure, teach fewer sections, publish as much as possible, or retire. This may seem to be a harsh assessment, and it doesn't mean that these people are evil. But the reality of the situation is that the vast majority of PE programs have no access to either the concept or the data of training, and cannot prepare their people to deal with it.

The upshot of this is that there is a giant hole in the literature regarding *training*, and the hole is filled by peer-reviewed articles about *exercise*. This is due to the fact that exercise, by its very nature, is accessible to PE departments, and training is not. With the current system in place, this situation will not change.

With the peer-reviewed literature dominated by articles on exercise, forming an "evidence-based practice" – the term fashionably applied to exercise prescription based only on evidence from peer-reviewed exercise science literature – devoted to the actual training of athletes is essentially impossible. Drawing conclusions about training for athletes based on a body of literature devoted to exercise for a few small subsets of the general public cannot be and has never been productive, and all the peer-reviewed publication-worship in the universe will not make it so.

Empiricism is a view of epistemology that holds that knowledge of a subject comes from direct sensory experience with it – empirical evidence. Empirical evidence is regarded by some people as data resulting from controlled experimentation in a formal study environment. These people are typically those involved in generating this type of data, and they may regard the absence of an experimentally-generated data set as an absence of knowledge. In contrast, *rationalism* is a competing epistemology that holds reason and logical analysis as a sufficient test of knowledge and truth. An absence of experimental data is not an insurmountable obstacle to a person capable of applying a rational analysis to a problem, since specifics can be accurately deduced from general principles.

The observations of experienced individuals – in this case, experienced coaches who have dealt with thousands of athletes over decades – are often regarded by academics in the exercise science publishing business as mere "anecdotal" reports, tantamount to hearsay and innuendo. This is a misunderstanding of the definition of "empirical," which most definitely includes the direct, informed observations of experienced coaches. Empirical evidence gathered from an experimental study is only one type of empirical evidence, and it is dependent on observation in precisely the same way an experienced coach gathers data through observation. It is therefore precisely as valuable, especially when you consider the fact that data from a study is only as good as the methods that generated it.

Exercise science has its problems. The populations it studies are typically small, often fewer than 20 people in the group. These people are very seldom trained athletes, and are most usually untrained college-age kids for whom any stress is adaptive. This makes for a poor way to study the effects of two different exercise methods, and completely precludes any questions regarding training. Often the methods themselves are poorly constructed, (doing a squat study on a Smith machine), completely omitting any quantification of the movement pattern being studied (precisely what is a squat? How deep is it? What is the hip angle? Does this affect muscle recruitment? How is this measured?), or display a failure on the part of the staff to standardize its interactions with the study population ("Try really *really* hard this time."). Sometimes the study duration is too short to reveal anything meaningful about the question being investigated, since we are dealing with students in the study population that will only be available for one semester. Most importantly, if the study is being directed by a person without the experience to know that the study question itself is stupid (Can more weight be bench-pressed lying on a bench or balanced on a swiss ball?), and if the review staff lacks the experience to know that the PI is asking a stupid question, then stupid peer-reviewed "evidence-based" research enters the literature and adds to the problem.

The observation that sets of 5 reps across for multiple sets is the most useful set/rep range for developing strength over a long career in the barbell sports is a conclusion based on the observed evidence, and is precisely as immune from prior belief *and* susceptible to experience bias as a controlled double-blind study. Both have their limitations, but both have their place. There may well be no such thing as a theory-neutral observation, but in the absence of other data, the informed observations of coaches are the best data we have, and conclusions drawn from them are far superior to extrapolations from very bad exercise studies. When a dearth of experimental data exists, as is the tragic situation regarding training methods beyond the scope of weight loss or thigh hypertrophy, the marriage of empiricism and rationalism yields the best result.

In the absence of any meaningful experimental data generated by peer-reviewed studies regarding the long-term effects of barbell training, we are forced to rely on the observations of hundreds of thousands of coaches and athletes who carefully picked their way through the mistakes made during the process of acquiring experience. This makes a rationalist out of every effective barbell training programmer. This process – if it is to be logical, effective, and productive, i.e. *rational* – must be guided by a thorough grounding in the sciences of physiology, chemistry, and physics, since the "exercise sciences" have proven themselves to lack the rigor and scope necessary for the task. The well-prepared coach has either a "hard" science degree or an otherwise extensive background in biology, anatomy, physiology, physics, chemistry, and probably psychology as well. Textbooks on these subjects should form the basis of the coach's library, with practical experience under the bar and many thousands of hours coaching on the platform rounding out his abilities as a coach of barbell training.

2

Adaptation

Training is predicated on the process of applying physical stress, recovering from that stress, and thereby adapting to the stress so that the processes of life may continue under conditions that include the applied stress. This is so fundamental a biological concept that the ability to adapt to stress is one of the criteria for defining life. An understanding of this phenomenon is critical for a coach or athlete who wishes to productively train instead of merely exercise. That understanding begins with Dr. Hans Selye.

On July 4, 1936, a paper was published in the journal *Nature* titled "A Syndrome Produced by Diverse Nocuous Agents." The basic premise of the paper is that an organism goes through a specific set of short-term responses and longer-term adaptations after being exposed to an external stressor. In our context, the stressor is lifting weights.

The General Adaptation Syndrome

Selye considered exercise to be a "nocuous" or poisonous stressor capable of causing death if the loading was too large or applied too frequently. His theory was the result of observations of animals under stress and optical microscope examinations of stressed cells. He was working without any knowledge of the basic details of human metabolism and the mechanism of skeletal muscle contraction, which was not yet understood when his paper was published. Despite the comparatively sparse information on which he based his observations, his reasoning was quite sound. A much more complete understanding of the physiologic mechanisms now allows us to better interpret and apply Selye's theory. Our understanding of the acute-phase response and the subsequent adaptation response, both possessing very identifiable time courses, along with modern insights into post-stress cellular events, has added weight to Selye's prescient concepts.

Selye's premise is that repeated sub-lethal exposures to a stressor lead to a tolerance of subsequent exposures to that same stressor, because the adaptation to a stress will be specific to that stress. This lends support to the concept of specificity – that a training stress needs to be relevant to the performance being trained for to elicit an adaptation that improves this particular performance. The theory holds that the body can go through three possible stages, the first two contributing to survival and the third representing the failure of the body to withstand or adapt to the stressor.

STAGE 1 – ALARM OR SHOCK

The Alarm phase is the immediate response to the onset of stress, in which a multitude of events occur. Selye noted that a major characteristic of stage 1 was a rapid loss of "muscular tone" lasting up to approximately 48 hours. We now know that other processes during this stage include inflammation and the acute-phase response, *and these effects are specific to the stress that produced them*, i.e. a burn to the hand does not produce blisters on the face, and a ten-mile run does not produce muscular soreness in the hands. One of the major results of these latter responses is a general suppression of basic cellular processes in order to stabilize cellular structure and metabolism until the withdrawal of the stressor. This is a survival process, and one that can also serve as a marker of effective training stimulus. Mild musculoskeletal discomfort may accompany this stage, indicating the disruption of homeostasis and events that stimulate structural and functional changes in the muscle after training. A trainee may not perceive soreness or pain in this stage; he is more likely to describe the sensation as "stiffness" or "fatigue." Regardless of the subjective perception, a transient reduction in performance accompanies this stage, although it may be imperceptible within the constraints of a barbell's typical 5-pound incremental loading system. Performance decreases will be more discernible in technique- and power-based exercises and less noticeable in absolute strength exercises.

Selye did not foresee his theory being central to exercise programming for healthy individuals. If he had understood the importance of his theory to training athletes, this first stage might have been more thoroughly described in terms of the current state of adaptation of the organism. With novice trainees, disruption of homeostasis occurs with smaller loads than those used by advanced trainees, since training has not yet developed either strength or work tolerance. As the level of advancement increases (from novice to intermediate to advanced), so does the magnitude and/or duration of stress needed to induce stage 1.

STAGE 2 – ADAPTATION OR RESISTANCE

In stage 2, the body responds to the training stress through the modulation of gene activity, changes in hormone production, and increases in structural and metabolic proteins, and the accumulated effects of these processes are known as *recovery*. In essence, the body is attempting to ensure survival by equipping itself to withstand a repeated exposure to the stress. The effects of the stress produce a group of reactions specific to that stressor, and recovery from the stress will be specific as well. In the context of training, performance increases when this occurs. Selye generalized that the Adaptation stage typically begins at about two days post-stress and that if the same stressor is reapplied periodically, complete adaptation could occur within four weeks or less.

We now understand that adaptation occurs on a sliding scale that varies with an individual's existing level of work tolerance, which essentially determines the proximity to one's ultimate physical potential. Someone far away from ultimate physical potential (the novice) will adapt quickly, a process which starts with the onset of the stress and may be completed within 24 to 72 hours. A stressor that is sufficient to disrupt such an individual's homeostasis need not be a gigantic physical insult, and it can be easily recovered from within that timeframe under even sub-optimal conditions. On the other end of the spectrum, the advanced trainee might require one to three months, and possibly longer, to adapt to a training stress sufficiently large and cumulative that it exceeds his highly developed work tolerance enough to disrupt homeostasis and drive further adaptation.

It is important to understand that the system is always in flux, with adaptation to numerous events that may act as stressors at various levels taking place all the time. Adaptation also occurs in response to the removal of a stress which had previously been adapted to, so that adaptation can occur in multiple "directions" depending upon the events that cause the adaptation. In this context, stress can be thought of as any event that causes an adaptation to occur.

Understand also that there is a good reason for the body to be able to change its state of readiness based on external conditions: it is metabolically expensive to maintain a constant state of high readiness if there is no external stress that justifies this expense. The reason we are all not as strong or as fast as our genotype permits – all the time, all of our lives – is that environmental conditions do not always warrant such a state, preparation requiring high amounts of precious metabolic resources that could be more thriftily expended on a lower state of readiness for a much longer period of time. Likewise, an inability to adapt would have rapidly disappeared from any gene pool in an environment capable of changing. Since an increase in readiness requires a response to stress that ends with the organism in a higher state of readiness than it previously occupied, the ability to adapt above the previous baseline evolved very early in the history of life.

STAGE 3 – EXHAUSTION

If the stress on the body is too great, either in intensity, duration, or frequency, the body will be unable to adequately adapt and exhaustion will occur. Selye proposed that an overwhelming stress of one to three months in duration could cause death. This arbitrary assessment was fine for purposes of illustrating the theory in 1936, but given our modern understanding of the application of this principle and the fact that people die while running a 3-hour marathon, it does not apply literally to our training extrapolation. If we consider that inappropriately-applied levels of training stress could produce this effect, the magnitude of this stress will be different for every level of training advancement. In practice, this concern is most applicable to intermediates and advanced trainees – novices usually lack sufficient strength and stamina to work at intensities and durations that would produce these levels of stress (although it is possible for an inexperienced coach to abuse a novice trainee) – and means that an extended period of excessively relentless maximum work should be avoided. The bottom line is that no one wants to be in stage 3, which we call *"overtraining."*

The application of Selye's theory to training is presented graphically in Figure 2-1. Progressive training within the context of the General Adaptation Syndrome requires that an increase in training load be applied in a way that produces an accumulating adaptation. Continued use of the initial, already-adapted-to load will not induce any disruption of homeostasis, since adaptation to it has already occurred, and therefore repeated use of the same training load cannot lead to further progress. Using the same training load repeatedly represents ineffective (but typical) coaching if performance improvement is the goal.

Of great importance is understanding the difference between Exercise and Training in the context of Selye. The process of stress/recovery/adaptation is a logical process that anyone can apply to their program of physical activity for an improvement in physical performance. It simply requires that stress be continually applied in a way that produces an *accumulating physiological adaptation* specific to the performance the trainee wishes to improve. Improvement requires, by definition, change. So an escalating stress is inherent in effective training.

At its most basic level, this means that training for a distance running event will be markedly different than training for weightlifting. The performance requirements for these two sports are essentially diametric opposites, and in order for the physiologic adaptations necessary for winning performance to occur, the training stress will have to reflect these differences. But within each sport, effective training will require the use of progressively-increasing stress specific to the adaptation required for competitive

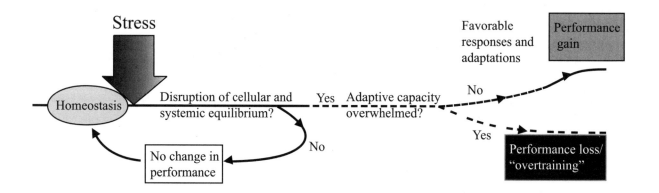

Figure 2-1. Within the parameters of Selye's theory, there are three possible outcome pathways following a training stress. Too little stress fails to disrupt homeostasis and no change occurs. Too much stress disrupts homeostasis, but overwhelms adaptive capacity, leading to performance loss. The appropriate amount of stress disrupts the system's state without overwhelming adaptive capacity, permitting progress to occur.

performance. A lifter cannot improve his lifting by running long distances, and a distance runner cannot improve his times by emphasizing strength training. Strength being a much more general adaptation than endurance, a runner can tolerate, and indeed benefit from, strength training, if it is done appropriately within the runner's competitive endurance schedule, while a competitive lifter has no reason to run as a part of his contest preparation.

If a lifter wants to get stronger, he must plan to do so. If a runner wants to get faster, he must plan to do so. A lifter gets stronger by planning a way to lift heavier weights, and a runner gets faster by planning a way to cover more ground in less time. The general process for creating both adaptations is rather simple, especially for those lifters and runners just starting the sport who have a lot of improvement left to obtain: lift heavier weights or run faster, and do so in a way that makes sustainable progress occur. Stress must be applied, recovery from that stress must occur, and the net effect will be an adaptation that causes improved performance. But it is easy to lose sight of the fact that the process of creating the improvement consists of *accumulating* the effects of the escalating stress/recovery/adaptation process over time – the individual workouts themselves are not the point; the *accumulated affects of the workouts over time produce the adaptation*. If this is not managed correctly, training is less than efficient. If it is not managed at all, we are not training. We are merely exercising.

The stress/recovery/adaptation cycle proceeds differently under different conditions and within different trainees. For a novice – a trainee who has all of his ultimate physical potential undeveloped – a single episode of weight training can make him stronger, after he has recovered from and adapted to the stress. From that point, subsequent stress can cause the process to occur again, producing more adaptation, provided that it occurs before the adaptation is lost to a lack of continued stress. For an athlete who has gone through this process and who is already strong from having accumulated years of adaptation, the process proceeds much more slowly, until a point is reached where it is virtually impossible to continue driving an adaptation (Figure 1-1). The interval between the rank novice's first workout and the advanced lifter's struggle to gain one more kilo of total is a continuum along which everyone who trains finds themselves, and their position along the continuum dictates their response to the stress/recovery/adaptation phenomenon.

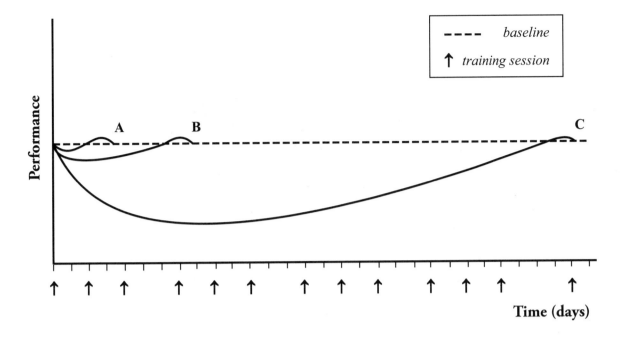

Figure 2-2. A longer stress/recovery/adaptation cycle is required as a trainee progresses from novice to advanced. (A) Novices can produce appropriate stress with a single training session and display performance above baseline within 72 hours. (B) Intermediate trainees require multiple training sessions and a longer recovery period to induce adaptation in a weekly cycle. (C) Advanced trainees require the cumulative stress of many sessions and recovery over a month or longer to drive progress.

In the novice, a single training session will disrupt biological equilibrium locally within the muscle and systemically within the body. If a single episode of weight training can disrupt homeostasis, a predictable set of outcomes can be detailed based on the degree of disruption. This model is presented in Figure 2-1.

In the novice, a single training session that disrupts biological equilibrium to an appropriate degree – utilizing a degree of overload that is within the athlete's capacity to both perform and recover from – results in a transient and very slight depression of performance. It is only slight because novice performance levels are already low, and small losses are hard to measure at this level. This depression occurs immediately after the training session and represents stage 1 of Selye's model. Subsequent to the training stress, performance ability will recover to the extent that an adaptation occurs to the stress, and then performance ability will exceed the pre-stress level to *approximately* the extent that the stress exceeded homeostasis. At this point the trainee has successfully completed Selye's second stage and has adapted to the new workload (Figure 2-2, line A).

It is important to understand that the trainee is not getting stronger during the workout. He is getting stronger during the recovery period *after* the workout. And since the stress/recovery/adaptation cycle has made him stronger, the next logical step is to increase the workload in the following workout by an appropriate increment within his capacity to both perform and recover from – i.e., to employ simple progressive overload, a regularly planned increase in the maximum weight lifted. Applying the same workload again produces no progress since this stress has already been adapted to, and repeating the same workload would no longer constitute a stress. At this point, a small increase in training load will once again take the trainee through Selye's stages 1 and 2 to repeat the stress/recovery/adaptation cycle at a slightly higher level. When the overload increment is approximately the same for each successive increase, the training program is referred to as a **linear progression**.

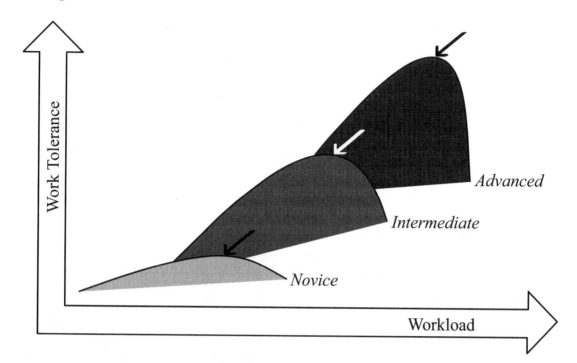

Figure 2-3. The relationship between workload and work tolerance. Regardless of training classification, there is a ceiling of work tolerance (designated by small arrows) that once breached decays into overtraining and a loss of work tolerance and performance capacity. Note that 1) work tolerance increases significantly throughout the training career, and increased tolerance is due to a progressive increase in workload, and 2) a descent into overtraining and manifestation of performance decrements will occur more rapidly and precipitously as the training career advances (note the sharper drop-off for more advanced trainees after the work tolerance peak is reached). Although overtraining can be a problem at every stage, prevention is critical at the advanced stage, as the rate of performance decay is very rapid once work tolerance is exceeded. Conversely, the diagnosis of overtraining may be a problem at the novice and intermediate stages, as the reduction in performance capacity occurs at a much slower rate after work tolerance is exceeded, and easily could be missed or misinterpreted.

     This organization of training can continue for many months, until the trainee's progress plateaus. At this point it is likely that it will require a series of two or three training sessions specifically arranged to have a cumulative effect, plus a longer stress/recovery cycle of perhaps a week's duration, to adequately take the trainee through Selye's first two stages. This represents the response of the intermediate trainee (Figure 2-2, line B). The intermediate period of a trainee's career, depending on the purpose of his training, can be quite long, possibly years.

     As the body gets better at producing force against a load, it is also getting better at recovering from that stress. As both performance competence and recovery ability increase with progressive training over time, eventually it will take weeks to adequately disrupt homeostasis to stimulate adaptation, and then another length of time for recovery and adaptation. The advanced trainee may require even up to a month's time to progress through stage 1 and stage 2 (Figure 2-2, line C).

     The more advanced an athlete becomes, the greater the importance of understanding the stress/recovery/adaptation model and its approach to balancing the two opposing forces of accumulating adaptation: 1) the workload must be sufficient to disrupt biological equilibrium enough to drive an adaptation, yet not excessive to the point of constituting an unmanageable level of stress, and 2) recovery must be sufficient to enable the adaptation to occur (Figure 2-3). The advanced athlete walks a knife's edge here. For the novice, it is very dull and wide, not really much of an edge at all, and rather easy to negotiate. The edge for the intermediate trainee is sharper, requiring a more complex approach. For the advanced trainee, it is razor sharp, and balancing on it without damage requires careful manipulation of all the programming variables.

Understanding Overtraining

Key to understanding progress in strength training is the concept of **overload**. Overload represents the magnitude of the stress required to disrupt physiological equilibrium and induce an adaptation. For progress to occur, the physiological system must be perturbed, and in weight training the perturbation is heavier weight, more training volume (sets and reps), or, perhaps for an intermediate or advanced trainee, less rest between sets than the athlete is adapted to. The overload is applied to the system through training, with the specific stress that disrupts equilibrium referred to as an **overload event**. For novice trainees, each workout constitutes an overload event. For intermediate and advanced athletes, the various elements of a week or more of training might collectively constitute the overload event.

But without recovery from an overload event, the overload does not contribute to progress. Overload without adequate recovery or excessively stressful overload induces overtraining. The term **microcycle**, traditionally defined as a week of training, is better thought of as the period of time required for the stress/recovery/adaptation cycle to be completed. This period will vary with the level of training advancement of the trainee. For a novice, a microcycle is the period of time between two workouts. The more advanced a trainee becomes, the longer the microcycle becomes, until the term loses its usefulness for advanced lifters, who might require a period of time for this process that would more traditionally be described as a **mesocycle**. These terms therefore lack the concision required for usefulness.

Overtraining is the bane of any program. When the stress of training outstrips the ability of the body to adapt, the trainee is at risk of not only ceasing to progress but actually regressing. To put it in the terms we have been using, the overtrained athlete has entered into Selye's stage 3. An imbalance between training stress and recovery has occurred, such that the trainee will not recover from the stress and adaptation cannot occur. The effects of fatigue are so pronounced that recovery processes, which may be either unaffected or diminished, are nevertheless overwhelmed, leading to persistent and potentially escalating fatigue. Performance will remain depressed from the initial overload and will suffer further decline with continued loading. The end result is the inability to train and perform at the previous level.

In the conventional exercise science literature, there are three possible versions of training stress: 1) fatigue, 2) overreaching, and 3) overtraining. Each of these is associated with a reduction in performance ability, but only one is an actual training problem.

FATIGUE

Fatigue is usually defined physiologically as a reduction of the force-production capacity of a muscle. It could be described as simple and transient "tiredness" resulting from physical effort – a necessary component of training which results from the stress necessary to enter Selye's stage 1. In the novice it is expected that fatigue will be recovered from within 48 to 72 hours in the most fundamental stress/recovery scenario. In the intermediate lifter elements of fatigue will be present until the full completion of the training week. And in the advanced trainee, complete recovery to adaptation may occur even in the presence of fatigue, and may occupy a period of a month or more. For the intermediate and advanced trainee it is neither expected nor desired that each workout begin free from fatigue. If a trainee is persistently fatigue-free, the loading scheme is not rigorous enough to induce homeostatic disruption and adaptation.

OVERREACHING

Overreaching has been described as the cumulative effects of a series of workouts, characterized by a short-term decrease in performance, feelings of fatigue, depressed mood, pain, sleep disturbances, and other miscellaneous effects that require up to two weeks to recover from. Hormonal changes such as a short-term reduction in testosterone and increase in cortisol occur at this level of homeostatic disruption, and in fact these are among the factors that produce the positive systemic effects of barbell training. A significant problem with this definition is that it differs from that of overtraining only in that "overreaching" can be recovered from with approximately two weeks of reduced work or rest – a rather arbitrary distinction – whereas recovery from overtraining takes longer.

This definition of overreaching also fails to consider the level of training advancement of the individual and the recovery abilities associated with that level, a problem typical of the conventional exercise science literature. The novice trainee will not experience overreaching on a properly constructed novice program, since recovery to adaptation occurs within the 48–72-hour period. It is important to understand that the novice trainee will not and cannot overreach unless far more than the recommended load is used, because the hallmark of novice status is the ability to recover quickly from the incremental increase in workload used to produce gradual, steady progress. Even when a late-stage novice plateaus within a simple linear progression, a single additional short-term reduction in training load is usually adequate to restore the athlete to normal recovery capacity. The intermediate trainee can recover in the time allotted for a weekly training period, since intermediate-level trainees characteristically respond to short-term cumulative training loads. The advanced trainee, after a long cumulative disruption of homeostasis, might require four or more weeks to recover and adapt, more than the two weeks allowed for by the definition. But this is a normal programming timeframe for an advanced lifter. The term "overreaching" is therefore not useful in strength training.

Moreover, the term "overreaching" defined as a negative training effect misses the point. An athlete must "overreach" to produce the stress necessary to disrupt homeostasis, intentionally breaching the maximum workload he has adapted to in order to induce adaptation to a higher level of stress and load. It is more relevant, practical, and understandable to discard the term and simply use the term "overload," since it describes both the load and the stimulus for driving adaptation in all trainees, regardless of advancement level. Every training program should include periods of overload, as is required by any practical application of Selye's theory; these periods should be understood as adaptive, not detrimental; and they should be appropriate to the trainee's level of advancement if they are to produce the desired effects. Judging this level of effort can be difficult and requires vigilant monitoring, especially for the advanced lifter, since a rapid descent into overtraining can occur if loading is too severe or recovery is inadequate.

OVERTRAINING

Overtraining is the cumulative result of excessive high-volume or high-intensity training, or both, without adequate recovery, that results in the exhaustion of the body's ability to recover from training stress and adapt to it. The primary diagnostic indicator is a reduction in performance capacity that doesn't improve with an amount of rest that would normally result in recovery. Although the American College of Sports

Medicine and U.S. Olympic Committee's definition of overtraining states that recovery from it requires no less than two weeks, overtraining is obviously relative to the advancement level of the trainee, and therefore there can be no hard and fast rules governing its onset or its abatement. Even the heinous abuse of a novice with an overwhelming workload, one that induces an immediate loss of performance ability, would resolve fairly quickly. Although the timeframe would be compressed, the symptoms observed by the coach would be those of overtraining. Although overtraining in the novice can occur, it may not be easily diagnosed because the magnitude of the loss of performance might be difficult to perceive, due both to a lack of training history for comparison and the low level of performance overall (as represented in Figure 2-3). Once again, as with overreaching, the overtrained intermediate fits the commonly accepted ACSM/USOC definition: an overtrained intermediate will not be able to recover in less than two weeks. For the advanced trainee, however, training periods are planned using longer time frames, rendering the accepted definition inadequate for these trainees. It is also easier to diagnose overtraining in advanced athletes since the performance reduction is quite noticeable against the background of an extensive training history.

A working definition of overtraining that applies to all levels of training advancement requires a better way to quantify recovery time in each stage. **Overtraining occurs when performance does not recover within one reduced-load training cycle.** The duration of that cycle will vary according to the athlete's level of advancement. For example, if a novice training every 48 hours has a workout that is markedly off due to excessive load in the previous workout, this will be apparent during warm-up. Range of motion will be decreased due to the soreness, and bar speed will be noticeably slower and more labored as the weight increases through the sets. The coach should then stop the workout, having determined the problem (in the last workout he did five extra work sets while another trainee was being coached in the other room, for example) and send him home with orders to rest until the next workout 48 hours later. He comes back in for his next workout, and warm-ups reveal that he is fine now, recovered and capable of the sets he should have done the previous workout. He was overtrained, and now he is recovered. This is possible because he is a novice, and this recovery timeframe is consistent with a novice's ability to recover, both from normal overload and from overtraining, since the mechanism is the same.

If an advanced trainee on a four-week cycle of loading declines below expected performance levels during a cycle, either the athlete has come into the cycle overtrained or the current cycle has exhausted his recovery capacity. In such a case, as much as four more weeks of reduced training load might be required to facilitate recovery. For both the novice and the advanced trainee, a repeated and dramatically reduced loading cycle of equal duration should immediately follow the diagnosis of overtraining in order to reestablish homeostasis. Advanced lifters using very long training cycles cannot afford the time required to deal with a programming error that might take months to notice, and even longer to correct.

Overtraining is yet another example of the profound differences between novice and advanced athletes, in that the more advanced an athlete becomes, the more costly overtraining becomes. A novice might be inconvenienced by a missed training session or goal, but that inconvenience lasts for a couple of days, and is of no consequence to anything other than the next workout. Intermediate athletes have committed to their training to the point of selecting a sport, and are in the process of becoming competitors. An advanced athlete is by definition always training for a competition, has invested many thousands of hours, many thousands of dollars, and many gallons of sweat in his training up to this point, and has much to lose as a result. Elite athletes may have titles, sponsorship money, endorsements, and post-competitive careers riding on their performance at the next competition. As careers advance, so does the price of failure, even if it is temporary.

Is consideration of overtraining important? According to the USOC/ACSM "Consensus Statement on Overtraining," 10 to 20% of all athletes are suffering from overtraining on any given day.

If this is true – it's probably not, because most athletes do not actually train hard enough to produce overtraining, and the USOC/ACSM should know this – it is a problem. How many coaches can afford to have 20% of their team performing below par on game day? Having a significant number of athletes overtrained at any given time would have important ramifications for team success, as well as for the careers of the individual athletes. Overtraining is the direct result of the failure to understand and apply the principles of stress/recovery/adaptation to the athlete's training, and to base that training on a correct assessment of the athlete's level of training advancement.

Diagnostic signs of overtraining in non-novices are severe, when finally apparent: obviously compromised performance, disrupted sleep, increased chronic pain, abnormal mood swings, chronic elevated heart rate, depressed appetite, weight loss, and other physical and mental abnormalities. (In fact, these are the same physical symptoms characteristic of severe depression, a clinical problem also arising from the accumulation of unabated stress.) However, not all trainees will display the same symptoms even if they become overtrained on the same program. Once again, the coach's eye is essential in determining changes in the performance and well-being of the trainee. Once overtraining is diagnosed, it is imperative to take remedial action, as longer periods of overtraining require longer periods of recovery. It quite possibly can take as much as twice as long to get a trainee out of overtraining as it took to produce the condition. Horror stories about severe overtraining abound, with examples of athletes losing entire training years. No effort must be spared in recognizing and treating this very serious situation.

Factors Affecting Recovery

The topic of overtraining is usually treated in a fairly narrow sense, with only the ratio of work to recovery discussed. These are the two controlling factors in disrupting homeostasis and forcing adaptation, but, ultimately, recovery is multifactorial and is affected by much more than just time off between workouts. It is popular among the hardcore lifting and bodybuilding communities to say, "There is no such thing as overtraining! Arrgh!" Most assuredly, there *is* such a thing as overtraining, but their attitude reflects an awareness of the other factors that contribute to recovery, and therefore the prevention of overtraining. The importance of attention to the details of diet and rest during recovery is of pivotal importance in avoiding overtraining. Unless the coach and trainee both understand and actively attempt to facilitate optimal recovery, no method of training can produce optimal results or prevent overtraining.

Aside from the work/rest ratio, several factors affect or contribute to recovery, the most important being adequate sleep and diet – the proper intake of protein, calories, water, and micronutrients. The problem is that each of these factors is under the direct control of the trainee, not the coach. A good coach will explain why these things are important for progress, will attempt to reinforce their importance on a regular basis, and then realize that better athletes will treat this responsibility as they should, and that average athletes will not. The best training program in the entire universe will be a dismal failure if athletes fail to hold up their end of the deal. The success of any program is ultimately the trainee's responsibility.

SLEEP

It should be intuitively obvious, but trainees and coaches alike often overlook the importance of sleep during periods of increased physical demand and stress. It would be hard to overstate the importance of sleep to the lifter – it may well be the most important anabolic factor within our control. While rather limited in scope, the scientific literature on this topic does support the following observations:

1) Lack of adequate sleep during recovery leads to a decrease in competitive ability, reduced determination, and lack of tolerance for intensity in training.

2) Lack of adequate sleep negatively affects mood state, leads to a greater level of perceived fatigue, promotes depression, and can induce mild confusion.

3) Lack of adequate sleep can reduce the capacity of the physiological mechanisms that enable adaptation to the stress of training.

A number of physiological changes occur during sleep. Among them, hormonal secretion is perhaps the most important for recovery from physical exertion. An increase in anabolic (muscle-building) hormone concentrations and a decrease in catabolic (muscle-wasting) hormone concentrations and activity take place during the sleep cycle. Levels of testosterone begin to rise upon falling asleep, peak at about the time of first REM, and remain at that level until awakening. This means that a disrupted sleep pattern probably limits the recovery contributions possible from testosterone. Another anabolic hormone, somatotropin or human growth hormone, also has a characteristic secretion pattern during sleep. Shortly after deep sleep begins, growth hormone concentrations begin to rise, leading to a sustained peak lasting 1.5 to 3.5 hours. A major function of growth hormone is the mitigation of the negative effects of the catabolic hormone cortisol. A disruption or shortening of the sleep period will reduce the beneficial effects of these important anabolic hormones.

How much sleep is required? The U.S. military at one time believed that four hours of continuous sleep per night allows for survival and the maintenance of basic combat function, but now recognizes the need for more, a recommended 7–8 hours per night for "sustained operational readiness." Your mom tells you that eight hours a night is needed to be healthy and happy. The average American adult gets somewhere between six and seven hours per night. The "average" sedentary person is not significantly stressing the body's recuperative capacity. But Mom knows. An average of eight hours of sleep, especially during very rigorous training, will aid in recovery. After all, the purpose of sleep is to induce a state of recovery in the body. The longer the period of sleep, the better the quality of recovery.

The number of hours of sleep is not necessarily the same thing as the number of hours spent in bed. Very few people go to sleep when their head hits the pillow. Going to bed at 11:00 and getting up at 7:00 may not be getting you eight hours of sleep. It is more realistic to add extra time to account for any delay in actually falling asleep, ensuring that eight hours is obtained.

Protein

How much protein do athletes really need? Recently, a growing pool of research has dealt with the protein needs of strength-trained athletes. The United States Recommended Daily Allowance (RDA) values call for a protein intake of 0.8 g/kg/day (grams per kilogram of bodyweight per day) for males and females fifteen years and older. The RDA is based on the needs of the average population, and the average American is sedentary. It is not logical to expect the nutritional requirements of a sedentary individual to be the same as the requirements of anyone undergoing a program of systematically increasing physical stress and adaptation, and in fact recent research has shown that even the sedentary population does not consume sufficient protein for their limited needs. It has been well documented that any type of exercise increases the rate of metabolism in the muscle and also accelerates the rate of muscle protein degradation and turnover. Research shows that resistance exercise stimulates muscle protein synthesis that lasts well past the end of the exercise bout, longer in novices than in advanced lifters.

Muscle protein synthesis (MPS), the process by which new muscle is built, requires a dietary protein source, as well as carbohydrates, which function synergistically to drive the process. The primary way muscles recover from stress and grow is for MPS to occur faster than the muscle protein breakdown that is the inevitable result of an effective training stress. If protein synthesis is to exceed protein degradation, anabolism, or constructive processes, must exceed catabolic, or breakdown, processes. If nutrients needed for other protein synthesis requirements – those needed to maintain or repair other damaged tissues – are not sufficiently available from dietary sources, the body will take them from its own protein stores; its existing muscle mass will serve as a protein repository. This is a perfectly normal process in times of starvation or chronic stress. In essence, the body robs Peter to pay Paul in order to maintain function. A training stress will still function as a stress in the absence of sufficient dietary protein and carbs. By ensuring adequate dietary protein intake, the trainee provides the body with the building blocks necessary for new protein synthesis. Failure to do so will prevent new muscle protein synthesis from occurring, thus blunting the training effect and wasting a lot of effort under the bar.

So, how much protein is needed to support training? The literature includes a broad range of recommendations that go as high as 2.5 g/kg/day. Some coaches and trainees don't like to do arithmetic, or aren't competent in converting pounds to kilograms. An easy way to ensure enough dietary protein, and the tried-and-true method used by the weightlifting and strength training communities for many years, is simply to eat one gram of protein per pound of body weight per day: a 200-pound athlete should try to get about 200 grams of protein per day, from various dietary sources. This works out to 2.2 g/kg/day, a value that, while in excess of the obviously inadequate consensus recommendation of between 1.2 and 1.8 g/kg/day, remains below the highest recommended value in the literature of 2.5 g/kg/day, and will ensure a target high enough that missing it a little will still be sufficient for full recovery. This calculation disregards considerations of lean body mass and therefore assumes an already "normal" body composition; individuals with a higher bodyfat percentage should take this into account when planning protein intakes.

The calculation also disregards the effects of poor quality protein sources and other caloric intake. A dependence on so-called "third-world" protein like soy protein, rice protein, hemp protein, beans, and other non-animal protein sources which have poor amino acid profiles based on their low content of the BCAAs (branch-chain amino acids: leucine, isoleucine, and valine), will necessitate even higher levels of protein intake than these recommendations. Muscle protein synthesis is also dependent on a surplus of non-protein calories, such that lower levels of carb/fat intake will make even higher protein intake levels necessary to drive MPS. Conversely, higher-quality protein sources coupled with enough high-quality carbs and fat can lower the total dietary protein requirements. And as people age, they become more sensitive to protein quality, making either more total protein or better quality protein an important factor in an older lifter's program.

It is important to note that there is absolutely no evidence to support the notion that "excessive" amounts of protein are harmful to normal kidneys with unimpaired excretory function, despite the ill-informed advice of most health-care professionals. In fact, for people without active kidney disease *there are no unsafe levels of protein consumption.*

Protein supplementation is useful in that it can help an athlete get a sufficient protein intake, making up the difference between that found in the normal diet and the recommended level. And a protein drink, being convenient to make and consume, is useful for post-workout recovery. There are high-quality whey-based protein supplements on the market with higher levels of the BCAAs and better bioavailability than beef, certainly better than any soy protein product ever made. But we eat food for reasons other than merely the BCAA profile. Other nutrients are found in a steak and a nice salad that are not present in high-quality whey protein. It may be tempting to allow supplements to become the staple of your training diet, and under special circumstances this may be necessary. But supplements are best used to *supplement* a good diet. If a high supplement intake is necessary for your protein requirements, it might be prudent to examine the quality of the rest of your diet.

CALORIES

Since calories are expended during exercise, mostly derived from the body's ready reserves of stored carbohydrate and fat, an obvious requirement for recovery after exercise is an increased need for energy to replace that consumed during training. There are two reasons exercise creates a need for calories: 1) exercise of all types, volumes, and intensities expends some fraction of the body's energy stores, and these must be replaced before the next workout, and 2) exercise of sufficient intensity disrupts homeostasis and muscle structural integrity, producing a requirement for both protein and fat/carbohydrate calories to facilitate repair and recovery.

During exercise, the muscles preferentially burn stored glycogen for fuel, and fat plays a very small role in the production of energy during resistance exercise. As recovery processes proceed within the muscle, carbohydrate remains the most significant source of energy for muscle protein synthetic processes. At rest, fat becomes the most important energy source for non-MPS metabolic processes. The source of the carbohydrate and fat is not terribly important as long as it is sufficient in caloric content and a protein source accompanies it. Fat requires a longer time for breakdown and utilization than carbohydrate, but the body's metabolic rate is elevated for many hours after exercise and having an energy-rich substrate (fat has more calories by weight than carbohydrate) slowly metabolized over a number of hours is beneficial. Given adequate caloric intake and adequate protein, the composition of the diet must also consider the requirements of vitamin intake, essential fatty acids, and fiber. The quality of the diet should be as high as the resources of the trainee permit.

It is important that the total caloric content of the diet be greater than the total caloric expenditure of the training day. Matching intake to expenditure will theoretically maintain homeostasis and strength, but will not support maximum strength improvement and increased muscle mass, the object of strength training. As a practical matter, a significant caloric surplus is needed to drive progress, and it is almost impossible to calculate daily energy expenditure with any degree of accuracy, due to the huge number of variables – training load, sleep, the sex of the trainee, the effects of the diet itself, and the age and growth status of the trainee – that affect the system. If we simply pay back the energy used during exercise and daily activities, we are not providing the extra energy required to drive homeostatic recovery and adaptation through muscle protein synthesis.

To get stronger, the conventional literature advises the consumption of around 200 to 400 calories more energy than we expend. This is woefully inadequate for most people who are serious about their training, and absolutely positively inadequate for an underweight male who is trying to gain muscular bodyweight. It has been the experience of the authors that a more reasonable intake to ensure recovery and strength gains would be *at least* 1000 calories per day over baseline requirements. If a gain in muscular bodyweight is the primary goal, a surplus of *at least* 2000 calories per day, and perhaps much more for some people who are inefficient metabolizers, will be needed. Considering the fact that calculating baseline expenditure is almost impossible, the way to accomplish this is to eat as much as possible from a diet based on high-quality protein, quality carbohydrates, and fat from both plant and animal sources, and adjust the quantities based on the results of this intake. Whole milk has long been the staple addition to the diet of young lifters who want to grow.

FATTY ACIDS

Another set of compounds that affect recovery are essential fatty acids (EFAs). Although a bias against dietary fat remains in vogue in some circles, fats are essential nutrients as well as efficient sources of energy. While there are no essential carbohydrates, there are several essential fatty acids – the body can synthesize many of the lipids it needs from dietary fat sources, but it cannot make omega-3 and omega-6 fatty acids. These two types of lipids play an important role in the maintenance of the body's structural integrity, are crucial to immune function and visual acuity, and are involved in the production of eicosanoids, the precursors of the prostaglandins which regulate the inflammatory process. Of the two, omega-3 fatty acids are the most important to recovery: they support anabolic processes and assist in the management of post-exercise inflammation and pain. They are also less likely to be present in adequate amounts in the diet. Omega-6 fatty acids may actually contribute to inflammatory processes if they are present in the wrong proportions.

Deficiencies in EFAs are fairly common in the United States, since fish, the primary source of omega-3 fats, has never traditionally been an important component of most American diets. Chronic profound deficiencies result in growth retardation, dry skin, diarrhea, slow wound healing, increased rates of infection, and anemia. Sub-clinical deficiencies would likely not produce symptoms that could be easily diagnosed by observation. Acute clinical deficiencies quickly develop in individuals with very low-fat diets, with symptoms evident in two to three weeks.

Only a few grams of omega-3-rich oils are required. This can be done with about one generous serving of fatty fish, such as salmon, per day. Many people find that taking an omega-3 fish oil supplement is helpful, since hard training benefits from higher dietary levels of EFAs. Cod liver oil too is an inexpensive source of EFAs, and is also very high in vitamins A and D.

HYDRATION

Water is essential for recovery from strenuous exercise. After all, nearly every biochemical process occurring in the human body takes place in an aqueous environment. Dehydration causes loss of performance, and when it is severe it can be catastrophic. An increased metabolic rate increases the requirement for water. Increasing storage of energy substrates (such as ATP, CP, and glycogen) in the muscle increases the need for intracellular water. A hydrated cell is an anabolic cell. In fact, if a cell – particularly a multinucleated muscle cell – is dehydrated it will synthesize proteins at a much slower rate than it would if it were well hydrated. Increasing hydration levels within the cell is one of the ways creatine supplementation works to increase skeletal muscle hypertrophy. But how much water do we need to drink to support recovery and avoid overtraining?

Everybody's physician, dietician, nutritionist, trainer, coach, and friend "know" that it is "absolutely necessary" to drink "8 × 8": eight 8-ounce glasses of water per day. This equals half a gallon, or about 1.9 liters, of water a day. Note that standard beverage cans or bottles are 12 ounces or 20 ounces, and that a 16-ounce cup is usually a sold as a "small" drink at a restaurant, so the requirement is not necessarily eight commonly available "drinks."

But do we really need to drink this much water? The 8 × 8 recommendation is not actually based on any scientific evidence obtained through research, but on a subjective viewpoint stated in a 1974 nutritional text that was seized upon by the clinical professions, and that has slowly entrenched itself in both clinical dogma and conventional wisdom. Most fluid intake values found in the research data indicate that between 1.2 and 1.6 liters per day, less than the 1.9 liters of the 8 × 8 prescription, is sufficient for maintaining hydration status in healthy humans who exercise mildly. These recommendations must of course account for different environmental conditions – the hydration needs of a person in Florida in June will be different than that of a person in Manitoba in October – so in reality there can be no absolutes with respect to fluid intake.

It is also hard to imagine that the human body has spontaneously lost the ability to self-regulate its hydration status since the bottled-water industry was born. After all, very few human societies previously developed the custom of sipping water every 5 minutes all day from a convenient container carried in the hand or the backpack. So, self-selected fluid intake in response to thirst probably represents an appropriate method for maintaining health and function under most circumstances. But does it represent an intake that can support recovery from intense training?

How much fluid is needed beyond the 1.2 to 1.6 liters per day that reportedly supports a mildly active lifestyle? Larger, more active individuals require more water intake to support their greater quantity of metabolically active tissue, the increased caloric cost of incrementally larger workloads, and their less-efficient heat dissipation characteristics. Smaller athletes, both male and female, require less water. The fluid content of foods also affects the total fluid intake, as does the intake of coffee and tea, and must be considered in the calculation. *One size does not fit all in terms of hydration.* If you need a gallon of water today to keep from being thirsty, drink it. But don't drink a gallon of water today because you think you are supposed to.

Your attention please: Excessive water consumption is extremely dangerous – hyponatremia being a potentially fatal condition, but the intake of toxic levels of water requires a conscious effort far above any effort to assuage thirst under any circumstances, and it cannot be done accidentally. It is, however, occasionally accomplished during organized endurance events, where the promoters make water available at every rest stop and where over-zealous and inexperienced participants incorrectly heed the un-moderated advice of "professionals" to start drinking water before you get thirsty, to "stay ahead" of dehydration.

One last consideration is which fluids count toward hydration. Many popular health practitioners will boldly state that only water and a few other "natural" beverages count toward hydration. They discount anything with caffeine or alcohol or even sugar as a viable rehydrating beverage. The statement has actually been made that "You wouldn't wash your car with a diet soft drink – why would you use it for hydration?" Such a ridiculous statement demonstrates a lack of understanding of the mechanism by which water is absorbed from the gut: anything that contains water counts toward water consumption if it provides water in excess of that which must be used to metabolize it.

Water itself is the best rehydrating fluid since, after all, it's *water*. It can be taken up by the gut faster than commonly consumed commercial beverages, if that is actually a practical consideration in normal hydration situations, but every water-based drink (are there any *drinks* that are not water based?) contributes to hydration. The water content of a 20-ounce diet cola counts toward hydration even though it contains caffeine and artificial sweeteners. A 20-ounce regular cola full of high-fructose corn syrup also counts even though it contains caffeine and sugar. Alcoholic beverages have been quite effective hydrating agents at various points in human history. Beer and wine, in more primitive times, were major rehydrating fluids necessary for survival, since they were safer than the available untreated water supply, as was the grog – 1 part rum mixed with 4 parts water and a little lime juice – of the British Navy in the eighteenth century. We are not proposing that soft drinks, beer, and wine should be staple components of the training diet, but honesty compels the consideration of the realities of the American lifestyle and how it may affect recovery. Aside from the question of their other benefits or detriments, moderate consumption of these beverages does in fact contribute to hydration.

VITAMINS AND MINERALS

Frequently, it is stated that the average American diet provides all the vitamins and minerals necessary for a healthy life, and that statement is almost always considered to extend to hard-training men and women. Virtually no one is ever tested for vitamin and mineral levels unless they display deficiency disease symptoms. Therefore, few individuals, sedentary or athletic, ever know for sure whether they have all the required vitamins and minerals present in sufficient quantities.

Severe vitamin and mineral deficiencies are not common in the United States, but they do occur. Mild deficiencies are much more common – the majority of American females are consistently iron and calcium deficient to a small but significant degree, for instance. Calcium has a tremendous variety of functions in nervous and muscular physiology, growth, and performance, and a deficiency can limit recovery from training. Iron has a crucial role in oxygen transport and metabolic function. A mild iron deficiency can have significant negative effects on the body's ability to recover after exercise.

Vitamins and minerals act as mediators of biochemical reactions in the body. Referred to as "micronutrients," they are needed in relatively small amounts and occur naturally in foods in varying concentrations. To obtain all the vitamins and minerals required for life – and certainly for training – we must consume a variety of foods. The average American kid does not. If parents were aware of the basic need to provide young athletes with a diet of high quality and variety, this might not be an issue. But we are a culture of convenience and habit, and it is common that people consume a very limited selection of foods and food types, often those that are processed to increase the convenience of storage and preparation. Such processing typically reduces the vitamin and mineral content of food to the extent that the quality of the diet – even though sufficient in calories and maybe even protein – is quite low.

The result is that while the typical athlete's diet may not be so inadequate that deficiency symptoms are present, it may contain less than optimal amounts of essential vitamins and minerals, nutrients needed to assist in recovery from rigorous training. Recent research on normal sedentary populations has concluded that vitamin supplementation has no effect on longevity; we are not concerned with longevity, but rather performance. After all, if it is logical that an athlete in hard training needs increased calories, water, and protein, then a higher vitamin/mineral intake would also be required. Given the diverse regional, ethnic, cultural, and economic tastes and habits within the U.S. population, and without specific and costly laboratory testing, there is no easy way for the coach or athlete to assess the vitamins and minerals present in any given diet. Thankfully, this is not necessary: nutritional supplementation to ensure that these important factors are present for training and recovery is safe, effective, and economical.

The best way is to start simple and cheap. An inexpensive generic vitamin and mineral supplement containing all the commonly supplemented vitamins and minerals is readily available at grocery stores or on the internet. More money will get you a better, purer, more readily absorbable product. Bill Starr in his famous book *The Strongest Shall Survive* advocated the use of the "shovel method": just take a lot, and the body will excrete what it doesn't use. Since vitamin toxicity is excruciatingly rare, especially among hard-training athletes, this is good advice.

How Hard and How Much

PERIODIZATION

Possibly having encountered Selye's theory and realizing that it had direct applications to the training of athletes, Soviet exercise physiologists fifty years ago proposed several methods of training that capitalized on the body's ability to adapt to increasing workloads. The roots of this method, called **periodization**, are often attributed to Leonid Matveyev in the Soviet Union in the 1960s (advanced versions of Soviet-style periodization can be traced further back to Hungary in the 1940s and 50s). Periodization was brought to the attention of the U.S. weightlifting community in the 1970s by Carl Miller and molded into a hypothetical model for weight training for sports performance by Mike Stone in 1981. Since then, periodization has become one of the primary tools of successful training program design, regardless of the sport.

The objective of all training for performance improvement should be to take the body through Selye's stages 1 and 2 of the stress model, providing enough training stress to induce adaptation without reaching Stage 3, exhaustion. Correctly designed programs achieve positive results by controlling the degree of stress placed on the body through the manipulation of the volume and intensity of training. It is therefore important to have a method of quantifying volume and intensity.

Volume is the total amount of reps performed in a workout or group of workouts, usually excluding warm-up reps. Volume is the number of reps performed at the weight to be used as the overload stress. But volume is not very useful as a singular quantity. A workout with a volume of 25 reps could be either 5 sets of 5 reps or 25 singles. These represent quite different types of stress. So for volume to be meaningfully quantifiable, it must be expressed as **tonnage** – the total amount of weight lifted in the workout:

repetitions × weight = tonnage

The following table shows an example of tonnage calculations for a squat workout:

Warm-up sets			Work sets			
45	95	135	185	185	185	Weight
5	5	5	5	5	5	Repetitions
225	475	675	925	925	925	Tonnage per set
	1375					Warm-up set tonnage
					2775	Work set tonnage
					4150	Total tonnage

For this one exercise, warm-up reps included, the trainee lifted a volume of 4150 pounds. This calculation is repeated for every exercise included in the workout session. In that way the total volume of stress applied can be quantified. It is usually more useful to consider only work set volume, since it is the work sets and not the warm-ups that are disrupting homeostasis and bringing about stage 1. As shown in the table, this significantly reduces calculated volume. If a trainee does an inordinately large number of warm-up sets, it would be important to consider their effect on training volume.

Intensity is the average weight lifted in a workout or group of workouts relative to the trainee's 1RM ("one-rep max," or the maximum weight that the trainee can lift for a single repetition):

volume / repetitions = average weight used

average weight used / 1RM × 100 = % intensity

For the example in the table above, the average weight used is 4150 pounds/30 reps, or 138.33 pounds per rep. If the trainee's 1RM is 225, the intensity is 138.33/225 × 100 = 61%. It is easy to see how excessive warm-up volume can affect the average weight of all the reps, and the average intensity, making it desirable to use only work sets in the intensity calculation. For only the work sets in this example, the intensity is 82%.

To reiterate: Intensity is considered as a percentage of 1RM. An intensity of 80% of 1RM is greater than an intensity of 50% of 1RM. While this is a simple concept, there are many different ideas about "intensity" in the scientific, medical, and popular literature. Intensity is sometimes equated with the level of power production in a given exercise. Things as abstract as the amount of mental focus given to a repetition ("Let's really focus on this next rep and get your *intensity* up!") or the individual's subjective perception of their effort during the exercise (the Borg Rating of Perceived Exertion scale, for example) have been proposed as definitions. Another proposed description is related to fatigue: if it fatigues the muscle, the exercise was intense. All these concepts have been elaborated upon in the literature, and they may work well for endurance training where an accumulation of very sub-maximum effort is the nature of the training stress. But without exception they are not practical for the strength training professional because they are not quantifiable, a characteristic that both scientists and practitioners regard as pivotal. Intensity, as defined with respect to percentage of 1RM may seem somewhat simplistic, but that is precisely its advantage. It is the most practical and useful method, especially for coaches and trainers who program for large groups and need a way to objectively assess work and improvement.

The simple calculation of a range of intensities of an exercise weight relative to 1RM:

$$
\begin{aligned}
\text{Squat 1RM (lbs)} \quad &225 \\
95\% = 225 \times 0.95 = \ &214 \\
90\% = 225 \times 0.90 = \ &203 \\
85\% = 225 \times 0.85 = \ &191 \\
80\% = 225 \times 0.80 = \ &180 \\
75\% = 225 \times 0.75 = \ &169 \\
70\% = 225 \times 0.70 = \ &158
\end{aligned}
$$

Traditionally, the manner in which periodization controls volume and intensity – and therefore the degree of stress placed on the body – is by dividing training into periods whose lengths and load characteristics vary according to the level of the trainee.

Interpretation of the literature on overtraining must be done with an awareness of the fact that much of it is based on aerobic exercise. The overtraining that can be induced by anaerobic training such as weightlifting has different characteristics than that induced by the quite different stress of aerobic work – referred to by lifters as long slow distance work, or LSD. The different ways in which volume and intensity are defined between the two disciplines have a bearing on the analysis of overtraining. Modern competitive road cyclists, for example, may spend hours each day on the bike, generating a huge volume of training. When they want to work harder, they add miles, hours, or training days, accumulating what have been termed "junk miles." They also tend to ride at a sustainable percentage of their VO_2max, and if this is used as a measure of road cycling intensity every training session typically averages out to be similar to the one before it. It is important to note that VO_2max occurs at about 30 to 40% of a muscle's maximum strength of contraction. So, intensity (measured as a percentage of absolute strength) is not a major training factor in the average self-coached American competitive cyclist's training program. But because volume is essentially the training variable that they manipulate with overload, road cyclists generally suffer from volume-induced overtraining. But be aware of the fact that "volume" to a cyclist and "volume" to a lifter are two completely different things. Cycling volume is always much more sub-maximal in intensity as we define it, while involving many thousands of times more repetitions than any workout under the bar.

Because weight training programs manipulate both the volume and intensity of training, trainees can experience either volume-induced or intensity-induced overtraining. Extremes in programming styles are represented by the "go-heavy-or-go-home" approach, which may precipitate intensity-induced overtraining, and the "train-to-failure" approach on the other, which may produce volume-induced overtraining. More common is overtraining that has elements of both types, since most programs manipulate both variables.

Understanding the rate of recovery from both types of resistance training stress is important. In well-trained weightlifters, intensity-induced overtraining – a function of the nervous system and its interface with the muscular system – is easier to recover from than its volume-induced counterpart, which affects primarily the contractile components and metabolic systems of the muscle cells. When peaking for a strength or power event, intensity continues to increase in the program, at greatly reduced volume, up to very near the event. When peaking for an endurance event, both the volume and intensity of weight training should be curtailed several weeks in advance, since the longer period required for volume recovery will directly affect the competition.

The basic cure for overtraining is the combination of time and a reduced workload. The time spent dealing with overtraining costs the coach and athlete valuable progress: reduced workloads do not produce improvement, or even maintenance; a complete layoff results in detraining to some inevitable extent. Since the costs of overtraining are high, prevention is the best approach. Correctly designed training programs appropriate for the athlete and the sport are the key. Although properly executed simple linear progression produces rapid progress without overtraining in the early stages, for more advanced trainees more complex programming – periodization – is necessary.

3

Strength: The Foundation of Performance

Any discussion about the improvement of human physical potential must start with a discussion of strength. The ability to produce force against an external resistance is, in essence, the ability to effectively interact with the environment. An improvement in physical capacity involves an improvement in strength, unless you are already very strong. If you are, you have gone though the process of getting that way, in which case you already know why it is important, or you are quite a bit luckier in terms of genetic endowment that most people. Let's assume you're not, so we'll have something to discuss.

STRENGTH

The strength of a muscle is the ability of the muscle to exert *force* – the quantity which causes motion to occur – against an external resistance, provided by the skeletal attachments of the muscle and the skeleton's ability to transmit the force of muscular contraction to the environment. The skeleton is a system of levers that provide an interface between the muscular contractile force and the objects we wish to move with our muscles. The system of muscles operating the system of skeletal levers comprises the totality of our physical existence – it is what our bodies are for, the most basic element of our lives.

The stipulation "against an external resistance" is important, in that both the body and the object the body moves must be considered as a system, since both move as a result of the force produced by the body. When you deadlift a bar, we measure your strength by the weight of the bar you overcome when it leaves the ground. But force is being created and applied within the system of levers – your skeleton – as well as against the loaded bar. For example, force was being applied between the separate components of your spinal column, to maintain the constant intervertebral relationships that allow the spine to act as a rigid, efficient transmitter of force, between the hips and legs that generate the motion and the bar being moved. No one would argue that force is not being expended to hold each vertebral segment in place, but such complex measurement is impractical to the extent that it is practically impossible. Therefore, we stipulate that we are measuring the force produced against the external resistance, to make the calculation both possible and meaningful.

In its broadest interpretation, strength is the ability to move a weight irrespective of the amount of time it takes, as with a heavy deadlift moving slowly to lockout. Maximum strength is thus measured without reference to the time it takes to move the load the required distance. Its inappropriate name notwithstanding, the sport of *powerlifting* measures strength in this way, using the squat, the bench press, and the deadlift as the tests of strength.

Powerlifters move heavy weights relatively slowly. The heavier the weight, the slower it moves, until a weight that exceeds one's strength cannot be moved, at any speed. Powerlifting is therefore a test of maximum strength, and training to lift heavier weights is the most basic expression of strength training. In a more indirect application of strength, consider the example of a football lineman trying to move an opposing player after the initial contact, the opposing player being the weight. Upon contact, the movement might stop completely, as force production ramps up against the opponent. As the opposing force is overcome, movement speed increases from zero but remains slow relative to the explosion off the line. Overcoming the resistance that the opposing player provides takes superior strength – the ability to hold position while better mechanical position is obtained, and the ability to produce more force than the opposing player once it is.

Strength is displayed in the three basic ways our muscles exert force upon our skeletal components. The force of muscular contraction is *tension*, described as a "pulling" force exerted by a string or cable on another object, without the source of the pulling specified. The contractile machinery that causes the shortening inside the muscle belly produces the tension of muscular contraction, applied at either end of the muscle against the attachments on the bones. This tension can be either:

Concentric: The muscular force results in the length of the muscle belly decreasing

Eccentric: The muscular force is applied while the length of the muscle belly increases

Isometric: The muscular force keeps the length of the muscle belly the same

A concentric contraction is most familiar to the public as a biceps curl, while eccentric and isometric contractions are never considered. The three forms of muscular action interact in complex ways to form the patterns of human movement. Strength is displayed using all three expressions of tension.

SPEED

Speed is the rate at which a moving object changes its position in space. It is the *scalar* version of the *vector* quantity **velocity**, in which the direction of the movement is specified. The amount of time it takes an object, or one's own body, to move a given distance is an important component of the majority of sports. In barbell training, we use the terms informally and interchangeably, since everybody knows which direction the bar is supposed to go. Speed is critical to the correct performance of many barbell exercises, specifically the Olympic lifts and their variants; bar speed is a critical factor in completing a snatch, a clean, and a jerk. In all three movements, the bar must be moving fast enough to rack at the lockout position, and if this doesn't happen, the lift is missed. Speed, in contrast, is not a requirement for the successful completion of a deadlift. Beating an opposing player to the ball requires speed. Once movement is initiated, strength is required for the continuing rapid transfer of force that maintains the velocity of the object against its tendency to slow down.

POWER

The production of power is the key to most sports. Power is the ability to exert force rapidly – to display strength quickly. Explosion is power. It is the amount of work performed per unit of time, specifically considered here in terms of short time frames. Work is the force applied to an object and the consequent distance it is moved by that force; an easily understood unit of work is the foot-pound, the energy needed to move a 1-pound load a distance of 1 foot. Therefore a unit of power would be 1 foot-pound per second – the rate at which the work of moving the object is performed. If a large muscular force is generated that moves a heavy weight very quickly, power production is high; the highest peak power outputs ever recorded in all of athletics have been produced during the second-pull phase of the snatch. It can be considered as the rate of force production, usually measured using a force plate.

On the other hand, if an athlete in training climbs ten flights of stairs faster today than he did last week, he has moved the mass of his body the distance of ten flights of stairs more quickly. Or if an athlete finishes the task of doing three rounds of 30 pull-ups and running 400 meters faster than she did it last month, the mass of her body has moved faster over a shorter period of time. These are examples of *rate of work production*, and could be improved by merely resting less between the components of the work without increasing the rate of the force production of the movements themselves. In other words, the density of the cumulative efforts increases – an increase in frequency without an increase in the amplitude of the individual component efforts. Improvements in rate of force production and rate of work production require different metabolic adaptations, which may or may not overlap. For our purposes here, power is the ability to generate high levels of force rapidly. The successful lineman comes off the line very fast, accelerating his bodyweight quickly enough to meet his opponent, completely stop the opposing forward momentum, and start the process of pushing him out of position. The effects of his power – the momentum created by his speed and the mass of his body moving at that speed, and his subsequent ability to quickly generate force against his opponent – determines more about his performance during the play than any other aspect of his movement.

Acceleration is inherent in the production of power. Acceleration is the change in velocity over time, the rate at which the object is increasing or decreasing (negative acceleration or *deceleration*) its velocity. Acceleration is what happens to the bar when it starts from a motionless position on the floor, moves slowly off the floor and increases its speed as it is lifted higher. A clean and a snatch both require that the bar display a certain amount of **momentum** (the product of the mass and the velocity of the bar), in order that the load continues upward while the lifter stops applying force to it between the end of the pull and the catch in the rack position. When the lifter's feet break contact with the ground to shift to the rack position, the velocity of the bar must be great enough to generate sufficient momentum to carry it upward high enough to get under it before its velocity returns to zero and starts back down. Acceleration is what produces this peak velocity, and this requires the ability to generate high levels of force in a short amount of time – the very definition of power. Therefore, the ability to accelerate the bar displays power, and increasing the clean and the snatch displays an increase in power.

This is of extreme importance to every athlete and coach: the ability to generate power directly affects performance in all sports. All other things being equal, the more powerful athlete will always beat the less powerful athlete.

Note that the calculation for power is the Force needed to overcome the load, multiplied by the Distance the effort moved the load, divided by the Time the action took, or

$$(F \times D)/T = P$$

Note the effect of decreasing the value of the denominator T on the value of the equation. The faster the bar moves at the same weight, the greater the power output of the effort. But examine the effect of increasing the weight moved, F, without increasing the speed – power improves this way also. Increasing the distance we move the load would increase power as well, but in the context of explosive exercise, a large increase in D would change the very nature of the movement. We are not interested in a longer bar path for the clean, or the effect of the accumulation of repeated efforts; we are interested in making a single clean occur either faster or with a heavier weight.

The power output of the deadlift and the clean can be compared with a simple set of calculations. Take the example of a very strong offensive lineman:

Bodyweight = 140 kg (308 lb)

Deadlift personal best (1RM) = 300 kg (660 lb)

Distance from floor to lockout = 0.65 meters

Time from floor to lockout = 4.0 seconds

To calculate his power output in the deadlift, first calculate the work performed (force × gravitational constant × distance):

Work = 300 kg × 9.8 m/s² × 0.65 m = 1911 Newton meters (N·m)

Next, calculate total power generated (work/time):

Power = 1911 N·m / 4.0 seconds = 477.75 watts

This can be expressed in a form that allows for the comparison of two individuals, by calculating watts per kilogram, or relative power output (power/bodyweight):

Relative power = 477.75 watts / 140 kg = 3.41 watts/kg

This measurement of relative power is now scaled for the mass of the athlete.

Figure 3-1. A comparison of the deadlift and the power clean. The deadlift (*above*) moves a heavy weight over a short distance slowly, while the power clean (*facing page*) moves a lighter weight over a longer distance quickly. Much greater power is produced during the power clean.

Next, calculate the power generated by using the power clean (from floor to shoulder):

> Bodyweight = 140 kg (308 lb)
>
> Power clean personal best (1RM) = 150 kg (330 lb)
>
> Distance from floor to lockout = 1.27 meters
>
> Time from floor to lockout = 0.6 seconds

Work performed (force × gravitational constant × distance):

> Work = 150 kg × 9.8 m/s² × 1.27 m = 1866.9 N·m

Total power generated (work/time):

> Power = 1866.9 N·m / 0.6 seconds = 3111.5 watts

Relative power output (power/bodyweight):

> Relative power = 3111.5 watts / 140 kg = 22.2 watts/kg

The main difference between the two is the time it takes to move the load. The work done in the two lifts is essentially the same: 1911 N·m for the deadlift and 1867 N·m for the power clean. The power clean is faster, so much faster that it generates more than six times the power despite the fact that it is only half the weight and moves only twice the distance of the deadlift (Figure 3-1).

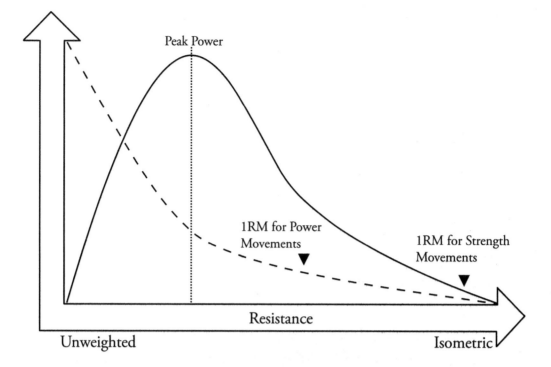

Figure 3-2. Velocity-power graph. The dashed line represents velocity, and the solid line represents power output. Peak power occurs at approximately 30% of maximum isometric force and 30% of maximum movement velocity. This would equate to 50 to 80% of 1RM, depending on the exercise.

But remember this simple rule: a man who deadlifts 600 pounds will *always* clean more weight than a man who only deadlifts 300 pounds. Always. This consideration is often overlooked by advanced coaches who are more impressed with their own ability to coach the clean than the understated importance of the deadlift. The simple act of increasing strength for the novice lifter will increase his power, since power depends on strength and strength improves rapidly for a novice. For example, an increase in the deadlift will immediately decrease sprint times for an inexperienced kid much more productively than time spent working on sprint mechanics. If we remember that the physiological capacity to explode – to rapidly recruit lots of motor units into contraction from a state of rest – is largely (and unfortunately) a genetically-predetermined capacity outside the trainee's ability to improve much more than about 20–25% (under the very best of circumstances, and usually the trainee does not find himself in the very best of circumstances), we begin to grasp the importance of strength development to the athlete, which does not have a narrow genetically-predetermined limit. Since strength is more trainable than explosion, and since strength can be developed for many years to a very high level, strength development is more important to the athlete than the now-fashionable focus on developing explosion – "rate of force development training" – which is an attempt to improve an ability that is neither very trainable nor as valuable to the athlete as a simple strength increase.

This is the reason that athletes take steroids. There are no technique steroids. Steroids make you stronger, and that increased strength is displayed as increased power. Any time you see the criticism of athletes taking steroids and beating athletes who are "clean," you are seeing the plainly-stated observation that strength is critical – especially if those athletes cannot depend on their training to make them stronger. Baseball players who take steroids and thereby risk their careers by doing so would be much better off doing an effective program of barbell-based strength training, a method which is not yet illegal.

So, strength is the most trainable aspect of power, and as strength increases its display as power should be trained to keep pace. This requires the use of exercises in which heavy loads *must be moved quickly*, such as the Olympic lifts – the snatch and the clean and jerk and their derivatives. Cleans and snatches cannot be done slowly – a slow clean is a missed clean, and a slow snatch is just a snatch hi-pull. The act of committing to the racking of the bar on the shoulders or overhead ensures that more acceleration will occur during the pull than if the lifter merely *intends* to pull the bar fast. This phenomenon – the difference between a clean and a clean hi-pull which intentionally does not rack – is familiar to all experienced lifters. This must be remembered when thinking about the use of "dynamic effort" deadlifts for training power off the floor: a racked clean was accelerated enough to rack – a PR clean was accelerated maximally, and a fast deadlift may or may not have been. You just don't know, because there is no way to "miss" a fast deadlift. A clean either racked, or it didn't.

Cleans and snatches, therefore, are inherently (and not volitionally) explosive, i.e. the movement pattern that produced a racked clean involved enough explosion to rack the clean. More importantly, these two important barbell exercises feature the primary advantage of using barbells in the first place: they are incrementally increasable to the extent that the gym has the small plates. We can precisely determine the athlete's current ability to display power – to clean the weight – and then we can increase that weight as much or as little as the athlete finds necessary. To the limited extent to which explosion can be specifically trained, this ability to finely discriminate the incremental increases allows the Olympic-derived movements to be the absolute best developers of power in the coach's repertoire.

MASS

Muscle size is normally associated with strength. We've all seen people who just look strong. They have an imposing muscular appearance. And there is truth in this perception: absolute strength increases as a muscle's cross-sectional area gets bigger. It is an inevitable consequence of weight training that muscles will get larger, and this is why most men do it, especially when they start. This growth happens whether the intent of the training is strength, power, or mass.

Advanced competitive bodybuilders perform five sets of twelve reps of an isolation-type exercise with minimal rest between sets for producing muscle hypertrophy in the muscle group trained in the exercise. The possible physiological reasons for this will be discussed later. But bodybuilding workouts are organized so that isolated muscle groups, not movement patterns, are trained. Since muscle groups are trained separately by most bodybuilders, their coordinated performance in systemic movement patterns that also display the ability to balance the load remains untrained, and thus their potential for the athletic application of the strength of the individual muscle groups remains largely untapped. For this reason, strength and conditioning programs based on isolated muscle-group exercises are far less effective for producing athletically-applicable strength than those based on the movement patterns found in the major barbell exercises. High-rep, low-intensity training of isolated muscle groups results in hypertrophy of those isolated muscle groups, but a coordinated strength and power adaptation relies on movements that demand more coordinated strength and power, and a body that functions as a balanced coordinated system. It is unfortunate that many strength and conditioning coaches, even at the college and professional level, fail to appreciate this fact.

The hypertrophy aspect of strength training is an important consideration for athletes involved in sports that favor size. Football, for example, is a different game today than it was many years ago, before 300-pound linemen and 245-pound defensive ends were common. Most heavy-implement throwers and strongman competitors are bigger athletes as well. It's simple: size is commonly associated with strength athletes because, in general, stronger is bigger. Bigger is also useful in team sports involving contact, like rugby and basketball, and even those traditionally played under endurance conditions, like soccer, because heavier players are harder to push around than lighter ones.

But bigger muscles also mean more efficient leverage around important joints. Knees, elbows, hips, and shoulders work better when the muscles that operate them are larger, since the angle at which the muscles cross the joint is more mechanically efficient for the joint's lever system: the steeper the angle of attack that the tendon has on the bone, the more efficient the pull. Big quads thus work better than small quads, both because they are stronger in terms of cross-sectional area and because at least a portion of the muscle mass is positioned to extend the knee more efficiently.

When training for strength, specialization is less effective than generalization. The same is true for hypertrophy. The endocrine system responds in a dose-dependent manner to stress. Large-scale, multi-joint (sometimes called "structural") barbell exercises are more effective in producing an anabolic hormonal stimulus than small-scale, single-joint, isolation-type exercises, even when using the same intensities and repetitions. In the context of non-chemically enhanced training, exercises such as the squat and the bench press are more effective in producing hypertrophy for athletes who train the body in a systemic, coordinated manner than for those who use isolation-type exercises such as leg extensions or the pec deck.

Training Specificity

The conventional wisdom holds that all strength training for sports should be done in a manner that mimics both the movement patterns and the metabolic demands of the sport as closely as possible, requiring specificity with respect to the energy systems used (ATP/CP vs. glycolytic vs. oxidative; see chapter 4), the muscle groups primarily involved in the sport, and the requirements for force generation, speed of movement, range of motion, and frequency of contraction. Training is the process of accumulating physiological adaptations that benefit the sport being trained for, and as with all other training program considerations, this must be informed by an understanding of the application of strength within the sport in question. For example, the marathon or any other long-distance endurance event would not benefit from the type of training an Olympic weightlifter would do. Endurance athletes require adaptations in oxidative metabolic capacity to improve performance, an adaptation that weight training at high intensity and low volume develops only peripherally. Increasing the number of reps under the bar does not turn strength training into endurance training, because higher repetitions and lower intensity do not develop oxidative capacity anyway.

Endurance athletes benefit from the increased strength provided by a typical novice program because the vast majority of endurance athletes are novices with respect to strength development, and increased strength decreases the percentage of the endurance athlete's absolute strength required to sustain the repeated submaximum efforts which accumulate into an endurance performance. An advanced sprinter, however, who operates entirely in anaerobic metabolism during performance, and who needs a great deal of explosion and power, would directly benefit from strength training. Every coach should be familiar with the metabolic demands of his sport: the longest and shortest effort, the intensity of these efforts, the recovery time between them, the normal duration of the event, and the typical length of its rest periods. He should also be familiar with the beneficial effects of a simple increase in strength, because the absence of sufficient strength limits the development of all other athletic parameters.

So the concept of training specificity has its limitations. Strength is a very generally acquired and utilized characteristic, developed through the process of lifting increasingly heavy weights over the course of time. Strength is developed by exercises that use lots of joints and lots of muscles moving lots of weight over a long range of motion. Fundamental strength exercises like the squat, the press, the deadlift, and the bench press, along with power exercises like the clean and the snatch, always form the basis of any strength and conditioning program that is actually useful to an athlete, irrespective of the level of training advancement. This is true precisely because these exercises are quite non-specific to anything other than increasing strength – they develop useful strength and power that can be applied in any athletic context. Sports *practice* involves motor patterns and metabolic pathways that apply this generally-acquired strength in ways extremely specific to the sport activity. It is neither necessary nor desirable to exactly mimic either a sport's movement pattern or the exact metabolic demands of a sport in the weight room.

Many Physical Therapists misunderstand the concept of training specificity, and this is because they misunderstand the value of strength and the process of its acquisition for athletics. I have personally witnessed a Physical Therapist prescribe 3-pound one-arm dumbbell swings with a bent elbow – at a normal curling tempo, no less – for a softball pitcher, on the assumption that the dumbbell was heavier than the softball and would therefore strengthen the pitching motion. In an attempt to be sport-specific with strength and power training, many practitioners have gotten so specific – with respect to both the movement pattern and the metabolic pathway – that an increase strength and power using the exercise is impossible.

Stated succinctly, strength *training* is best acquired through the use of the exercises which are best at building strength – basic barbell exercises that use lots of muscle mass over a long range of motion while standing on the ground in a balanced position, thereby allowing the use of heavy weights that develop the ability to generate high amounts of force while balancing the load and controlling the position of both the load and the body in space. *Practice* is where the athlete learns to apply strength to the motor patterns specific to the sport. Trying to mimic sports-specific positions, poses, stances, and movement patterns while under a heavier-than-normal load cannot and does not allow for the most efficient strength development, because while these positions are where strength is displayed on the field, *they are not the best positions for its development* – the positions designed for best handling the heaviest amount of weight are found under the barbell. Furthermore, attempting to do so is detrimental to the execution of the sports skill under load, because a heavier-than-normal throw/swing/push is a slower-than-normal throw/swing/push and a less-accurate throw/swing/push.

Motor specificity refers to the degree of similarity in movement pattern between the sport activity and the strength training movements being used. If we consider three superficially similar exercises for the shot put – the press, the incline press, and the bench press – we might visually select the incline press as the most specific, since it most closely mimics the angle of primary effort and release of the shot. Many trainers and athletes regard the incline press as an important exercise, but the press and the bench press develop both the horizontal and vertical ability to generate force, and completely overlap the area trained by the incline. The bench press allows the use of the heaviest weights, thus building absolute strength most effectively. And the press is the only one of the three with an important characteristic for the throw – the use of the whole body all the way to the ground as an active component of the exercise. And remember that the athlete will be *practicing* throwing the shot. So the incline press is actually the least useful of the three for strength *training*, even while superficially appearing to be the most specific.

Consider another example: a cyclist and the squat. A cyclist's knee is never flexed beyond 90 degrees, so if specificity is considered only in terms of knee flexion, the conclusion would be that squatting above parallel is specific to cycling performance, and that full squats are not. This, in fact, is what most sport coaches believe and advise their athletes to do, in more sports than cycling. The problem here is a misunderstanding of the exercise and its relationship to the sport skill. At the detailed level, a partial squat does not produce a strong hamstring contraction. Any cyclist who does partial squats is not developing balanced strength around the knee and is neglecting the muscles used in the hip-extension aspect of a properly executed pedal stroke.

At a more generalized level of analysis, this is a misunderstanding of the difference between *training* and *practice*. While the partial squat may superficially look more specific, the more generalized full squat is more applicable to the activity. This is fundamental to understanding strength and conditioning for sports: full squats are more applicable to cycling – and all sports in which strength is an important component – because strength is more efficiently and effectively developed with full squats than with partial squats. **The similarity in movement pattern between any sport movement and the squat is utterly irrelevant. The squat's ability to develop strength is the relevant criterion for its inclusion in the program.** Prowess in movement skill on the field must be developed on the field, and strength is best developed in the weight room using the best exercises for the task, and the squat is the most important exercise for strength.

It has become popular among "functional training specialists" to apply unilateral exercises to training for sports with a dominant unilateral component. This is another version of misunderstanding of training and practice, and a fundamental misunderstanding of strength and its development and application. Lunge-derived exercises like split squats, exercises utilizing unstable components as the base of support, ipsilateral/contralateral movements using light weights, and exercises that feature an attempt to isolate "the core" with partial unilateral contractions that cannot be quantified all have one thing in common: they cannot be used to develop strength as effectively as the barbell exercises, because they substitute the mere display of balance for progressively increasing load. Strength improvement cannot occur using light weights for more than a very few weeks in a completely untrained individual, and lunges and balancing exercises cannot be done with the weights that can be eventually lifted in the deadlift, press, and squat. An athlete with a 500-pound deadlift has a stronger "core" than an athlete with a 200-pound deadlift, because all the muscles used in the deadlift are strengthened by the deadlift in the process of getting the deadlift strong. And the stronger the athlete, the better the athlete can balance – control the position of his body – while applying improved strength and power on the field.

Metabolic specificity refers to the degree of similarity between the energy substrate used in the sports performance and that used in the training activity, and is a more important consideration for intermediate and advanced athletes who have already developed their basic strength. For example, a shot put lasts between 1 and 3 seconds, uses all the muscles in the body from the hands to the ground, is powered by ATP (adenosine triphosphate) stored in the muscle (more on this later), and never even remotely approaches a state of muscular fatigue. It depends entirely on the ability to generate force rapidly in a coordinated manner, one very brief attempt at a time and consistent with the technique the athlete has practiced. Strength training for the shot put would focus on getting the athlete very strong if a very high strength baseline had not already been established – a big thrower should be squatting 600, benching 400, pressing 300, deadlifting 650, and power cleaning 350. After this base has been established, more attention can be focused on cleans and snatches done for single reps at high effort. Note than none of these exercises look like the shot put, but they all develop the physiological adaptations used in the performance. Middle-distance running or 100 pushups/situps/pullups, powered by carbohydrate or fat metabolism and lacking a rapid high-force-production component, do not. Metabolic preparation must fit the task, and must be specific to the effort being trained for, whereas the movement pattern itself is *practiced specifically* on the field using strength *generally* acquired through *training* in the weight room.

High-rep training may seem more applicable to a sport that requires sustained effort, but it is an inferior way to develop strength, and for an athlete who is not very strong, strength is the limiting factor in the ability to sustain an effort. High-rep exercise by definition entails the use of light weight,

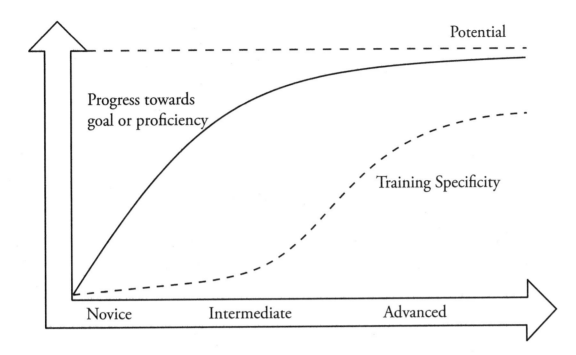

Figure 3-3. Specificity of training is a function of proximity to goal performance in a task. As a trainee comes closer to achieving a performance goal near his full potential, the training stimulus must more closely mimic the physical nature of the goal. Whereas a novice can make substantial progress with generalized training, an advanced trainee must use more specific methods, although absolute specificity is not productive.

and light weights cannot drive an increased force production adaptation because it doesn't require high force production to lift light weights. This seems astonishingly simple, perhaps even simplistic, but no more complicated analysis need be applied. Strength is developed by lifting heavier weights, and weights that can be lifted for 20 reps are not heavy. Specificity in programming must be considered in terms of the optimal way in which the most fundamental athletic attribute – strength – is acquired, and the needs of the athlete relative to his level of training advancement.

The degree of specificity exists on a sliding scale. Compare, for example, push-ups for 50 repetitions, bodybuilding-style bench presses with lighter weights at 12 to 15 reps, and bench presses with heavy weights at 3 reps. For the shot putter, the push-ups, which may take 60 seconds, lack any metabolic specificity, and the 15-rep bench press is less specific than the heavy bench press. Work-to-rest ratios must also be considered within this metabolic context. An obvious example is a football play, which usually involves 6–8 seconds of intense activity followed by 45 seconds of very low-intensity activity and recovery. Training in the weight room or on the track with similar periods of exercise and rest better prepare the athlete for the demands of on-the-field performance, while longer durations of rest during barbell workouts allow the better development of maximum strength, also useful on the field. The coach must use his judgment in order to select the best work-rest ratio to augment the performance of his athletes, often on an individual basis.

In a novice, the need for any type of specificity in training is low, since an untrained individual is so far removed from his ultimate potential for performance. For a trainee at this stage, any type of exercise will improve performance, and well-designed progressively increasing barbell training will markedly increase his performance in a very short time. In contrast, an elite athlete must be trained with a high degree of specificity for his sport, being very close to his physical potential in strength and sport performance. *Practice* that contributes directly to maintaining expertise in the sport activity is required but is insufficient in and of itself – *training* is also necessary (Figure 3-3). It is very important to understand that absolute specificity – playing only the sport itself – is not adequate for the vast majority of the athletic population, especially when all your competitors are training hard in the weight room. For everybody except a tiny fraction of the genetically gifted (who quite unfortunately come to represent the norm to the general public), performance skill is developed by repeatedly practicing the sport activity, but higher-level expression of that skill requires the improvement of other physical parameters that are best affected by training – like strength.

In the clean & jerk, for example, the training/practice paradigm is in full operation. Simple performance of the exercise beyond the novice level will at some point fail to drive adaptation. The lift itself must then be approached as *practice*, with strength *training* driving up the levels of force production necessary to clean & jerk heavier weights. Once maximum technical performance has been well established, continued work at maximum clean & jerk weights in the absence of strength increases in the squat, press, and heavy pulls will fail to satisfactorily disrupt homeostasis. This is because at maximum weights for the clean and jerk, both skill and strength are required. The components of skill – technique, psyche, and explosion – must be practiced. Strength must be trained, just like in any other sport.

4

The Physiology of Adaptation

Muscular Contraction: The foundation of movement

To understand how to train the body for improved performance, you must understand how the performing body actually works. Muscle is the basic physiologic unit of movement. The structure of muscle controls its function, and training changes both structure and function. A familiarity with basic physiologic principles related to muscle and to its training for peak performance is essential for effective program design.

MUSCLE STRUCTURE

The largest structural unit of the muscular system is the muscle itself, which attaches to the skeleton at a minimum of two points by connective tissues called *tendons*. The contractile mechanism of muscle generates the force of tension between these points of attachment on the skeleton. This force operates the system of skeletal levers which multiply the contracting muscle's limited ability to shorten as a percentage of its own length. The use of mechanical advantage by the musculoskeletal system enables our bodies to interact with the environment – to run fast, throw far, and lift heavy weights explosively.

Individual muscles are separated from each other by a thin sheet of another type of connective tissue called *fascia*. An individual muscle is an organized mass of thousands and thousands of individual muscle cells, also called *muscle fibers*. These cells are arranged in bundles, and separated from other bundles by more connective tissue. The muscle cells that make up the bundles contain hundreds of myofibrils – organelles which contain the contractile components. These structures are repetitively organized into the basic contractile units, the *sarcomeres*. Sarcomeres are composed of protein strands that interact with each other to produce a net shortening (contraction) of the entire muscle fiber. It is in aggregate that all the contracting muscle fibers of a muscle generate the high levels of contractile force necessary to produce movement. Muscle cells also contain *organelles* required for normal metabolic function: cell membranes, cytoplasm (called sarcoplasm in muscle cells), nuclei, mitochondria, ribosomes, endoplasmic reticulum, etc., all of which are important contributors to muscle function and all of which also adapt to training.

The myofibrils within a muscle cell have a characteristic striated appearance due to the structural arrangement of each sarcomere. The major contractile proteins, actin and myosin, are aligned in an

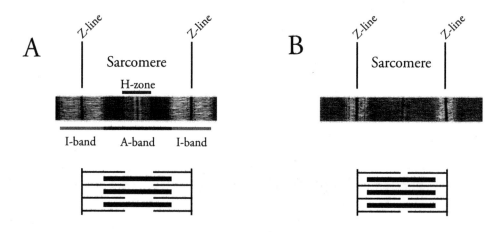

Figure 4-1. Sarcomeric structure (A). Z-lines form the boundary of each sarcomere which repeat in series to form the myofibril. Note that in the relaxed sarocomere, the thin actin-containing filaments and thick myosin-containing filaments only partially overlap, creating distinct I- and A-bands seen in the electron micrograph. Huxley's sliding filament theory holds that expenditure of ATP will cause actin and myosin to transiently interact with each other to pull the thick and thin filaments past each other, causing Z-lines at each end of the sarcomere to move together (B).

overlapping thin/thick filament pattern (Figure 4-1). There are several other proteins associated with the thin filament, actin. Two of these proteins, troponin and tropomyosin, are major parts of the regulatory mechanism of muscle contraction, the details of which are important but outside the scope of this book.

There are several types of muscle fibers. These different types are often generally referred to as "fast-twitch" and "slow-twitch" muscle fibers, but this classification scheme does not indicate the actual breadth of difference between the types. A better system of categorizing fiber types is by their primary method of fueling metabolic activity, i.e. fatty acid metabolism/beta-oxidation vs. glycolytic metabolism. Table 4-1 illustrates the continuum of fiber types, with a range of anatomic and metabolic properties. These properties dictate how a muscle composed of varying percentages of the different fibers performs and responds to training. Weight training can dramatically change muscle architecture and metabolism, thereby altering function.

MUSCLE FUNCTION

The muscle is composed of several functional units, the largest being the entire muscle itself. When a muscle contracts, it pulls the bones attached at either end toward each other, resulting in movement around the joint between them. Improving this large-scale ability to move is the ultimate goal, and the smaller-scale components of muscle tissue are the elements that must actually adapt to training.

Actin and myosin, proteins of the myofibril (usually referred to as "contractile proteins"), are two of the major players in muscle contraction. When actin and myosin bind to each other, there is a shape change in the myosin molecule that pulls the ends of the myofibrils – and the cells that contain them – toward the centerline. When adequate numbers of these units interact, enough force is generated to cause the entire muscle to shorten, but the percentage of its own length by which it can shorten – 25% or so – is limited by the structure of the sarcomere itself. To compensate for this, the distance between the joint and the muscle attachment is very short compared to the distance along the bone to the other end, and this difference in length provides the leverage effect that we depend upon to multiply this short muscle length change into large movement radii around the joints.

The energy needed to induce the configurational change in myosin comes from adenosine triphosphate (ATP), the high-energy product of a variety of metabolic pathways. ATP is the stuff of life, and is responsible for the transport of nearly all chemical energy within all the cells of our bodies. As such, it is the basis for the conversion of chemical energy into kinetic energy – the basic function of muscle tissue. Its importance in biochemistry cannot be overstated.

The amount of force a muscle can potentially exert is generally considered to be proportional to its cross-sectional area. This means simply that the bigger around a muscle is, the more force it can generate. This is because all of the muscle fibers basically start at one end of the muscle belly and extend all the way to the other end, so that as the contractile filaments in the muscle fiber increase, the diameter of the aggregate increases. All other factors being equal, the only way to make a stronger muscle is to make a larger muscle, one that contains more contractile protein. But all other factors are seldom equal, and there are several that contribute to effective muscle function. One factor directly related to muscular function is the availability of ATP and the efficiency of the mechanisms by which ATP is utilized and regenerated within the muscle. Low concentrations of ATP or a poor ability to synthesize or utilize it will diminish muscular function, and training induces an increased ability to store and synthesize ATP.

As previously mentioned, there are several types of muscle fibers, each with a characteristic set of metabolic properties that relate to ATP utilization. Type I fibers are described as slow oxidative, or "slow twitch," meaning that they rely primarily on aerobic or oxygen-dependent metabolism and its associated pathways which take more time than non-oxygen-dependent processes. These fibers are smaller, are capable of generating less force, and have less potential for enlargement than other fiber types. But they are extremely fatigue resistant since they preferentially rely on enzymes that enable the use of an essentially inexhaustible energy substrate: fatty acids. The enzymes that break down fatty acids are dependent on the presence of oxygen for their function. Type I fibers are the first to be recruited

Characteristic	Type I	Type IIA	Type IIB
Contraction speed	Slow	Fast	Very fast
Fiber diameter	Small	Intermediate	Large
Size of motor neuron	Small	Large	Very large
Resistance to fatigue	High	Intermediate	Low
Activity used for	Aerobic	Long anaerobic	Short anaerobic
Force/Power capacity	Low	High	Very high
Mitochondrial density	High	High	Low
Capillary density	High	Intermediate	Low
Aerobic capacity	High	Intermediate	Low
Anaerobic capacity	Low	Intermediate	High
Major fuel source	Triglycerides	CP, Glycogen	CP, Glycogen

Table 4-1. Muscle fiber types and their properties. Type I ("slow twitch") fibers are chemically, structurally, and functionally distinct from the two categories of type II ("fast twitch") fibers: fast oxidative (IIA) and fast glycolytic (IIB). While there are other fiber-type classifications in common use, this one applies best to the discussion of adaptation for strength and power.

and the last to relax – they function in all situations where prolonged contraction occurs at low levels of intensity, like standing, sitting, and walking.

Type II fibers depend to a greater extent on energy production from the breakdown of glucose – *glycolysis* – than do Type I and are far less dependent on the presence of oxygen than Type I fibers. Type IIb fibers are termed fast glycolytic or "fast twitch," meaning that they primarily use the process of glycolysis, by which glucose is broken down to yield ATP, a process that does not require the addition of oxygen, and which takes place faster within the cell. Type IIa fibers are intermediate between Type I and Type IIb. Their function can be skewed toward either purpose, depending on the training stimulus. Type IIa and IIb are much larger than type I fibers, have higher enlargement potential, metabolize ATP more rapidly, and are less fatigue-resistant. But training can change how all of these muscle fiber types behave. Strength training drives an adaptation toward larger fibers that produce more contractile force, and endurance training drives a metabolic adaptation toward more efficient use of oxidative mechanisms that enable fatigue resistance at lower intensities. Fibers which are trained to *simultaneously* increase their force production capacity *and* fatigue resistance will increase these properties to a lesser extent than fibers which are trained to increase these two parameters separately.

Energy Metabolism: Powering the muscle

ENERGY SOURCES

Muscle contraction, and in fact all intracellular activity, is powered by ATP. Our bodies produce ATP from the breakdown of food. Everything we eat – carbohydrate, fat, and protein – can serve as a source of ATP. (Fat and protein are less important in power performance energetics, since carbohydrate is selectively utilized for this purpose, when supplied in adequate amounts, by the type IIb muscle fibers which dominate this type of activity.) This indispensable molecule is produced during a series of biochemical events that occur after the breakdown of food in the body. For the purposes of this discussion, ATP is produced in three ways: 1) through the regeneration or recycling of previously-stored ATP by creatine phosphate, 2) through non-oxygen-dependent glucose metabolism (glycolysis), and 3) through oxygen-dependent metabolism that utilizes both fatty acids and the end products of glycolysis (oxidative phosphorylation). Conventionally, the first two mechanisms for ATP production are termed "anaerobic" and the third "aerobic." Each of these distinct pathways provides ATP at different rates and contributes a greater proportion of the required ATP under different circumstances.

ENERGY UTILIZATION

Stored ATP is always the energy source utilized during muscular contraction. During contraction, ATP loses one of its three phosphate groups and becomes adenosine diphosphate (ADP), liberating energy stored in the molecule and allowing its use in muscle contraction. As ATP reserves are depleted, which takes just a few seconds, ADP is rapidly recycled back into ATP by the transfer of a replacement high-energy phosphate ion from a creatine phosphate (CP) molecule back to the ADP. Creatine phosphate thus serves as a carrier of this replenishing energy for ATP.

ATP, utilized and resynthesized by this two-part mechanism, powers intense, short-duration exercise (less than 10 to 12 seconds) such as sprinting and weight training. If the exercise is longer than this few seconds worth of stored ATP can cover, the ATP that would normally serve to replace that just used becomes the ATP that now must power the exercise. Sources for these slightly longer efforts are

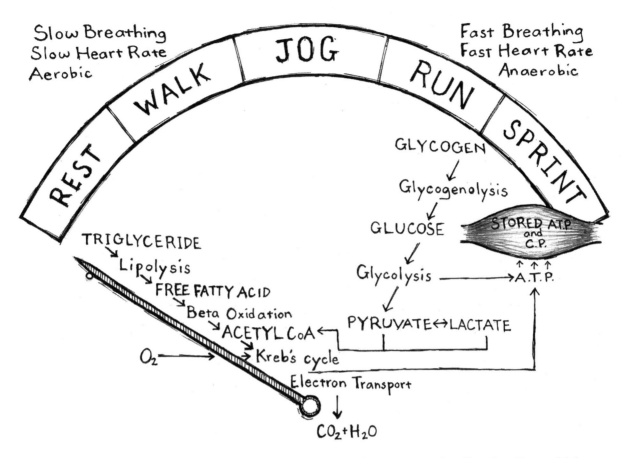

Figure 4-2. The metabolic speedometer. How hard and low long we exercise directly affects which metabolic pathways our bodies primarily use to fuel the activity. All physical activity lies along a continuum, from rest to all-out maximum effort. All activities are powered by the ATP already present in the muscle, and all bioenergetic activity acts to replenish these stores. Low-intensity exercise depends on cardiopulmonary delivery and muscular uptake of oxygen, the ready availability of which enables the body to utilize aerobic pathways and fatty acids as substrates. These aerobic processes take place inside the mitochondria within the muscle cells. As activity levels and energy requirements increase, the ability of oxidative metabolism to meet the increased demand for ATP replenishment is exceeded. Weight training and other forms of high-intensity training exist at the anaerobic end of the continuum, utilizing substrate that does not require added O_2. The diagram above represents the relationships between the energy substrates and the metabolic pathways in which they are used in different types of exercise. With the exception of very short-duration, all-out 1RM effort, no activity uses only one metabolic pathway, so the scale above represents a sliding scale of continually increasing intensity of activity. (*Starting Strength: Basic Barbell Training 3rd Edition*, Aasgaard, 2011)

1) ATP produced through glycolytic metabolism, if the effort lasts up to a couple of minutes, and 2) ATP produced by oxidation of fatty acids and glycolytic products, if the effort is of very long duration. However, *all the ATP utilized during muscle contraction comes from this stored ATP pool*, and the other processes function to replace it there.

The form of energy stored within the muscle is glycogen, the storage form of glucose, which is made up of long branched chains of glucose molecules stuck together. Intense exercise longer than 12 seconds and up to a few minutes in duration, such as longer sprints and high-repetition weight training, requires the breakdown of glycogen molecules into glucose, a process called glycogenolysis. The resulting individual glucose molecules are further broken down through the processes of glycolytic metabolism. Steps in this process generate ATP, and the ATP produced by glycolysis is available as a fuel for continued intense exercise.

In addition to ATP, glycolysis produces pyruvate and lactate as end products. These glucose breakdown products can be further used to produce ATP through oxidative metabolism. Lactate is able to move out of the cell and be taken up for use by other cells as a fuel for oxidative metabolism or, in the liver and kidney, as a precursor to new glucose formation. Under conditions of very high energy demand, lactate levels in the blood rise as release outstrips uptake.

Of lesser importance to individuals who train for strength and power is the production of ATP through oxidative metabolism. Lower-intensity rhythmic repetitive exercises that can be sustained for minutes to hours, like jogging, walking, or distance cycling, depend on the processing of fatty acids and glycolytic end products through the Krebs cycle and then the electron transport chain (ETC). Fatty acids are broken down into acetyl coenzyme A (Acetyl-CoA) through the process of beta-oxidation before entry into the Krebs cycle. Pyruvic and lactic acids also enter this system after they are converted to Acetyl-CoA. Both beta-oxidation and oxidative phosphorylation take place in the organelles known as mitochondria. Large amounts of ATP are produced by oxidative metabolism. Oxygen is required for this process.

But since a single set of a weight training exercise takes considerably less than a minute, is very intense, and consumes a lot of ATP, oxidative metabolism is not a factor in this type of training. Even though it does operate (all of the various processes of ATP production are always operating), oxidative metabolism contributes very little to the actual performance of a heavy set, since it transpires over a much longer timeframe and yields ATP more slowly. An overview of basic energetics is presented in Figure 4-2.

Training-Induced Muscle Adaptations

Strength training elicits numerous changes in both muscle structure and function. If the training program is well planned and the exercises are correctly performed, exercise-induced changes will enhance strength and power. If workouts are poorly planned and/or incorrectly performed, improvement may be absent, or performance may actually decay. Figure 4-3 illustrates the continuum of responses to different organizations of training programs with respect to reps per set.

When it comes to understanding the effects of various repetition schemes in training programs, there is a difference of opinion between those who rely on practical experience and those who assume that the interpretation of inadequate research is sufficient, as long as it is interpreted by tenured academics. Several academic sources have proposed that, in essence, all repetition schemes will result in the same gains in strength, power, mass, and endurance – that is, that doing a set at 3RM will yield the same result as doing a set at 20RM. This is in stark, obvious contrast to the observations of practitioners familiar with training athletes for performance. It ignores the basic tenets of metabolic specificity, the same principles that are enthusiastically applied to running and cycling. A 40-meter sprint is a much different race than an 800-meter event. Running a mile is different from running 26.2 miles. Sprinting a kilo is different than a 100k road race. Training for these events requires some degree of specificity, and no exercise physiologist would suggest that all running yields the same result. Why would anyone with even a passing interest in the training of athletes suggest that a 3RM squat, which takes a few seconds and exists entirely within the ATP/CP (adenosine triphosphate/creatine phosphate) end of the metabolic spectrum, yields the same training result as a set at 20RM that takes 60–120 seconds and exists squarely within the glycolytic middle of the spectrum? There are decades of fundamental research that supports the validity of the repetition continuum presented in Figure 4-3 and provides for a thorough understanding of the physiologic basis for the concept. That data has the added benefit of more than a century of recorded practical application to back it up. The failure to correctly apply this information results in wasted training time and ineffectively designed programs.

One of the results most closely associated with weight training is an increase in muscle size. This phenomenon, *hypertrophy*, is the result of increased protein synthesis and decreased protein degradation, which leads to an increased accumulation of proteins within the muscle cell and a resulting increase in the size of the whole muscle. Theoretically, there are two basic types of hypertrophy. In myofibrillar hypertrophy, more actin, myosin, and other associated proteins are added to those already existing in the cell. More contractile elements within the cell mean more actin/myosin interactions and more force production. This type of hypertrophy is typical of low-repetition, high-intensity training. It adds less mass but produces greater increases in the force generated per unit area of muscle than the second type of hypertrophy, sarcoplasmic hypertrophy. In sarcoplasmic hypertrophy there are more cytoplasmic and metabolic substrate accumulations than in myofibrillar hypertrophy. Lower-intensity, high-volume training produces a significant addition of myofibrillar elements but less than that added by high-intensity, lower-volume work. In the novice trainee, both types of hypertrophy occur simultaneously because the same stress produces both adaptations in the unadapted muscle.

Bodybuilding-type training utilizes very high-volume lower-intensity repetition and set configurations that cause a decrease – and subsequent increase – in metabolic substrate stores in the muscle. The addition of glycogen – and high-energy phosphates (the mechanism behind the effectiveness of creatine supplementation) – to the cell causes additional water to be stored. This effect, combined with minor accumulations of fat droplets, enzymes relevant to the additional activity, and a moderate increase in contractile proteins, causes the cell volume to increase. However, since this type of training lacks a significant force-production component, it explains why some individuals with smaller muscle mass are stronger than individuals with much more extensive muscular development derived from bodybuilding training.

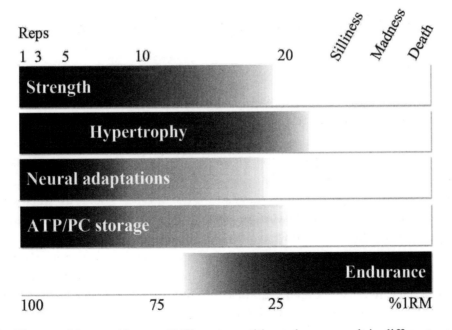

Figure 4-3. The repetition continuum. Different repetition schemes result in different anatomical and physiological adaptations.

Concentrations of the enzymes responsible for driving ATP production also increase as a consequence of training. Several researchers in the 1970s independently demonstrated increases in the concentrations of enzymes responsible for catalyzing all three of the ATP pathways discussed earlier. Of primary interest is the finding that concentrations of enzymes driving the resynthesis of ATP from ADP and creatine phosphate, as well as those responsible for glycolytic metabolism, can be increased with weight training. The degree of increase in enzyme concentrations is related to the duration, frequency, and intensity of training. Programs that elicit increased enzyme concentrations enhance performance through more efficient production and utilization of ATP.

Energy stores within the cell also increase in response to weight training. ATP and CP reserves increase by about 20% after a prolonged training program, resulting in more energy immediately available for contraction. Larger stores of ATP and CP correlate with improved power output. Glycogen stores are also increased as a result of prolonged training, which increases the amount of rapidly available energy and contributes to muscle hypertrophy.

Measures of contractile properties, such as power output, absolute strength, and rate of force production are obviously improved by training. These changes are likely related to the effects weight training has on the fiber-type composition of muscle, since the rate of ATP utilization differs according to fiber type. In decades past, changes in muscle fiber types were thought not to occur, but more recent research has shown that shifts in fiber type do in fact occur in response to various types of exercise. Furthermore, even in the absence of a fiber type change, fibers with slow-twitch contractile properties can assume more fast-twitch properties following strength training. Resistance training of four to six weeks in duration has been shown to reduce the number of muscle fibers classified as slow-twitch. It is also interesting to note that the intramuscular concentrations of ATP and CP are related to the fiber composition of a muscle; if ATP and CP are depleted in the muscle for long durations, there will be a switch from fast-twitch contractile properties to slow-twitch properties. It is also likely that the elevated ATP/CP stores associated with heavy weight training may drive this relationship in the other direction, toward fast-twitch characteristics.

Neural Integration: Stimulating the Muscle to Move

STRUCTURE AND FUNCTION

While the muscle fiber is the basic unit of contraction, without its intricate link to the nervous system, coordinated movement could not occur. The central nervous system is linked to muscle fibers by way of motor neurons. These neurons vary in size and innervate varying numbers of muscle fibers depending on fiber-type and muscle function. Slow-twitch fibers are innervated by smaller motor neurons. Fast-twitch fibers are innervated by larger motor neurons. In terms of speed and magnitude of conduction, think of the motor neurons for type-I fibers as drinking straws and those of type-II fibers as fire hoses.

The number of fibers innervated by a single neuron depends on the muscle and its function. Large muscles responsible for large-scale movements, such as the rectus femoris muscle of the thigh, have a low ratio of motor neurons to fibers, with a single motor neuron innervating a large number of fibers, up to one neuron for as many as 1000 fibers (1:1000). Muscles responsible for fine motor activity, such as certain eye muscles, may have a high ratio of neurons to fibers, nearing 1:10. The term **motor unit** is used to describe a motor neuron and all of the fibers it innervates, and the term **neuromuscular system** describes the functional integrated whole of the body's nerves and muscles. The motor unit is the basic functional unit of the neuromuscular system, since muscle fibers "fire" (go into contraction upon nervous stimulation) only within motor units as a group and never individually. Heavy, high-velocity training over time improves *recruitment*, defined as the number of motor units activated in the muscle and generating force during contraction. A higher percentage of recruited motor units within the muscle results in more force production by the muscle, and a higher number of motor units recruited within a shorter period of time results in more *power* production. The ability to recruit more motor units into contraction, and the ability to recruit motor units into contraction faster is one of the hallmarks of effective strength training. Neuromuscular improvement is one of the main reasons strength and power can be gained in the absence of muscle-mass increases, although hypertrophy normally accompanies a strength increase *because the adaptation to the stress of training involves both hypertrophy and increased neuromuscular efficiency.* This is why novices grow in both size and strength from the immediate onset of training.

The number of fibers innervated by a motor neuron dictates the maximum amount of force the motor unit can produce during contraction. The more fibers contained in the motor unit, the higher the force production. An active motor neuron stimulates all the fibers it innervates to contract. The amount of force a muscle generates will vary with the number of motor units recruited. If all the motor units in a muscle are recruited simultaneously – an event that occurs only as a result of a planned 1RM in training – maximum force is generated.

Motor units are recruited in a specific order, according to each one's threshold of stimulus required for the contraction to occur. Lower-threshold slow-twitch motor units are recruited initially regardless of the intensity of the exercise. These motor units are associated with the maintenance of normal posture when sitting and standing, and they fire when the body is not lying at rest. Walking increases low-threshold motor unit recruitment, since posture is being maintained while the body propels itself forward. The muscles associated with posture and walking – the calves and spinal erectors, for example – would therefore be expected to have proportionately higher percentages of slow-twitch fibers, and they do. During low-intensity aerobic-type exercise, slow-twitch motor units are preferentially recruited, but as intensity increases higher-threshold fast-twitch motor units get called into contraction. Low-threshold fibers continue to be recruited at high intensities but their contribution to the net force being produced is negligible relative to the contribution of the high-threshold fibers. If high power output is the objective of the training program, it must be designed to improve the ability to recruit high-threshold fast-twitch motor units.

NEURAL ADAPTATION

One of the tragic problems of human physical existence is the stubbornness of the neurological system, both to heal itself when damaged or diseased and to adapt to the stresses imposed by performance athletics and a life lived the hard way. We are born with a constrained ability to make our nervous system more efficient: for example, the standing vertical jump (SVJ) is the gold-standard for measuring neuromuscular efficiency. Its value lies in its diagnostic ability – it is not very trainable, and as such it is a very good test of genetic potential for explosion. In fact, training the SVJ misses the point of why it is used. A freak-level SVJ for a male would be 36 inches, and average is about 22 inches. A guy with a SVJ of 10 inches will never improve this ability much more than 25%, no matter how hard he trains. This is because the nerves that control neuromuscular efficiency don't adapt very well or very fast, nerves being among the most specialized tissues in the body. Add to this the other genetically controlled aspects of explosion – fiber-type allotment, anthropometrically-controlled leverage arrangement, height, sex, and other factors – and it becomes obvious that genetic gifts usually determine who we see at the pinnacle of human sports performance.

But still, an individual becomes more efficient in neuromuscular function – to the extent possible – by improving both technical competence and motor unit recruitment, so these aspects of performance must be trained. As performance increases, strength and power gains become more directly related to gains in muscle mass than to neural function, since muscular growth can occur long after technical and neural improvement plateaus. Nevertheless, whether for novices or for elite athletes, a primary training objective should be more complete, coordinated, and effective recruitment of motor units in the working muscle.

Hormones: Mediators of Physiologic Adaptation

Hormones are compounds produced by glands, and they are the regulators of the vast majority of the physiological functions in individual cells, the organs, and the body as a whole. Hormones are secreted into the entire body systemically, and their specific function is produced in the tissues that contain receptor sites sensitive to those particular hormones. Each hormone system is capable of responding to external stress, since the body uses these systems to cope with stress and to facilitate adaptation to future stress exposure. As such, hormone systems are an integral part of the mechanisms by which the processes in Selye's theory of adaptation operate. Each hormone has a characteristic effect or effects on specific target tissues (Table 4-2). Muscle magazines are filled with ads and articles about hormones and how to manipulate them through exercise, diet, and supplementation to get bigger and stronger, huge and muscular, more massive and powerful. As you might imagine, not all of these ads are accurate.

HORMONE FUNCTION

Hormones affect physiologic events in two basic ways. First, hormones can change the rate of synthesis of specific substances. Examples of this are an increase in contractile protein synthesis or increased enzyme production. Second, hormones change the permeability of cell membranes. Membranes are selective barriers, allowing certain molecules to pass into the cell while keeping other molecules out. Hormone-induced changes in membrane permeability affect cellular function in many ways, all of them important, since substances outside the cell are usually necessary for the modification of the environment inside the cell.

Training program composition (frequency of workouts, duration of workouts, exercises, sets, repetitions, and rest periods) affects hormone production in the body. Effective program design capitalizes on the body's innate hormonal response to these changes.

HORMONAL ADAPTATIONS

There has been considerable research in the area of hormone-specific exercise physiology. While exercise in general affects numerous hormone systems, a few hormones have a direct effect on muscle structure and function as they relate to weight training.

Testosterone. This hormone has been the center of much scientific and popular attention for many years as its role in anabolism – protein synthesis and tissue growth – is well known. It is also associated with neuromuscular efficiency, bone growth, metabolic rate, glycogen reserves, red blood cell production, and mineral balance. Elevated levels have a beneficial effect, but there is limited experimental evidence that exercise or training of any type elicits increased testosterone production.

Researchers have produced many studies of high-intensity, short-duration exercise such as weight training, which show increases, decreases, or often no changes in testosterone levels over the course of a workout. The inconsistency and lack of a clear pattern between these studies may be due to the relatively complex nature of resistance training. Protocols used have varied widely in the volume, load, intensity, rest intervals, and total muscle mass involved in the exercises. Each of the factors interacts with the others to affect the nature of the exercise stress and thus the response produced. Study design and its interpretation are further complicated by the normal circadian fluctuations of testosterone which may make changes more difficult to elicit, observe, and interpret, especially where few time points were selected for analysis.

Cortisol. In contrast to testosterone, the net effects of cortisol are catabolic – it acts as an anti-inflammatory by dismantling damaged tissues and ushering them in the direction of the excretory pathways, thus making room for the synthesis of new tissue. As a catabolic hormone it counters the effects of the anabolic hormones testosterone, growth hormone, insulin-like growth factor (IGF-1) and its isoform mechano-growth factor (MGF). Cortisol also likely suppresses protein synthesis by interfering with the cellular machinery responsible for protein replication, probably so that it doesn't have to tear down tissue that was just synthesized. Cortisol is secreted in response to both the physical stress of a hard workout, and the psychological stress of the many factors that play upon our psyches, such as personal relationship problems, sleep deprivation and insomnia, psychological issues related to disease processes, the loss of a loved one, or simple disruptions in lifestyle like job loss, schedule change, or even a vacation.

At any rate, when stress is applied to the body, cortisol production goes up, because of its role in removing damaged tissue, which is the normal consequence of training that is sufficiently stressful to cause an adaptation. Normal cortisol secretion promotes protein degradation and the conversion

Hormone	Function & Characteristics
Testosterone	Promotes muscle growth and development of male sex characteristics; anabolic; increases metabolic rate.
Cortisol	Increases in times of stress; catabolic; chronic elevation associated with decreased performance.
Growth Hormone	Develops and enlarges all tissue types; maintains connective tissue integrity.
Insulin	Drives glucose transport into cells; anabolic.
Glucagon	Drives movement of glucose into blood; catabolic.
Insulin-like Growth Factor I	Mediates growth factor action; anabolic.
Epinephrine	Mobilizes glycogen; increases muscle blood flow; increases cardiac contractility.

Table 4-2. Hormones of specific interest to training.

of proteins into carbohydrates, and conserves glucose by promoting fat utilization. At higher levels it promotes hyperglycemia, depresses immune function, produces perceptions of fatigue, and is probably one of the mechanisms that produce the symptoms of clinical depression often associated with severe overtraining.

It is important to understand that cortisol *will increase* with training that is sufficiently hard to produce an adaptation. An *overload event* is a training stress that is sufficient to disrupt homeostasis. An overload event elevates cortisol, every time and for every trainee, irrespective of the level of training advancement, and that elevation returns to baseline shortly after the workout that produced the overload event. A novice produces an overload-event-level cortisol elevation with his simple novice workout (see chapter 6), and that level returns to baseline in time for his next workout. The intermediate lifter produces his major cortisol elevation with the volume of his Monday workout, and the intensity day on Friday (see chapter 7) adds to cortisol elevation, but the level following both perturbations of homeostasis has returned to baseline in the hours following these workouts. An advanced lifter may require the accumulation of several weeks' training volume (see chapter 8) to produce the stress associated with an overload event. In all three cases, the cortisol elevation was the marker for a stress adequate to disrupt homeostasis and produce an adaptation.

Since exercise-induced cortisol levels are elevated transiently, a chronic elevation in cortisol could be the result of the effects of overlapping workouts that may not allow sufficient time for levels to drop back to baseline. This, coupled with the adverse psychological factors associated with overtraining, i.e. the worry associated with a competitive event and the implications of failure, and chronically elevated cortisol levels become a major potential contributor to overtraining.

Growth Hormone. Human growth hormone (GH) is a peptide (configured from amino acids, as opposed to a steroid) hormone that has numerous physiologic effects: it increases bone growth, cartilage growth, cell reproduction, and protein deposition in the cells. It stimulates the immune system, promotes gluconeogenesis in the liver, and drives metabolism toward fat utilization. It is thus elevated in situations of fasting or chronic caloric deprivation. Its primary anabolic function seems to occur in growing children and adolescents, and in adults its functions are primarily maintenance of connective tissue integrity. GH levels increase 8- to 10-fold after high-volume training involving multi-joint exercises. It plays a role in connective tissue repair after injury, and elevated levels thus aid in recovery from heavy training in a systemic way.

The role of training stress in growth hormone secretion remains unclear. Its relationship to fasting and low blood-sugar levels may have produced cause-and-effect/correlation confusion in previous analyses. It is clear that GH levels are elevated in circumstances where the body is under the environmental stress of caloric deprivation (easily simulated by the acute effects of a hard workout), but these elevated levels are quite probably managing the use of substrate, rather than promoting growth in adults. GH has not been demonstrated to elevate lean body mass in adults, and this comports with the absence of higher-than-normal levels of muscle mass in adults suffering from acromegaly, a disease caused by the overproduction of GH which results in large increases in bone and visceral organ mass.

Insulin. A highly anabolic peptide hormone, insulin regulates the permeability of cell membranes and facilitates the transport of glucose and other substances into the cell. This function is crucial for recovery from training, since depleted glucose and amino acids must be replaced so that comprehensive recovery processes can occur. Animal research has demonstrated that hypertrophy can proceed in the absence of insulin, so other mechanisms are also at work, but insulin remains one of the most potent, abundant, and easily manipulated anabolic hormones.

Insulin-Like Growth Factor. IGF-1 is a another peptide hormone similar to insulin in configuration. Insulin-Like Growth Factor-1 has a strong anabolic effect in both children and adults. It is secreted by the liver in response to growth hormone, and low levels of GH as well as inadequate protein and calorie intake can inhibit its release. It affects almost every cell in the body, and is a potent regulator of cell growth and DNA synthesis, primarily through the action of its important metabolite mechano-growth factor (MGF). MGF is the primary IGF-1 variant seen in circulation following heavy training, and its effects on the promotion of skeletal muscle hypertrophy are probably due to its influence on the proliferation of muscle cell nuclei.

Epinephrine/norepinephrine. These catecholamines have widespread effects all across human physiology as both neurotransmitters and hormones, and are largely responsible for the "flight-or-fight" response familiar to all humans. Epinephrine (EPI or adrenaline) and norepinephrine (NE or noradrenaline), acting as endocrine hormones, are produced in the adrenal glands located on top of the kidneys, and are secreted directly into the bloodstream. In its role as the neurotransmitter, NE is released at the sympathetic nerve endings. Among *many* other things, the combined effects of direct sympathetic nervous system stimulation and EPI/NE released into the blood cause an increase in the amount of blood the heart pumps each minute and promote the breakdown of glycogen. During intense bouts of training, epinephrine concentrations can increase a dozen times over. This may help the body cope with the rapid onset of exercise by quickly increasing blood supply to the working muscle and by helping provide a rapid energy source (glycogen/glucose/ATP). This response is transient, with exercise-induced increases returning to normal within six minutes of the cessation of exercise.

The bottom line for the athlete is that the body reacts to the stress of training with a specific sequence of hormonal responses. These responses derive from the body's general stress-response/adaptation mechanisms, as predicted by Selye's theory. If the coach designs an appropriate training program and the athlete adheres to it and gets adequate rest and good nutrition, the body will respond optimally to training – largely through hormonal mechanisms, and improved performance will be the result. Coaches can attempt to employ training methods that induce and capitalize on short-term hormonal responses and long-term hormone-mediated adaptations. However, with very few exceptions, coaches are forced to approach this task by the seat of the pants, as it were. Blood tests are not widely available or useful to the average coach; he must rely on his own observations of his athletes and correlate those observations with the signs and symptoms of what he knows to be the effects of desirable and undesirable hormone responses. Every athlete responds differently to stress to some degree, and age, sex, and recovery status will produce wide variations in these hormonal responses. Essentially, a coach must make an educated guess as to how to tailor the training program to induce the necessary hormonal changes required to drive improved performance.

Cardiovascular Considerations

When a heavy weight is lifted, several events occur that stress the cardiovascular system. One of the first is that the contracting muscles compress the blood vessels and thus increase their resistance to blood flow. This increase in resistance causes a dramatic increase in blood pressure. There are reports of blood pressure increases as high as four times their normal values. These pressures place a tremendous load on the heart, which has to pump harder to compensate and to continue to deliver blood not just to the compressed working muscle but to all areas of the body.

As a result of long-term weight training, the heart adapts to this stress by increasing the thickness of the muscular wall of the left ventricle. The increase in heart muscle mass enables the heart to deliver blood efficiently in spite of temporary blood pressure increases during exercise.

CARDIORESPIRATORY ADAPTATIONS

Cardiorespiratory adaptations are sometimes confused with aerobic or endurance adaptations. Aerobic/endurance adaptations relate directly to the efficiency of oxygen-dependent metabolism, and while endurance training may drive cardiorespiratory adaptations, they are not the same as those produced by strength training. Specifically, cardiorespiratory adaptations affect the capacity to efficiently deliver oxygenated blood to working muscles. Aerobic/endurance adaptations affect the oxygen-dependent mechanisms of ATP generation for prolonged, low-intensity exercise. Maximum oxygen consumption (VO_2max) is used as a measure of this ability. The development of more-efficient aerobic processes does not contribute to strength or power performance, either directly or indirectly. Exercise scientists trained in academic programs where aerobic exercise is the focus will usually say that aerobic training is necessary for all athletes, despite the fact that many studies have shown that aerobic training actually interferes with maximum strength and power development and expression.

These arguments should be evaluated with four things in mind. First, cardiorespiratory "fitness" is primarily a health issue, of concern to the medical community regarding the general public; competitive athletes do not fall within the population that should be concerned about heart attack prevention. (The fact is that elite competitive athletes are not concerned about their health – they are concerned about winning.) Individuals with below-average levels of cardiorespiratory capacity are in fact at a higher risk for developing high blood pressure and cardiovascular disease, both of which are certainly detrimental to performance. Competitive athletics has already selected against these individuals. People for whom aerobic training – doing "cardio" – addresses a problem that does not exist would be better served by devoting the time to skill acquisition, more complete recovery, or a hobby.

Second, although a degree of cardiorespiratory capacity is needed to more efficiently recover from sets or workouts, supply needed oxygen and nutrients to the working muscle, and carry away waste products fast enough for adequate recovery, strength training itself – by providing this specific stress – provides the mechanism for this adaptation without the need for any help from a treadmill. And in fact, anaerobic training alone has been demonstrated to develop aerobic capacity to above-average levels, thus reaffirming the stress/recovery/adaptation paradigm. The adaptations required for successful strength and power performance are supplied quite adequately by the stress of the work itself, thus invalidating the argument for including aerobic training in strength and power athletes' programs.

Third, even if an increase in VO_2max were desired, long slow distance-type endurance training is not as efficient a way to obtain it as a more intense approach to training would be. A concentrated dose of high-intensity glycolytic-type work lasting several minutes, utilizing exercises that incorporate a full range of motion for a large amount of muscle mass, which produces significant O_2 desaturation and subsequent a very high heart-rate and respiration-rate response, has been shown to drive improvement in VO_2max better than low-intensity long slow distance exercise that produces no oxygen desaturation at all.

Finally, research regarding the use of endurance training for strength and power athletes strongly suggests that endurance work *interferes with all the parameters such athletes are concerned with developing*. Aerobic training has a demonstrated tendency to reduce the magnitude of anaerobic improvement when the two are done together or in close sequence. Furthermore, when done together, the improvement in both aerobic and anaerobic is blunted considerably. The two adaptations compete for metabolic resources, and both cannot be trained to a high level simultaneously. Strength training for endurance athletes is quite beneficial for weaker endurance athletes, as has been previously discussed. The converse is not true: it has been well known since the 1980s that a program of endurance training will cause large reductions in vertical jump height, and all well-constructed studies done on the subject have concluded that power production is diminished by endurance training, in both the long and short term. For athletes whose sport requires a mix of anaerobic and aerobic/endurance training, separating the two by as little as an hour spares some of the negative effects of the endurance workout. Practical experience indicates that aerobic training may be included at low volumes and intensities if desired by the athlete or coach, but doing so contributes nothing to effective strength training and time management. The upshot of this is that many gifted and talented athletes have for decades excelled in their sports in spite of the unnecessary and counterproductive clutter of endurance training, not because of it.

The distinction between cardiorespiratory capacity and aerobic capacity is particularly important. Anyone who has ever done a 20RM set of squats knows that there is a cardiorespiratory component to the work. The depression in O_2 saturation produced by this high level of glycolytic intensity is much more disruptive to the homeostasis of oxygen transport and utilization than traditional low-intensity types of aerobic ("cardio") training. This is probably what drives both the moderate improvement in VO_2max seen in traditional weight training programs and the high degree of improvement associated with high-intensity glycolytic exercise: if you want to get better at breathing, breathing harder in your training is a pretty good approach.

Physical Potential

"Genetics" is a term bandied about fairly loosely in sports. A good definition of genetic potential is whether the athlete possesses the active genotype necessary to excel in sport. In simpler terms, does the athlete have a suitable set of genes, and enough of them turned on, to be good in the sport of choice? And how does the development of the organism within the environment affect the expression of the genotype?

Genetic endowment is strongly associated with athletic performance. While humans all swim in the same genetic pool, there is a huge amount of variation in both the genes possessed and the genes actively expressed. These variations lead to differences in performance potential. And so, like it or not, here is the rule: DNA → RNA → protein → function. The reality is that genetic potential ultimately affects the performance of every individual, and as such is an important part of the individual's physical potential.

Genotype – the genetic endowment of the organism – ultimately controls the limits of the phenotype – the physical expression of the organism in its environment – in that anything *not* coded will *not* be present. But it is crucial to understand that this does not mean that every gene present will always be expressed; it does mean *that which is not present cannot be expressed*. More importantly, the expression of a genetic trait depends on its presence in the genotype, but it is also quite dependent on the environmental conditions that determine whether or not it gets expressed during the development of the organism. It is quite possible to inherit all the genetic traits necessary for the ability to demonstrate a standing vertical jump of 38 inches, but to also contract polio as a child. In this tragic case, the genotype cannot be expressed in the phenotype. An individual may inherit the genetic endowment equivalent to that of a champion racehorse that remained locked in a stall all its life. For the ultimate phenotypic expression of an above-average genotype, the environmental conditions must permit *and favor* its expression.

Conversely, an individual may inherit the genetic endowment of a donkey. There are some fine donkeys, wonderful animals with lovely personalities and handsome faces, but there are no fast donkeys, no matter how they are fed, trained, threatened, or cajoled. (We will leave discussion of the breeding of racehorses vs. donkeys for another venue.) The average SVJ – the gold standard for the identification of genetics for explosive power – is about 22 inches for men ages 21–30. This means that about half the population jumps lower than this, and that some of the population jumps *much* lower than this. A 21–30 year-old male with a SVJ of 7 inches may be a fine golfer, but he will never be a power-dependent athlete of any outstanding ability.

But not all athletes are power athletes. Elite marathon performance is just as dependent on a particular physical potential as is elite Olympic weightlifting performance. Muscle fiber type allotment, stature, VO_2max, a psychological penchant for pain tolerance and the ability to deal with repetitive motion for long periods of time, and the ability to hold bodyweight down yet eat enough to recover (certainly not an exhaustive list) are examples of characteristics of both genotype and the optimal phenotypic expression for a successful marathon competitor. Many very good powerlifters are not particularly explosive, because strength is so highly developable over time. Different types of physical potential are obviously required for different sports.

Therefore, the ultimate physical potential of an athlete is determined by genetic endowment and the ability of the athlete to optimize its expression. This occurs when all the conditions for the greatest possible efficiency of this expression can be provided. These conditions include proper coaching of strength, conditioning, and sports expertise, optimal recovery circumstances such as the perfect diet and perfect rest and recovery, and the absence of interference with these things by variations in daily routine that disrupt these optimal conditions.

Occasionally an athlete possesses an excellent genetic profile, is highly motivated to succeed, is provided with optimal coaching and recovery conditions, responds well to training, and improves beyond expectations. These are the exceptions – those rare individuals that can make an average coach look exceptional as well. But most coaches and trainers must deal with all types of athletes, genetically gifted or not, with varying degrees of control over their circumstances and therefore varying degrees of control over their own physical potential. Only coaches who work at the highest levels of sports have the luxury of working with many gifted athletes. Most coaches must learn to deal with the average athlete, since they will make up the bulk of any normal team or clientele, and must relish the rare opportunity presented by the occasional genetic freak.

While coaches cannot alter an individual's "genetic potential," they can program appropriately to capitalize on each trainee's genetic endowment and environmental circumstances, to allow the optimum expression of physical potential – if that potential is correctly assessed and recognized. An athlete will progress faster and ultimately reach higher levels of performance if the nature of his potential is correctly identified and trained for. Everyone responds to training in much the same way, through the same mechanisms; only the rate of progression and the magnitude of the result will vary. This is why it is possible to define useful generalizations about training and coaching. But it also means that individualized training is necessary and that you must know your athletes – their strengths, their weaknesses, and the nature of their physical potential.

Frequently, individuals with great physical potential fail to train optimally, since success has always come easily. A lack of work ethic is sometimes *the result* of exceptional genetics, and cockiness occasionally allows a gifted athlete who trains inappropriately to be beaten by a less-gifted athlete who is receiving proper coaching, and who is motivated to succeed.

As is often the case, sports preparation can shed light on the human condition. Humans are built to move. We evolved under conditions that required daily intense physical activity, and even among individuals with lower physical potential, that hard-earned genotype is still ours today. The modern sedentary lifestyle leads to the inactivation of the genes related to physical performance, attributes that were once critical for survival and which are still critical for the correct, healthy expression of the genotype. The genes are still there, they just aren't doing anything because the body is not stressed enough to cause a physiological adaptation requiring their activation. The sedentary person's heart, lungs, muscles, bones, nerves and brain all operate far below the level at which they evolved to function, and at which they still function best.

Going Backward: Detraining

When an athlete stops a strength training program, there will be a regression in strength levels. Strength is a much more persistent adaptation than endurance. Strength declines much more slowly than VO_2max does, and the reasons for this are due to the differences in the nature of the two adaptations. Strength as an adaptation includes changes in the architecture of the muscle mass, the neuromuscular system, and the skeletal architecture. These changes take time to occur, and likewise they take time to reverse. In fact, a man who has gotten strong through an effectively designed program of barbell training will always respond more robustly and more quickly to a return to training than he did the first time as a novice, no matter how long a period of detraining he is subjected to.

In contrast, endurance adaptations are transient, in that they come on fairly quickly and go away quickly as well. You have probably noticed that the second time you ran 3 miles was noticeably easier than the first time, provided they were not done more than 4–5 days apart. This is due to the fact that adaptation to VO_2 max-dependent activity takes place within the extant metabolic machinery of the cells – we don't have to build new tissues to run faster and longer than we did last time, we just have to "tune up" the chemistry that's already present.

Endurance performance depends on the effective delivery of oxygen and substrate to the working muscles, their efficient use of oxygen and substrate, and the transport of waste products out of the area. In elite distance competitors, structural changes to the cardiovascular system have taken place over time, as well as a loss in muscle tissue extraneous to the specific performance, and other histological changes such as an increase in the number of mitochondria. But for the typical athlete who wishes to retain a more generalized physical capacity, the increase in endurance can occur without the large-scale loss of other abilities. An endurance adaptation for more general purposes, i.e. the ability to run 3 miles a couple of times per week, can be obtained and retained in a very short period of time, because the adaptations do not require extensive structural modifications – they work with what's already there.

The differences between these two types of adaptation are profoundly important for applied physical performance in a non-sport-specific situation. For example, a deployed soldier in a battlefield scenario must often depend on his physical preparedness to stay alive. Strength has been universally reported to be a more valuable capacity than the ability to run 5 miles in 30 minutes, because at the time of this writing our combat troops are *mechanized.* They don't have to walk or run into combat, since we have machines for that now. If a limited endurance capacity is necessary – and some could successfully argue that it is – that capacity can be readily developed in a few weeks prior to deployment, while a much more valuable strength adaptation takes many months or years to acquire, is more important to combat readiness than endurance, *and is a much more persistent adaptation in the face of forced detraining than the ability to run,* which you're not going to use on the battlefield anyway. The stubborn insistence on an endurance-based preparation for combat readiness is an unfortunate anachronism that should be reevaluated soon.

A trainee's ability to generate force slowly decreases after the last overload event. The longer a lifter has been training, the longer it will take to completely detrain, but everyone experiences a loss of strength if training stops. This loss of strength is perfectly consistent with what we know about the stress/adaptation response. In this case, the stressor is a lack of activity, and the corresponding adaptation is detraining.

If an athlete stops training for a period of a few months and restarts training again, he should start back one level (see chapters 6, 7, and 8) below where he was when he stopped. For example, an intermediate trainee who stopped for 6 months would re-start using a novice's program. He would continue using this program until his previous levels of strength were regained, and then move to a program consistent with where he was before he quit training. This process will occur much faster than the first time, due to a group of phenomena collectively referred to as "muscle memory." A combination of persistent neuromuscular adaptations and increased numbers of muscle cell nuclei make the rebuilding process proceed quickly. The replacement of the layoff-depleted glycogen stores and cytoplasmic volume are the main reasons muscle size returns as quickly as it does. In other words, the presence of all the metabolic machinery originally built during previous training and a diminished but quickly replaceable level of the substrate that makes it work are the factors that make regaining previously acquired muscle size and function occur in a fraction of the time it originally took.

A longer training hiatus requires a different approach. If an advanced or elite trainee "retires," and then a year or two later decides to once again start training and competing, it would be best to begin with a version of a novice program, rather than reducing just one level to an intermediate program. This athlete has regressed far enough away from his physical potential and previous physical capacity that a short period of simple progression will be the fastest and safest way to restore lost performance ability. After the gains from simple linear progression begin to plateau, the athlete would follow an intermediate program for the short time it would be useful, and then, when improvement plateaus or when the coach judges him ready, he would move on to an advanced training organization again. This entire process might take anywhere from 3 months to a year, depending on the athlete, the sport, and the length of the layoff, but in any case, the process would take a fraction of the time originally invested in the progress from baseline.

It is very important to understand that previously-trained athletes returning from layoffs – even relatively short layoffs – must be handled with care. Ambition is useful, greed is dangerous: We're happy that you're back to your training, but try to remember that *you're out of shape now*, and you have to do some homework or you'll get hurt. Maybe badly. Athletes with even an intermediate training history have developed a neuromuscular system that is far more efficient than that of an untrained individual; this athlete can still recruit a high percentage of his available motor units, although they are not prepared to be used very hard. An athletic neuromuscular system enables the muscles to generate more force than they are currently conditioned to produce. In practical terms, this means that these trainees are going to be very, very sore, unless marked restraint is used for the first few workouts. The athlete or coach ignores this fact at his peril. Extreme cases of soreness, to the point of loss of function, disability, or even rhabdomyolysis (the breakdown of muscle caused by mechanical, physical, or chemical injury that can lead to acute renal failure due to the accumulation of muscle breakdown products in the blood) can and certainly do occur. So coaches and trainees need to resist the urge to push to the limit when returning to training after a layoff. During the recommended simple progression we are rapidly redeveloping the mechanical and metabolic adaptations within the muscle to match the neural abilities that have persisted over the period of detraining. But this still takes some time. Patience here is a priceless virtue.

5

Training Program Basics

Strength training programs may vary considerably depending on the sport, the goal, the athlete, and the coach. But all strength training is based on the use of a few basic tools. These have been developed over the past hundred or so years out of the experiences of millions of smart folks who paid attention to what worked and what didn't while they were getting strong.

Repetitions

Organized training programs are based on the concept of the "repetition maximum" (RM or max) or personal record (PR). This is the maximum weight that an individual can lift for a specific number of repetitions:

1RM = maximum weight that can be lifted one time

10RM = maximum weight that can be lifted ten times in a single set

All RM tests that are lighter than a 1RM are, by definition, done with a submaximum weight, since a 1RM defines maximum. A 5RM will be done with a weight that is 85 to 90% of the 1RM, and is thus submaximal. It is very heavy relatively – the maximum that can be done for 5 reps – but it is still submaximal to 1RM.

There is no single repetition scheme that is appropriate for achieving all training goals (Figure 5-1). The number of reps per set is important because **different numbers of reps produce different types of adaptations.** This is an extremely important principle of exercise programming, and it often goes unappreciated by those without a background in the subject, and misinterpreted by those who do.

Strength is the ability to produce force: high force production requires heavy weights, and maximum force production requires 1RM effort. So sets consisting of single reps, doubles, and triples using 90 to 100% of 1RM loads involve the highest force production and build the most strength. In fact, if we are to produce an effort that comes as close as possible to 100% of motor units recruited into contraction, we must perform a 1RM, because there is no other way to ensure that as many motor units as possible come into contraction.

Muscular hypertrophy is traditionally trained by using higher reps (8 to 12 or more) at lighter weights (65 to 80% of 1RM) while restricting rest between sets so that subsequent sets are performed in a state of fatigue and vascular occlusion – the "pump." If the vessels that carry blood to the muscles in longer sets are squeezed shut – *occluded* – by the engorged muscle mass, the breakdown products are prevented from being immediately removed, thus prolonging their effects on the occluded tissue and thus increasing the signaling for growth and repair factors in the area of the occlusion.

However, the fastest muscular hypertrophy any trainee will ever experience is during his initial novice progression where he uses sets of 5 reps to get strong as rapidly as possible – and therefore to get bigger as fast as possible. A stronger muscle is a bigger muscle, since strength is proportional to the cross-sectional area of the muscle belly, and the way a muscle makes itself capable of producing more contractile force is to grow the myofibrils, which also makes the muscle larger. Sets of 12 do not accomplish this objective for a novice as fast or as effectively as 5s do, so in this particular and very common situation, 3 sets of 5 reps works better for hypertrophy than the plan typically used by advanced bodybuilders who have progressed past this phase of training. As we shall see, sets of 5 reps are very useful.

Power, the ability to demonstrate maximum force production as quickly as possible, can be displayed and practiced by using lower numbers of reps (1–3) performed at maximum velocity with loads between 50 and 75% of 1RM. The rapid recruitment into contraction of as many motor units as possible is the component of power utilized when each individual repetition is performed at maximum velocity. The other component of power – the amount of force produced – is developed using heavier weights, and this strength is applied as power when the acceleration of the load becomes the primary feature of the exercises used. Movements such as cleans and snatches that incorporate acceleration of the barbell as inherent features of the movement pattern are the best exercises for pacing power production with a strength increase. Volitionally-accelerated movements such as "dynamic effort" deadlifts are less effective than cleans and snatches because the acceleration of the bar is not an inherent part of completing the movement.

The load range of 50 to 75% of 1RM allows most people to develop maximum power in each rep, and this is not coincidentally the percentage range of the 1RM deadlift that most people can clean. This weight is heavy enough that a high amount of force must be used to accelerate it, but light enough that the velocity can peak at a level that is sufficiently high for power production.

In power sports that involve lengthy competition periods that are comprised of an accumulation of higher-intensity bursts of effort (football, basketball, some field positions in soccer and hockey), endurance represents the ability to produce many consecutive bursts of anaerobic effort, as opposed to the more conventional understanding of the term "endurance" to mean long durations and low intensities. This type of anaerobic endurance is dependent on strength, and for the already-strong athlete it is best prepared for by increasing the number of low-rep sets, which more closely mimics the metabolic demands of the sport. The common misunderstanding of endurance in this context leads to the use of increasing numbers of reps per set, mistaking low-intensity endurance for what actually happens on the field. An example would be the use of multiple short sprints, perhaps 40 reps of 20 meters, as opposed to doing the whole 800 meters at a slower pace.

Although endurance is usually associated with long slow distance (LSD)/aerobic exercise, it is important to understand that there are different types of endurance. LSD is one example, but endurance can mean several things. Local muscular endurance – the ability to tolerate the pain that develops in the muscles during intense efforts lasting 30 seconds to several minutes – can be very effectively improved through weight training. High-rep sets are used for this purpose. And by increasing the absolute strength

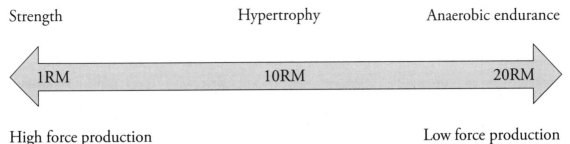

Figure 5-1. The repetition continuum. Different numbers of reps have different training effects, and it is important to match the correct reps to the goal of the trainee.

of an endurance athlete, it is possible to quite effectively increase the time to fatigue by reducing the relative effort required for each submaximum contraction. High reps, in excess of 15, can be used effectively for such athletes to increase pain tolerance and the ability to contract while fatigued, and sets of 5 reps with heavier weights can be used on alternating workout days to increase absolute strength. Even though neither of these rep schemes directly improves any aspect of oxidative metabolism, both do in fact improve aerobic endurance performance.

Sets of 20 or more reps will significantly improve muscular endurance, but will not produce large strength gains due to the lighter weights necessarily involved, and this is certainly not optimal for any athlete with the primary goal of improving either power or strength. Athletes for whom power must be produced repeatedly for extended periods must still be trained to produce power in the first place, and high-rep sets do not accomplish this. The advantage of using multiple low-rep sets is that both power and strength are trained in the precise metabolic context in which they will be used in competition.

But in the final analysis, sets of 5 reps have proven over the decades to be the most useful number of reps per set for strength training. Strength coaches rely on 5s for training lifters from the novice to the world-class levels of training advancement for several reasons. They allow the use of sufficiently heavy weight to be an effective strength stimulus, without the injury potential of near-1RM loads. They are better for general training purposes than singles across because they allow more technique practice with more reps. They are enough reps that a coach can effectively interact with the lifter during the set, and the lifter can make corrections and embed them into his movement pattern, thus improving technique in real time. When done for 3–5 sets across, they allow the accumulation of enough volume and workload to be an effective endurance and hypertrophy stimulus. For these reasons, successful athletes and lifters will use sets of 5 for their entire careers under the bar.

Sets

Most national exercise and credentialing organizations recommend 1 to 3 *sets* (groups of repetitions) per exercise, irrespective of the fitness goal. This is an Exercise approach, not a Training approach. It is generally acceptable in that it works better than no exercise at all, and therefore improvements will occur for those people who have never exercised before, but the results would be better if the number of sets is actually designed to produce a specific result and achieve a definite training objective. Doing 1 to 3 sets of 8 to 12 reps may be enough to achieve the exercise goal of a typical health club member, or it may be adequate for assistance exercises after a barbell training workout. It is inadequate for athletes trying to improve strength and power.

As with other aspects of training, the number of sets must produce the metabolic effect desired as an adaptation. One set of an exercise is not capable of producing the stress that multiple sets can produce, because *stress is cumulative*. If one set is all the work that is necessary to force an adaptation, then the athlete has not been training either very long or correctly, because an athlete's ability to adapt to training volume is itself one of the aspects of physiology that adapts. As an athlete progresses through the stages of advancement, more stress is required to disrupt homeostasis. One set of an exercise – no matter how hard, or long, or heavy – is not enough stress to cause a strength adaptation in an already-adapted athlete. As an athlete progresses past the novice stage, his adaptive capacity becomes advanced to the point where stress must be accumulated, not just with multiple sets during one workout but over several workouts, and training complexity must accommodate this fact. This will require programming more complicated than one-set-to-failure, one set of twenty, or other types of single-set training organizations.

Multiple sets are required to make the best use of a trainee's gym time. Basic exercises that are critical for enhancing sport performance should be done for multiple sets. Depending on the trainee's level of advancement, this could be as few as 3 sets for novices or as many as a dozen sets for the advanced athlete. Numbers of sets, as mentioned above, can accumulate for an emphasis on endurance for sports that involve long periods of time under competitive stress, such as football or boxing.

When referring to the number of sets, a distinction must be made between warm-up sets, the lighter preparatory work that readies the trainee for heavier work, and work sets, which accomplish the training objective for that workout. Warm-up sets prepare the tissue and the motor pathway for the coming work. As such, they should not fatigue or interfere with the work sets: their purpose is to facilitate the work sets, not function as work themselves. *When properly planned, warm-up sets need not be counted as work, since they will always be light enough that in the absence of the subsequent work sets no adaptation would result from their having been done.*

Work sets are the heavy sets that produce the training effect of the workout; they constitute the stress that causes the adaptation. They may be progressive – they may go up five or ten pounds per set until they are all done – or they may be done "across," with the same weight for all sets. Progressive sets are a good way to explore an athlete's capabilities with a load if uncertainty exists about his ability with it. For instance, coming back from a missed week, an injury, or an illness might indicate the need for small progressive jumps at work-set intensity. Sets of 5-rep squats at 285, 295, 305, 315, and 325 are an example of progressive sets for an athlete otherwise capable of 315×5×5 (5 sets of 5 reps each, all done with 315 pounds on the bar), which is an example of sets across. Sets across is a marvelous way to accumulate total volume of high quality, since the weight chosen is repeated for all the work sets, producing a higher average load at the limit of the trainee's ability.

Rest Between Sets

The time between sets is an important variable in workout configuration. Several exercise organizations recommend 30 seconds to 2 minutes between sets. If strength gains are the primary training objective, rests of greater than 2 minutes are not only okay, but quite necessary. While partial recovery from anaerobic exercise is rapid, complete recovery doesn't occur for several minutes, depending on several individual factors such as the intensity of the set, the fatigue and nutritional status of the lifter, as well as the trainee's age, the temperature of the facility, and injury status. Competitive strength and power athletes often use rests between sets of 10 minutes or more, depending on the load. In contrast, if muscle hypertrophy is the only concern, rests of 45 seconds or less are often used. If training is designed to increase muscular endurance and conditioning, very little, if any, rest is taken between the sets of different exercises.

It is also important to consider which sets the rest occurs between. Warm-up sets function as preparation for work sets, and they should be approached with this in mind. The lightest warm-ups will not be heavy enough to produce any fatigue, and no rest need be taken longer than the time it takes to load the bar for the next set. As they get progressively heavier, more time should be spent between warm-up sets. Remember: warm-ups facilitate work sets – they should not interfere with them. If three heavy sets across are to be done after warm-up, 15 warm-up sets done as fast as possible up to 5 pounds away from the work set would obviously be counterproductive, since the fatigue produced by the warm-up would interfere with the work-set intensity.

Workout Frequency

The American College of Sports Medicine (ACSM) prescribes training two days per week for improving "muscular fitness." Many exercise organizations propose a three day per week schedule, yet the vast majority of elite weightlifters train six days per week, with multiple workouts per day. Why such a discrepancy? First, the ACSM's guidelines are minimal recommendations for the sedentary, completely unadapted-to-exercise general American public, not for athletes who have been training for years. It is wise for athletes in training to ignore exercise recommendations for the general public. Second, textbook recommendations almost always fail to account for individual differences in ability, level of training advancement, training objective, and all the other parameters that may influence the ability to recover from more frequent training. Finally, elite athletes are highly adapted to training and can not only tolerate, but in fact require, much higher training loads than novice or intermediate trainees to sufficiently disrupt homeostasis and facilitate further adaptation. This level of training stress cannot be administered in three sessions per week – it must be distributed more uniformly over the week. This will require many more than three workouts per week and possibly multiple daily workouts for some athletes. These specific details are addressed in subsequent chapters.

Too few workouts per week will not adequately stress the body, and no positive adaptation will occur. A common way to organize training among recreational lifters and bodybuilders is a "split" routine, where one body part or "muscle group" is worked each day, until the entire body has accumulated a workout. If "chest" is trained only once a week, even though training may occur several days per week, "chest" will not receive enough work to constitute overload, and optimal adaptation cannot occur. By the same token, "chest" will usually include triceps, since the bench press is the favorite chest exercise; if "shoulders" involves pressing, "arms" get their own day too, and "back" to people like this really means lats, and therefore lat pulldowns or chins. It is therefore possible to expose the triceps to four or more workouts in a week. This is an example of poor training organization producing a schedule that includes both *inadequate* and *excessive* exercise frequency at the same time.

It is also important to note that the incidence of training injury is not significantly increased with greater strength training frequency. However, it is quite high with more than 5 aerobic workout days per week. These kinds of aerobic exercise programs involve thousands of identical, repetitive movements over a short range of motion, and are thus inherently different from weight training, even when weight training workout frequency is very high. The end result is a higher incidence of repetitive use injuries in endurance training than in strength training.

Exercise Selection

The combinations of exercises included in a workout and in a long-term training program directly affect progress. The most important consideration is to select exercises that have a direct application to the training objective. For a novice, the primary consideration is strength, since strength is the most effective way to improve the performance of any athlete who is not already very strong. Strength applies in a general way to any athletic performance, and a novice needs no particular specialization in exercises since an increase in strength applies to any sport in a general way.

Strength and its corollary power are developed by a very few exercises that are very general in nature – the squat, press, deadlift, bench press, and the power clean and power snatch are the best developers of strength and power. The improved capacity for strength and its explosive application applies to every sport that demands it, irrespective of how it was specifically acquired, because strength and power are applied specifically on the field through *practice* of the skill used on the field. Strength is *trained* most effectively through the use of these specific exercises that are the most efficient at developing strength. No consideration should be given to making the strength exercises look like the sport, because this will mean that the effectiveness of the exercise for training strength has been made a secondary consideration.

This is critical to the understanding of the very basis of strength and power for athletics: strength, and its corollary, power, are best acquired in ways that best develop strength and power, *not in ways that look like the application of that strength and power on the field.* The very general characteristics of strength and power are developed by *training* for strength and power, and then applied specifically to the sport during the *practice* of that sport. Squats, for example, are the best way to build general strength. So we squat in a way that produces the strongest squat for the greatest amount of muscle mass over the longest efficient range of motion (ROM), because that is the way to produce the strongest squat, and therefore the most strength. We do *not* squat in a way that mimics positions or stances encountered in, for example, football, because that would mean a less-efficient squat, and would compromise the ability of the squat to produce the greatest strength. Which is more useful: a lineman that squats 550 pounds with a full ROM and the stance that best facilitates that full ROM, or a lineman that quarter-squats 650 with a stance that mimics his stance off the line? This is an important question, and the answer may not be obvious, so be careful how you answer it. (Hint: How much can the 550-pound full-squatter do at a quarter-squat, and in any stance or at any depth below that?)

Virtually every single effective exercise program for sports performance will include the following rather short list of weight room exercises: squat, press, deadlift, bench press, clean or power clean, jerk, snatch or power snatch, and chin-ups or pull-ups. And few, if any, other exercises are ever necessary for the effective strength and power development of an athlete at any level of training advancement. Novices and advanced athletes use the same exercises, because these are the movement patterns that must get stronger to drive increases in strength and power. The differences in programming lie in variations of load, intensity, frequency, and rest.

This has pivotal implications for strength and conditioning for athletics. Contrary to popular representation by the "functional training" community, the variables to be manipulated for strength and power training for athletes are load, intensity, frequency, and rest – not the number or variety of the exercises used in training. The purpose of strength and power training is to get stronger and more powerful. This can be done most effectively with 7 or 8 exercises and their variations programmed for an increase in intensity and volume over time. It cannot be accomplished with 30 different exercises that cannot be revisited frequently enough to strengthen them significantly, or that, more importantly, lack sufficient muscle mass and neuromuscular resources to create a systemic stress that drives systemic adaptation. There are only a few barbell exercises that fit the needs of athletes to become stronger and therefore more powerful, and those are the ones that must be *trained*. The others can only be *exercised*.

The next consideration in exercise selection is how many times per week an exercise, or type of exercise, should be done. This would be based on the lifter's level of training advancement. Novices will train 3 times per week, squatting, pressing or bench pressing and deadlifting or power cleans each workout, with some chins done once per week. Novices do not benefit from training more frequently, and the details will be examined in chapter 6.

Once the novice phase of training is completed and a strength base has been firmly established, other considerations become important. By this time, the trainee has some idea about the direction his training will take. Competitive Olympic lifting, powerlifting, or sports that a strength and power base enables him to play are different expressions of the continued reason to train. The approach he takes will be determined by which path toward the application of his training he follows. Olympic weightlifters typically train more often than powerlifters, perhaps 5 to 6 days per week, because of the need to practice the technically challenging lifts, the fact that these lifts are not as fatiguing as absolute strength movements, and the need to continue to train for strength at the same time. Powerlifters tend to train 3 or 4 days per week, and players of field sports must work their strength training into a practice schedule determined by team activities.

As a general rule, the more advanced the athlete, the more frequent the training, but this is not always the case. Extremely advanced powerlifters – due to their accumulation of many years of experience, a few injuries, and a considerable level of strength, may decide that twice a week is sufficient to be under the bar. This is probably not representative of competitive athletes in most other sports, which tend to see advanced open competitors in their late twenties who have to train frequently to continue driving adaptation.

Workouts should consist of three to five exercises, with the most emphasis placed on basic exercises, and any assistance exercises done at the end of the workout. Athletes seldom need more exercises than this, but if circumstances warrant, say, 6 exercises, it may be more effective to do them in 2 workouts per day rather than all in a single session. Few coaches and athletes are afforded the luxury of unlimited time in the gym, so if 6 exercises are required and they must be done in one workout, try to do them efficiently – perhaps by doing your warm-ups for the next exercise between the work sets of the previous exercise – or reevaluate your program.

Exercise Variation

It is normal to vary the individual exercises and total number of exercises included in a training program at several levels: the individual workout, the training cycle, and according to the advancement of the trainee. For the novice, effective workouts are short, basic, intense, and rapidly progressive. Exercises are chosen to accomplish the program's specified goal in the most efficient manner possible. This means large-scale, multi-joint exercises that will always include the squat, deadlift, press, bench press, and power clean, unless there are injuries that prevent the inclusion of one that cannot be performed. But again, productive training is facilitated by the use of movements that can be trained, and not all exercises fit this description.

The reason is simple and obvious: squats, presses, deadlifts, bench presses, and the Olympic lifts work the whole body at one time, and therefore allow the use of enough weight to make dramatic levels of stress and subsequently adaptation possible. Chopping the body up into its constituent components and then working these components separately lacks the capacity to make things change. The stress that can be applied to one piece at a time never adds up to the same stress that can be applied to the whole thing working as a system. And the whole body has evolved to work as a system by the selective processes that have accumulated the genotype, and consequently the phenotype.

The term "synergy" is the interaction of multiple elements in a system to produce a coordinated effect greater than the sum of the individual effects of the separate elements. The accumulated action of the parts functioning in their anatomically and biomechanically predetermined roles as components in a complex system of levers and motors is the very definition of synergy. It's also the very definition of coordination. The normal functions of the different components of the musculoskeletal system can't be simulated by isolating them and making them work independently of their roles in the system, because such a large part of their function involves their coordinated relationships with all the other components.

So the basis of effective programming for strength training is the use of multi-joint barbell exercises, large muscle masses working in a coordinated manner. These exercises are simply normal human movement patterns that are loaded using a barbell with progressively heavier weights. As the weight increases, it becomes more important that the movements be performed correctly. Effective strength training therefore requires that coaches be effective teachers of movement skills, and that athletes become better at learning them. As trainees proceed from the novice stage to the intermediate stage, the number of exercises in the program increases. This is because they have gained strength and motor skill and can now tolerate and directly benefit from exposure to a wider variety of movement patterns.

However, effective strength training programming will never devolve into the rotation of exercises for the sake of variety and excitement. The variables in effective strength training are always load, volume, intensity, and rest; variety for its own sake is a hallmark of Exercise, not Training. Progress in strength training means a progressive increase in force production, and this requires the use of exercises that permit that progressive increase. Basic exercises like the squat, press, deadlift, bench press, and the Olympic lifts can be used with progressively heavier weights for years at a time, and *assistance exercises* cannot.

Assistance exercises are the usual culprit when variety is introduced inappropriately into programming. Assistance exercises use less muscle mass, a shorter kinetic chain, or are some variant of the parent exercise that is less efficient at allowing as much weight to be lifted, or more weight to be lifted through a partial ROM. In *Starting Strength: Basic Barbell Training, 3rd Edition*, these exercises are categorized as either *assistance exercises*, which are variations on the parent exercise, like rack pulls, stiff-legged deadlifts, RDLs (Romanian deadlifts), close-grip benches, and low-box squats, or *ancillary exercises*, which work a group of muscles in a way that the primary exercises do not, like a chin-up or a back extension. Assistance exercises can be very effectively used to address a weakness in a particular part of the ROM of the primary movement.

Partial movements, like rack pulls, partial benches, and press lockouts in the rack, that use heavier weights through a shorter portion of the ROM of the parent exercise, can be improved right alongside their parent exercises, and can be used to drive progress for as long as they are trained. But they do not constitute a replacement for the parent exercise, because they are not using the full ROM; rather, they are used to drive continued progress on the primary lifts for more advanced trainees.

An exception to this is the use of partial squats, perhaps the most common distraction in any weight room. Half-squats allow the use of much heavier weights because of the shorter ROM, but they fail to recruit the elements of the posterior chain that come into play at the bottom of the ROM – the adductors, external rotators, and the full loading of the hamstrings – because of the knees-forward/back-vertical technique used to do them, and the anatomical fact that the use of these muscles is dependent upon a full-ROM to call them into contraction. Below-parallel squats paused on a box are a quite useful variation for advanced trainees, but partial squats should never form *any* component of an athlete's training. Remember: a lineman who squats 550 with a full ROM is always stronger than a lineman who quarter-squats 650.

Novices should make progress on the primary exercises for as long as possible, and when the level of advancement reaches the point at which progress becomes difficult on the basic exercises, variety is introduced with the addition of these assistance exercises. For a novice, the premature substitution of assistance movements for the primary exercises is the fastest, easiest way to stall progress in a strength program.

Even more distracting are the types of assistance exercises that have no ability to drive long-term progress in strength and power. Isolation movements for single muscle groups, like preacher curls and leg extensions, utilize the changing length of the lever arm to produce the resistance against the isolated joint they are working. **One muscle or muscle group is never used in isolation in athletics**, and it is pointless to train its strength and neuromuscular function in isolation. In contrast, the primary barbell exercises all feature the load moved through a straight vertical line over the center of balance of the body against the floor – the middle of the foot – or the scapulas against the bench in the case of the bench press. This balanced movement pattern is typical of the way humans always handle loads – it is safer for the body to keep an external load nearer to the center of balance than it is to expose a single joint to a long moment arm.

In addition, all the basic barbell exercises can be assessed with a one-rep maximum effort. This doesn't mean that they *should* be tested for 1RM – it just means that they can be. Novices will have a new theoretical 1RM every workout, since they are getting stronger every workout by doing sets of 5, so 1RM testing is pointless for novices, and for intermediates too, since they are still getting stronger every week. In contrast, assistance exercises cannot effectively be done for 1RM. Imagine a 1RM preacher curl or dumbbell fly, or even a 1RM RDL (try it sometime – it cannot be quantified precisely), and you can easily see the point.

Increases in exercise variety are therefore constrained to the use of movements that have the capacity to contribute to the objectives of the program. During the late novice and intermediate phases, an athlete who will ultimately proceed to the advanced level defines the course of his career, choosing a sport to train for and compete in. Many decisions are required of the athlete at this point. Strengths and weaknesses, abilities and interests, time and financial constraints, and the support of family and friends are gauged. This involves experimentation with training and its application to the chosen sport, and it requires a greater variety of exercises than a novice either needs or can tolerate. An intermediate's skills are developing as fast as his strength, power, and recovery ability. It is at this time, when the ability to learn is peaking, that an athlete benefits most from exposure to new movement patterns and new types of stress. This would be the time to introduce the Olympic lifts as regular features of the program – they fit the criteria for effective training exercises, and exposure to them hones the athletic skills of the athlete, challenging the ability to effectively move the barbell through space efficiently as well as with more force and power. They are an important addition to the preparation for any sport, not just for competitive Olympic weightlifting.

Advanced athletes already know the things an intermediate is learning, and have by definition developed their competitive careers into a specialization in one sport. These athletes use fewer exercises, because they know exactly which ones are relevant to competitive success and know how to manipulate their well-developed stress/adaptation mechanisms. An elite athlete is an accomplished competitor, an expert in his sport, and is far along his training trajectory, approaching the limit of his potential. He has developed a highly individual training program that might involve only four or five exercises but that very specifically develops critical aspects of his already highly-adapted muscular, neuromuscular, and psychological abilities.

For advanced athletes, programming for strength training may also become more specialized with respect to the metabolic demands of the sport. Most athletes in most sports will never need training complexity beyond the intermediate level, because they are unable to devote sufficient time to the strength program during the training year to exhaust the potential of the intermediate weekly overload event. An advanced lifter is a competitor in powerlifting or Olympic weightlifting. But the advanced phases of programming may also be reached by competitors in strongman, the field throwing events, Highland Games competitors, and some football players, depending upon the way they were coached in the weight room. If the sport requires brief, explosive bouts of high power generated by the whole body, the training program must be capable of producing this adaptation, either on the field or in the weight room. If the sport requires pulses of explosion for several seconds repeated over a longer period of time, the exercises used in either the strength program or the field practice – perhaps both – must challenge the depth of the ATP-CP system's ability to provide for this. If the sport demands muscular endurance at intensities near anaerobic threshold for extended periods, the program must be capable of producing this glycolytic stress in a controllable, programmable way. All these requirements are predicated on the athlete's strength, which must be adequate to the task before more elaborate preparations are necessary.

This type of specialization, both in terms of exercise variety and metabolic specificity, is completely irrelevant until the athlete has advanced well beyond the novice phase of training and is already very strong. And "very strong" means different things to different athletes. A 300-pound lineman cannot be considered "very strong" until he is squatting 600×5, while a 135-pound marathoner might well be "very strong" at 185×5. Keep in mind that strength is the basis of power and most other things as well, and though it might be tempting to do a "football-specific" program when your squats are only 225×5, the time wasted in an attempt to be prematurely specific is very expensive in terms of performance on the field. A lineman who squats 225×5 against a lineman who squats 600×5 gets mashed *every single time*, no matter how specifically he has prepared. Remember: getting strong is the best general preparation for any sport where power is a factor – so general, in fact, that it becomes the most important thing you can do.

New exercises added to a program should have a purpose other than just being new. For example, for an Olympic lifter, reasonable squat variations might be below-parallel pause squats and front squats. The leg press would not be reasonable because it does not work enough muscle mass under the conditions in which a strength adaptation is used in sports. Again, this does not mean that the exercise copies the precise movement pattern used in the sport – it must, however, duplicate the conditions in which the desired adaptation will be used, e.g. cycling and swimming are not productive exercises for sprinting. The leg press does not provide training specificity to sports played on your feet: any major strength exercise has one important feature – you should be able to fall down while you're doing it, so that you have to make sure that you don't. This balance aspect of the movement, along with the fact that it can be done with heavy weights, is a critical criterion in exercise selection.

If an intermediate trainee needs to add another workout – a medium or light day – to his week, or if the decision is made to cut heavy pressing work back to twice per week and substitute a variant for the third day, it might be appropriate to introduce a grip or stance variation to the parent exercise as the variant workout. This is what is meant by "variation," where the quality of the workout remains high due to the careful choice of substitute exercises that accomplish the same purpose as the basic movement but in a slightly different way. Or the purpose may be well served by doing the standard form of the exercise at 80% intensity, an approach which can reinforce technique while allowing for active recovery from the heavy volume or intensity of a previous workout.

For the novice lifter, each training day of a three-day week should be a heavy day, since this is consistent with linear progression. As intermediate status is achieved, more variation becomes necessary, and light and medium days become part of the week. New exercises should be initially included on light and medium days because the neuromuscular novelty of these exercises will produce beneficial adaptations at lower intensities. This way, a light day of training can produce a significant training stimulus while still allowing for recovery from the preceding heavier workouts.

It is important to note that with any new exercise, the weight that can be used increases quickly, much like the general response seen in a novice trainee. Adaptations in neuromuscular efficiency and motor coordination are responsible for much of this early improvement. When adding a new exercise, allow time for the motor pattern to ramp up in efficiency, and avoid trying to go as heavy as possible the first few workouts, as tempting as this might be. Many injuries have occurred through the pursuit of such greed.

Exercise Order

Workouts should be ordered in a way that allows the most important exercises to be done first. Basic strength for a rank novice is the primary training consideration, and this means that squats should always be done first. Between strength movements that use some or most of the same muscle groups, it is useful to insert exercises that use other muscles so that some measure of recovery can occur. Bench presses or presses are commonly done between squats and deadlifts, so that the best performance can be obtained from both of these lower-body exercises after some rest between them. Power cleans can be performed effectively by novices after the short break from squats provided by benches or presses, since these trainees are not yet proficient enough at power cleans that a small amount of fatigue will adversely affect them. Any other assistance work would be done after the primary exercises, but they would only be used for more advanced novices if time and energy levels permit, since rank novices need no assistance exercises, and even for more advanced trainees their inclusion in the workout is not as critical to the training program.

As the trainee advances, other considerations complicate the scenario. If the practice of power display becomes a primary training objective, as it will for Olympic lifters and throwers, the emphasis will shift to those exercises and they will be performed first, with squats moving to the end of the workout. As a general rule, the faster the movement, the more precise that movement must be, because of the decreased amount of time during the rep in which position adjustments can be made; and the more precise the movement must be, the more important it is to perform it without the interference of fatigue. For intermediate and advanced athletes, snatches, cleans, jerks, and their related movements should be done early in the workout, with slower strength-focused movements done later.

Fatigue decreases the precision with which motor unit recruitment patterns can be managed and has a direct bearing on the skill with which a movement can be executed and practiced. Movements that are highly dependent on skill of execution should be done first in the workout, before fatigue has blunted the unimpeded contribution of efficient force production to the movement. A snatch is limited by the ability of the lifter to accelerate the bar through the pull in as close to a vertical bar path as possible. If the athlete's strength – and therefore his power – is compromised by fatigue, the ability to apply that strength in the correct way will interfere with the technical execution of the lift. Correct technique depends on

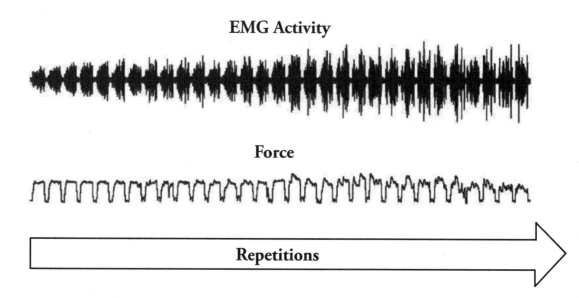

EMG Activity

Force

Repetitions

Figure 5-2. Electromyogram (EMG) and force production tracings from a high-rep set. Note that the muscle fatigues as more repetitions are completed and that motor control erodes with fatigue, as evidenced by the amplitude scatter of the EMG tracing. This effect can result from a single set, as presented here, or can be the cumulative result of repeated sets.

the ability to deliver maximum power to the bar at the right time in the right position, all of which are affected by the ability to produce maximum force, the very thing that fatigue affects (Figure 5-2).

Speed of Movement

There is a persistent belief among the public, many personal trainers, some coaches, and even a few exercise scientists, that weight training exercises must be done slowly. The intentional use of slow movement in weight training reflects an inadequate understanding of the nature of efficient power production, the physics of work, and weight-room safety.

A slow cadence increases the "time under tension" (how long the muscle spends in contraction) and is thereby thought to increase the amount of work the muscles do and the resulting amount of muscular development. An examination of the physiology of power production is necessary to understand this.

Power is strength displayed quickly, the ability to explode against a resistance (see chapter 3). High power production depends on the rapid recruitment of a maximum number of motor units to generate the high amount of force necessary to produce that power. More power requires an increased efficiency in the recruitment of high numbers of motor units and the quickness with which they come into contraction together.

Most importantly for the person interested in more muscle, high numbers of motor units working at the same time means an increase in the actual amount of muscle tissue involved in the work. As more "high-threshold" motor units – the ones that get recruited only by the highest level of stimulus, to produce the highest amount of force – are recruited to generate more power through increased force production, more of the muscle fibers in the muscle go to work. This uses more ATP that must be replaced through active metabolic recovery processes. Studies have found that longer duration repetitions with a longer time under tension actually demand less metabolic work when compared to fast-moving repetitions powered by higher numbers of motor units firing together. This is because in slow movements only the lower-threshold motor units are recruited and fatigued by lower-movement-speed exercise.

It is true that motor unit fatigue produced during sustained contractions or with higher repetitions (8 to 12 or greater) produces a "burn," a sensation that is perceived by many personal trainers to be an indicator of high-quality stimulation. But the fact is that more motor units and more total muscle mass is recruited and worked by higher-velocity movement than by slow exercise speeds. In the interests of both muscle mass and power training, higher velocity works better.

The commercial emphasis on exercise with machines may be the source of a lot of the misinformation about weight training, due to considerations other than the physiology of exercise. Because of their construction, exercise machines generally have limitations in their use, one of which is that if the stack is dropped, the plates may fracture. Over the decades since the invention of Universal and Nautilus machines, this limitation has resulted in the dogma that a slow exercise cadence (a count of 2 up and 4 down or something similar) is needed for optimal results from weight training. This also controls the noise level in the spa. It is merely good fitness club management, not effective strength training. The conventional wisdom has actually developed from the desire of club management to extend the life of their machines and make for a more placid business environment.

Safety also gets dragged into discussions of movement velocity, under the assumption that fast is dangerous, as in driving a car. "Speed kills," after all. But just as in driving, it really depends on the ability of the operator. The more experienced an athlete becomes with barbell exercises, the more efficiently and safely he can perform them at higher speeds. Squats can be dangerous for novices at high speeds, but for advanced athletes high-speed squats are a very productive exercise. If technique is correct, all multi-joint exercises can be performed in a way that enhances power production. Safety is the result of *correct technique*, at any velocity. High-speed exercise is necessary if power production is to be practiced. This obviously means that power training is not inherently dangerous; if it were, all power-trained athletes would be injured. Bad technique is inherently dangerous, whatever the speed or load. Good technique increases safety, and that should be the emphasis in every weight room.

The correct movement velocity of an exercise should be determined by the movement pattern of the exercise and the effect the exercise is intended to produce, not by arbitrary notions of intensity or safety. The Olympic lifts and their variations cannot be performed slowly. A slow clean is not a clean; in fact, a clean cannot be performed without an acceleration through the middle of the pull that produces sufficient momentum in the load that it continues upward long enough to shift the feet to catch the bar. On the other hand, some single-joint exercises cannot be performed both quickly and correctly. A strict barbell curl cannot be performed rapidly through the entire range of motion. In fact, one might argue that the more slowly an exercise must be executed, the less valuable it is for sports training. Also, the closer a weight is to 1RM, the slower it moves. This is true for any exercise, regardless of its nature – a heavy snatch comes off the floor more slowly than a light one, although it will still have to be accelerated if it is to be racked at the top. Movements that are limited by absolute strength will approach zero velocity in a true 1RM, and will always be slower than a 1RM explosive movement. Many factors affect movement speed, and blanket statements about what is best are seldom useful – except for this one: *for exercises useful to strength training for a sports application, faster is always better.*

Warm-up

Warming up is an essential component of training, but it need not be a tremendously histrionic affair, with lots of arm waving, hopping around the gym, contortions, demonstrations of movement proficiency, and exhaustion. Once again, the warm-up should fit the workout, and if weight training is the workout, then the warm-up should prepare the body for weight training. Preparation is both muscular and neuromuscular: it elevates the temperature of the muscles and associated tissues, making them more flexible and less prone to injury, and it improves muscular contractile properties while at the same time allowing the movement pattern to be practiced so that it is familiar, comfortable, and more automatic at work set weights.

Begin temperature elevation part of the warm-up with a simple 2–5 minutes on an exercise bike or, best of all, the C2 rower. The time will depend on the temperature of the room – in winter in a cold room, more is necessary; in summer in Houston, none at all may be necessary. A couple of minutes with a gradual increase in intensity is sufficient. Then move directly to the first barbell exercise, to prepare the movement pattern. Do the complete range of motion for that exercise with an empty bar, for as many sets as necessary to warm the range of motion (this might be as many a five sets for an injured athlete, or a creaky old masters guy). Then increase the weight in even increments for 3 to 5 sets until you are ready to handle the work set weight. After the work sets, repeat the process without the aerobic part for every exercise in the workout.

After the novice's first couple of weeks, warm-up reps can be tapered down to two or even to a single rep for the last warm-up set, saving gas for the work sets. But for the first few workouts, novices need the motor pathway practice and should stay with the full number of reps all the way up, until skill level permits the taper.

The athlete should understand the proper role of warm-ups: they prepare for the work sets – they must not interfere with them. If the last warm-up set is too heavy, i.e., too close to the weight of the work set, it will fatigue rather than warm. Warm-ups are valuable in that they prepare the body for the work sets, but *they do not themselves make anything stronger.* If 295×5×3 are the bench press work sets, 290×5 is not a good idea for the last warm-up. If 295 is heavy enough to constitute an adaptive load, 290 will reduce the likelihood of succeeding at all 15 reps of work, since it is close enough to be tantamount to another heavy set done before. By the same token, if 295×5×3 will actually go for all 15 reps, 290×5 will not produce a strength increase, because that adaptation has already occurred or 295 would not be feasible.

Stretching

Flexibility is traditionally defined as having complete range of motion around a joint. It is probably more usefully described as the ability of the muscles that limit motion around a joint to extend beyond their resting length, which affects the range of motion around the joint. The ability to relax a muscle group is an important part of flexibility; the ultimate expression of this is seen during general anesthesia. Stretching increases flexibility by increasing the ability to lengthen the muscles, and it should not be thought of as acting on the connective tissue of the joint itself. Stretching has traditionally been included as part of the pre-training, pre-event preparatory ritual. It is thought that stretching before exercise prepares the joints to move through their complete range of motion, thus improving performance and reducing the incidence of injury. A great deal of money has been spent on posters and books dealing with how to stretch effectively, and it is nearly universally accepted among exercise professionals that stretching must precede exercise. But hang on...

An examination of the scientific and medical literature paints a different picture. The majority of the data available indicates that pre-training stretching neither reduces the frequency of injury nor effectively improves flexibility, the two areas in which it is supposed to provide benefit. Other studies have demonstrated that stretching after the onset of delayed-onset muscle soreness (DOMS) does not diminish soreness, and that overly-vigorous stretching can produce soreness quite effectively. DOMS is an inflammatory process, the body's method of healing damage produced in the eccentric portion of training movements, and all the stretching in the world cannot reduce inflammation. More importantly, evidence from studies on vertical jump and broad jump performance indicates that pre-event stretching actually reduces power output, and other studies suggest that this is true for other explosive activities, such as weightlifting, as well.

If pre-training stretching doesn't increase flexibility, what does? Proper range of motion in the barbell exercises does. The loaded human body moving through its maximum range of motion actually provides a stretching stimulus for both the agonist and antagonist muscle groups – an agonist causes motion around a joint, while an antagonist resists or decelerates that motion, or stabilizes a related joint to facilitate the agonist's motion. A number of studies have shown an increase in flexibility as a result of complete-range-of-motion weight training. Improvements in hip and knee flexibility on the order of 40% or better are commonly experienced. This is because proper form requires complete range of motion of the involved joints and, if proper position is maintained, the weight puts the body into a properly stretched position at the bottom (or top) of each rep, exposing the antagonists to a stretch stimulus each time the load is moved.

This obviously requires good form, and good coaching. Properly done, each weighted rep provides a better stretch than an unweighted traditional stretch, because the complete range of motion is easier to reach with the help of the weight. More importantly, and most especially for the hamstrings, the postural position of the back – the very critical lumbar extension that must be maintained to fully stretch the hamstrings – is best accomplished with a loaded spine, since the load gives the spinal erectors some resistance to contract against to maintain proper lumbar curvature. It is common to see athletes attempt to stretch the hamstrings with a rounded lower back, and this cannot be done effectively.

It must also be noted that badly detrained populations – the elderly, the untrained morbidly obese, and those exhibiting pathological frailty – may be unable to display a normal range of motion around a system of joints entirely because of a lack of strength. If a person cannot safely occupy a position, they will not assume that position, because people are quite averse to falling and injuring themselves. This protective mechanism may not even be a conscious process, and inexperienced coaches often mistake muscular weakness for a lack of flexibility.

If traditional stretching exercises are desired, they should be done at the end of the workout, when the muscles are warm and the stretch will not interfere with performance. There are several methods of stretching currently practiced, but the only type of stretching really needed, beyond the active flexibility work inherent in full-ROM strength training, is static stretching. Move the joints into a position of mild discomfort and hold the position for 30+ seconds. Repeat 2 to 3 times for maximum benefit. Problem areas – hamstrings often need extra attention from both very young and older lifters – should be stretched after every workout. If flexibility is severely inadequate and critical to improved performance, the fastest route to more ROM is an experienced therapist trained in Active Release Therapy or myofascial release. Manual manipulation of the tight fascial components of the muscle bellies immediately acts on the source of the problem, and one treatment can produce more improvement than months of stretching on your own.

Be aware of the fact that many older people – some of whom may wish to become athletes – often display bony changes inside the joint capsules, most frequently the shoulders. If stretching and massage is not immediately effective in improving the ROM, the situation may not be correctable, and the intelligent approach would be to work around it. Arthritic shoulders can be injured badly by overzealous attempts to fix what cannot be fixed.

But a more critical question might be: how flexible does an athlete need to be? If full range of motion in all the positions encountered during training and performance can be properly expressed under load and during skills execution, the athlete is sufficiently flexible. Training through a full range of motion and the correct practice of sport skills will maintain flexibility, just as they have established it to begin with, and an attempt to further increase flexibility is at best a waste of time.

The Training Log

A training log is kept by every serious trainee as a record of his history under the bar. It is an important source of data for determinations regarding staleness, overtraining, the effectiveness of newly added exercises, and the overall effectiveness of the training program. Sometimes it may be necessary to make large-scale changes in the program due to an unexpected lack of response, the inability to recover from the program because of individual lifestyle factors outside the trainee's control, or a change in the athlete's training goals. The log records trends in both training and schedule compliance that have a definite bearing on progress. It should include the athlete's impressions of that day's workout, useful cues discovered, and any other subjective information that might serve a purpose later. It might also include notes about sleep, diet, and other information pertinent to recovery. A training log is an essential tool for both trainee and coach, and as such *is not optional.*

The best way to log workouts is to follow a column format, top to bottom, using a small enough hand that the whole workout fits in one column, and that at least four or five workouts fit on one page. This way it is possible to display up to three weeks training data on two open pages, so that trends over time are visible.

This means that a good quality book will be needed. It should be a good enough book to last at least a year, so use a notebook with a decent binding. It need not be expensive, but it should be better than a spiral. Spiral-bound books don't last very long because the pages tear out easily. The best training logs are ledger books with relatively plain paper, but simple composition books, the kind with the mottled covers, work just fine. It is popular now – and in fact the norm – to use an online training log. A paper log cannot crash, so keep this in mind.

6

The Novice

Programming for the novice is the most important task a coach will encounter and the most important task an athlete can undertake. Done correctly, it sets the stage for a lifetime of proper training habits, long-term progress, and athletic achievement far above what would be possible without it. Insufficient attention to detail, and to the trainee's response to training during this phase, can cost valuable progress that may not be recoverable later.

In one very important respect, training novices is easy: **virtually anything that makes a novice work harder than bed rest will produce positive results.** And this is true of essentially every human endeavor: you always make rapid progress when you start, especially relative to the progress you will make after you've been doing it for a few years. As a result, many people have an erroneous impression of the quality of their training system. Single sets, multiple sets, high volume, high intensity, super slow, supersets, giant sets, gnarlmonster sets – quite literally anything resembling a training program will produce better results than no program at all in novice trainees. This is known as "the novice effect," and must be considered when training this population.

Ignorance of this simple principle has produced profound confusion among both academics and coaches in the strength and conditioning profession, and has sold millions of exercise programs, and millions of exercise devices that fold up and store under your bed. Many coaches believe that there is only one right way to train all athletes, and many academics believe that research conducted on untrained eighteen-year-old males is relevant to all populations, including athletes. The simple fact is that people who are *not* already strong get stronger faster than people who *are* already strong. A college S&C coach who only deals with accomplished, talented athletes may be as ignorant of the novice effect as personal trainers who only teach "Exercise" to the general public – neither of them has seen the process of progression from novice to advanced lifter occur, because neither of them are concerned with the process, and neither of them know how to make it happen. The coach thinks everyone is "advanced" (or they wouldn't be in his program, right?) and the Personal Trainer has no idea that there is a difference between what he does and *training*.

Most research into weight training has been done on the untrained populations commonly found in college weight training courses – unfit young adults eager to earn bonus points by participating in a study. Unfit and inexperienced people are by definition far removed from their physical potential for

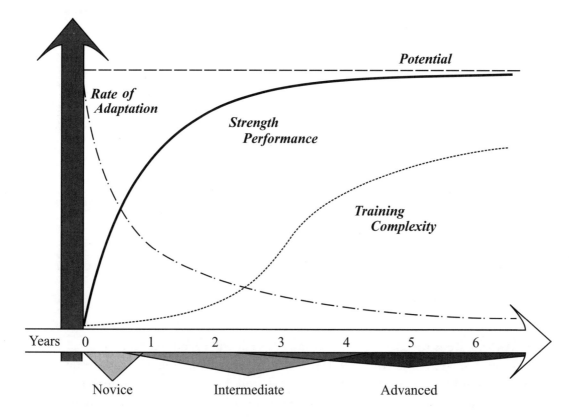

Figure 6-1. The generalized relationship between performance improvement and training complexity relative to time. Note the steep slope during the novice phase.

athletic performance. Older adults, middle-aged women, large populations of nurses, active 30-year-old walkers, and any other relatively sedentary population that has never trained with weights for any significant period of time or with any degree of organization – the groups most commonly studied – will never have gone through the process of getting stronger efficiently with a barbell training program. The subjects used in these experiments, and all novice trainees for that matter, will exhibit large increases in strength following a short series of exposures to weight training, regardless of the nature of that exposure. The literature provides many, many examples of statistically significant increases in strength – typically referred to as "fitness" in this literature – within a very few weeks using virtually *any* training program. Figure 6-1 illustrates the steep slope of performance improvement for the novice trainee. It is quite easy to produce an adaptation in a previously unadapted organism.

These studies may be valid for the populations studied, depending upon the training experience of those designing the study protocol. Quite often, however, even this is not the case – as hard as this may be to understand, many researchers in the area of exercise physiology have no real experience in the weight room. They are runners or cyclists themselves, and their role as Principal Investigators in an exercise physiology department may well mean that guidance over student researchers (who may themselves be devoid of experience) is poor in quality and devoid of a practical background in the questions that might be investigated regarding strength training. These people often design studies using unrealistic, impractical methods that an experienced coach would consider bizarre.

But this is not really the biggest problem. Frequently, the data acquired from these badly-designed studies on essentially novice populations has been generalized as valid for all training populations, from novice to Olympian, from healthy to diseased, young to old. It would be a gross understatement to characterize this as merely "inappropriate." The results of a study done on a specific population – one with specific characteristics that make it very different from other specific populations – *apply only to that specific population*. These results cannot be applied to other populations, because their differing characteristics will change the results. In the same way that a training program must be specific to the sport that it is designed to produce an adaptation for, the program must also be specific to the athlete's level of adaptation.

This would, of course, require that the individuals conducting the research be aware of the fact that different levels of training adaptation/advancement *actually exist*. Few of them apparently do. The very essence of training is the correct application of the stress/recovery/adaptation cycle, and the outcome of this cycle is extremely dependent on the physiological characteristics of the individual to whom it is applied. As the characteristics of the individual change, so must the stress, if the adaptation is to continue. Novices eventually become adapted past the usefulness of novice programming and thus move to the intermediate, and possibly advanced stages. Diseased populations respond differently depending on their pathologies; the elderly adapt to stress less efficiently; children and adolescents adapt more efficiently, but only to certain stresses; males respond differently from females; motivated athletes progress faster than casual trainees. Specific training organizations are necessary for each population and for each stage of life and of training advancement, and the blanket application of one program across all populations is absurd, illogical, and unprofessional.

Yet we claim above that all novices respond to any stress by adapting – an apparent contradiction. The point is that *in an unadapted trainee, any stress serves to cause an adaptation, but a program that makes optimal use of the novice trainee's ability to adapt quickly is better than a program that doesn't*. And as the novice trainee becomes more adapted to stress and more closely approaches the limits of physical potential, the stress must become more and more specific to that individual's level of advancement in order for adaptation to continue.

The Basics of Novice Programming

The result of the universal "novice effect" is that there are nearly as many training programs for beginners that produce at least marginal improvement as there are coaches. They all produce results because the novice trainee adapts to an *overload event* quickly, in as little as 24 to 72 hours (Figure 6-2). This means that, as long as the novice training program provides overload at some point, performance improvement will be the result.

This actually means that any programming model fits within the context of Selye's General Adaptation Syndrome theory when applied to novices. Any stress causes an adaptation, because so little adaptation has already taken place.

So what's the problem? If everyone is right, can't we all just get along? Actually, everyone is right, but some are much more right than others. And most are right only accidentally. Being "more right" means basing the training program on the optimal stress/recovery rate of the athlete being trained, so that time and potential are not wasted. To be most effective and efficient at improving strength for novices, a program must progressively increase an appropriate training load as rapidly as the novice recovers from the overload event – a period of time that experience has proven to be 48–72 hours.

Most people arrive at this conclusion intuitively. In gyms all over the world, inexperienced people training by themselves know they can successfully add weight to the exercises they did last time, and that last time was just a couple of days ago. Most will do so unless told they can't by someone who is supposed to know more than they do. Most individuals enjoy testing themselves with heavier loads or more reps.

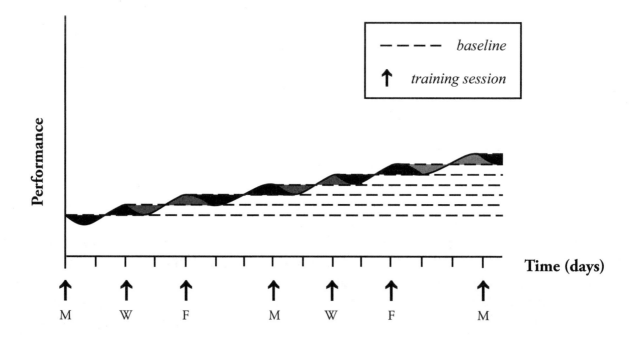

Figure 6-2. The novice stress/recovery/adaptation cycle. Each training session represents a stress that can be recovered from and adapted to within 48-72 hours. Effective programming takes advantage of this rapid ability to improve by applying an overload event in each training session using linear progression.

They derive a sense of pleasure and accomplishment from the improvement, and only become frustrated with lifting weights when improvement stops. Simple progression is everyone's friend. It works well, and it's how many weak people have gotten very strong very fast.

The keys to maximum efficiency in using simple progression are selecting the correct amount to increase the load each time and timing these increases to coincide with recovery from the previous training session. This is where the role of a coach becomes important: applying the discipline of a program to an eager trainee who might otherwise not exercise discipline or the judgment that comes from experience.

Novice trainees adapt to stress more quickly than is usually recognized by the typical exercise science academic or strength coach. As illustrated in Figure 6-2, the best time to train again after the first session would be somewhere between 48 and 72 hours later: train Monday, rest Tuesday, train again at the same time on Wednesday or Thursday. The goal is to drive adaptation as quickly as possible. For a rank novice, a 48 to 72-hour recovery can generally be expected, meaning that 3 workouts per week will produce optimum results.

All successful and productive training relies on the body's innate ability to adapt to stress. Novice training may very well be the athlete's first exposure to truly hard work done in a planned, logical, progressive manner. This regimented approach to work is not necessarily fun, and it may be perceived as boring and repetitive to those with a short attention span, but the results it produces are something that motivated people find rewarding and encouraging. The desire to test one's limits is harnessed for the first time in a program of this type, where hard work is done in a logical manner to produce a predictable, directable outcome. Athletes' responses to this phase of training – in several different ways – determine their ability to move to the next level.

Novice trainees, by definition, have little or no weight training experience. Having been a member of a health spa, using the machines at the Y, or curling with the plastic-coated weights in the garage doesn't count. Novices lack the motor skills to perform the basic barbell exercises that form the core of the program, and they must learn proper and safe exercise execution. The novice is also unexposed to systemic exercise stress and has not developed the ability to respond to the demands of exercises that cause whole-body adaptation. The squat, deadlift, press, and bench press should be learned first, with the power clean and, later, the power snatch, introduced as skill and ability permit.

It may be tempting for people who are active or have been playing sports to assume that this translates to the barbell exercises. **People who have not trained with weights before, no matter what other activities have been engaged in, are novices, and their programs should be designed accordingly.** More importantly, *even people who have trained with weights extensively but who have never followed a program that drives progress in a linear fashion are still novices* with respect to their response to linear programming. Progress through the novice stage occurs very rapidly for everyone since an increase in weight every workout generates the fastest possible progress mathematically, and this therefore constitutes the most efficient possible use of training time. But if the trainee is placed immediately into a program that calls for less frequent increases in work set weights, the rapid initial improvement of the novice *will not occur.* Weekly or even monthly increases are commonly recommended by many uninformed coaches, if increases in load are programmed at all. The fit trainee can tolerate incremental increases in loading every 48 to 72 hours just like a deconditioned person, and rapid initial progress is the objective of a well-designed program.

There are two important differences for the already-strong novice. First, a stronger trainee might be able to make bigger initial incremental increases through the first couple of weeks of the novice phase than a poorly conditioned person. Second, and as a result, the period of time before intermediate-type training programs are necessary may be shorter, since the initial progress has occurred more quickly. This is because a person who has obtained some level of conditioning from sports, while still unadapted to barbell training, is closer to his physical potential than a completely unconditioned person and thus has less far to go. However, strong novices may be able to maintain linear progress for 6–7 months, with sets-of-5 squats into the 500s.

Basic Program Variables

The first goal for the novice should be the development of basic usable whole-body strength. At this stage in a trainee's development, even short-term goals unrelated to getting stronger are irrelevant. Sports performance, conditioning, and improved aesthetics all depend, first, on the acquisition of basic strength. It is the foundation for all other physical improvement, and it must be the trainee's first concern.

EXERCISES

The core of the novice program includes just the "big" exercises to develop the novice trainee's strength base: the squat, the press, the bench press, and the deadlift. After a few weeks of successful training – or sooner, depending on the initial strength and aptitude of the athlete – the power clean can be added to the program. Power cleans are considered a core exercise for most sports, but they not are included in a beginner's program until the basic strength and motor skills have developed enough that they can be done with reasonable technique. The four basic exercises have been used for many decades by strong men and women to improve basic strength, and no substitutes exist for them. Together they form a complete package of loaded movements that stress the whole body in exactly the proportions that produces the strength used in sports and in life. It is critical to a program's success that everyone involved learn to perform and coach these exercises correctly.

Once the basic exercises have been mastered, chin-ups can be added into training. The most valuable assistance movements are those that fill in the very few holes in the program, and that are also multi-joint exercises. Chin-ups (with hands supine) are the staple upper-body assistance movement, since they work the entire arm and the upper back muscles in a way that closely duplicates the pulling and grasping functions of the arms and hands in sports and work. They are also a very good basic strength indicator; a trainee who cannot do many chins needs to work on them, since chinning strength is closely related to pressing strength and improving a weak chin-up will improve the pressing movements. Chins provide enough arm work and additional lat work – satisfying the normal male concerns about appearance – that they can be considered the first and most important assistance exercise to include in the novice program.

A coach who is responsible for a large number of beginning trainees at one time, such as a PE teacher or a public school sports coach, should consider using only the four basic exercises. The power clean does not lend itself well to some programs due to the limitations imposed by time, coaching experience, and equipment.

Focused abdominal exercises are the least important assistance movements to include. The lower back is supported from the anterior by the abs, and squats, deadlifts, presses, and chins all provide enough work for the abs that it is not necessary to include dedicated ab work in the program. In fact, lots of time gets wasted on abs in the vast majority of weight rooms across the planet. If you are squatting, deadlifting and pressing heavy weights, *you are already working your abs*. Additional time spent exercising them separately is better spent recovering from the heavy work, and may indicate narcissistic tendencies that can be detrimental to a focus on strength.

REPS AND SETS

Figure 4-3 illustrates the continuum of physiological responses to varying repetition and intensity schemes. Absolute strength is gained by using very low reps, mass is increased with higher reps, and local muscular and systemic endurance is developed with even higher reps (20+). For the novice, a repetition scheme that is right in the anaerobic middle works best: sets of 5 reps. Fives are close enough to the strength end of the continuum to provide tremendous increases in strength, the primary goal of the novice. Fives are also enough reps to develop a tolerance for elevated work levels, and provide for a good amount of hypertrophy so that muscular weight gain occurs too. This mix of adaptations provides a very good fitness base that allows for progress. Fives are optimal for most novices; they effectively stimulate strength gains and other forms of progress without producing sufficient muscular or neuromuscular exhaustion to cause technique deterioration at the end of the set. The exceptions would be novice women and some older lifters, for whom 3s would be more appropriate. More on this later.

Some training programs advocate the use of a set to failure on the last of the work sets across. The purpose of this would either be to test the capacity today, or to add a volume stress under the assumption that the scheduled 5s are inadequate to the task. This might result in 2 sets of 5 and one set of 9, depending where the lifter is in his novice progression. Think with me here: sets of 9 have a different training effect than 5s, today's workout is valuable only in that it is a preparation for the next workout in which heavier weight will be lifted, and anything that might interfere with the next workout's incremental increase in terms of fatigue or an inability to adequately recover is not useful. We are *training*, not *performing*. Stay with the process – it works just fine the way it's written.

As mentioned in chapter 5, sets across have several advantages. They allow sufficient tonnage to be accumulated to produce the necessary adaptive stress, more than is possible with only one work set. But they also allow a coach to observe enough reps to analyze any form problems a trainee might be having, and then observe the effectiveness of the correction in the next set. Gross technique problems can be seen immediately by anyone familiar with the movement; less pronounced or intermittent form problems need more reps for diagnosis. Sets across provide that opportunity.

Assistance exercises, when finally integrated into the program, may be done with higher reps. Chin-ups, for instance, might be done with up to 15 reps before weight is added, at which time they may be converted to weighted sets of 5 across if desired.

The number of sets to be done varies with the athlete's circumstances: first workout ever, or second month of training; sore from the previous workout, or fresh as a garden tomato; perfect form, or in need of technical practice to hone a skill. It also varies with the exercise being done: core lift or assistance exercise, presses, which do not tap in too deeply, or heavy deadlifts, which are hard enough at 5RM that one set is plenty for most people. These decisions must be made on an individual basis each time, but it is possible to establish some general guidelines. As a rule, work sets for squats, bench presses, and presses should be three sets across (three sets at the same weight) for novices, but in some special circumstances as many as five sets across or as little as one work set might be appropriate.

The number of sets per exercise is the sum of the warm-ups and the work sets. Warm-up sets are done as necessary, more if the trainee is sore, inflexible, or in need of movement practice, fewer if he is already warm from previous exercises. Warm-up sets add to the total number (and total work done), which might, in atypical cases, be as high as twelve sets if extensive light warm-up sets and three work sets across are done. Warm-up set volume can be held to a minimum even if it is necessary to do extra warm-up by using lower-rep sets. As a general rule, warm-up set volume is controlled by tapering toward doubles and singles before the work sets, for most trainees that have more than a couple of weeks experience.

Note: This text uses the following format when specifying training loads: Weight × reps × sets. Example: 45 pounds × 5 reps × 2 sets. Unless otherwise specified, weights are in pounds. For examples without weights specified, the format is: number of sets × number of reps. Example: 3 × 10 = 3 sets of 10 reps.

	Squat	Bench Press	Deadlift
Warm-up	45×5×2	45×5	135×5
	75×5(×1)	65×5	165×2
	95×3	85×2	195×5
	115×2	105×1	
	135×1	120×5×3	
Work	155×5×3		

SCHEDULING

For a novice trainee, the adaptation to a new training load occurs within 48 to 72 hours. Three days per week yields a training session every 48 hours with one 72-hour interval at the end of the week. Three days per week fits well into most people's work schedule, an important factor for most novices just getting started, trying to integrate a training schedule into their lifestyle.

Monday, Wednesday, and Friday are the most obvious training days for most people on a three day-per-week program. In fact, Monday and Wednesday are the busiest days in all gyms everywhere, Monday being referred to as Guilty Conscience Day since so many people show up on Monday to apologize to themselves for Friday's missed workout. Depending on the facility, this might be an excellent reason to use a Tuesday/Thursday/Saturday schedule, or Sunday/Tuesday/Thursday.

Depending on individual scheduling flexibility, recovery ability, and personal preference, a trainee might decide to use an every-other-day schedule, where each week is different but each break between workouts is the same 48 hours. This schedule does not allow for a longer break between two workouts, sometimes a handy thing in the event that incomplete recovery has occurred between a couple of previous workouts.

WORKLOADS

Any novice learning a new exercise, regardless of training history, apparent fitness level, aptitude shown on previous exercises, or protestations to the contrary, should begin with an empty bar. And that empty bar may need to be a lighter one than the standard 20-kg/45-lb type, depending on the trainee. For the novice, the law is: learn first, and then load. There will plenty of time to put weight on the bar later; the first task is to learn the movement pattern without having to worry about how heavy it is. *Heavy* always competes with *correct*, and at this point correct is much more important.

The vast majority of the time, a trainee will learn the movement well enough that the load can be increased during the first workout, but it is important that a good command of the movement pattern be established before any plates are added to the bar. This process may take three sets, or it may take three workouts, depending on both coach and trainee. Do not rush this process: this is not the place for impatience. If the first workout for a 150-pound trainee progresses through the empty bar for three sets of five, then 75×5, 95×5, and 115×5, and then ends with 135×5×3 sets, all with good form and the bar speed on the work sets slowing down just a little, it is a very good first day. This is enough work to disrupt homeostasis and bring about Selye's stage-1 response.

The trainee has done more work than he is accustomed to already, and adding more weight is pointless on the first day of training. If the trainee has worked through the entire range of motion of an unfamiliar exercise, he will experience some muscle soreness from the eccentric work in the new ROM. The result for the first workout will be a little soreness, but not so much that daily activities are markedly impaired. It accomplishes absolutely nothing for a novice trainee to wake up the day after the first workout unable to get out of bed, and many, many people are discouraged to the point of quitting when faced with what they think will be a second workout with the same result. An exercise professional will *never* cause this intentionally, although it sometimes occurs accidentally.

After the first workout has established the trainee's starting point, subsequent workouts should progressively increase the work-set weights of all the exercises. This should occur at every workout. Weight is the only variable in the progression that is adjusted to increase stress. The number of reps is fixed by the physiologic effects that the training program is designed to improve, as discussed earlier, and if five reps is the assigned workload, rest cannot be decreased without compromising the ability to do all the reps. The increments by which the weight of the work sets increase are determined by both the exercise and the ability of the trainee.

As a general rule, the fewer muscles involved in the exercise, the longer it takes to gain strength for the lift. Exercises that use large numbers of large muscles, such as deadlifts and squats, result in much faster gains in strength than upper body exercises like the bench press. Exercises such as the press, clean, and snatch, which use a lot of muscles but are limited by the ability to manage the mechanical efficiency of all the components of a very long kinetic chain result in a slower gain in strength for those lifts as well. Chins and assistance exercises that involve only one joint like triceps pressdowns result in very slow gains in strength; progress is expected only on a monthly basis.

People of different sexes, sizes, ages, levels of experience and athletic ability, and levels of motivation make progress at different rates. As Selye's theory predicts, those populations most capable of adapting to external stress will make the fastest progress. People whose hormonal, dietary, rest, and motivational circumstances are optimal for recovery from physical loads – well-fed young men on sports teams, for example – will make more rapid gains than any other population when subjected to intense training. All other groups will progress more slowly, and will attain commensurately lower levels of absolute performance, although their relative performances may certainly be comparable.

So, for young males who weigh between 150 and 200 pounds, deadlifts can likely move up 15 pounds per workout, and squats 10 pounds, with continued steady progress for 2 to 3 weeks before slowing down to half that rate. Bench presses, presses, and cleans can move up 5 to 10 pounds for the first few workouts, with progress on these exercises slowing down to 2.5 to 5 pounds per workout after only 2 to 3 weeks. Young women tend to progress on the squat and the deadlift at about the same rate as young men, adjusted for bodyweight (which would mean 5–10 pounds instead of 10–15), but more slowly on the press, bench press, clean, snatch, and assistance exercises. Progress can be made for quite some time, and specific strategies to maximize it and delay the onset of a training plateau should be employed as progress starts to slow. These methods are discussed below.

Linear progress, for as long as it is possible, is the most efficient way to utilize a novice's training time, since every workout can yield a strength improvement. This is true even if the increases are very small; two pounds per week on the press still adds up to 104 pounds per year, pretty good progress if you can make it. As progress begins to slow, i.e. as work sets become harder to do and to complete, or as reps begin to get missed, smaller incremental increases should be used. Smaller jumps will allow for more linear progression, so that more progress is accumulated before a radical change in programming is necessary. Smaller jumps waste time at first, but become absolutely essential later.

Small plates are necessary for small jumps, and small jumps are necessary for progress. An understanding of this very practical matter is fundamental to continued improved performance under the bar.

As training progresses, the ability to adapt to the stress of training slows, as discussed at length previously. What were once easy 10-pound jumps for sets of 5 reps become difficult 5-pound jumps for 5 reps. With standard 2½-pound (or 1.25 kg) plates, sets of four are the inevitable result. The object is to use sets of five, for the physiologic effects produced by five reps, and training is designed around a certain number of reps for this specific reason. So it is necessary to be able to make incremental increases while holding the reps constant, and this requires that the increments be small enough that an adaptation can occur during the time allotted. A novice trainee who has correctly followed the program will eventually not be able to adapt to 5-pound jumps between sets.

But that trainee can get strong 1 pound at a time, or 1.5 pounds or 2 pounds at a time, depending on the exercise. Certainly for technique and power-dependent exercises like the clean and snatch, and small-muscle-group exercises like the press, bench press, and chin-ups, small jumps are the only way progress will accumulate smoothly. And if a 2-pound jump is required, it will have to be loaded with 1-pound plates.

Several companies make small plates, in both pounds and kilos. Or they can be made in the garage out of 2-inch washers glued, taped, or welded together in varying increments. Or 2½-pound plates can be shaved down at a machine shop. In pounds, the range should be ½, 1, and 1½; in kilos, 0.25, 0.5, and 0.75.

It is also important to understand how the small plates relate to the rest of the equipment. Standard "Olympic" barbell plates are castings, and castings are inherently inaccurate. Even good-quality calibrated plates, which are milled to tolerance, are not dead-on. When loading a bar, which will itself have a small error, with several plates, all of which have a small error, it is likely that the face value of the loaded weight is not actually what is on the bar.

This is not important for warm-ups, or for back-off sets, or for anything else during the workout that does not represent a measured incremental increase over the previous workout. But when the load on the bar is supposed to be 173.5 pounds, and it actually weighs 175.5 due to plate error, the target has been missed. It may not be possible, or even necessary, to have dead-on plates; it is possible to have the same big plates on the bar as last time, so that the increase made with the small plates is exactly what it is supposed to be. That is the concern anyway – *that the amount lifted today be exactly the specific intended amount more than last time*. If training is done in a commercial gym or school weight room, number or mark the bar and a set of plates so that they can be identified for use at every workout, and buy and bring with you your own small plates. This way, the amount of the increase can be exactly what it needs to be, the increase will be exact every time, and progress can be better ensured.

The Starting Strength Model

As outlined in *Starting Strength: Basic Barbell Training*, a novice starts with three or four basic whole body exercises and after warm-up does three work sets (except for the deadlift) at a weight that is based on the performance during the previous workout. When the prescribed sets and reps are completed at the assigned weight, the load is increased for the next workout. This is very simple, and it works for quite a while for most normal novices. In the presence of adequate rest and nutrition, it would be so unusual for someone to fail to add quite a bit of muscle and strength before any changes to the workout are needed that you would have to assume that adequate rest and nutrition are not actually taking place. In fact, this program works so predictably that the failure of a novice to progress means that it was not followed precisely.

For a rank novice, the simplest of workouts is in order. This short program can be followed for the first few workouts:

A	B
Squat	Squat
Press	Bench Press
Deadlift	Deadlift

The two workouts alternate across the Monday-Wednesday-Friday schedule for the first couple of weeks, until the freshness of the deadlift has worn off a little and after the quick initial gains establish the deadlift well ahead of the squat. At this point the power clean is introduced:

A	B
Squat	Squat
Press	Bench Press
Deadlift	Power Clean

After this program is followed for a short time, chin-ups can be added, along with back extensions or glute/ham raises for a break from pulling every workout. This somewhat more-complicated program looks like this:

A	B
Squat	Squat
Press	Bench Press
Deadlift/Power Clean	Back extension
	Chin-up

In this variation, the deadlift and power clean alternate every time workout A is done. The 2-week schedule would look like this:

Week	Monday	Wednesday	Friday
1	Squat	Squat	Squat
	Press	Bench Press	Press
	Deadlift	Back extension	Power Clean
		Chin-up	
2	Squat	Squat	Squat
	Bench Press	Press	Bench Press
	Back extension	Deadlift	Back extension
	Chin-up		Chin-up

The squat, bench press, and press are done for 3 sets of 5; note that the bench press and the press alternate in all variations of the program. The deadlift is done for 1 set of 5 reps every fifth workout, due to its harder nature at heavy weights, and alternates with the power clean, which is done at 5 sets of 3 reps across. Squats continue each workout uninterrupted; this is possible because they start lighter than the deadlift due to a longer range of motion but are less fatiguing due to the inherent stretch reflex at the bottom. Unweighted (bodyweight or BW) chin-ups, done with a supine grip for bicep involvement, are done to failure for 3 sets unless the trainee can complete more than 15 reps per set (unlikely for a rank novice), in which case weight is added. If the athlete can maintain his chin-up numbers as his bodyweight increases, he is actually getting stronger.

This is a reasonable exercise selection for a novice, and a reasonable weekly plan. It can be followed for several months if careful attention is paid to the increments of increase, rest, adequate nutrition, and the elimination of activities that compete for recovery resources during this important period of rapid strength increase.

WELL-EXECUTED NOVICE LINEAR PROGRESSION

The following numbers are based on an actual client, male, age 35, former Division I college football player.

Week	Monday	Wednesday	Friday
1	Squat 135×5×3 Press 95×5×3 Deadlift 185×5	Squat 145×5×3 Bench 155×5×3 Deadlift 205×5	Squat 155×5×3 Press 100×5×3 Deadlift 225×5
2	Squat 165×5×3 Bench 165×5×3 Deadlift 235×5	Squat 175×5×3 Press 105×5×3 Deadlift 245×5	Squat 185×5×3 Bench 175×5×3 Deadlift 255×5
3	Squat 195×5×3 Press 110×5×3 Deadlift 265×5	Squat 205×5×3 Bench 185×5×3 Power Clean 115×3×5	Squat 210×5×3 Press 115×5×3 Deadlift 275×5
4	Squat 215×5×3 Bench 190×5×3 Power Clean 125×3×5	Squat 220×5×3 Press 120×5×3 Deadlift 285×5	Squat 225×5×3 Bench 195×5×3 Power Clean 135×3×5
5	Squat 230×5×3 Press 125×5×3 Deadlift 295×5	Squat 235×5×3 Bench 200×5×3 Power Clean 140×3×5	Squat 240×5×3 Press 130×5×3 Deadlift 305×5
6	Squat 245×5×3 Bench 205×5×3 Power Clean 145×3×5	Squat 250×5×3 Press 135×5×3 Deadlift 315×5	Squat 255×5×3 Bench 210×5×3 Power Clean 150×3×5
7	Squat 260×5×3 Press 140×5×3 Deadlift 325×5	Squat 265×5×3 Bench 210×5×3 Power Clean 155×3×5	Squat 270×5×3 Press 145×5×3 Deadlift 335×5
8	Squat 275×5×3 Bench 215×5×3 Power Clean 160×3×5	Squat 220×5×3 Press 147.5×5×3 Deadlift 345×5	Squat 280×5×3 Bench 220×5×3 Power Clean 165×3×5

Week	Monday	Wednesday	Friday
9	Squat 285×5×3 Press 150×5×3 Deadlift 355×5	Squat 230×5×3 Bench 225×5×3 Power Clean 170×3×5	Squat 290×5×3 Press 152.5×5×3 Deadlift 360×5
10	Squat 295×5×3 Bench 230×5×3 Power Clean 175×3×5	Squat 235×5×3 Press 155×5×3 Deadlift 365×5	Squat 300×5×3 Bench 235×5×3 Power Clean 180×3×5
11	Squat 305×5×3 Press 157.5×5×3 Deadlift 370×5	Squat 245×5×3 Bench 240×5×3 Power Clean 185×3×5	Squat 310×5×3 Press 160×5×3 Deadlift 375×5
12	Squat 315×5×3 Bench 245×5×3 Power Clean 190×3×5	Squat 255×5×3 Press 162.5×5×3 Deadlift 380×5	Squat 320×5×3 Bench 250×5×3 Power Clean 195×3×5
13	Squat 325×5×3 Press 165×5×3 Deadlift 385×5	Squat 265×5×3 Bench 255×5×3 Chins BW×11,8,7	Squat 330×5×3 Press 167.5×5×3 Power Clean 200×3×5
14	Squat 335×5×3 Bench 260×5×3 Chins BW×12,9,6	Squat 275×5×3 Press 170×5×3 Deadlift 390×5	Squat 340×5×3 Bench 265×5×3 Chins BW×12,9,7
15	Squat 345×5×3 Press 172.5×5×3 Power Clean 205×3×5	Squat 285×5×3 Bench 270×5×3 Chins BW×12,10,7	Squat 350×5×3 Press 175×5×3 Deadlift 395×5
16	Squat 355×5 (335×5×2) Bench 275×5×3 Chins BW×13,8,8	Squat 295×5×3 Press 177.5×5×3 Power Clean 210×3×5	Squat 360×5 (340×5×2) Bench 280×5×3 Chins BW×13,9,7
17	Squat 365×5 (345×5×2) Press 180×5×3 Deadlift 400×5	Squat 305×5×3 Bench 285×5×3 Chins BW×14,9,6	Squat 370×5 (350×5×2) Press 182.5×5×3 Power Clean 215×3×5

Week	Monday	Wednesday	Friday
18	Squat 375×5	Squat 315×5×3	Squat 275×5×3
	Bench 290×5×3	Press 185×5×3	Bench 295×5×3
	Chins BW×14,11,7	Deadlift 405×5	Chins BW×15,11,7

Starting bodyweight = 175 (skinny-fat), final bodyweight = 220 (lean-muscular)

The above linear progression was executed almost flawlessly by an outstanding former athlete. It is not necessarily the norm to make progress this rapid and consistent, but is an illustration of what is possible with good planning, a conservative pace, and hard work. The athlete had previous exposure to squats, bench presses, and power cleans as a collegiate athlete, although almost a decade had elapsed since his last exposure to the movements. A very conservative starting point on all exercises allowed him to avoid debilitating DOMS and make steady progress through an 18-week period with no resets and no microloading. A genetic propensity for explosiveness and power provided very good progress on the power clean.

The Advanced Novice

BACK-OFF PERIODS

Inevitably, progress will stall. There are three basic scenarios: 1) an unavoidable absence from the gym, 2) one in which the trainee does everything right but still fails to stimulate further progress, and 3) progress stalls or regresses because of greed for faster-than-possible increases, or because of a lifestyle factor that affects recovery. In either case, something must be done to salvage the novice's ability to use simple linear progression and milk all possible progress from the first level of training advancement.

Missed Workouts. Unfortunately, training plans do not always run as smoothly as was illustrated in the previous sample program. Life happens, people get sick, and unexpected travel often forces a trainee to miss valuable time in the gym. Missed training sessions are often negatively compounded by the weight loss and poor nutrition that results from illness, missed meals due to travel, and the physical and emotional stress that accompanies events that force schedules to change.

In the event of a very short absence from the gym – just one or two training sessions – there isn't necessarily a need to take any remedial action. In fact, sometimes for the hard-training athlete who is grinding through the end of his linear progression, the extra recovery days afforded by a missed workout can actually bring about a slight performance increase. However, in general, if the athlete is out of the gym more than a week, there will be a detraining effect, and a reset must accompany the athletes re-entry into the training program.

A simple method is to just redo the previous 2 weeks' worth of training, set by set, rep by rep. This approach will work, but is generally more time consuming than it needs to be. If the athlete misses more than a week's worth of training, it is a good idea to start back at about 10% less than the last workout prior to the layoff. This percentage could be as high as 20% if the layoff was due to severe illness, or in the case of a very emotionally stressful event such as the death of a family member.

So, the lifter who left his linear squat progression at 315×5×3 would re-enter the program at 285×5×3. In all likelihood, the first time the lifter went from 285 to 315, he used 5-lb incremental jumps. Progress will generally be faster the second time; most likely, he would probably go up 10 lbs per workout. Or if the lifter really felt strong at 285, it may be that he only needs to do one more light workout, at say 300 or 305, before picking back up at 315. It is generally a good idea to repeat the weight that was used in the final workout before the program went on hiatus. This will give the lifter and coach the most accurate data about his strength levels.

Example Reset Methods:

Last full week before vacation:
    Squat 305×5×3   Squat 310×5×3   Squat 315×5×3

First week back from vacation:
    Squat 285×5×3   Squat 295×5×3   Squat 305×5×3

Second week back from vacation:
    Squat 315×5×3   Squat 320×5×3   Squat 325×5×3 (previous PR)

In this example, the lifter bounced back rather quickly and smoothly and was setting new PRs about a week and a half after returning from vacation. In this case, it can be assumed that the trainee ate well, slept well, and was not under any severe emotional or physical stress during the layoff.

In the next example, the lifter missed gym time, but not for vacation. The lifter got severely ill with the flu and was out of the gym for about 10 days. Upon return to training he will re-enter the program at about a 20% reduction from where he left off. In this case, it can be assumed that the trainee wasn't eating or sleeping well during this period and the severity of the detraining effect will be greater.

Last week in the gym before illness:
    Squat 305×5×3   Squat 310×5×3   Squat 315×5×3

First week back in the gym after 10 days off:
    No workout   Squat 245×5×3   Squat 265×5×3
                    (23% reduction) (16% reduction)

Second week back after 10 days off:
    Squat 285×5×3   Squat 295×5×3   Squat 300×5×3
    (10% reduction)

Third week back after 10 days off:
    Squat 305×5×3   Squat 310×5×3   Squat 315×5×3

In this example, the lifter did his first workout back at a 23% reduction from where he left off, followed by 16%, and then 10%. He was able to make a 10-lb jump from there, but had to revert back to 5-lb increments before he ever reached his previous PR weight. This slower rate of increase is due to the prolonged length of time that the trainee had spent away from his old work set PR weight of 315, and the fact that his illness forced him to re-enter the program at a much lower starting point.

For women, resets will follow the same pattern, except that lower percentages and poundages will be used. For the woman who was microloading a press at 2-lb increments, she may be able to re-enter the program at a 10% reduction, and work her way back to PR weights in 3–5 lb increases rather than 2-lb increases.

Legitimately Stuck. The second scenario assumes proper application of all the progression principles, adequate attention to recovery, sleep, and nutrition, and proper technique on all the exercises. This may be a bit of a stretch, since few novice trainees execute all parts of the plan without flaw.

If the trainee correctly follows the simple progression program, does not get greedy, and eats and rests correctly, then he will be able to add weight to the bar at every workout for quite some time. He might start by adding weight in 5-pound increments at each bench press workout and progress to 1- to 3-pound increases. At some point, adding weight will cause missed reps in one workout (usually in the last set), followed by all three sets of 5 completed at that weight the following workout. Finally, he will begin to miss the last reps in the work sets for two to three workouts in a row.

Quite a few things could be changed about the workout, but the correct approach will accomplish two things. First, it will offer the highest probability of restoring linear progress as quickly as possible and, second, it will keep the trainee as close as possible to his most recent 5RM, thus avoiding the loss of hard-won progress. The trainee needs a change but will do best with a change that disrupts the essence of the program as little as possible. A slight back-off in training weight with the immediate resumption of slow and steady progress identical to what has taken place in previous months is appropriate.

Any time a trainee working very hard is allowed a bit of extra rest and recuperation, performance will increase. This is evidence not of a dramatic unexpected increase in overall physical ability, but of the increased ability to display it on a given day. It's not that he's actually stronger; he's just not tired. "Peaking" for a contest or testing procedure works the same way: no dramatic increase in strength occurs at a peak, just the ability to demonstrate the strength that is actually present as a cumulative effect of the training program. And, in this case, this is exactly what is necessary. A trainee at this stage is not terribly "stuck" and will not take much unsticking to get back on the road to progress. A little extra rest will always allow a small increase in the weights that can be handled afterward, and the accumulation of strength through progressive loading can resume from there.

Let's assume that a hypothetical trainee is following the very basic A/B Novice rotation:

A	**B**
Squat 3×5	Squat 3×5
Bench 3×5	Press 3×5
Deadlift 1×5	Power Clean 5×3

For the sake of clarity and illustration, we will assume that our hypothetical trainee stalls out on all five lifts at the same in his programming. It is important to understand that this scenario is purely hypothetical and it is very *very* rare for all five lifts to stall at the same time.

Example Reset: The following illustrates how a trainee can stall out, reset, and set new PRs in 5 weeks.

Week	Monday	Wednesday	Friday
1	Squat 255×5×3 Bench 170×5×3 Deadlift 300×5	Squat 260×5×3 Press 110×5×3 Power Clean 150×3×5	Squat 265×4,3,3 Bench 172×4,4,3 Deadlift 300×3
2	Squat 265×4,3,3 Press 112×4,3,3 Power Clean 152×3,3,2,2,2	Squat 245×5×3 Bench 160×5×3 Deadlift 275×5	Squat 250×5×3 Press 100×5×3 Power Clean 152×3,3,3,2,2
3	Squat 255×5×3 Bench 165×5×3 Deadlift 285×5	Squat 260×5×3 Press 105×5×3 Power Clean 140×3×5	Squat 265×5×3 Bench 170×5×3 Deadlift 295×5
4	Squat 270×5×3 Press 110×5×3 Power Clean 145×3×5	Squat 275×5×3 Bench 172×5×3 Deadlift 300×5	Squat 280×5×3 Press 112×5×3 Power Clean 150×3×5
5	Squat 285×5×3 Bench 175×5×3 Deadlift 305×5	Squat 290×5×3 Press 115×5×3 Power Clean 152×3×5	Squat 295×5×3 Bench 177×5×3 Deadlift 310×5

The extra rest and recovery – the small "peaking" effect from the temporary reduction in training load – should allow success with a weight slightly above that which the trainee was successful with previously, and the act of lifting this heavier weight should spur further progress for several more workouts.

Impatience and Greed. The third scenario, in which progress stalls because of impatience with a slow, steady pace of incremental increase, is different. Here, the trainee has actually regressed slightly, or possibly more than slightly. The build-up of fatigue is more pronounced, and the back-off should therefore be more drastic.

The following illustrates how a trainee gets himself into trouble by being too aggressive, and digging himself into a recovery deficit. In this example, the trainee makes an enormous programming mistake when he attempts to push ahead and add weight even when he was failing to make all 3 sets of 5 reps. This scenario generally takes longer to get into, and longer to get out of.

Week	Monday	Wednesday	Friday
1	Squat 255×5×3	Squat 260×5×3	Squat 265×4,3,3
	Bench 170×5×3	Press 110×5×3	Bench 172×5,3,3
	Deadlift 300×5	Power Clean 150×3×5	Deadlift 305×3
2	Squat 265×5,3,2	Squat 270×3,2,2	Squat 270×2
	Press 112×4,3,3	Bench 175×3,2,2	Press 115×3,2,1
	Power Clean 152×3,3,2,2,2	Deadlift 310×1	Power Clean 155×2,2,1,1,1
3	Squat 240×5	Squat 250×5	Squat 250×5×3
	Bench 145×5	Press 95×5	Bench 150×5
	Deadlift 280×5	Power Clean 140×3	Deadlift 290×5
4	Squat 255×5×3	Squat 260×5×3	Squat 265×5×3
	Press 100×5	Bench 155×5×3	Press 100×5×3
	Power Clean 140×3×5	Deadlift 300×5	Power Clean 145×3×5
5	Squat 270×5×3	Squat 275×5×3	Squat 280×5×3
	Bench 160×5×3	Press 105×5×3	Bench 165×5×3
	Deadlift 305×5	Power Clean 150×3×5	Deadlift 310×5
6	Squat 285×5×3	Squat 290×5×3	Squat 295×5×3
	Press 110×5×3	Bench 170×5×3	Press 112×5×3
	Power Clean 152×3×5	Deadlift 315×5	Power Clean 155×3×5
7	Squat 300×5×3	Squat 305×5×3	Squat 310×5×3
	Bench 172×5×3	Press 115×5×3	Bench 175×5×3
	Deadlift 320×5	Power Clean 157×3×5	Deadlift 325×5

One aspect of back-off workouts is that, to the extent possible, intensity should not drop more than absolutely necessary. This is an important concept to follow if the back-off period is to be kept short and new personal records for 3 sets are to be set afterward without much time elapsing. Again, the key feature of novice training is linear progress – the ability to steadily increase the weight on the bar at each workout – and every effort should be made to keep this from stopping.

The reason intensity is kept relatively high while the volume of training is dropped is to maintain neuromuscular efficiency, the ability of the neural system to fire the motor units in a way that allows all the muscles to work together to efficiently display strength in a movement pattern. Basic muscle strength remains relatively constant even with reduced training. Neuromuscular efficiency, however, is much more influenced by short-term changes in training. This is why we keep intensity relatively high and cut volume drastically: *high intensity with low volume develops and maintains neuromuscular efficiency, while high volume with low intensity does not.* (This is why kettlebell training and high-rep light-weight conditioning do not produce significant increases in strength.) Keeping the weight within 10% of where it was while drastically dropping volume maintains a high state of neuromuscular readiness, while at the same time allowing for some additional recovery. It allows the trainee to resume personal record performance after the back-off period.

A simple recycling of the training intensity will work once, and maybe twice. If training has been going well in the context of proper progressive programming and proper recovery, more than two training-intensity back-off periods usually will not be productive. A need for a third usually indicates a need for more complex programming. If, however, there were problems the first and/or second time through, with progress stopping suddenly because of lack of rest, improper or inadequate diet, or greed for unreasonable incremental increases, one more back-off period might correct a sticking point. After the second back-off period, a different approach is necessary if all the possible linear gains are to be realized within the capacity of the novice lifter to milk the potential of rapid linear progress.

This back-off method is an important tool that will be used throughout the lifter's career, from novice through advanced. For each different rep and set program and level of fatigue there is a different "ideal" way to do it. But the basic concept is simple: rest, but don't detrain. The more fatigued the trainee, the more his performance has dropped, the longer the progress lasted before reaching the sticking point, the more gains that were made, and the longer the training history, then the longer the back-off period will have to be. A novice who has trained 3 months and then simply stalled in his progress and not regressed will need only a short back-off period and a moderate reduction in load, while an advanced athlete who has trained 7 years, has hit a serious wall at the end of a very hard training cycle, and has regressed quite a bit due to fatigue over his last 2 to 3 workouts will need a much longer back-off period and much lighter workouts to begin it.

ADVANCED NOVICE PROGRAMMING

Once a back-off period has become necessary, other changes can be made in the program that are appropriate for the more advanced novice. The squat can go from 3 days of increasing load per week to 2, with the introduction of lighter squats at 60–80% of Monday's work set weight into the program. They provide a break in the intensity due to the unloading, which helps to prolong linear increases. The program would now look like this:

Week	Monday	Wednesday	Friday
1	Squat	Light Squat	Squat
	Bench Press	Press	Bench Press
	Back extension	Deadlift	Back extension
	Chin-up		Chin-up
2	Squat	Light Squat	Squat
	Press	Bench Press	Press
	Power Clean	Back extension	Deadlift
		Chin-up	

Deadlifts are still done for one set of five. Deadlifts are very easy to overuse; they are important for basic strength, but too many sets make recovery difficult because of the weights that can be used and the amount of stress they can produce cumulatively. Chin-ups should have improved, or at least kept pace with added bodyweight. If chin-up reps are consistently above 10 on all of the three sets, they should be done every other workout with weight added, either hung from a belt or with a dumbbell held in the feet, so that failure happens at 5 to 7 reps. This will increase the reps on the bodyweight-only days and increase arm and shoulder strength for the presses.

At the very end of the novice progression a trainee will exhaust his ability to do 3 sets of 5 reps across on the squat, bench press, and press. Very efficient trainees will often be able to mount one herculean set of 5 on each exercise, but will be physically spent after that. Sets 2 and 3 will often yield only 2–3 reps each. At this point, there are a few techniques that can be employed to sneak a little more weight on the bar in a more-or-less linear fashion for a few more weeks. It is important to understand that at this point, the novice is still capable of adding weight *almost* every workout, he just isn't capable of adding weight to his 3×5 maximum.

The first option for the trainee is to continue to try and hit a new 5RM at every session, but for only one set, keeping the light squat day in the middle. It is a good idea to try and add in two back off sets of 5 after the 5RM, at about a 5–10% reduction. So with this method, the trainee is still hitting 3×5, but he is doing it with a 5RM and 2 back-off sets. It looks like this:

Monday	Wednesday	Friday
Squat 380×5, 360×5×2	Squat 280×5×3	Squat 385×5, 365×5×2
Bench Press 265×5, 255×5×2	Press 170×5, 165×5×2	Bench Press 268×5, 258×5×2
Deadlift 415×5	Chin-up 3×10	Power Clean 225×3×2, 215×3×3

The second option, is to simply reduce the 3×5 goal to 3×3. This slight tapering effect will also allow the trainee to continue to linearly progress for a few more weeks, albeit for sets of 3 and not sets of 5. Either way, more weight will be added to the bar. Power cleans can also benefit from a reduction in training volume. If cleans are stagnant at the standard 5×3, a simple 50% adjustment to 4×2 can work well in this tapering phase.

Whichever method is used, the late stage novice can also benefit from a reduction in training frequency. This may be the most powerful adjustment of all. For the trainee who has been training Mon-Wed-Fri, he can prolong his novice progression for quite some time by reducing frequency to a "one on, two off" schedule. In this set up, the trainee would train on Monday, then again on Thursday, and then again on Sunday. If he had a light squat day in his schedule, he will continue to squat light every other squat workout. This will mean that a heavy squat workout is only done once every 6 days, with a light squat day in between.

Example Trainee: Using 3×3 method and frequency reduction
(5-lb increments used on all exercises for illustrative purposes)

Last Week of Standard Novice Program

Monday	Wednesday	Friday
Squat 380×5×3	Squat 280×5×3	Squat 385×5×3
Bench Press 285×5×3	Press 175×5×3	Bench Press 290×5×3
Deadlift 425×4	Chins BW×10×3	Power Clean 205×3×5

First "week" of novice taper:

Monday	Thursday	Sunday
Squat 390×3×3	Squat 285×3×3	Squat 395×3×3
Press 180×3×3	Bench Press 295×3×3	Press 185×3×3
Chins BW×10×3	Power Clean 210×2×4	Chins BW×10×3

Wednesday	Saturday	Tuesday	Friday
Squat 290×3×3	Squat 400×3×3	Squat 295×3×3	Squat 405×3×3
Bench Press 300×3×3	Press 190×3×3	Bench Press 305×3×3	Press 195×3×3
Deadlift 430×3-5	Chins BW×10×3	Power Clean 215×2×4	Chins BW×10×3

This taper could be run for as long as the trainee is able to continue to add weight to the bar.

Example Trainee: Using 5RM + 2 back-off sets and frequency reduction. Below, the same reduced-frequency model is run using the 5RM + 2 back off sets at a 5% reduction.

Monday	Thursday	Sunday
Squat 390×5, 370×5×2	Squat 285×5×2	Squat 395×5, 375×5
Press 180×5, 170×5×2	Bench Press 295×5,	Press 185×5, 175×5×2
Chins BW×10×3	280×5×2	Chins BW×10×3
	Power Clean 210×2×4	

Wednesday	Saturday	Tuesday	Friday
Squat 290×5×2	Squat 400×5,	Squat 295×5×2	Squat 405×5, 358×5×2
	380×5×2		
Bench Press 300×5,	Press 190×5,180×5×2	Bench Press 305×5,	Press 195×5, 185×5×2
285×5×2	Chins BW×10×3	290×5×2	Chins BW×10×3
Deadlift 430×3–5		Power Clean 215×2×4	

The 3×3 and/or back-off methods do not necessarily have to be run for every lift. In fact, it has been observed that the back-off method works better with squats, and the 3×3 method works better with bench presses and presses. Additionally, the two methods do not have to be employed simultaneously with the reduction in frequency. It could be that frequency is reduced for several weeks and the trainee continues to make progress on his 3×5 work. Moving to 3×3 or 1×5/2×5 could be prolonged for several more workouts.

This is a rough outline of the first three to nine months of training for most novices. Starting with three work sets, the weight increases steadily until progress stalls. The weight drops 10% to get unstuck, the exercises are changed slightly, and progress is made again until another plateau occurs. Finally the point is reached where the amount of work needed to disrupt homeostasis exceeds that which the trainee can recover from between workouts, and more elaborate programming is needed. The key to the novice level of training advancement is the workout-to-workout increases that are possible during these first months. The trainee has made rapid progress and is now much stronger in a much shorter period of time than he would have been had simple linear progression not been used.

At some point, usually between the third and ninth month of training, the standard variations on linear progression will have been exhausted, and training will need to be organized into weekly periods instead of the workout-to-workout periods that characterize the novice phase. At this point, the trainee can be considered an intermediate.

Novice Programming Considerations for Special Populations

THE UNDERWEIGHT MALE

For the underweight novice trainee, overall progress and loading will occur at a much slower rate than for a trainee with an already-athletic build or even an overweight trainee. Mass moves mass, and leverages are very poor for skinny people – especially tall skinny people. For the press, the bench press, and the power clean, microloading will be required very early in the program, before the trainee has had time to gain mass. There is absolutely nothing inherently wrong with microloading a movement during a linear progression, but it wastes time when it is unnecessary, and for a skinny kid, this necessary slow progress should serve as motivation to eat enough to make progress faster.

For the underweight trainee, a high calorie diet will of course be the main catalyst for gains in muscular bodyweight, and will be responsible for preventing early stagnation and premature microloading. Gains in muscular bodyweight will generally be accompanied by gains in bodyfat, although for very skinny kids the bodyfat gains may be imperceptible. It is a misconception to think that trainees must get "fat" in order to get strong. It is perfectly reasonable for a trainee to lose their "six pack" when they are attempting to go from 165 lbs to 225 lbs in bodyweight, but it isn't necessary for the trainee to become a sloppy fat mess either. "Eating big" doesn't have to mean eating bad. The quality of the food in the trainee's diet will generally determine the body composition.

To gain muscular weight, a meal consisting of a steak and baked potato will be superior to a cheese pizza. A box of Lucky Charms for breakfast does not accomplish the same thing as 6 whole eggs and a bowl of oatmeal. Likewise snacks should be focused on things like fruit and nuts rather than crackers and candy. And whole milk has long been the novice weightlifter's friend.

A sample daily menu is given below:

Breakfast (7am)

Whole eggs & bowl of oatmeal with
blueberries
16-24 oz of whole milk

Midmorning (10am)

16-24 oz of whole milk with scoop of
protein powder, blended with banana

Lunch (1pm)

Large turkey & cheese sandwich with
lettuce/tomato/onion
16-24 oz whole milk

(Training at 2:30pm)

Post Training (4pm)

16-24 oz whole milk with scoop of
protein powder and 50 g of waxy
maize or maltodextrin

Dinner (6-7pm)

Steak or filet of fish
Large serving of grilled vegetables
16-24 oz whole milk

Before Bed (10pm)

16-24 oz whole milk, 1 scoop protein
powder

This diet provides the trainee with 1 gallon of whole milk per day broken up into six ~20 oz servings. This is a very manageable way to drink a gallon of milk per day without having to drink an absurd quantity at any one sitting. If the trainee is not gaining weight on this program, calories could be added in, in the form of more carbohydrates in the evening meal. Additionally, fat calories can be "snuck" into the menu by adding things like olive oil or peanut butter to any of the 3 daily protein shakes. This adds significant caloric value without forcing the trainee to ingest more solid food. On top of this diet, the very hard-gaining trainee should also consider at least 1–2 weekly extremely high-calorie meals. Something like a Double Quarter-Pounder, a large order of fries, and a milk shake can add a significant amount to the trainee's overall weekly caloric intake. This approach tends to work well in younger trainees, under 40. As a lifter ages, he becomes less efficient at processing this many calories productively. Very high calorie meals (McDonald's, pizza, etc) should generally be reserved for the last meal of the day. A very large, high calorie meal eaten early in the day tends to stifle the trainee's appetite and makes it difficult to get in the rest of the day's scheduled meals.

It is a good idea for underweight trainees to keep deadlifts in the training program for as long as possible before introducing the power clean. Along with squats, deadlifts have the potential to add more muscle mass than any other exercise. If he can recover from deadlifting 3 times per week, he should do so for as long as possible.

THE OVERWEIGHT TRAINEE

For trainees who are starting a novice strength program and who are significantly overweight, there are a few potential stumbling blocks. First, progress on the squat may be slow at the beginning of the program for several reasons. Being that an overweight trainee is very heavy already, even a bodyweight squat to full depth offers quite a bit of resistance to the rank novice. Adding even a small amount of weight to the trainee can dramatically increase the difficulty. It may be that some novices are so heavy that they cannot do even one bodyweight squat to full depth. The chances for this scenario are greater in heavy trainees that are older and/or female. In this case, it is best for the trainee to use a linear progression on the leg press machine while focusing on the other lifts and a tightened dietary approach.

Second, an obese trainee may have anthropometric issues that prevent squatting with good mechanics. Range of motion limitations often accompany severe obesity, and it may be that squat mechanics will be compromised until some bodyweight is lost. This can also be true for the deadlift and the power clean. Excessive bodyfat around the waist, thighs, and chest area can make the correct start position of the pull difficult, and can interfere with a vertical bar path on the clean. If a trainee cannot squat or pull with good mechanics, then the coach must be extremely careful about loading the movement. Generally, limitations are not as profound for upper body movements, and indeed, in most cases upper-body strength will be relatively disproportionate to the lower body for the overweight novice. It is not uncommon for the overweight male to bench press quite a bit more than he can squat in the early training stages.

Weight training is a critical tool for the overweight trainee's return to a favorable body composition. Adding muscle mass should be the primary goal for significant changes to the overweight trainee's metabolism.

For this reason, a serious commitment to getting stronger on the basic barbell exercises is absolutely necessary if his weight loss is to be primarily a loss of bodyfat. But because of the possible limitations described, it may be that the overweight trainee's initial strength program relies almost as much on machines as it does barbells.

It may be that the trainee's program looks like this:

Monday	Wednesday	Friday
Leg Press 3×10	Leg Press 3×10	Leg Press 3×10
Bench Press 3×5	Press 3×5	Bench Press 3×5
Deadlift 1×5	Deadlift 1×5	Deadlift 1×5

As the trainee's deadlift progresses (or if poor mechanics prevents faster load increases) he may need to rotate another exercise with the deadlift. A good choice might be the lat pulldown, an exercise he can do safely, load fairly heavily, and use to work a large amount of muscle mass. Lat pulls can rotate every other workout with the deadlift.

Workout A	Workout B
Leg Press 3×10	Leg Press 3×10
Bench Press 3×5	Press 3×5
Deadlift 1×5	Lat Pulldown (chin grip) 3×8–10

As the trainee progresses, every attempt should be made to move off the leg press machine and learn to squat. Experience has shown that when work sets of 10 reps on the leg press reach a load equal to the trainee's bodyweight, a correct barbell squat can be performed.

Although the overweight novice is trying to build strength and muscle mass as fast as possible, he should also be trying to reduce bodyfat through dietary manipulation. Obviously, the high-calorie diet used for normal and underweight trainees is wildly inappropriate for an overweight trainee. His diet should largely consist of meals that are based on lean sources of protein and vegetables. Both fat and carbohydrate should be restricted. A fast-digesting carbohydrate such as Gatorade is a good idea just prior to training, and *only* then. This will give the carb-restricted trainee the energy he needs to have productive training sessions without raising overall intake.

A sample menu for the overweight strength trainee is below:

Breakfast (7am)
| Egg omelet with vegetables

Pre-training
| Half-bottle of Gatorade

Midmorning (10am)
| Protein shake (made with water),
| one apple

Mid afternoon (4pm)
| Protein shake (with water),
| oranges

Lunch (1pm)
| Grilled chicken and a large salad

Dinner
| Lean steak or grilled burger patties
| Large serving of grilled vegetables

FEMALE TRAINEES

Women who are young, old, fit, or fat will progress at a slower rate than men. Females will progress at a disproportionately fast rate on squats and deadlifts as compared to bench presses, presses, and cleans. Females will progress with 5- and even 10-lb increments on the squats and deadlifts for several weeks but will almost immediately require microloading for the upper body exercises. And the profound differences in neuromuscular efficiency between men and women are significant contributors to the differences in response to sets of 5, the staple of men's training. After a couple of months, women do better on 5 sets of 3, and this change can contribute to a much longer linear progression, as discussed in chapter 9.

Extremely high-calorie diets are not as effective for women as they are for men. The female body simply cannot process the excess calories for productive muscle building purposes as quickly as male trainees, due to the profound hormonal differences in the two sexes. Progress will always be slower, absolute strength improvements will always be lower, and upper-body strength will always lag behind lower-body strength when compared to men of even the same bodyweight. Sorry. We can't have a multiple orgasm.

7

The Intermediate

After several months of steady workout-to-workout incremental progress, weight being added to all of the primary barbell exercises with no layoffs and uninterrupted steady progress, all trainees will get stuck. This is the normal, inevitable result of progress having advanced the trainee closer to the limits of his physical potential. By this point both strength and muscular bodyweight have improved quite a bit. So has the trainee's ability to recover quickly from heavy training, but this is offset by the fact that increased strength levels allow heavier and therefore more taxing loads. This more advanced trainee is more efficient, in both recovery and in the ability to tax recovery capacity. And with increased efficiency comes change: simply increasing the workload at each workout can no longer be relied on to spur continued progress. When the training overload of a single workout and the recovery period allowed for by the 48- to 72-hour schedule does not induce an adaptation adequate to drive a performance improvement, the novice trainee needs a change of program. A single training stress constitutes an overload event for a novice, and this overload and the recovery between that training stress and the next one is enough to disrupt homeostasis and induce a gain in strength for the beginner. Once this is no longer the case, the trainee is no longer a novice. His program must be adjusted accordingly.

An important characteristic of intermediate trainees is that they have specific training goals developed from their experience at the novice level. The high school kid who wanted to "learn how to lift" and get bigger and stronger for sports might now realize that he wants to concentrate on training that will increase his performance in the shot put. The 35-year-old who started off wanting to get back in shape might have decided that he wants to go to an Olympic weightlifting meet. Even competitive athletes who knew from the start that they were training for a sport – but were well-enough informed that they realized they were novices to strength training and decided to begin with a novice program – will find that this is the time to tailor their training to their now more-specific needs.

Simple progression works for months when the trainee is new to a program of organized training. At this level, the amount of work that disrupts biological equilibrium and results in an adaptation – the overload – can be applied in one workout. As the trainee adapts to the stresses of training, he becomes capable of applying enough stress in one workout that he will not be recovered from it before the next one. A "heavy" load for an athlete at this level is relatively more stressful on the body than a "heavy" load for a novice, and so requires a longer recovery period. At this point, if progress is to continue, training must be reorganized into periods of work that constitute a recoverable overload for the trainee at this

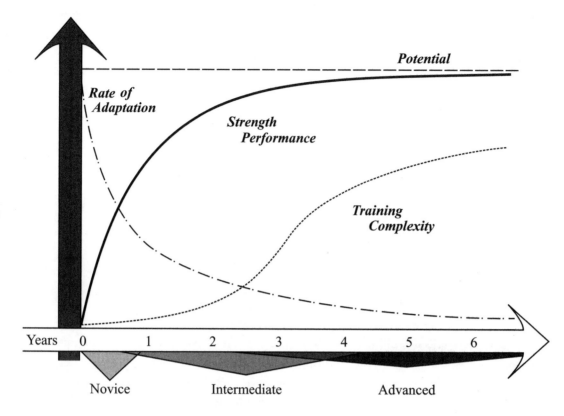

Figure 7-1. The generalized relationship between performance improvement and training complexity relative to time. Note the decreased rate of adaptation in the intermediate relative to the novice.

level of adaptation. This involves training periods that include more than one workout – enough work to accumulate into sufficient stress to constitute an overload event and enough built-in recovery time to allow adaptation to take place. At the intermediate level of adaptation, training organized in week-long periods functions well for this purpose.

There is nothing magical about one week of time. It might very well be that 96 hours (4 days) might suffice to allow enough work to accumulate and be recovered from, since the previous work/recovery period was 48 to 72 hours. But it is likely that more than 4 days will be necessary, because only one workout in 72 hours has probably been barely sufficient – in terms of both sufficient stress and sufficient recovery – for some time. The trainee has not suddenly flipped a switch and become unable to produce an overload/recovery in 3 days, so increasing the cycle period to 4 days will probably not solve the problem. Five days might, and 6 days probably will, but given the fact that society is organized along weekly timeframes, one week works most easily into most people's schedules.

The intermediate program must differ significantly from the novice program. A novice using 3 sets of 5 repetitions on the squat three days per week will find that those 3 sets are sufficient to stimulate progress, and that recovery from that quantity of work occurs quickly enough that each subsequent workout can be done with heavier weight. A novice bench press program might be 3 work sets of 5 reps on Monday and Friday, with the press done on Wednesday. An intermediate lifter using 3 work sets of 5 reps on Monday will not receive sufficient stimulation to spur progress. Five sets might be enough, but it also presents a problem. Doing 5 work sets across at an intensity high enough to drive progress may exceed recovery when done twice per week. Some variation of the work must be introduced to

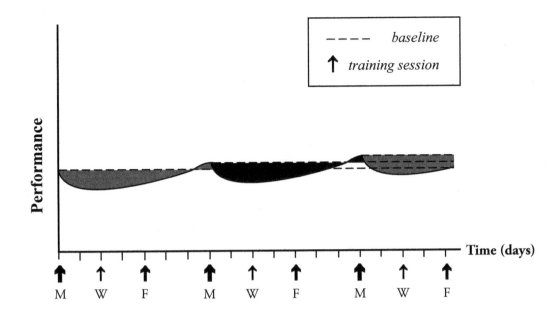

Figure 7-2. The intermediate stress/recovery/adaptation cycle. An intermediate requires a greater stress to disrupt homeostasis and a longer time to recover and adapt than does the novice. Effective programming balances these demands over the course of a longer cycle, using variations in stress to allow progress to occur.

accommodate the intermediate trainee's need for both more work and sufficient recovery from that work (Figure 7-2).

There are many ways to accomplish this and produce the desired variation across the week. Three methods will be presented later in this chapter, all proven to work well for different applications. But first, let's look at the general principles guiding intermediate programming.

General Considerations

EXERCISES

The most important consideration for programming at the intermediate level is the selection of exercises, which will be determined in large part by the trainee's choice of sport or training emphasis. If powerlifting is the sport of choice, training will be based around the squat, bench press, and deadlift; if it is weightlifting, practicing the snatch and the clean and jerk will be emphasized in the program along with the basic strength movements. Athletes training for heavy field events will incorporate power exercises such as clean, jerk, and snatch variants into the basic strength program. Those interested primarily in hypertrophy will use more isolation exercises with higher reps and shorter rest intervals along with the basic strength program.

It is likely that athletes in sports that are less dependent on strength – the lighter field events, sprinters, basketball and baseball players, non-grappling martial artists, etc. – will never have a need to advance much beyond this initial phase of intermediate training. Strength acquisition is perhaps the most important part of any athlete's preparation because it has such a profound impact on the ability to efficiently develop and express all the other parameters of athletics. But these athletes are engaged in activities that are more dependent on skills acquired in the practice of their sport than the strength and power provided by training in the weight room under the bar. One reason it is important to identify training goals is that the level to which a trainee is intentionally advanced depends on the need for such advancement.

The degree of specialization in exercise selection is therefore also determined by the need for more than basic strength enhancement, not usually the correct role of the strength program. A javelin thrower might opt for a 3-day program that involves squats, presses, cleans, snatches, and chins; any more complexity than this is unnecessary and would take away time better spent on this highly practice-dependent sport. And the very definition of "ineffective" would be engaging in weighted activities that look like the javelin throw – using a dumbbell to mimic the movement, for example, is essentially practicing to throw slower and wrong. This attempt to make strength training movements copy the specific motion of the sport reveals a fundamental misunderstanding of the general role strength plays in a sports application, where strength best acquired through training the general exercises is applied specifically in the practice of the sport. Make the athlete *strong under the bar*, make the now-stronger athlete *better at his sport on the field.*

Exercise selection will, to a certain extent, determine sets and reps. The basic strength exercises – squats, presses, bench presses, deadlifts – can be used at a variety of rep ranges, from singles to sets of twenty. This is one of the reasons they are so useful: they can be used throughout the repetition continuum to obtain the entire range of physiologic response, from absolute strength to power to hypertrophy to endurance.

Less versatile are the weightlifting-derived movements, the snatch and the clean and jerk, and their variants the power snatch, the power clean, the jerk from the rack, and hang snatches and cleans. These exercises cannot be used for high reps in programs specifically designed for strength or power development, because high reps require light weights, and light weights do not require power, merely speed. And their technique-dependency means that under conditions of high-rep fatigue they will always be done with technical imprecision. The fact that they cannot be done slowly is both an asset and a limitation. It is best to restrict snatches and cleans to singles and doubles, occasionally using sets of 3 reps for cleans; since fatigue causes technique to break down, the reps should be restricted to 3 or less so that fatigue is not the limiting factor.

Assistance exercises will be used by intermediate-level trainees. These movements are more valuable here than at any other period in a training career. An intermediate trainee is developing a feel for the direction he wants his training to take, and assistance exercises are a necessary part of learning the ropes. There are thousands to try, but only a few are valuable. The most useful assistance movements are functional in nature (they utilize normally encountered human movement patterns), use multiple joints, incorporate a balance component, and contribute to the performance of the basic exercises. Chin-ups satisfy these criteria, for example; wrist curls do not.

The best assistance movements are always those that most closely resemble their parent movements in both performance of the lift and in load. These high-quality assistance exercises will almost always be barbell-based. Many of them are so close to their parent movements that they can create the same level of stress on the body, so care must be taken when adding these types of exercises into the program in addition to the basic movements. They are probably better used as short term replacements to the parent exercises, for a period of time that could be as little as one workout or as long as several weeks or months, depending on the lifter's purpose for using them.

Some of the most useful barbell-based exercises are done inside of a power rack for the purpose of training a very specific range of motion, or initiating the movement from a very specific starting point. For the bench press and the squat, the lifter can do "dead-stop" sets, with each rep started at the bottom of the movement where leverage is the least advantageous. For presses and deadlifts, partial rack presses, rack bench presses, and rack pulls can be very powerful tools for working the lockout portion of both of those lifts. Other barbell assistance exercises, such as the Close-Grip Bench Press or the Snatch-Grip Deadlift, mimic the parent lift very closely, but slightly change the mechanics of the lift so that the range of motion can be manipulated to alter the stress.

The important point to remember is that rack presses and rack pulls are far more taxing on the lifter than things like isolation triceps work or weighted back extensions. More thoughtful care and planning must be used when programming these types of very stressful assistance movements. By and large, it usually interferes with nothing to add 2–3 sets of light weighted back extensions after a deadlifting workout or 2–3 sets of cable triceps pressdowns after presses. A well-conditioned lifter will be able to add this additional workload without any disruption to the program and get the extra work he needs. However, haphazardly adding in sets of 500+ lb rack pulls to any already heavy pulling schedule will throw the lifter's program completely off course.

Front squats can be used by intermediate trainees interested in Olympic weightlifting as a squat variant; they are regarded by Olympic lifters not as an assistance exercise, but as another core lift. They are a critical component of training for Olympic weightlifting, but their omission of significant hamstring involvement limits their consideration as a primary exercise for strength training. Chin-ups are an important upper-body exercise that supports pressing strength and functional arm strength for sports that involve throwing or pulling with the hands – so important that they have already been introduced in the novice program. Romanian deadlifts (RDLs), a deadlift variant that starts at the top instead of on the floor, and barbell rows (pulled from the floor on each rep) can be added at this stage of training.

Lower-back-specific exercises such as glute/ham raises and heavy abdominal work such as weighted sit-ups can be used by intermediate trainees to improve trunk stability for the basic movements. These exercises can be varied along the repetition continuum depending on the result desired, but generally they are used at higher reps than the basic strength movements, since they cannot be trained in the same sense that the primary exercises can. They function more as extra work and active "rest" than as critical components of the programming, and in the event of a back injury they should be discontinued because of their tendency to irritate an injured spinal component that should be kept stable while it heals.

There are times when non-barbell-based assistance exercises are appropriate. Barbell exercises are very stressful, and there is only so much that a lifter can recover from within the training program, and only so much he can do within a given workout. There are no strict guidelines that govern exactly when a lifter should employ dumbbell, bodyweight, or even machine exercises, but there are instances where they are appropriate. Dumbbell presses at all angles (flat, incline, and seated) can be useful tools to add mass to the shoulder girdle. Knocking out 3–5×10 after heavy barbell work, can be a powerful stimulant for growth. Isolation triceps work is good for lifters who are focused on building up bench and pressing strength, and can be done with e-z curl bars, dumbbells, or machines for multiple sets of 10–12. For the lower body, exercises like glute-ham raises and back extensions can add a little work without the stress of heavy stiff-leg deadlifts, RDLs, or good mornings.

SETS AND REPS

The number of sets will also vary with the exercise. The bulk of the work should always be focused on the exercises that produce the majority of the disruption in homeostasis. This means that the core lifts will receive the majority of the work in terms of sets per week and time devoted to them, since they deliver more results for the time spent doing them. Cleans and snatches, being used at lower reps, will need more sets per week to equal the volume of work; to match the reps from 5 sets of 5 squats with that from cleans, you would have to do 8 sets of 3 cleans. But keep in mind the fact that volume/tonnage in the primary exercises and volume/tonnage for the snatch/clean/jerk have very different overload effects. A 5RM deadlift PR is a vastly different physiological event than a 3RM power clean PR, and it takes far more volume for exercises that are limited by technique and explosion to equal the effects of even one bone-on-bone set of deadlifts or squats.

Assistance exercises using higher reps per set might accumulate more total reps than the core lifts. If squats are done for 5 sets of 5 across after 3 warm-up sets of 5, and 5 sets of 10 glute/ham raises are done afterward, more reps of glute/hams have been done than squats. But in terms of total tonnage (weight × reps) – and in terms of their contribution to homeostatic disruption – the squats are far more significant.

So, within the framework of the exercises used, our training goals will generally determine the nature of the sets and reps. Strength work needs up to five sets of 1 to 5 reps on the core lifts, hypertrophy calls for five sets of 12 to 15 reps with little rest between sets, and power work requires five to ten sets of 1 to 5 reps at weights light enough to move fast but heavy enough to be hard to complete. Cleans and snatches will be done with 5 to 10 sets of 1 to 3 reps. Assistance exercises will be done with higher reps, usually 10 to 15, and fewer sets, usually 3 to 5.

SCHEDULING

At the intermediate level, the weekly schedule conforms to the trainee's individual needs with regard to continued progress, not to the calendar. At the advanced level, quite often the training cycle will be tailored to a competitive schedule, but intermediate trainees are still making relatively rapid progress and they should be allowed to do so as long as possible with minimal interference from scheduling factors external to the training program. If a competitive calendar is superimposed on the training program at the intermediate level, the disruption to both the competitive performance and to the training schedule itself can be planned so as to be relatively minimal. High school football players are often in this position: they are making good progress on a training program despite the fact that football season is on, and with adequate rest and nutrition are able to do both, to the benefit of both. Intermediate trainees are not so far along in their training that an occasional game day will destroy the delicate balance between stress and recovery; the balance is not yet that delicate, as it will be at the more advanced, more specialized levels.

The time allotted for a training session will obviously vary with the number of exercises, sets, and reps. Rest time between sets should be adequate for recovery but not enough to allow "cooling off," or a decrease in preparedness for the next set. Too much time between sets represents wasted training time and, in institutional contexts, an inefficient use of the training facilities. Too little time between sets causes failed reps and missed work sets and defeats the purpose of training. Make sure that enough time is allotted that the whole workout can actually be done in one session. Any workout that takes longer than two hours probably involves too many exercises, too many sets, or too much talking.

INTENSITY

In typical strength training programming, the intensity of the work is usually calculated as a percentage of the 1RM for the number of reps performed (Table 7-1). This means that for the core lifts and the explosive lifts, the percentage of 1RM and the numbers of reps are calculated for each workout. "Light," "medium," and "heavy" correspond to different percentages, depending on the number of reps used for the exercise, as the table shows. If several sets across are to be done, the weight will have to stay a little below the corresponding RM to allow for accumulating fatigue: 355×5 done as a 5RM would need to be reduced to 330 or 335×5 for 5 sets across.

While a measured 1RM is nice and makes workload calculation easy, it is so often inaccurate as a prescriptive tool that it is not terribly useful to most lifters. A 1RM performed by a novice is useless as a data point because 1) a novice cannot perform a true one-repetition maximum effort, and 2) if he could perform a 1RM, it would not be valid for exercise programming.

Novices, by definition, lack the motor skill to perform a valid 1RM on any barbell exercise. They have been performing the movements only a short time and have not had a chance to develop the motor pathway of the movement to the point where *the effort* can be the focus instead of the movement pattern. So, by definition, any heavy one-rep attempt at any barbell exercise by a novice is submaximal. Such a test proves nothing, tests nothing, and is of no value as data for the calculation of subsequent training loads.

One very good reason that the percentages calculated from such a test are invalid for determining work loads for the novice is the fact that novice trainees get stronger every time they are exposed to an effort they have not previously performed. If the test itself makes the trainee stronger, then the test has functioned as a training stimulus and the assumption that the value obtained is actually a 1RM is wrong. If a novice's ability improves every time he trains, he is essentially a different athlete than the one for whom the test is supposed to determine workloads.

It should be understood that a 5RM test yields a 5RM, and a 5RM is not terribly useful for predicting a 1RM. There are many formulas that have been developed, none of which can take into account the factors peculiar to the individual test situation: the neuromuscular efficiency, experience, fatigue, mood, and sex (see chapter 9) of the athlete, not to mention the differences with which individual exercises convert from 5 reps to max single. Many factors influence the efficiency with which an individual converts a sub-maximal RM to a 1RM, and it is not an exact science.

There is no point in doing a 1RM unless it is at a competition, because an intermediate-level trainee is still making progress every week, and 1RM testing implies the need for data upon which a

		Volume (reps)		
	100	—	—	1
	90	—	1	3
Intensity (%1RM)	80	3	5	8
	70	5	8	10
	60	8	10	15
	50	12	20	25+
		Light	Medium	Heavy

Relative Intensity

Table 7-1. The difficulty of a repetition scheme is a function of both the intensity and volume used. The number in the table represent reps. A set of 3 repetitions with 90% 1RM is heavy, as is a set of 15 with 60% 1RM. As such, 60% for 15 reps cannot be considered a recovery workout any more than 90% for 3 reps can. Recovery during periodized training requires a reduction in relative intensity. For example, if sets of 3 are being used to train for strength, 90% would be a hard workout, and 70% for 3 reps would be considered an easy workout that will allow for recovery.

longer cycle of training – involving a back-off period and a run-up back to the 1RM and beyond – will be constructed. Intermediates use weekly training periods, making progress and new PRs each week, so 1RM testing is useless for them too.

Even then, a 1RM performed at a recent competition by a competitive lifter was done under meet conditions, usually at a different – sometimes *much* different – bodyweight, always under different rest and psychological circumstances, at a different time of day and different day of the week, with different equipment, clothing, and surroundings. It cannot serve as an accurate data point for a program that might start anywhere from 1 to 3 weeks after it was established, due to detraining, recovery differences, and different levels of motivation. The percentage of 1RM is often depended-upon, but is never very reliable, as evidenced by the fact that programs derived from 1RM data have to be subsequently adjusted most of the time.

In this book we will refer to percentages in a general sense when discussing programs in a broadly descriptive manner, to introduce the concepts of relative intensity – no other way exists to illustrate the relationships between varying loads when the loads are unknown. This does not mean that the actual application of the program will proceed exactly from these percentages. The loads used in these programs must be derived from the actual capacity of the lifter and the individual lifter's ability to apply the concept of the program that the percentage illustrates. The only time a calculated percentage is always useful is when doing back-off sets immediately after work sets that have just been performed. As illustrated in the advanced novice programming section, back-off sets are applied as additional work after what might be a very heavy limit set, to keep training volume up but permitting it to be done in a precisely manageable way. Since the work set has just been performed, it is an accurate data point, and a percentage of that work set is an accurate gauge for the stress to be applied afterward.

An accurate evaluation of performance through titration is a much better way to assign loads, because variations – sometimes minor, sometimes quite profound – in technique, strength, and fatigue are the realities of training human athletes. This is one of the most important functions of the experienced coach, and one of the best reasons to have one. Performances vary widely for many reasons, and human response to stress varies with the human. A coach with a good eye can judge a "relative maximum," the weight the individual trainee can lift on a given day under specific individual circumstances. This coach/ athlete interaction involves a great deal of experience and feedback from both the coach and trainee, and is perhaps the most valuable input into the lifter's programming.

This variability becomes even more important when training older clients or competitive athletes in sports other than barbell training. Older trainees (50–80) tend to be much more sensitive to outside influences on their training, such as a new medication, a bad night's sleep, a head cold, or some missed meals. Even a hard day of physical labor that is not normally in the daily routine can throw his recovery cycle off significantly. Trainees in their 20s and 30s can usually overcome these types of external interference and adapt as though nothing is different. The coach should be aware of older trainees' sensitivity to schedule abnormalities and program accordingly. Trying to force the regularly scheduled heavy day onto an under-recovered geezer is a recipe for a bad workout, or worse, an injury.

Competitive athletes are in a similar situation, in that they often have to deal with the physical demands placed on their bodies from practice and play of their chosen sports. Often these "outside" activities will negatively impact their weight training sessions. The more physically demanding the sport, the greater the impact on their strength training. Often the strength coach is not working in sync with the sport coach and cannot consistently predict the athlete's performance in the gym. As a general rule, the athlete's weight room performance will be based on the severity of the most recent practice or game. Sports that involve lots of running such as distance track events, basketball, and soccer may be especially hard to couple with heavy squat training. Sports that affect the entire body such as swimming or grappling may have a negative carryover to all the lifts.

The strength coach should also consider the effects of weight training on the performance of the athlete's sport, particularly prior to games and competition. The heaviest and most demanding weight training sessions should obviously not be done immediately prior to competition. If it is at all possible, the heaviest workouts should be scheduled when the athlete is most recovered and when the workout will have the least interference with the competition. Remember: athletes train for strength to *improve* performance, not interfere with it. In some instances, this time window may directly follow a competition or game. This is especially true in sports where the training or practice of the sport is more demanding than the actual game itself.

An example of this would be high school football and a 2-day in-season strength program. Typically games are played on a Friday, and teams will hold a weight training session on Saturday morning following the game. The majority of players on the team will have done very little during the game itself, and even those who did may have actually played fewer downs, run less, and had less contact than they did in practice the week prior to the game. Keeping with this example, in the world of high school football Monday and Tuesday are typically the hardest practice days in terms of repetition, contact, and conditioning work. Wednesdays are generally toned down a bit, and Thursdays are a walk-through prior to Friday's game. Wednesday is a sensible time to hold the second weight training session during the week, although this will typically be a lighter session than Saturday. Legs are beat up from Monday and Tuesday and the coach shouldn't risk creating any new soreness for Friday's game by trying to train too heavy. Thursdays are the easiest day of practice, but are only 24 hours removed from game time and it is best to save that day for complete rest and recovery. The high school football scenario is an example of programming intermediate training around sport, but the planning process can be applied to any competitive schedule.

It is important to understand that many competitive athletes can be classified as *situational intermediates*. They have not truly exhausted the novice progression, but external circumstances (such as sports practice) have forced them into intermediate-style programming. The physical demands outside the weight room are significant enough that simple workout-to-workout linear progression is not possible and not programmable. The high school senior whose 5RM squat is 435×5 is likely to have his training be more affected by the imposition of a practice and conditioning schedule than the freshman who just began weight training and is squatting 95×5.

As training progresses and strength and power are developed, the rate of improvement slows down. The closer the trainee is to his ultimate physical potential, the slower the progress toward it will be. The squat may advance 5 pounds per week, instead of 5 pounds per workout, and the bench may go up only 2 pounds per week, if that much. The more an exercise depends on smaller muscle groups, the more slowly that exercise will get strong. It is prudent to keep this in mind. There is no point in getting frustrated when the press moves up only one pound. Any steady progress is good progress for the intermediate trainee, and this becomes more true as the athlete advances and progress inevitably slows.

There will be many times over the months and years of using this weekly training model that a change within the program will be required to continue adaptation and improvement. Many things can be done to accomplish these changes, as we shall see. Reps and sets can be varied as needed, and will be changed by the observant coach or the perceptive trainee to accommodate changing conditions as they arise. Warm-ups will vary almost daily, in accordance with soreness and minor injuries; more work sets should be added as they can be successfully handled and until the need for more sets finally justifies an additional training day. Exercise selection and frequency can be varied. As noted in chapter 5, workout frequency will change progressively, but it's also possible that training frequency will need to be decreased temporarily as a result of a brush with overtraining. And the workouts themselves can be manipulated to produce varying physiologic effects by controlling the rest time between sets.

There is a tremendous amount of possible variation in training stress that can be used to drive weekly adaptation for a long time. Only creativity limits the possibilities, as long as the physiologic requirements of the goal are kept in mind and trained for.

As training progresses in intensity and volume, the role of the coach changes from that of a teacher of movement patterns to a consultant in movement, and from that of the planner to the planning adviser. The maturing trainee will eventually have enough experience – from being coached and helping coach others with whom he trains – that the kind of coaching he needs will change. A more experienced trainee needs the coach's eye to check what he himself cannot see, since he has been taught the movement correctly and has had months of experience doing it correctly. Technique needs just checking or cueing, not from-the-ground-up teaching, at this point. The coach becomes a source of advice about the application of the program instead of the controller of all its elements. Coaching input becomes more subtle, and should become more precise regarding detail as the trainee acquires finer skill. The coach should provide input about exercise variation after all the exercises have been taught correctly, guidance about load and intensity variation after it has been determined how the trainee responds to it, and constant, absolutely necessary reminders about technique on all the lifts, long after technique has been learned.

VARIATION

The intermediate stage is the place where most athletes make their biggest training mistakes. It is very true that many novices start out on terrible programs, training with no reason or logic, or adopting programs that are designed for more advanced trainees which prevent them from progressing as quickly as they could. But the magical adaptability of the novice is often strong enough to overcome even the poorest of decisions. Novices can often make progress under even the worst of circumstances. But for the intermediate trainee, progress is harder to come by, and the body is much more particular about what it responds to when it comes to improving an already-honed performance.

Many intermediate trainees get caught up in an endless cycle of changing routines, constantly messing around with the weekly schedule of exercises, sets, and reps. In an effort to feel that progress is being made, they often talk about changing even their core goals. How many times does someone in the gym (or, for God's sake, on the Internet) who hasn't really progressed in years talked about how they are going to concentrate on "cutting" now instead of "bulking"? Most often, that person still just wants to get bigger and stronger, but after a long period of no progress and therefore boredom, frustration sets in and the goal is changed to something perceived as more attainable – or perhaps merely easier. Or someone stuck on the bench press for months decides to just quit doing it and instead focus on the IsoLateral DynoPressMaster. People can ride the merry-go-round of different exercises, different routines, and different set and rep systems for years with no real progress.

When a lift gets stuck, the lifter should ask himself a very important question: does this lift need more work, or less work? Almost always, the answer is one of those two things. *It almost never involves adding more and different exercises.* Generally a little bit of common sense and review of the training log will provide the answer. If the lift is being trained once per week for 3 sets, there is a good chance it needs more work. If the lift is being trained 3 times per week for 5 sets, it probably needs less work. Exercise variety is not the problem – the programming of the primary exercises being used is the problem.

The proper way to include variety in the program is to use it in ways that reinforce training goals, so that different types of training during the week have a functional purpose. This means that the variety lies in the way the basic exercises are applied, and not in a bunch of new exercises. Sets of 5 on the basic exercises will always be useful as a part of every strength program, and constructive variations will involve different interpretations of sets, reps, and movement speed. If an athlete is training for a sport that requires speed and power production, including some additional explosive-type exercises is a good idea. After the novice stage, some sort of training that involves moving a moderate weight quickly is very useful for these trainees. For those whose main goal is increased muscular weight and size, keeping a higher-volume day in most training cycles is necessary. For those who want increased strength, and especially an increase in strength-to-bodyweight ratio, the focus must be on power development and lower-volume, higher-intensity training.

A specific example might be the trainee who is mostly interested in gaining muscular weight. He has completed the novice stage, and has finished an intermediate-level training cycle with 5 sets of 5 for one workout and dynamic effort sets for the other. He wants to gain weight, so he will keep the 5 sets of 5 portion of the workout and add in a higher-volume workout for the second session. The choices might be 5 sets of 10 across, 5 sets of 12, or even 3 to 4 sets of 15. The first set of the 5 might be a 10RM effort, with the last 4 sets done to failure and the rest between sets controlled so that full recovery does not occur. Or each set might be done for the full 10 reps, with enough rest between to ensure this. Rep schemes for the volume workout could change for each of the next few cycles, while the 5 sets of 5 keeps pace with and drives improvement on the volume training days.

Another example might be the trainee who is mostly interested in speed and power. As workouts are added or variety is introduced, singles, doubles, and triples will become more important. Dynamic effort sets – squats, benches, and presses done with 60–70% of the 5RM for very explosive doubles or triples – are a component of this type of training, as are cleans and snatches and their derivatives. Experimentation in subsequent training cycles would include multiple sets across of heavy singles or doubles, and 3 sets of 3 across or ascending or descending in weight through the work sets, along with a continued emphasis on sets of 5. The focus is always on force production, with explosive work the secondary objective and training volume held down as much as possible.

The problem is that most people, at various points in their training careers, lose sight of the basis for all productive training. They forget that the goal is always to produce a stress that induces adaptation through recovery and that, as advancement continues, the increased timeframe of this stress-response cycle must be factored in. Variety for variety's sake is pointless. All training must be planned, and success must be planned for.

The following are a sample of the many possible interpretations of basic weekly programming. They are used as a guide to your own discovery of a solution to the problem – a starting point on the way to understanding the most important period in the development of a strong athlete.

The Texas Method

This method uses a sharp contrast in training variables between the beginning and end of the week. High volume at moderate intensity is used at the first of the week, a light workout is done in the middle for maintenance of motor pathways, and then a high intensity workout at low volume ends the week. A classic example of this variation would be a squat program where, after the warm-ups, Monday's workout is 5 work sets of 5 across, Wednesday's workout is lighter – perhaps 5s at 80% of Monday's load, and

Friday's is a single heavier set of 5. This simple program is probably the most productive routine in existence for lifters at this level. It looks like this:

Monday	Wednesday	Friday
Squat, 5 sets of 5 across	Squat, 2 light sets of 5	Squat, 5RM

As with all the following example programs, the sets enumerated are work sets, with adequate warm-up sets of increasing weight and decreasing reps done beforehand. It is usually the first program to use when simple linear programming doesn't work anymore. The trainee in transition from novice to intermediate is unable to make progress with either a not-sufficiently-stressful workload that he can recover from enough to do 2 to 3 times per week, or conversely, a workload that is stressful enough to induce the stress/recovery/adaptation cycle, but that he cannot recover from quickly enough to be able to do 2 to 3 times per week.

The Texas Method is a grueling program. Particularly after the first several weeks of beginning the program, the volume day in particular becomes very difficult to complete. Two-hour sessions on volume days are commonplace, and the heavier weight 3 days later is a genuine test of the lifter's mental and physical toughness. Workouts on both volume and intensity days are both time consuming and extremely demanding physically.

For this reason, it can't be stressed enough that **the Texas Method is a program for serious strength training and competition in the barbell sports**. This style of programming requires that time outside of the gym is spent focusing on rest and recovery. Trying to couple Texas Method-style programming with sports conditioning, practice, and field competition is likely to lead to poor performance in both the weight room and in competition. **For the competitive athlete, and indeed for most people, transitioning from novice programming to intermediate style programming is best done through the Split Routine model**, dealt with later in this chapter.

However, for those serious lifters who are transitioning into intermediate training for the first time, the Texas Method presents an opportunity to make that switch very smoothly. Aside from a few adjustments on the volume and intensity of each lift, the basic structure of the program is remarkably similar to what the lifter has already been doing as a novice. Each day will still consist of about 3 multi-joint lifts and the full body will be trained at each session by squatting, pressing, and pulling.

The primary mistake that novices make when transitioning into the Texas Method is starting off too heavy. The end of the novice phase will not be a walk in the park. It is likely that the trainee has been struggling to complete all his sets and reps on each lift for several weeks. Workouts have been slow and heavy, and the trainee has been attempting sets-across for 5 reps with weights approaching 5RM levels. No athlete can continue to push at this level once novice progression has been exhausted. Better long term gains will be yielded if the trainee is allowed to throttle back on the severity of his training for at least a few weeks, to allow the body to rebound a bit and adapt to a new style of programming.

In the Texas method, the first workout of the week is the primary "stress" workout, the lighter midweek workout comes during the recovery period, and the last, higher-intensity/lower-volume workout is done when the trainee has recovered enough from the first day to show an increase in performance with a different type of stress. Both the Monday and Friday workouts increase in weight each week by 5 pounds. The total weekly training volume and training stress is low enough that as each week begins, the trainee has no accumulated fatigue from the previous week, yet the one "stress" workout on Monday is high enough in volume to trigger an adaptation, the heavy single set on Friday provides enough intensity that neuromuscular function is reinforced without fatally upping the volume, and each week produces a small net increase in strength.

Volume Day weights will be approximately 80–90% of the weight done on intensity day. It cannot be sufficiently emphasized that *the volume day does not start where the novice linear progression left off.* This is far too aggressive an approach and will stifle progress immediately. Typically 90% at 5 sets of 5 works well as a starting point for most lifters, but this must be titrated. It is impossible to know prior to starting the program exactly how much volume and at what weight yields the optimal result. Remember, the purpose of the volume day is to drive progress on the intensity day. The 90% estimate is a ballpark guess, but after that, the experience provided by trial and error will become more useful.

The best way to make the transition into the Texas Method is to use the lifter's 3×5 weight from the end of his linear progression for the first intensity day set of 5. This will represent a slight offload for the lifter at the upper end of his strength level. Previously he had been doing this weight for 3 sets across, now he uses it for one set of 5. This is a significant reduction in volume at this percentage of his absolute strength. It is important for the sustainability of the program that this reduction occurs. From this point on in the lifters career, he will primarily gauge his progress by higher-intensity low-volume work – a 1 to 5 RM for one set will be the yardstick of absolute strength. Lifters will still try to set PRs for 5×5, but generally only for the purpose of driving a 1–5RM.

Typically, lifters will begin their volume days at approximately 90%×5×5 of the intensity day load for the squat, press, and bench. After a period of time, however, some may find that lower volume works better and only 4 sets are required to set PRs on intensity day. Others have found that slightly higher percentages work better for bench presses and presses on volume day, and some have found that slightly lower percentages work better for squats. A great benefit to training with the Texas Method is the ease of manipulation from week to week to yield the desired result. As the lifter advances in strength, he may find that volume day offsets need to be adjusted from time to time. The lifter squatting 350×5 on intensity day might be fine using 90% of that weight for 5×5 on volume day, which is about 315. However, the lifter squatting 500×5 on intensity day, may find that squatting 90% (or 450 lbs) for 5×5 is a little too much to recover from on volume day. He may obtain better performance on Fridays by keeping a 15–20% offset from Monday to Friday and focusing on bar speed and good technique.

Aside from starting the training cycle too heavy, a second mistake that many lifters make with the Texas Method is trying to stay with the 5RM on intensity day for far too long. Heavy sets of 5 will generally always be involved in the strength program of all novice, intermediate, or advanced trainees, but one can only progress their 5RM for so long before things must change. The initial stages of the Texas Method begin with a 5RM on the intensity day, but within several weeks, it is likely that progress on the 5 rep set will stagnate, and it is wise to change things up. Continuous resetting of work set weights over and over again often results in ending up at the same spot he stalled the first time or two through the cycle. Multiple resets in order to PR the intensity day 5RM are not advised.

At some point, sooner rather than later, intensity day sets should transition to triples ×2 sets across, doubles ×2–3 sets across, or singles across for 3–5. These 3 rep schemes should be rotated each week, so that singles, for example, are done every fourth week. This makes each week a bit different, yet has PRs being reestablished weekly in keeping with the intermediate template. A similar approach will be detailed later.

Example transition from novice programming to the Texas Method:

Assume the last week of the Novice Program ended with the following PRs (using the Squat as an example): Squats 335×5×3

The first week of the Texas Method might look like this:

Monday	Wednesday	Friday
Squat 300×5×5 (90% of Friday)	Squat 275×5×2–3	Squat 335×5

Here is another example of this basic intermediate template, this time for pressing exercises:

Monday	Wednesday	Friday
Bench Press, 5×5 across	Press, 3 sets of 5	Bench Press, 1RM, 2RM, or 3RM

Like the sample squat workout, this bench press workout uses a high-volume session on Monday, a related but less-stressful exercise (because lighter weights are used) on Wednesday, and a high-intensity session on Friday where training volume is low but PRs are attempted. Once again, the plan is pretty simple. The Monday workout should be stressful enough to cause homeostatic disruption. Any trainee who has gotten to this point in training should be able to make a pretty good guess at what is needed, and sets across is a proven strategy, one that has worked for many people for decades. The second training session is a different exercise that contributes to the development of the primary muscle groups being trained, working the muscles and joints involved through a different range of motion, but at a load that does not add significantly to the disruption caused by the first workout. In fact, this light workout might stimulate recovery by increasing blood flow to sore muscles, in effect reminding them that they will have a job to do on Friday. The third day should be an attempt at a personal record (whether for 1, 2, or 3 reps) on the first exercise.

This is the simplest level of periodization, and this is the first appropriate time to use it. While the trainee was making progress with simple linear progression, this type of variation would have wasted training time: more progress was being made each week using the simple incremental increase every workout than could be made with this smaller weekly increase punctuated by the mid-week offloading. But at the intermediate level, the trainee's ability to progress that fast has diminished, and in order for progress to continue, the midweek offload and the Monday/Friday load variation become necessary.

Most intermediate trainees will be able to make progress for months on programs set up like this one. Different set and rep schemes can be used, as long as the basic template of a volume workout, a light workout, and an intensity workout is followed.

Again, this is the key to intermediate level training: workout-to-workout progress is no longer possible, since much of the distance between completely untrained and absolute physical potential has been covered in the novice months. What is possible is weekly progress, and Friday's workout is the opportunity to demonstrate it. Every effort should be made to choose weights carefully so that the PR can actually be done. Much is riding on the trainee's ability to stay unstuck during this phase of training. The reps each Friday do not have to be the same; it is quite useful to try for a max single, double, or triple on Friday, and rotate between all three. There is enough difference between singles and triples that the variation helps with staying unstuck.

When a program like this is started, the goal is to make progress on both Monday and Friday, just as in the novice program. When all the prescribed sets and reps on Monday are accomplished, raise the weight for the next week. If a new 1RM is set Friday, next week try for a new 2RM. In essence, linear progress is still being made, but the line is now being drawn between Monday and Monday and between Friday and Friday, instead of between Monday and Wednesday.

It is always possible to exceed recovery, just as it is always possible to under-stimulate. Balance between the two must be achieved, or progress does not occur. The novice has little chance of chronically exceeding recovery ability unless somebody gets stupid, in the form of crazy numbers of sets and reps due to inexperienced or absent supervision. And if any increase in weight at all is occurring each workout, progress is being made, although slower progress than might be possible with more aggressive loading. (The novice can exceed his lifting ability – the limits of strength – in which case the weights chosen cannot actually be done for the prescribed reps and sets. This error will also lead to no progress, but is so obvious that it can be immediately corrected.) The intermediate phase of training, then, is the first opportunity for the serious misapplication of training variables that would result in an imbalance between stress and recovery.

The ability of the body to recover from a workload increases with training, but even with the same sets and reps, the workload increases as strength – and the weight on the bar – goes up. The novice squatting 200 pounds for 3 sets of 5 was challenged by the task of recovery from that workload. Now, the intermediate lifter squatting 300 pounds for 5 sets of 5 several months later is still being challenged. Of course 200 pounds for 3 sets would be very easy to recover from at this point, but doing that doesn't accomplish anything since it now does not constitute an adaptive stimulus. Can 300 pounds for 5 sets be recovered from as easily as 200 pounds was months ago? Maybe, maybe not. That is why Monday's workout has to be adjusted as necessary, and not always adjusted up in a simple stepwise manner as with earlier workouts. Sometimes as strength goes up, a set must be dropped from the workout, or the percentage of max slightly lowered to keep residual fatigue from creeping in. The more advanced the trainee, the finer the line between not enough and too much.

Stalled Progress. In chapter 6 we discussed three possible remedies for stalled progress in a novice's linear training cycle. Those principles can be applied at the intermediate level as well, specifically to the task of keeping Monday's training stress from going too high or too low.

If progress stalls, with no reduction in the ability to complete Monday's workouts but the absence of completed PRs on Fridays, the stress needed to spur progress is probably not being applied on Monday. Often an increase in Monday's workout load will restore progress. Adding a set is a good idea. Holding the total number of reps constant while using more lower-rep sets with slightly higher weight also works well. For example, Monday's 5 sets of 5 (25 total reps) with 300 pounds becomes 8 sets of 3 (24 total reps) with 315 pounds. The addition of one or two higher-rep sets done after the regular work sets is another option; these are referred to as *back-off sets*. The trainee doing 5 sets of 5 with 300 pounds could follow that with a set of 10 at 250, or even at 225 if done with a pause or some other alteration that makes the reps harder at lighter weight. There are several possibilities, but they should not all be explored at the same time; stress should be added in small increments.

If, however, actual regression occurs, not only in Friday's workout but with staleness carrying over into Monday, then usually the workload on Monday is too high, and residual unrecovered fatigue is creeping in. Possible solutions could be to eliminate excessive warm-up volume, to drop a set or two from the sets across, reduce the work-set weight, or reduce the reps in the work sets – from 5 sets of 5 with 300 pounds to 5 sets of 4 with 300, for example.

With intelligent, careful use, it is not uncommon for this type of program to yield many months of continual progress.

TEXAS METHOD PHASE I: A BASIC TEXAS METHOD PROGRAM

The following program is appropriate for the early intermediate trainee who has just successfully completed a linear novice routine. The focus of the program is to continue to increase the foundation of strength, size, and power by increasing the 5RM on the basic exercises. The most significant changes to the program are the fluctuations from workout to workout in volume and intensity, and the introduction of the Power Snatch.

The intensity day workout will pick up where novice progression left off, but with only 1 set of 5 instead of 3 sets. Volume day weights for squats, bench presses, and presses will be approximately 90% of the same week's intensity day 5RM. The light or recovery day squat will be a 10–20% reduction from the same week's volume day workout. The recovery day presses, bench presses, cleans, and snatches will be a 5–10% reduction from their last volume day.

By placing the deadlift on the intensity day, the trainee will benefit from pulling in a fresher state than in the novice program, and progress should continue on this exercise without a reset even though no actual changes are being made to the set/rep framework. If a reset is necessary, use a 5–10% reduction in load.

Week 1

Monday – Volume Day

Squat 90% of Friday's weight ×5×5

Bench Press 90% of Friday's weight ×5×5

Power Clean 5×3

Wednesday – Recovery Day

Squat 80–90% of Monday's weight ×5×2–3

Press 90%–95% of the last workout of novice LP and thereafter of Monday's volume weight ×5×3

Power Snatch 90–95% of the last workout of novice LP and thereafter of Monday's volume weight ×2×3–4

Friday – Intensity Day

Squat 5 lbs over last workout of novice LP ×5

Bench Press 2–3 lbs over last workout of novice LP ×5

Deadlift 1×5

Week 2

Monday – Volume Day

Squat 5×5

Press 90% of Friday's weight ×5×5

Power Snatch 6–8 x 2

Wednesday – Recovery Day

Squat 80–90% of Monday ×5×2–3

Bench Press 90–95% of Monday volume weight ×5×3

Power Clean 90–95% ×3×3 of Monday's volume weight

Friday – Intensity Day

Squat 1×5

Press 1×5

Deadlift 1×5

Sample 8 Week Progression using the Basic Texas Method Template

Hypothetical Lifter ended his novice progression with the following lifts:
Squats 310×5×3, Bench Press 250×5×3, Deadlift 400×5, Press 160×5×3, Power Clean 190×3×5

Note: For the sake of simplicity, all weights are shown to increase at five pounds per week. In actual practice, it is likely that many of the exercises will have to be increased at a slower rate dictated by the strength of the individual lifter.

		Week 1	Week 3	Week 5	Week 7
Monday	Squat	285×5×5	295×5×5	305×5×5	315×5×5
	Bench Press	230×5×5	235×5×5	240×5×5	245×5×5
	Power Clean	195×3×5	200×3×5	205×3×5	210×3×5
Wednesday	Squat	225×5×2	235×5×2	245×5×2	255×5×2
	Press	135×5×3	140×5×3	145×5×3	150×5×3
	Power Snatch	125×2×4	130×2×4	135×2×4	140×2×4
Friday	Squat	315×5	325×5	335×5	345×5
	Bench Press	255×5	260×5	265×5	270×5
	Deadlift	405×5	415×5	425×5	435×5

		Week 2	Week 4	Week 6	Week 8
Monday	Squat	290×5×5	300×5×5	310×5×5	320×5×5
	Press	150×5×5	155×5×5	160×5×5	165×5×5
	Power Snatch	135×2×8	140×2×8	145×2×8	150×2×8
Wednesday	Squat	230×5×2	240×5×3	250×5×3	260×5×3
	Bench Press	210×5×3	215×5×3	220×5×3	225×5×3
	Power Clean	185×3×3	190×3×3	195×3×3	200×3×3
Friday	Squat	320×5	330×5	340×5	350×5
	Press	165×5	170×5	175×5	180×5
	Deadlift	410×5	420×5	430×5	440×5

TEXAS METHOD PHASE II: RUNNING IT OUT

The following program is generally the second phase of Texas Method-style programming. It may be used instead of the method noted above that follows the exhaustion of the potential for a 5RM on intensity day. At this time in the trainee's career, the switch should be made to higher intensity training on Fridays, with the continued use of sets of 5 on volume day. The first time through this phase, the trainee should keep progression as simple as possible. He will "run out" his strength on the intensity day, starting with triples and progressing all the way down to singles over the course of several weeks.

The trainee will still seek to complete a total of about 5 reps on the intensity day, but now, he will be using multiple sets of triples, doubles, and singles to reach his target volume for the day. Volume day should still be kept at 5×5, with the weight adjusted so that the trainee can complete all 5 sets with no more than 8–10 minutes between sets and quality form and technique. A slight reset on volume day (5–10%) weights is permissible if warranted when this phase begins.

Essentially, when the lifter feels like he can no longer complete another 5RM on his intensity day, then he will attempt to get the next increment for 2 sets of 3. This should provide some mental and physical relief for the trainee who has been pushing through limit sets of 5 for quite some time. After a period of just a few weeks (generally just 2–4, as triples don't last very long) the lifter will scale his reps down to doubles aiming for 2–3 sets across. Perhaps the lifter will increase his 2s for another 3–4 weeks, and then it will be time to pare down to singles, generally aiming for 5 across. The lifter will continue to increase the weight on the bar for 5 singles until it becomes apparent that he can no longer do so. He may decide on the final week of this cycle to take out just one heavy single. This will probably not be his true 1-rep max because of the fatigue he has accumulated over this entire training cycle, but it will be a useful number to know.

An Example of this Method is below (only intensity days are shown):

425×5
430×5
435×5
440×5
445×5 (barely made this set)
450×3×2
455×3×2
460×2×2
465×1×5
470×1×5
475×1×3
480×1×3
485×1×3
1RM attempt = 505

At this point, the lifter might start the cycle over with a set of 5 on intensity day that reflects his new 1RM and maintains the volume-day load. Now, having an accurate recent training history, the lifter can set some realistic goals for each phase that he can confidently assume will yield a new 1RM at the end of the training cycle.

A Note on Failure. Ideally, the trainee will not fail on any sets in a rep-range on intensity day before making the transition to the next. In other words, do your first workout with triples because you *planned* on doing so rather than because you *failed* your 5RM. The transition downward in reps should allow a slight physical and mental break for the lifter – failure on an intensity day load does not accomplish this. Reaching absolute failure on an exercise like the squat is a tremendously taxing event, and makes recovery for the next week very difficult.

At this point in the lifter's career he has done very little work outside of the 5-rep range. Both his body and his brain have likely soured on heavy 5RM attempts, and he will welcome the change to something different. Even this slight change in programming can spark some renewed vigor and enthusiasm in a tired lifter. The first adjustment to the intensity day should be the drop from a 5RM to a heavy triple. There are no highly-technical percentage calculations for determining the weight of the triple – 5 lbs up from wherever the 5RM left off is a good starting point. Typically, lifters don't make very long runs on sets of 3. They are useful in that they allow the lifter to slightly let off the gas for a week or two from heavy 5RM attempts. They make a nice bridge into the singles training that is to come. This first 2–3 weeks of triples will feel relatively easy for the lifter, but they tend to get heavy quickly; expect only a few weeks worth of progress. Once the lifter reaches the point where he can no longer PR a triple, he can drop to doubles or singles. Often a switch to singles-across makes sense, primarily because they provide a great deal of physical and mental relief from the 5s and 3s, even though they are heavier. The time usually spent progressing on singles-across is far longer than the time spent on triples. This is especially true if this is the lifter's first exposure to heavy singles training.

This is a very important part of using the Texas Method for the long haul: when a lifter makes the shift from one rep range to another on the intensity day, it can be useful to "skip a rep" on the way from 5s to singles. There is absolutely nothing wrong with sets of 4 or sets of 2, but dropping from a 5RM to a 4RM isn't much of an offload. The same is true with dropping from a heavy triple to a heavy double. If 5s, 4s, 3s, 2s, and singles are all performed on the way down, it prolongs the process excessively. And when a lifter has exhausted a certain rep-range, he should perceive a physical and mental break for the next few weeks while still adding weight to the bar. Dropping down two reps (from 5s to 3s and from 3s to 1s) allows weight to be added while still allowing the lifter to experience a somewhat significant break from very heavy limit sets. Again, this is in no way a hard-and-fast rule. It is simply a programming tool, and the basic concept can be very useful, especially to those trainees who are driving limit weights on a weekly basis.

Example Texas Method Phase II Program. In Phase Two, our trainee will be making the transition to higher intensity training on Friday over the course of the next 12 weeks. The 12-week time frame is being used *for illustrative purposes only*, as is the duration of each cycle of triples, doubles, and singles. The actual duration of this phase, as well as the duration of each mini-cycle of 3s, 2s, and 1s, could be quite a bit shorter or longer depending on how well the trainee executes the program. We will also assume that our hypothetical trainee has undergone a 5–10% reset on all volume day weights. This will allow for some built-up fatigue to dissipate at the beginning of the cycle, but will still culminate in the lifter setting weekly volume-day PRs, consistent with the intermediate level of training advancement.

Deadlifts will reset 5% and resume for sets of 5 until new 5RM PRs are set. About halfway through this second phase deadlifts will drop to triples, doubles, and ultimately singles. Power cleans will also reset, and the aim of the exercise will be to keep the pulling volume high, not necessarily to work towards a 1RM. Therefore, multiple resets of cleans and/or snatches may be required during the course of this hypothetical 12-week cycle in order to keep the volume high. Snatches will not initially undergo a reset in this program since the trainee was just recently introduced to them, relative to all other exercises.

Week	Monday	Wednesday	Friday
1	Squat 290×5×5 Bench Press 240×5×5 Power Clean 200×3×5	Squat 230×5×2 Press 135×5×3 Power Snatch 145×2×4	Squat 355×3×2 Bench Press 275×3×2 Deadlift 425×5
2	Squat 295×5×5 Press 150×5×5 Power Snatch 155×2×8	Squat 235×5×2 Bench 225×5×3 Power Clean 185×3×3	Squat 360×3×2 Press 185×3×2 Deadlift 435×5
3	Squat 300×5×5 Bench 245×5×5 Power Clean 205×3×5	Squat 240×5×2 Press 140×5×3 Power Snatch 150×2×4	Squat 365×3×2 Bench 280×3×2 Deadlift 445×5
4	Squat 305×5×5 Press 155×5×5 Power Snatch 160×2×8	Squat 245×5×2 Bench 230×5×3 Power Clean 190×3×3	Squat 370×3×2 Press 190×3×2 Deadlift 450×5
5	Squat 310×5×5 Bench 250×5×5 Power Clean 210×3×5	Squat 250×5×2 Press 145×5×3 Power Snatch 155×2×4	Squat 375×2×3 Bench 285×2×3 Deadlift 455×5
6	Squat 315×5×5 Press 160×5×5 Power Snatch 165×2×8	Squat 255×5×2 Bench 235×5×3 Power Clean 195×3×3	Squat 380×2×3 Press 195×2×3 Deadlift 460×5
7	Squat 320×5×5 Bench 255×5×5 Power Clean 215×3×5	Squat 260×5×2 Press 150×5×3 Power Snatch 160×2×4	Squat 385×2×3 Bench 290×2×3 Deadlift 465×3
8	Squat 325×5×5 Press 165×5×5 Power Snatch 170×2×8	Squat 265×5×2 Bench 240×5×3 Power Clean 200×3×3	Squat 390×1×5 Press 200×2×3 Deadlift 470×3

Week	Monday	Wednesday	Friday
9	Squat 330×5×5	Squat 270×5×2	Squat 395×1×5
	Bench 260×5×5	Press 155×5×3	Bench 295×1×5
	Power Clean 220×3×5	Power Snatch 165×2×4	Deadlift 475×2
10	Squat 335×5×5	Squat 275×5×2	Squat 400×1×5
	Press 170×5×5	Bench 245×5×3	Press 205×1×5
	Power Snatch 175×2×8	Power Clean 205×3×3	Deadlift 480×2
11	Squat 340×5×5	Squat 280×5×2	Squat 405×1×5
	Bench 265×5×5	Press 160×5×3	Bench 300×1×5
	Power Clean 225×3×5	Power Snatch 170×2×4	Deadlift 485×2
12	Squat 345×5×5	Squat 285×5×2	Squat 410×1×5 or 1RM
	Press 175×5×5	Bench 250×5×3	Press 210×1×5
	Power Snatch 180×2×8	Power Clean 210×3×3	Deadlift 495+ ×1

TEXAS METHOD PHASE III: CYCLING INTENSITY DAY

After many weeks or months of Texas Method-style programming, the lifter will have grown quite a bit stronger and more experienced. He will have built up a good database of training PRs at various rep ranges and will have learned much about his body's individual tolerances to training at different volumes and intensities. At this point, it might make sense to move on to a less-fatiguing system of training than the Texas Method, such as a split routine. But if the lifter has had good success with this style of programming thus far, then change for the sake of change itself makes no sense. In fact, staying within this system longer means the possibility of more subtle alterations, which in turn means less risk of losing valuable training time through the trial-and-error process that accompanies major overhauls in programming. The next step for the trainee at this point is to attempt to "run out" the Texas Method again. Our hypothetical lifter would essentially repeat the approximately 20-week process that he just completed, with the only change being significantly more weight on the bar. The second time through this process should be much smoother. The lifter now has good data and experience to work with, and isn't feeling his way through the program as he goes. He can set things up on a more predictable schedule this time around, perhaps organizing an 18-week cycle that uses 6 weeks of 5RM, 4 weeks of triples, 4 weeks of doubles, and 4 weeks of singles, while still using 5×5 for his volume work.

However, at this point the lifter may benefit from adopting a more cyclical approach to his training – a continuing theme as the lifter advances through his training career. Up to this point, the trainee's novice and intermediate program have basically followed a pattern of heavier and heavier training week to week. This is very taxing physically and mentally. The Texas Method has introduced some fluctuation in workload within the week, but the weight on the bar continues to rise weekly, and this continues through Phase III with the volume day's 5×5. The trainee's first introduction to a cyclical approach to training should come on the intensity day of the Texas Method.

In the following example, intensity days will be intentionally cycled between triples, doubles, and singles *each week*, instead of running out each rep-range over several weeks. This is occurs while the trainee continues to add weight to his 5×5 volume-day work. Any time a new phase of training begins, it is permissible for the trainee to re-evaluate the load for his volume-day work. Continued progress on his 5×5 is important, but the point of the training program is to set continual PRs on Intensity Day. If volume work is allowed to creep up too heavy for too long, stagnation or regression can occur on Fridays. This is defeating the purpose of the program. There should generally be at least a 10% offset between volume day and intensity day, and an occasional 5×5 reset may be necessary to keep this relationship viable.

This program generally works best for a trainee that has already completed several weeks/months of basic Texas Method-style programming and ideally has already "run it through" once or maybe twice. Recent data regarding the trainee's performance in the 1–3 rep range will help him set realistic goals for his intensity day work sets.

At this point in his training program, the trainee may also benefit from slightly reducing the volume of work on his intensity days. The trainee is likely strong enough that performing just one all-out triple is plenty of work on Fridays. Doubles can likely be done for just two sets, while singles can still be done for 3–5 sets across.

For illustrative purposes, the program will be outlined using percentages, but as always, percentages are guidelines only. They are useful reference points, but common sense and his immediate training history should ultimately determine a trainees starting point in a new program. Starting weights should be adjusted up or down accordingly.

Sample Template for a Lifter Focusing on the Squat, Press, and Deadlift:

Monday
Squat 70% ×5×5
Press 70% ×5×5
Stiff-Leg Deadlift 3×5

Wednesday
Squat 80% ×5×2 of Monday
Bench Press 3×5
Power Clean 3×3

Friday
Squat 90% ×3 / 93% ×2×2 / 96% ×1×5
Press 90% ×3 / 93% ×2×2 / 96% ×1×5
Deadlift 1×3 / 1×2 / 1×1

The following is a nine-week snapshot of a lifter using this approach. Assume the hypothetical lifter ended his last training cycle with 1RMs of 475/225/515. By the end of the third cycle (week 9) the lifter will be doing his old 1RM for 5 singles across. These 3-week mini-cycles could be repeated for as long as the lifter is progressing.

Week	Monday	Wednesday	Friday
1	Squat 335×5×5	Squat 270×5×2	*Squat 425×3*
	Press 155×5×5	Bench Press 300×5×3	Press 200×3
	SLDL 365×5×3	Power Clean 205×3×3	Deadlift 465×3
2	Squat 340×5×5	Squat 275×5×2	*Squat 440×2×2*
	Press 157.5×5×5	Bench Press 302.5×5×3	Press 207.5×2×2
	SLDL 370×5×3	Power Clean 207.5×3×3	Deadlift 480×2
3	Squat 345×5×5	Squat 280×5×2	*Squat 455×1×5*
	Press 160×5×5	Bench Press 305×5×3	Press 215×1×5
	SLDL 375×5×3	Power Clean 210×3×3	Deadlift 495×1
4	Squat 350×5×5	Squat 285×5×2	*Squat 435×3*
	Press 162.5×5×5	Bench Press 307.5×5×3	Press 205×3
	SLDL 380×5×3	Power Clean 212.5×3×3	Deadlift 475×3
5	Squat 355×5×5	Squat 290×5×2	*Squat 450×2×2*
	Press 165×5×5	Bench Press 310×5×3	Press 212.5×2×2
	SLDL 385×5×3	Power Clean 215×3×3	Deadlift 490×2
6	Squat 360×5×5	Squat 295×5×2	*Squat 465×1×5*
	Press 167.5×5×5	Bench Press 312.5×5×5	Press 220×1×5
	SLDL 390×5×3	Power Clean 217.5×3×3	Deadlift 505×1
7	Squat 365×5×5	Squat 300×5×2	*Squat 445×3*
	Press 170×5×5	Bench Press 315×5×3	Press 210×3
	SLDL 395×5×3	Power Clean 220×3×3	Deadlift 485×3
8	Squat 370×5×5	Squat 305×5×2	*Squat 465×2×2*
	Press 172.5×5×5	Bench Press 317.5×5×3	Press 217.5×2×2
	SLDL 400×5×3	Power Clean 222.5×3×3	Deadlift 500×2
9	Squat 375×5×5	Squat 310×5×2	*Squat 475×1×5*
	Press 175×5×5	Bench Press 320×5×3	Press 225×1×5
	SLDL 405×5×3	Power Clean 225×3×3	Deadlift 515×2 (attempt to double old PR)

When using this model (Texas Method Phase III: Cycling Intensity Day), it is possible to use larger increments on the intensity-day increases than on volume days. For instance, on presses, the 5×5 work increases at a rate of 2.5 lbs per week in this program. Yet the triples, doubles, and singles increase 5 lbs each cycle. So when the lifter arrives at triples on week 4 he can increase 5 lbs from his previous triple instead of just 2.5. The same thing occurs on the squat. In this example, the lifter is increasing his volume work by 5 lbs per week. His intensity day work increases 10 lbs each time he hits a new triple, double, or single. This is possible because by the time the lifter repeats the cycle and arrives back at a given rep range, his volume weight has since increased on 3 different occasions. This provides enough stimulus to allow for larger jumps at each rep range.

TEXAS METHOD PHASE IV: INTRODUCTION OF THE DYNAMIC EFFORT METHOD

Dynamic Effort Sets. A valuable training tool that fits very well into the Texas Method template is dynamic effort (DE) sets, as popularized by Louie Simmons in his "Westside method." The authors are grateful to Louie and his athletes for this extremely important contribution to the strength training portfolio.

High-intensity training, i.e. using a very high percentage of your force production capacity, is very productive but difficult to recover from in large doses. Any reps done, where maximal force is applied, train the efficiency of motor unit recruitment. The most common way to generate maximal force is to use maximal weights – 3, 2, or 1RMs. The problem with using maximal weights is that it is extremely taxing and hard to recover from. Lifting heavy weights is obviously a useful thing, but heavy weights must be respected and used properly and sparingly or chronic injuries can develop. Tendinitis, ligament injuries, bursitis, tendon avulsion, cartilage damage, and long-term changes in bony anatomy can accompany the misuse of heavy weights at low reps.

Another way to increase the number and efficiency of motor units recruited to generate force is to generate that force quickly and explosively, requiring the coordinated, simultaneous firing of high numbers of motor units. DE sets increase neuromuscular efficiency, in effect making it easier for the body to regularly recruit this larger number of motor units by teaching the neuromuscular system to do it on demand. The most useful way to turn on more available motor units each time the bar is lifted is to use a lighter weight, somewhere between 50 and 75% of 1RM, and push the bar as fast as possible. This has advantages over using maximal weights: it allows far more reps to be done, practiced with, and recovered from, and it can be used for long periods of time without injury due to the lighter weights involved and the reduced stress on joints and connective tissue.

Three disadvantages of DE are:

1) The acceleration of a lighter-than-max weight in an exercise that does not *require* acceleration for the rep to be completed – like a bench press versus a clean – is limited by the concentration and focus of the lifter. Especially for the inexperienced, this will always be only a percentage of the possible acceleration, even if it is a rather high percentage. Cleans must be accelerated to rack on the shoulders, and a 1RM power clean represents the limit of the lifter's ability to accelerate the bar. A DE deadlift, on the other hand, represents the lifter's *desire* to accelerate the bar, but not necessarily his *maximum ability* to do so, since there is no way to "miss" a DE deadlift.

2) There is no physiological possibility of generating an absolutely maximum motor unit recruitment event in an absolute strength exercise without performing a true 1RM.

3) A third disadvantage potentially lies within the lifter himself. We have discussed the highly individual nature of the ability to express power, and that some individuals are not terribly efficient at recruiting large numbers of motor units rapidly – some people are just not very explosive. For these people, DE will not work very well due to the fact that their inability to *recruit* motor units into contraction rapidly means that they will not be able to *work* as many motor units with weights in the DE range. These people will only be able to recruit and train sufficiently large numbers of motor units with weights heavy enough to preclude the use of DE-level acceleration. That said, DE work is still an extremely valuable adjunct to standard exercise execution for most lifters.

A proven way to use this method is with timed sets, usually done with about 10 sets of 2 or 3 repetitions with a short, controlled rest between the sets, moving the bar as fast as absolutely possible each rep. It cannot be stressed enough that even though this type of training is usually done with lighter weights, each repetition must be done with *maximum effort*. The magnitude of the force production is determined by the degree of acceleration of the load, not the amount of weight on the bar, and acceleration is completely volitional – the lifter must actively try to move each rep faster than the previous one. Herein lies the difficulty: this level of focus is hard for many people to maintain, and it must be maintained for all ten sets or the benefit is lost. A 65% weight is of no use moved slowly, but, when moved explosively for 20 reps in 10 minutes, it becomes a very powerful tool for the development of strength and power.

When beginning this type of training, it is normal to continue to use 5 sets of 5 on Monday and replace Friday's workout with DE sets. A lifter ready to try this on the bench press might have done 250 pounds for 5 sets of 5, 275 for 1 set of 5, and might be assumed to have a 1RM of around 300. A good first week for this type of program might be 240 for 5 sets of 5 on Monday and 185 for 10 explosive triples on Friday, with 1 minute between sets. The weight to use for the sets is the most weight that allows all 30 reps to be done explosively. If even the last rep of the last set slows down, the weight is too heavy. In fact, the first couple of times this workout is used, the last set of 3 should be noticeably faster than the first set.

The object is to maximally accelerate the bar and complete each set as quickly as possible. It is normal to take 2 to 3 workouts to find the correct weight, and then stay at that weight for several weeks while the weight increases on the sets-across workout. For instance, 185 on the bar for Friday's DE sets might work for 4 to 5 weeks, while normal progression on Monday's workout carries the weight incrementally back up to and past the previous 250 for 5 sets of 5. Remember, the object on Monday is heavy weight for sets across that goes up a little each week, and the object on Friday is moving the *same weight* as last Friday *faster*.

This is probably the best way to utilize this method the first time. It's the hardest to screw up, and the very act of trying to accelerate the bar, even without increasing the weight every week, will improve the ability to fire more motor units, which helps drive progress on the 5 sets of 5.

DE sets can be used with most multi-joint exercises, although different exercises customarily use different reps and sets. Squats use 2 reps, usually for 10 sets, while bench presses and presses typically use sets of 3, again for 10 sets; both are done with a one-minute rest between sets. Deadlifts work well with 15 singles on a 30-second clock. Weighted chin-ups have even been done this way. It works best to take each set out of the rack on the minute, re-rack it quickly after the set, and focus on the next set during the rest.

DE sets work well within the general intermediate template, because the ability to do relatively light weights fast will be underdeveloped initially, and the speed workout will not be that stressful. The speed workout is substituted for the PR workout on Friday, with the high-volume workout remaining as the primary stressor on Monday. The unique neuromuscular stimulus of this type of training should allow steady progress on Monday's workout for a while without subjecting the body to more stress than it can recover from. But as proficiency at DE sets increases, this workout can become stressful enough to replace 5×5 across on Monday, with a lower-stress workout, possibly several heavy singles across, at the end of the week.

Much confusion exists regarding the dynamic effort method, primarily on the appropriate percentages to use for the optimal amount of force production. This is due to the dynamic effort method's association with training for heavily-geared (suit, wraps, shirt, power undies, etc.) powerlifting, accommodating resistance (bands and chains), the use of the box, specialty bars, and the other trappings associated with the Westside Method. Across the literature and the internet there are recommendations for dynamic effort work ranging from 50–85% of 1RM, quite a broad range. The recommendations given for the following program assume that suits, shirts, wraps, accommodating resistance, boards, and specialty barbells are not used. A belt, perhaps knee sleeves or light wraps, and straight bars with barbell plates have been producing legendary strength athletes for many decades.

Because we are not using powerlifting gear, or bands and chains that alter the load, dynamic effort percentages work well between 60–70% of 1RM. Some lifters may go up to 75% for squats and even 70–80% for deadlifts. Power cleans should be used instead of DE deadlifts if the lifter is explosive enough that his power clean is more than 50% of his deadlift. But if the lifter is unable to generate good acceleration at loads lighter than 60%, the effectiveness of DE training for that lifter may not justify its use, and more traditional methods should be adhered to.

The dynamic effort method is first introduced on the intensity day of the Texas Method. The lifter will continue to train his 5-rep sets heavy on volume day, and then spend several weeks learning how to squat, bench, and press explosively. The more practice he gets, the faster he will become, within the context of his explosive potential. It may also take some time to figure out the optimal load for each lift. Some lifters may do better working closer to 60% and others closer to 70%. This will vary with the exercise and the lifter. The best weights are heavy enough that they force the lifter to push very hard to accelerate the barbell, but light enough that the weight should not slow down during the rep. If in the squat, for example, the weight is flying off the lifter's back more that a tiny bit, then it is probably too light, and if he can't make the plates rattle at the top, it's too heavy. Once again, percentages do not predict loads with enough certainty to be anything but a starting place.

When 1–5RM is being used on intensity day, the trainee must be careful to not push volume work too hard. But because this program is actually lighter on the intensity day, especially at first, this is an excellent program to use when the lifter is seeking to set new PRs on his 5×5 work until efficiency increases on DE day after a few weeks. This is therefore a high-volume training program and makes an excellent lead-in to the heavier, high-intensity training programs to follow.

A Sample Template for Introducing the Dynamic Effort Method. This program has been very successful for track & field, particularly shot put. Assume the hypothetical lifter has a 500-lb squat, 250 press, and 550 deadlift.

Monday	Wednesday	Friday
Squat 5×5 across	Power Snatch 4–6×2	Dynamic Effort Squat
Press 5×5 across	Bench Press 3×5	60/65/70% ×2×10
Power Clean 15×1 (singles on a 60-second clock)	Front Squat 3×3	Press 60/65/70% ×3×10
		Deadlift 1×5

In the above example, DE sets are cycled over a 3-week wave based roughly on percentage: if the lifter's titrated percentage of 1RM ends up being 60% *after experience with the method*, the wave starts there and goes up 5% each workout the following 2 weeks. Instead of DE deadlifts, power cleans are used due to the fact that they are quantifiable. Additionally, the pulling schedule is opposite that of the squatting and pressing schedule – dynamic pulling is done on Monday (after heavy squats), and heavy pulling is done on Friday (after dynamic squats). This allows the trainee to do his heavy pulling on slightly fresher legs.

Sample six week snapshot of this program (Two 3-week waves)

Week	Monday	Wednesday	Friday
1	Squat 400×5×5	Power Snatch 4–6×2	*Squat 300×2×10*
	Press 200×5×5	Front Squat 3×3	Press 150×3×10
	Power Clean 205×1×15	Bench Press 3×5	Deadlift 440×5
2	Squat 405×5×5	Power Snatch 4–6×2	*Squat 325×2×10*
	Press 202.5×5×5	Front Squat 3×3	Press 162.5×3×10
	Power Clean 207.5×1×15	Bench Press 3×5	Deadlift 450×5
3	Squat 410×5×5	Power Snatch 4–6×2	*Squat 350×2×10*
	Press 205×5×5	Front Squat 3×3	Press 175×3×10
	Power Clean 210×1×15	Bench Press 3×5	Deadlift 460×5
4	Squat 415×5×5	Power Snatch 4–6×2	*Squat 300×2×10*
	Press 207.5×5×5	Front Squat 3×3	Press 150×3×10
	Power Clean 212.5×1×15	Bench Press 3×5	Deadlift 470×5
5	Squat 420×5×5	Power Snatch 4–6×2	*Squat 325×2×10*
	Press 210×5×5	Front Squat 3×3	Press 162.5×3×10
	Power Clean 215×1×15	Bench Press 3×5	Deadlift 480×5
6	Squat 425×5×5	Power Snatch 4–6×2	*Squat 350×2×10*
	Press 212.5×5×5	Front Squat 3×3	Press 175×3×10
	Power Clean 217.5×1×15	Bench Press 3×5	Deadlift 490×5

The program would end when PRs on the 5×5 squats cease.

A Sample Template for the Dynamic Effort Method #2. The next logical step is the use of DE sets as the volume day stressor. After pushing very hard for multiple weeks of PRs on his 5×5 work, a switch to DE sets will be a welcome relief. It is acceptable to slightly increase the load for the DE work when it is being used as the volume day stressor. The lifter should know by now how much to increase for this effect. For the intensity day, the program should start with an attempt at a new 5RM. This will be an effective strategy to follow the heavy 5×5 work. Then for each 3-week cycle the trainee can lower the target rep-range for the intensity day goal. Deadlifts will start the cycle for heavy triples, since they have been used for 5RMs in the previous program. An overview of this model:

Monday	Wednesday	Friday
DE Squat 65/70/75%×2×10	Power Snatch 4×2	Squat 1–5RM
DE Press 65/70/75%×3×10	Front Squat 3×3	Press 1–5RM
Deadlift 1–3RM	Bench Press 3×5	Power Clean 15×1

A sample 9-week cycle of this method (Three 3-week waves)

Week	Monday	Wednesday	Friday
1	Squat 325×2×10	Power Snatch 4×2	Squat 445×5
	Press 165×3×10	Front Squat 3×3	Press 220×5
	Deadlift 500×3	Bench Press 3×5	Power Clean 220×1×15
2	Squat 350×2×10	Power Snatch 4×2	Squat 455×5
	Press 175×3×10	Front Squat 3×3	Press 225×5
	Deadlift 510×3	Bench Press 3×5	Power Clean 222.5×1×15
3	Squat 375×2×10	Power Snatch 4×2	Squat 465×5
	Press 185×3×10	Front Squat 3×3	Press 230×5
	Deadlift 520×3	Bench Press 3×5	Power Clean 225×1×15
4	Squat 325×2×10	Power Snatch 4×2	Squat 475×3
	Press 165×3×10	Front Squat 3×3	Press 235×3
	Deadlift 530×2	Bench Press 3×5	Power Clean 227.5×1×12
5	Squat 350×2×10	Power Snatch 4×2	Squat 485×3
	Press 175×3×10	Front Squat 3×3	Press 240×3
	Deadlift 540×2	Bench Press 3×5	Power Clean 230×1×12
6	Squat 375×2×10	Power Snatch 4×2	Squat 495×2
	Press 185×3×10	Front Squat 3×3	Press 245×3
	Deadlift 550×2	Bench Press 3×5	Power Clean 232.5×1×12

Week	Monday	Wednesday	Friday
7	Squat 325×2×10	Power Snatch 4×2	Squat 505×1
	Press 165×3×10	Front Squat 3×3	Press 255×1
	Deadlift 560×1	Bench Press 3×5	Power Clean 235×1×8
8	Squat 350×2×10	Power Snatch 4×2	Squat 515×1
	Press 175×3×10	Front Squat 3×3	Press 260×1
	Deadlift 570×1	Bench Press 3×5	Power Clean 237.5×1×8
9	Squat 375×2×10	Power Snatch 4×2	Squat 525+ ×1
	Press 185×3×10	Front Squat 3×3	Press 265+ ×1
	Deadlift 580+ ×1	Bench Press 3×5	Power Clean 240×1×8

A Sample Template for the Dynamic Effort Method #3. Used together, the last two programs can be melded to make an extremely powerful training plan that will last anywhere from 12–18 weeks in length. The first program feeds into the second program, and the second back into the first. Once the trainee has a feel for this type of training, it is likely that the program could be repeated again and again with only small alterations each time through.

Complete Overview:

Phase I: 3–9 weeks total.

Week	Monday	Wednesday	Friday
1	5×5	Recovery Day	DE 60%
2	5×5	Recovery Day	DE 65%
3	5×5	Recovery Day	DE 70%

Run cycle 1 to 3 times with focus on building PRs for 5×5

Phase II: 9 Weeks

Week	Monday	Wednesday	Friday
1	DE 65%	Recovery Day	5RM
2	DE 70%	Recovery Day	5RM
3	DE 75%	Recovery Day	5RM
4	DE 65%	Recovery Day	3RM
5	DE 70%	Recovery Day	3RM
6	DE 75%	Recovery Day	3RM
7	DE 65%	Recovery Day	1–2RM
8	DE 70%	Recovery Day	1–2RM
9	DE75%	Recovery Day	1RM

A Sample Template for the Dynamic Effort Method #4. The next program is a slightly different variation that could be used by any experienced lifter or general strength trainee who knows his body and his capabilities. In this example routine, the power clean now becomes the training focus and the trainee will attempt to set PRs on a weekly basis. In the previous programs, the power clean's primary function was for the accumulation of pulling volume. Now, power clean PRs will be followed by a moderate amount of volume work with about 90% of whatever the athlete PRed on that day. Dynamic effort deadlifts will be introduced and used as a volume exercise, with heavier singles (above 90%) being used every third week, so the trainee does not get too far away from heavy pulling. As in the previous program, the pulling schedule will fall on alternate days from the squatting and pressing schedule.

The intensity days are handled a little more subjectively than in some of the other programs introduced thus far. In this phase of training the athlete will "work up" to just one triple, double, or single on a given day. This attempt may or may not be a PR, but the athlete will try and break a PR if possible. If not, then the athlete will hit the maximum weight he can, for the prescribed rep range, on that day. Both the volume and intensity days in this program are set up for the athlete to perform to his full potential on any given day. Dynamic effort training allows the trainee to move the weight as fast as he can, on that day. The intensity day allows the lifter to lift as much weight as possible, within a given rep range, on that day.

This is an appropriate style of training for athletes who are heavily involved in other sports and cannot always accurately predict the impact of their sports training and conditioning on their strength program. This is also a good program for athletes who compete within a weight class: weight-class athletes often have to start dropping bodyweight in the weeks prior to competition, and this will impact their gym performance. Progression will become somewhat less predictable under these circumstances.

Week	Monday	Wednesday	Friday
1	Squat 65% ×2×10	Squat 2×5	Squat 3RM
	Bench Press 60% ×3×10	Press 3×5	Bench 3RM
	Clean 3RM (90% ×3×3)	Chins 3×10	Deadlift 70% ×1×10
2	Squat 70% ×2×10	Squat 2×5	Squat 2RM
	Bench Press 65% ×3×10	Press 3×5	Bench 2RM
	Clean 2RM (90% ×2×3)	Chins 3×10	Deadlift 75% ×1×10
3	Squat 75% ×2×10	Squat 2×5	Squat 1RM
	Bench Press 70% ×3×10	Press 3×5	Bench 1RM
	Clean 1RM (90% ×2×3)	Chins 3×10	Deadlift 80% ×1×10
			85% ×1×1
			90% ×1×1
			95% ×1×1

This very simple cycle could be repeated multiple times. At the end of week 3, the athlete will pull 3 heavier singles after his DE work, up to 95%. Every 2nd or 3rd time through a three-week cycle the athlete might decide to reduce the number of DE deadlift sets and attempt to set a new 1–3RM on the deadlift. Additional alterations might include switching from a bench-focused program to a press-focused program. Benching would be done for 3×5 on Wednesday while Pressing was used on Monday and Friday. Perhaps chins are replaced with barbell rows. It's a somewhat versatile program.

In the most recent examples, volume days were performed using the dynamic effort method in place of the volume 5×5 approach that had been used earlier. The lifter does not necessarily have to choose DE or sets of 5 as the blanket prescription for volume on *all* exercises. For example, with experience, he may find that dynamic effort work is effective for squat training, but that sets of 5 are better for benching and pressing. Perhaps on volume days, this hypothetical trainee would train 10 explosive doubles for squats, and 5×5 for bench presses or presses.

Max Effort Work & Rotating Exercises. After a period of many months of training nothing but the basic exercises, the lifter may benefit from the rotation of assistance exercises in place of the parent movements, using 1, 2, and 3RM efforts. The combination of Dynamic Effort work on Monday and high intensity/low volume work (1–3RMs) on the primary exercises on Friday is a very productive way to train for absolute strength, but it is very stressful for both joints and muscles, and generally the trainee can only engage in this type of work for short periods of time before progress begins to stagnate and PRs can no longer be set. Sometimes a cycle of lower intensity training will be necessary if stagnation – or worse, regression – occurs. This stagnation can often be avoided by keeping intensity high, continuing to train for 1–3RMs, but switching out similar exercises. The trainee may benefit from the introduction of some basic variants of the core group of movements – assistance exercises, using a partial ROM of the parent exercise, or some other alteration of the basic movement pattern, like a below-parallel squat paused on a box. This enables the use of either heavier weights or less-effective mechanics, making the assistance variation harder.

It is recommended that the number of exercises included in the rotation be kept reasonable. If all the basic variants of each basic barbell exercise were included, there would be dozens of different exercises that could fill up a rotation, and this would be an unproductive distraction. To start this type of training, only a few variants should be introduced. As the trainee gains experience, he can introduce new exercises and possibly eliminate those that proved to be ineffective. A good strategy is to introduce 2–4 assistance exercises along with the basic parent exercises and repeat them for several cycles.

A popular variation of this that many are already familiar with is alternating rack pulls with halting deadlifts on a weekly basis. This has proven to be a powerful way to train the deadlift without actually training the deadlift. Using a simple rotation like this allows the lifter to train at high intensity, but the variation in loading on the partial ROM each week keeps the lifter from getting stuck.

In phase III of the Texas Method, the cycling of rep-ranges was introduced to the trainee as a way to vary the stress of the intensity day to prevent the burnout that accompanies the same exercise done for the same reps every week. The max effort rotation essentially seeks to accomplish the same thing. Here is a comparison:

Option 1 (same exercise, vary loading)	Option 2 (variant exercise)
Week 1: Squat *3RM*	Week 1: *Squat 1RM*
Week 2: Squat *2×2*	Week 2: *Box Squat 1RM*
Week 3: Squat *5 singles*	Week 3: *Dead stop Rack Squat 1RM*

One method is not necessarily better than the other. Over the course of a training career, the lifter can experiment with both approaches to training. The response tends to be highly individual.

It is also important to understand that this approach does not have to be applied to every exercise at the same time. If the lifter is going to use this approach to squatting, it is very important that regular squats done in standard fashion are still trained another day of the week. It is very easy to "fall out of the groove" on squats, and regular practice is required. It is common to find that deadlifts respond best to this rotational concept. Deadlifts are very taxing to train for the advanced or late stage intermediate trainee, even when rep ranges are fluctuated, and this is why rack pulls rotated with haltings work so well.

Again, the trainee does not necessarily have to create a rotation of exercises for squatting, pressing, and pulling all at the same time. Many trainees find that a rotation of variant assistance movements work for one lift but not necessarily for the others. There can also be variability in the length of the rotation for each exercise. This trainee might set up 6 different deadlift variants (using different rack pull heights and grip widths for snatch-grip deadlifts) but maybe only two new exercises to train the bench press. The trainee is also not limited to training singles as illustrated in the example above. He may find that certain variant exercises respond better to heavy singles while others are best performed using up to a 5RM. At this point in training, the amount of variability that can be used is almost infinite.

A Sample Template Introducing Max Effort Work to the Texas Method

	Basic Split	Split with Alternate Squat Schedule
Monday	Squat 60–70% ×2×10	Squat 5×1
	Bench Press 60–70% ×3×10	Bench Press 60–70% ×3×10
	Deadlift 70–80% ×1×10	Deadlift 70–80% ×1×10
Wednesday	Squat 2×5	Squat 2×5
	Press 3×5	Press 3×5
	Power Clean 3×3	Power Clean 3×3
Friday	Squat 5×1	Squat 60–70% ×2×10
	Max Effort Bench	*Max Effort Bench*
	Max Effort Deadlift	*Max Effort Deadlift*

The alternate split works well for the very strong later stage intermediate trainee. The only change is that the squat follows a different schedule than the bench or deadlift. This prevents the lifter from having to go extremely heavy on all 3 lifts on Friday.

Sample 3-Week Rotation (using alternate split, and no max effort work for squat)

Week	Monday	Wednesday	Friday
1	Squat 5×1	Squat 2×5	Squat 60–65% ×2×10
	Bench Press 60% ×3×10	Press 3×5	Bench Press 1RM, 1×5*
	Deadlift 70% ×1×10	Power Clean 3×3	*Rack Pull* 1RM, 1×5*
2	Squat 5×1	Squat 2×5	Squat 65–70% ×2×10
	Bench Press 65% ×3×10	Press 3×5	Close Grip Bench 1RM, 1×5*
	Deadlift 75% ×1×10	Power Clean 3×3	*Halting Deadlift* 1RM, 1×5*
3	Squat 5×1	Squat 2×5	Squat 70–75% ×2×10
	Bench Press 70% ×3×10	Press 3×5	Rack Bench Press – 1RM, 1×5*
	Deadlift 80% ×1×10	Power Clean 3×3	*Snatch-Grip Deadlift* – 1RM, 1×5*

*Denotes the addition of a back-off set of 5 after the 1RM set. Back-offs are generally done at 85% of 1RM

The above 3-week rotation was an example snapshot of a program using this method. It is not necessarily a program prescription. The lifts chosen for the max effort rotation would be unique to the lifter.

How to Select Max-Effort Movements. As stated before, it's a good idea to not get carried away with the number of exercises in the rotation. To keep things simple, start with a three-exercise rotation for each lift. Use the parent exercise for one spot in the rotation and pick an alternate lift for the other two weeks. As the lifter grows in experience he can add or take away from the rotation as appropriate. A good strategy is to pick one lift that overloads the movement, and one lift that "underloads" the movement. Using the deadlift as an example, a rack pull is loaded heavier than a conventional deadlift. This would be an overload movement, and gives the trainee a chance to handle very heavy weights. A snatch-grip deadlift will use less weight than the conventional deadlift; this would "underload" the movement.

For the bench press, rack lockouts overload the bench, and long-pause bench presses underload. Often, overload movements are done for a partial range of motion, and don't address all potential areas of weakness in a lift. Underload movements are typically done for a longer range of motion or from a position of less advantageous leverage. Generally, increases in strength on underload movements are better indicators of progress than overload increases. So if the lifter adds 50 lbs to his best 5-second-pause bench, he can be fairly certain that his regular bench press has also gone up. The same isn't true with partial rack lockouts.

A lifter makes a tremendous mistake by doing nothing but overloading with max effort exercises. If the focus is only on the assistance overload lifts, he may set several PRs on those but make very little progress on the basic parent exercise. By keeping more focus on the weakest assistance exercises, he can have more confidence in the method's carryover to the primary movements.

Back-Off Sets. As the lifter becomes stronger and more advanced he will often become less dependent on 5-rep sets across as a means of accumulating volume. He may do so for short periods of time throughout the year, but methods like 5×5 across as a regular part of training will become much too taxing when done on consistent basis. This is why dynamic effort sets are so popular with very strong lifters. But always remember that the best way to build strength is with the basic set of 5 – whether novice, intermediate, or advanced. Lifters who are focusing most of their efforts on dynamic and max effort work should touch base with their sets of 5 several times per year.

An excellent way to work the 5-rep set into a more-advanced program is to use them as back-off sets after high intensity work has been done. Many lifters have found that they actually set the majority of their 5-rep PRs when they are done after a heavy single. Singles do not build a tremendous amount of fatigue, so the energy is there to do the back-off set. After taking out the heavy single, the neuromuscular system is "primed" to exert a high level of force. The lifter can take advantage of this by stripping some weight off the bar, and trying to set PRs in the 5-rep range. The first time he walks it out of the rack, 455 might feel heavy. When he walks it out after doing 2 singles with 500, that same 455 lbs will feel much lighter, and he may find that he can do more reps as a back-off set than he could if he had warmed-up to the weight in standard fashion.

A HYBRID MODEL FOR OLYMPIC LIFTING

This example program is appropriate for the intermediate-level trainee who is trying to build strength and focus on training the Olympic lifts. The trainee may be interested in being a competitor in Olympic weightlifting – an intermediate lifter can decide to compete too. And even though he is still getting stronger every week, he can benefit from a taper that peaks his strength and power on the Saturday of his choosing. Many sports benefit from training explosively, and even in the absence of a meet, a program like this allows the trainee to devote more time and energy to the clean, the jerk, and the snatch. If desired, the trainee can follow up this training cycle with a week of reduced volume and intensity and schedule a test or competition at the end of that lighter week.

The squatting portion of the program is built upon the model of the Texas Method, with volume back squats on Tuesday, front squats on Thursday, and high intensity back squats on Saturday.

Volume day in this program is essentially divided up into two training days. Monday is for the Olympic lifts, and Tuesday is for squats and presses. The Intensity day is divided between Thursday and Saturday, with Friday as a break from training between these two very demanding workouts. The structure of this program makes it essentially a hybrid between the Texas Method and a split routine.

On Monday's volume day, the snatches and clean & jerks are done for about 15 total repetitions. Emphasis during these workouts should be to try and go as heavy as possible without missing reps, taking only about 2 minutes between sets. Fifteen singles work well for clean and jerks and 8 doubles for the snatch, although singles can be used exclusively to train both lifts. A good starting point for each day's workout is about 90% of what the trainee did on the previous Thursday workout and work up in weight from there. If tapering for competition, 6–8 singles for the final week or two of the program works well.

Volume squats and presses begin the training cycle with 5×5 for the first six weeks, and in the final 3 weeks volume is accumulated via the Dynamic Effort method. Both volume and intensity are slightly reduced to allow some tapering and the introduction of speed into the squat training will enhance the peaking effect leading towards the competition or testing date.

Intensity day squats and presses use heavy singles for the first 6 weeks, and in the final 3 weeks the lifter will actually reduce weight on the bar and hit some nice 5-rep maxes. The first 6 weeks of volume sets of 5 and heavy singles are an excellent combination to set the stage for 5-rep maxes leading up to the testing date. The introduction of the DE squats and setting new 5-rep maxes on the back squat is a powerful stimulus, and the lifter's strength should be surging while he actually reduces the absolute load just prior to competition. Deadlifts will start the cycle for heavy sets of 5 for the first 6 weeks. Hopefully peaking a 5RM in week 6, the lifter will use the final 3 weeks to work up to a heavy deadlift single over the course of about 5 sets. Pulling back off the heavy 5-rep deadlift sets and increasing the load should produce a tapering and peaking effect in the lifter's pulling strength.

Thursday will have the lifter working up to a training max in each of the two Olympic lifts. The actual max may vary from day to day, but the trainee should work to set PRs as frequently as possible. Missed reps are acceptable on this day, but should be kept to no more than 3 attempts at a weight.

Expanded Texas Method for Olympic Lifting Example

Week	Monday	Tuesday	Thursday	Saturday
1	Snatch 8×2 C&J 15×1	Squat 75% ×5×5 Press 75% ×5×5 Chins 3×5–8	Snatch Max C&J Max Front Squat 3×3	Squat 5×1 Press 5×1 Deadlift 1×5
2	Snatch 8×2 C&J 15×1	Squat 75% ×5×5 Press 75% ×5×5 Chins 3×5–8	Snatch Max C&J Max Front Squat 3×3	Squat 5×1 Press 5×1 Deadlift 1×5
3	Snatch 8×2 C&J 15×1	Squat 75% ×5×5 Press 75% ×5×5 Chins 3 × 5–8	Snatch Max C&J Max Front Squat 3×3	Squat 5×1 Press 5×1 Deadlift 1×5
4	Snatch 8×2 C&J 15×1	Squat 75% ×5×5 Press 75% ×5×5 Chins 3×5–8	Snatch Max C&J Max Front Squat 3×3	Squat 5×1 Press 5×1 Deadlift 1×5
5	Snatch 8×2 C&J 15×1	Squat 75% ×5×5 Press 75% ×5×5 Chins 3×5–8	Snatch Max C&J Max Front Squat 3×3	Squat 5×1 Press 5×1 Deadlift 1×5
6	Snatch 8×2 C&J 15×1	Squat 75% ×5×5 Press 75% ×5×5 Chins 3×5–8	Snatch Max C&J Max Front Squat 3×3	Squat 5×1 Press 5×1 Deadlift 1×5
7	Snatch 8×1 C&J 8×1	Squat 70% ×2×10 Press 60% ×3×10 Chins 3×5–8	Snatch Max C&J Max Front Squat 3×3	Squat 5RM Press 5RM Deadlift 5×1

Week	Monday	Tuesday	Thursday	Saturday
8	Snatch 8×1	Squat 75% ×2×10	Snatch Max	Squat 5RM
	C&J 8×1	Press 65% ×3×10	C&J Max	Press 5RM
		Chins 3×5–8	Front Squat 3×3	Deadlift 5×1
9	Snatch 8×1	Squat 80% ×2×10	Snatch Max	Squat 5RM
	C&J 8×1	Press 70% ×3×10	C&J Max	Press 5RM
		Chins 3×5–8	Front Squat 3×3	Deadlift 5×1

TEXAS METHOD FOR POWERLIFTING

The term "sport-specific conditioning" has become popular in personal training and athletics circles over the last decade or so. This has led many trainers and coaches to mistakenly try to mimic the movements and demands of a given sport in the weight room. They assume because endurance sports such as swimming or cycling require long drawn out bouts of exertion, that all weight room activity should do the same thing. They may even have a pitcher, for example, "throw" a dumbbell. The critical point they miss is that strength, by and large, is a general adaptation and improves performance across the metabolic spectrum. Conditioning is a much more specific adaptation. Swimmers must swim. Runners must run. Adding strength training to the program will improve the performance of each, and the most effective way to get strong is with the basic barbell exercises done for sets of 5. In general the shorter the duration of the activity, the more strength training will improve the performance of that activity. In other words, a 100 m sprinter will benefit more from heavy squat training, than will a marathon runner.

The Texas Method is an extremely effective program for general strength training, but the downside of the Texas Method is that it is very difficult to recover from, and many of the workouts can take a long time to complete. For most competitive athletes, the Texas Method is probably not the best option, due to its physical demands. Athletes who are balancing sports practice and conditioning work may find it difficult to devote the time or energy to a 2-hour volume day training session. However, the Texas Method may be the most "sport-specific" and productive method for training for one sport in particular: powerlifting.

Like a typical Texas Method workout, powerlifting meets are long, difficult to recover from, and follow the familiar pattern of squat/press/pull. For this reason, training with the Texas Method will give the lifter an accurate predictor of his actual strength and will condition him for the demands of a meet.

It is popular for many powerlifters to follow a program that assigns one day per week to each lift, such as:

Monday – Squat Training
Wednesday – Bench Training
Friday – Deadlift Training

For many lifters, training in this manner has yielded great results in competition. But many lifters who train this way encounter a problem: they are not in "meet shape." Because they only train one lift per day, they cannot accurately gauge bench press and deadlift strength under meet conditions – having squatted

3 heavy attempts beforehand. Three heavy squat attempts are taxing, both on the lower body and on the system as a whole. If the lifter is used to benching and especially deadlifting as the first exercise in the session every week, he may be surprised to find that the weights seem heavier at the meet. Anyone who has ever done a powerlifting meet can attest to the fatigue that can build up in the legs, glutes, and low back after the squat. Often bench press flights are very long (due to the annoying number of lifters who compete in the "bench-only" divisions) and often several hours can pass between the last squat attempt and the first deadlift attempt. At this point the lifter is not feeling fresh for his deadlifts, at all. The meet-prep cycle should obviously condition the lifter for pulling at the conclusion of a workout, or at least after squatting.

Traditionally, the Texas Method calls for weekly progression based on the previous week's performance. Laying out preplanned cycles in advance is something that is generally reserved for the advanced lifter. However, when prepping for a meet – especially for a lifter's first meet – it is generally a good idea to be conservative and to make sure that progress doesn't grind to a halt just a few weeks prior to competition. Unless the cycle is somewhat planned, there is no way the lifter can know for sure what is likely to happen, and no way to direct the progress. It is no fun to try to fix a broken program a couple of weeks before a meet. Planning out an 8–12 week cycle with conservative PRs set in the final few weeks of the program is an excellent way to ensure that this doesn't happen. Since it involves a reset, it's not a strictly intermediate approach, but if a lifter can make it through an entire training cycle without any misses or bad training sessions, it will go a long way towards building confidence on his first competition platform.

The following is an example of a meet preparation cycle. It is not necessarily intended for this particular cycle to be followed to the letter year-round, but for an 8–12 week period prior to competition this type of program can be extremely beneficial. The lifter will be well conditioned to squatting, bench pressing, and pulling in the same workout, and will have a very accurate idea of what his actual strength will be on meet day.

Training Cycle Overview

Volume Day
Squat 70% ×5×5 (starting at 70–75%)
Bench Press 70% ×5×5 (starting at 70–75%)
Stiff-Leg Deadlift or Goodmornings 3×5
    OR Power Clean (10–15 total reps) or Dynamic Effort Deadlift 10×1
    OR No Pulling

Recovery Day
Squat 2–3×5 (light)
Press 3×5
Light Power Clean 3×3

Intensity Day or Mock Meet Day
    Squat 90% ×1×5
    Bench 90% ×1×5 (with pauses)
    Deadlift 90% ×1, Back-off Deadlift 70–75% ×5×2–3

Volume Day obviously starts with squats, and sets of 5 are used because they are the best builders of strength and muscle mass. Three to five sets of squats are used depending on the age and strength of the lifter. Sometimes, lifters over 30 will benefit from a slightly lower volume (3–4 sets). Likewise, lighter lifters squatting double their bodyweight or more for sets of 5 across, will probably generate enough stress with 3×5 and need not risk overtraining with 4 or 5 sets. And a lifter may start the training cycle with up to 5 sets and drop the volume to 3 sets as the weight on the bar increases and meet time gets closer, in order to complete the program without missing reps.

The bench press generally follows the same guidelines as the squats. Although the lifter is less likely to overtrain by doing too many sets of bench presses, older lifters or very strong lifters may receive the same or more benefits from doing 3 or 4 sets instead of 5. Again, the lifter may start the training cycle with up to 5 sets of bench presses and finish with 3 sets as the weight increases and recovery becomes more difficult. For the volume bench presses, it is not necessary to pause every rep. As long as form is strict, touch-and-go reps are fine in the bench press.

The example program used here is somewhat conservative and starts volume day at around 70% of 1RM, which is most likely a reset for most lifters using the program. For the bench press, the lifter will likely find these weights very easy to do. In order to "make the light weight harder" the lifter may decide to begin the first few weeks of volume training by doing all the work with a close grip (index finger on the smooth). As the weeks go by, and weight on the bar increases, the lifter can begin sliding his hands out, closer and closer to a competition grip. Close-grip benches make a wide grip stronger and this is a good way to get them into the program. Some lifters may like a close grip so much that they "split" the volume day work into sets of competition-style benches and close-grip benches. In this instance, the lifter may do 3 sets of competition-style benches, and then 2 sets with a close grip and slightly less weight on the bar.

The final volume day exercise is the pulling movement. Heavy deadlifts will be saved for intensity day, so there are several options for volume day. The first option is to pull dynamically with either DE Deadlifts or Power Cleans. The main advantage of the power clean is that progress on the lift is quantifiable: if you rack the bar, you pulled it fast, while the subjective nature of DE deadlifts makes them difficult to precisely assess. However, for those lifters who aren't very strong or technically sound on the power clean, a dynamic effort deadlift may prove to be more beneficial due to the heavier weights being moved. Seventy percent of a 500-lb deadlift is 350 lbs – it is unlikely that most 500-lb deadlifters are power cleaning 350 lbs. If the power clean weight is low due to technical inefficiency or a lack of explosive capacity, it may be that dynamic deadlifts have better carryover. Either way, learning to pull hard with legs that have just squatted sets of 5 across will go a long way towards conditioning the lifter for a long, tiring meet.

The second option for volume day pulling is to pick a "slow" pulling variant. The preferences for this would include Stiff-Leg Deadlifts, Snatch-Grip Deadlifts, or Goodmornings. Either exercise works well for building strength in the posterior chain. The downside to this method is that many lifters cannot recover from the "grind" of two "slow" pulling movements in the same week, and heavy deadlifts will be done on Friday. For these, 2–3 sets of 5 reps are appropriate. As a way to improve logistical efficiency in the gym, the goodmornings can be done immediately after squats (and before the bench press) since the bar and rack is already set up for the lifter, and he is already warmed up. All the lifter has to do is drop the weight after the squat work sets and move directly to goodmornings.

The final pulling option on Volume Day is simply to not pull at all. Particularly for a very strong lifter who is working at the high end of the volume range, 3–5 sets of 5 squats with weights approaching a 5RM will be enough homeostatic disruption to drive progress on both the squats and deadlifts on the intensity day. It may be that the lifter is better served by not digging himself too deep a hole on Monday. However, in the course of a long meet-prep cycle, there still needs to be some pulling volume in the program. A simple solution is to add a back-off set of 5 at the end of the intensity day workout. So if the lifter finishes his deadlift single at 500 lbs on Friday, he would back off to perhaps 405 and do a set of 5, or even use a deadlift variant such as a stiff-leg or a snatch-grip deadlift. The point is to accumulate some pulling volume after the deadlift singles, instead of at the beginning of the week. Many lifters will find this schedule more favorable from a recovery standpoint than trying to pull heavy multiple times per week.

Recovery Day is fairly self-explanatory. Squats are done for 2–3 sets with a weight that is about 20% less than Monday's weight. The exact number of sets is not critical, nor is the exact percentage of offset from Monday – the work should be through the whole ROM and light enough that no significant stress is added to the week. Pressing is the ideal light day exercise here because it can be trained hard but still be considered a "light day," because the absolute weight on the bar will be far less than what is used for either bench press workout. Additionally, presses will help safeguard the shoulder joint from injury and should be considered as much a preventative "prehab" movement as an assistance lift. Pressing is also a tremendous exercise for the development of the long head of the triceps, as much as any isolation exercise the lifter could choose from. For bench pressing strength, this is a critical area to keep strong. Three sets of 5 is appropriate for pressing.

Pulling on the recovery day is optional. It may be that a third day of pulling, however light, will be of no benefit to many lifters. If pulling is to be done, it should be done dynamically with light cleans or snatches.

Intensity Day in the meet-prep cycle could also be referred to as a "mock meet." Especially as the competition date moves closer, every effort should be made by lifter and coach to simulate meet conditions as closely as possible. It isn't being suggested that the lifter take 2 hours between exercises, but it is a good idea to know the rules of the federation sanctioning the meet. What commands are given for each lift? How long is the typical pause on the bench press? What equipment is permissible on the platform? If equipment such as knee wraps are to be worn, the lifter should practice the sequence of wrapping the knees, know how long it takes, and be prepared with an extra pair of wraps in case one gets dropped. In competition the lifter cannot rush the wrapping process, nor does he want to wrap too soon and then have to squat with numb feet. Commands for squatting and benching should be used in training by coaches and training partners, or rehearsed in the lifters mind if training alone.

The simulation that matters most is the training stimulus. This organization of training superbly conditions the mind and body of the lifter to squat, bench, and deadlift heavy in the same session. Additionally, since powerlifting is a sport of singles, singles will also be used in the meet-prep cycle. Five singles across is a practical place to start for the squats and bench presses; deadlifts will be done for just 3 singles across, and then perhaps just one top single as the meet draws nearer and weights begin to feel heavy. In the final weeks prior to the meet, squats and bench presses may also drop down to just 3 singles across. *But at no point should the training singles be 1RM attempts.* If a lifter is missing reps or straining against max weights prior to the competition, then the cycle was planned too aggressively, and the lifter is likely to miss his peak for the meet.

Tapering & peaking. The key to an effective meet prep cycle is timing the peak to occur on the day of competition. If proper planning is not in place it is very easy to show up at the meet overtrained or detrained. Both states will produce sub-optimal results on the platform. Overtraining generally occurs when the lifter has either failed to drop enough volume from the training taper, or when the lifter has tried to go too heavy too close to the meet. Detraining occurs when the lifter does not attempt to taper his training, but merely stops training altogether.

An advanced lifter plans a taper in advance of the meet day that may last for several weeks, depending on his training history, strength, and injury status. Our intermediate trainee needs a much shorter taper, since he is still making substantial progress each week anyway. Advanced lifters have planned each meet for months – our intermediate has just decided to go to a meet, and can approach it effectively in the short-term. An advanced lifter plans his PRs for the meet on a yearly schedule, while our intermediate is still making them weekly, in one form or another. In effect, the intermediate competitor is going to PR the Saturday of the meet anyway – he just needs to ensure that they will be spectacular. To that end, there must be a reduction in both volume and intensity starting about 10 days out from the competition. In the week to ten days prior to the meet, the lifter should not be grinding out high volume sets of 5, nor should he be taking out maximum attempts. Most intermediate-level lifters will perform a better total by continuing to train right up until meet time, but with a volume and intensity that allows recovery to take place and strength to peak.

The best way to taper for a meet is to work backwards from the date of the competition when designing the program. Most meets are held on Saturdays, so we will make the final training day on either Tuesday or Wednesday of meet week. This will be a volume day workout, but the total volume and the weight on the bar will be greatly reduced from what had been used during the prep cycle. Working backward from there, the Saturday before the meet will be a light "mock meet." Typically, lifters may use this day to figure out what they want their openers to be for meet day. The idea is to work up to one moderately heavy single on each of the main lifts. This is the first workout of the training cycle where volume and intensity are reduced. Up until this point, all training will be heavy and hard. This method of tapering gives the lifter approximately a week and a half of enhanced recovery prior to competition.

Below is a snapshot of the last two weeks of training:

Saturday: Last Heavy Mock Meet (ideally a PR)

Tuesday: Last Heavy Volume Day – set PRs for sets of 5 across

Thursday: Recovery Day

Saturday: Light Mock Meet – work up to openers (90–95%)

Tues or Wednesday: Light volume day (80% ×2×3)

Saturday: Meet Day

A Percentage Based Sample 12-Week Powerlifting Meet Prep Cycle

Week 1

Monday	Wednesday	Friday
Squat 70% ×5×5	Squat 60-65% ×5×3	Squat 90% ×1×5
Goodmornings 2 × 5	Press 3 × 5	Bench Press 90% ×1×5
Bench Press 70% ×5×5	Power Clean 3 × 3	Deadlift 90% ×1, 75% ×5

Notes: The weights for both volume and intensity day should feel fairly light. The lifter should be focused on using this week to dial in technique and good bar speed. Volume day bench presses may be done with a close grip. Intensity day bench presses should be practiced with competition grip and technique.

Weeks 2–6

Monday	Wednesday	Friday
Squat 5×5	Squat 3×5	Squat 5×1
Goodmornings 2×5	Press 3×5	Bench Press 5×1
Bench Press 5×5	Power Clean 3×3	Deadlift 1×1, 75% ×5

Mid-Cycle Adjustments. The lifter has reached the halfway point in his training cycle, and has decided to make a few adjustments to the program going forward. He can no longer do all of his volume day bench pressing work with a close grip, but would like to keep close-grip bench presses in the program. So he has decided to split up his volume day work into 3 sets of competition-style benches and 2 sets of close-grips. So he will continue his progression on the program for the first 3 sets, and then strip enough weight off the bar to allow him to complete 2×5 for close-grips. Close-grips will continue to progress for the rest of the training cycle at approximately 2.5 lbs per week.

The lifter has also started to experience quite a bit of cumulative low back fatigue from pulling 3 times per week, so the decision has been made to do all his heavy or "slow" pulling on just one day per week. Goodmornings will be dropped from the program and a back-off set of Stiff-leg deadlifts will be added after his deadlift single on Friday. The main reason for the change of exercises is for logistical efficiency. It is more efficient in the gym to do the goodmornings after squats, and easier to do the stiff-leg deadlifts right after regular deadlifts. The lifter has also decided to work up to just one top single on Friday, instead of 3 for the deadlift, with no pulling done on his recovery day. Power cleans will be moved to the volume day for approximately 10 singles. This will actually help to further condition the lifter to the sequence of squatting, pressing, and pulling. The switch from triples to singles will make it easier for the tired trainee to pull explosively and with good form after a brutal squat session.

The final adjustment to the program is the scheduling of the training week. Because most meets occur on Saturday mornings, it is a good idea to start letting the body adapt to lifting in the morning. If the lifter regularly does his training in the late afternoon or evening, trying to squat heavy at 10 am on meet day might come as quite a shock, and he might find that the weights feel a little heavier than they normally do in training. This schedule change allows the lifter to start teaching his body to perform at this new time of day, as well experiment with variable factors such as what time to wake up, when to eat breakfast, etc.

Weeks 7–9

Tuesday	Thursday	Saturday (at 10am)
Squat 5×5	Squat 3×5	Squat 5×1
Bench 3×5	Press 3×5	Bench 5×1
Close-Grip Bench 2×5		Deadlift 1×1
Power Clean 10×1		Stiff-Leg Deadlift 1×5

Week 10

Tuesday	Thursday	Saturday*
Squat 5×5	Squat 3×5	Squat 5×1
Bench Press 3×5	Press 3×5	Bench 5×1
Close-Grip Bench 2×5		Deadlift 1×1**
Power Clean 10×1		Stiff-Leg Deadlift 1×5

* Last Heavy Intensity Day for the Cycle
** Don't Max Out

Week 11

Tuesday*	Thursday	Saturday**
Squat 5×5	Squat 3×5	Squat 1×1 – Openers
Bench Press 3×5	Press 3×5	Bench 1×1 – Openers
Close-Grip Bench 2×5		Deadlift 1×1 – Openers
Power Clean 10×1		

* Last Heavy Volume Day Workout
**Light Mock Meet, to 90–95% of projected meet PRs

Week 12 (Meet Week)

Wednesday	Saturday
Squat 75–80% ×2–3×3	Competition
Bench 75–80% ×2–3×3	

The above program is a hypothetical percentage-based program used to illustrate the taper, not as an actual planning calculator. Percentages are useful to lay out the framework for a program such as this, but weights should be adjusted to reflect the individual lifter's capabilities.

Sometimes, as the lifter works his way through the meet-prep cycle, it becomes apparent that continued progress on his 5×5 volume work is not going to be sustainable all the way through to the meet. If the lifter becomes unable to complete 5×5 across on his volume days, back-off sets can be used to keep his volume high while slightly reducing the total load. The lifter can often successfully complete the first set of 5, but sets 2–5 are not feasible, due to the fatigue that was generated from the first set. This problem becomes more pronounced with stronger lifters. The solution is to continue to work up to a heavy set of 5 and then do 4×5 with about a 5–10% reduction in load.

Another option is to continue using 5 sets across, but reduce the reps to triples. This is less desirable. Heavy triples fade out very quickly, and if at all possible the lifter should try to keep progressing on the 5-rep sets. Sets of 5 have proven themselves over the decades to be the primary catalyst for strength gains. Below is an example:

Week 8:   455×5×5
Week 9:   460×5 (460×4,3,3,3) – lifter fails to make 5 reps on sets 2–5
Week 10: 465×5 (445×5×4)
Week 11: 470×5 (450×5×4)
Week 12: Meet week

Assistance Work. In a powerlifting-specific program, any lift that is not a squat, bench press, or deadlift is considered an assistance exercise. There are only a few viable assistance exercises that should be included in the meet-prep plan. All of them should seek to add to the lifters performance, and nothing should detract. It is very important that both volume and intensity be controlled closely on the assistance exercises such as presses, cleans, SLDLs, close-grip bench presses, etc. Generally, assistance work should never be more than 2–3 sets, and in most cases done for sets of 5 (cleans are triples or fewer). Higher reps in the 10–12 range on other barbell exercises runs the risk of creating excessive soreness which can bleed over into subsequent training days. Going below 5 reps on other barbell exercises creates excessive demand on the neuromuscular system, which is already being taxed heavily by weekly singles on the three competitive lifts. So when the program says to Press for 3×5, then that means ***3×5***. The weight must be adjusted on a weekly basis so that the lifter isn't failing reps and dropping below sets of 5. This may mean several resets on the assistance lifts throughout the course of the program

The Split Routine Model

The three-day-a-week, whole-body workout plan that has been used up to this point is a very effective way to organize training. In fact, most people would be well served by continuing this basic program design through their whole training career. It is an efficient use of time, and it provides a complete workout. There are, however, reasons to change from this model.

One possible reason is simple boredom. Training should be fun, and more progress will be made if it is. Different people have different psychological needs for variety and different levels of tolerance for repetitive scheduling. For some, the prospect of continuing on for years and years training the whole body three times a week is not a welcome prospect. These people will respond better to a program that varies more during the week, or one that varies weekly.

For some, a shift in training goals or the need to combine gym workouts with more specific training for a competitive sport will prompt a change. This could be caused by time constraints, or by the need to avoid the systemic fatigue that a whole-body workout causes so that it doesn't interfere with sport-specific training. *Split routines* address this problem by dividing the workload into more manageable segments along the lines of the functional and anatomical differences in the exercises.

Generally, trainees switch from the Texas Method to a split routine as their strength increases over time. It is not uncommon for a very strong trainee to need 2.5 hours to complete a very difficult volume day training session using the Texas Method. Many people cannot commit this amount of time to a strength training session, nor do they have the ability to recover from it. Splitting long workouts up over multiple days by "bodypart" is often the best solution.

Split routines also allow lifters to focus their efforts more on each individual lift. A very strong lifter doing 500+ lb squats for 5×5 probably doesn't have much gas in the tank for anything else. Even his performance on upper body lifts would be greatly compromised were he to attempt to train them in the same session.

Split routines are also much more flexible than traditional full-body Texas Method routines. Because the lifter is doing less work each session on the core group of lifts, he generally has the ability to start adding in assistance work if and when it is warranted. However, this flexibility can also be a drawback. Assistance exercises are powerful tools when used appropriately, but too much flexibility in a program can allow a lifter to drift away from the basics and get distracted by too many assistance movements, many of which will not be productive. If a lifter is spending more time on his assistance work than his primary barbell lifts, "mission creep" has occurred, and he probably needs to rethink his training.

There are many ways to organize or "split" up the training routine. Most of the time, the lifter will do pressing exercises on one day and squatting and pulling exercises on another day. This makes perfect sense from a recovery standpoint. Then there are a couple of different ways to organize assistance work. First is to do all upper-body movements on pressing days and anything for the lower body on squat/pull day. Lat work – chins and pulldowns – use the arms just as heavily as the lats, so they get done on upper-body day:

Upper Body – Monday/Thursday	Lower-body – Tuesday/Friday
Bench or Press	Squats
Chest/Shoulder assistance	Pulls
Lats	
Arms	

An alternate method creates additional fluctuation in how stress is distributed. In the following four-day split, the lifter will have 2 days that are relatively "easy" and 2 days that are relatively "hard." Fluctuation in stress across the week is a good thing for long-term progress. This fluctuation is maximized by placing all lat and upper-back work on the lower-body day. This makes sense, since the back is heavily involved in all pulling exercises anyway, and it also ensures that there is always time and energy available for triceps assistance exercises which are important for building a big bench and a big press.

A program organized along these lines would look like this:

Day 1 – "easy" day	Day 2 – "hard" day
Bench or Press	Squat
Chest/Shoulder Assistance	Pulls (DL, cleans, etc.)
Triceps Assistance	Upper back assistance (pull-ups, rows, etc.)

A good example of a different type of weekly schedule change would be that of a competitive shot-putter changing from 3 days per week to a 4-day-a-week program, as follows:

Monday
> Squats and pressing exercises

Wednesday
> Pulling exercises such as cleans and snatches, and other back work

Thursday
> Squats and presses

Saturday
> Explosive exercises

This can be appropriate for several reasons. Trainees involved in sports like the shot put normally do technique-oriented training several days a week, throwing various implements and using some form of plyometric training and sprint work. Good quality technique training is difficult the day after a whole-body workout, just as thirty throws would interfere with squats, pulls, and presses if done within an hour or two of throwing practice. What many would consider the most important exercises for the shot put – dynamic exercises such as snatch, the clean, the jerk, and related movements – are placed by themselves so that the trainee can devote an appropriate amount of attention to them.

Many competitive powerlifters use a training schedule like this one:

Monday
> Bench press and related exercises

Tuesday
> Squatting and deadlifting exercises

Thursday
> Bench press and related exercises

Friday or Saturday
> Squatting and deadlifting exercises

For the powerlifter, the split serves a different purpose than for the shot-putter. The specialized equipment used in the sport lengthens time it takes to train each lift. Training all three lifts in one session would often mean an enormous stress on the body and a 4-hour session, something neither desirable nor possible for many people. The bench press is best trained the day before the squat so that it is not affected by the fatigue produced by squatting and deadlifting. As functionally/anatomically related movements, squatting and pulling exercises can be combined. With the focus on very heavy weights and the use of squat suits, bench press shirts, and wraps in the sport, these two lifts cannot be trained heavy more than once per week by most competitive lifters. Since the same basic muscle groups are used, it is convenient to have a heavy squat/light deadlift workout, and another that is heavy deadlift/light squat.

"Four-day texas method"

A very logical transition from Texas Method-style programming into a split routine is to keep the same pattern of high volume/lower intensity at the beginning of the week and work towards high intensity/ low volume training at the end of the week. This is known as "The Four-Day Texas Method" because the setup is so similar. Essentially any Texas Method program can be split up into four training sessions and trained in this manner. Within this very basic structure there are dozens of ways to organize exercises, sets, and reps. But for the most part, all the rules that applied to a Texas Method template will apply to this split as well. The one major difference in this program is the lack of a recovery day in the middle of the week. Individual differences and tolerances will ultimately determine how much effect this has on programming.

In the Texas Method section, several methods were discussed to progress the basic lifts, with the two basic methods being, 1) "running it out" and 2) cycling the intensity day. Below is a brief overview of what this method looks like in the context of a 4-day split. The first version of the 4-day split will look very familiar to many trainees, and it attempts to keep either a light bench or press on alternate weeks when not being trained heavy. This program does not attempt to train both the bench press and the press for volume and intensity in the same week. Later programs will.

Basic 4-Day Texas Method Split

Week 1

Monday–Volume Bench	Thursday–Intensity Bench/Light Press
Bench Press 5×5	Bench Press 1×5 – 2×3 – 3×2 – 5×1
Bench Assistance	Light Press 3×5

Tuesday–Volume Squat/Pull	Friday–Intensity Squat/Pull
Squat 5×5	Squat 1×5 – 2×3 – 3×2 – 5×1
Power Clean 5×3	Deadlift 1×5 – 1×3 – 1×2 – 1×1

Week 2

Monday–Volume Press	Thursday–Intensity Press/Light Bench
Press 5×5	Press 1×5 – 2×3 – 3×2 – 5×1
Press Assistance	Light Bench Press 3×5

Tuesday–Volume Squat/Pull	Friday–Intensity Squat/Pulls
Squat 5×5	Squat 1×5 – 2×3 – 3×2 – 5×1
Power Clean 5×3	Deadlift 1×5 – 1×3 – 1×2 – 1×1
(or Power Snatch 6–8×2)	

When using this program, the trainee would follow the same pattern as he did when using the very basic version of the Texas Method. Starting in week one, he would try to set new 5RMs on the intensity day for as long as possible. As progress for each lift begins to fade, he would continue to add weight to the bar while dropping the reps down to two sets of triples, then 2–3 sets of doubles and ultimately singles. After running it through several times, the lifter could begin cycling his reps on the intensity day (this was illustrated in the Texas Method section too). Below is a brief overview of how 6 weeks of a cycling program would be structured (using the squat and press as an example):

Week	Monday	Tuesday	Thursday	Friday
1	Squat 5×5	Press 5×5	Squat 2×3	Press 2×3
2	Squat 5×5	Press 5×5	Squat 3×2	Press 3×2
3	Squat 5×5	Press 5×5	Squat 5×1	Press 5×1
4	Squat 5×5	Press 5×5	Squat 2×3	Press 2×3
5	Squat 5×5	Press 5×5	Squat 3×2	Press 3×2
6	Squat 5×5	Press 5×5	Squat 5×1	Press 5×1

FOUR-DAY TEXAS METHOD: VERSION #2

The second method is a more difficult version of the four-day split, and presents a new wrinkle – training both the bench press and the press in a volume and intensity fashion each week, and training them together in the same workout. This differs from the previous example program, where only the bench or press was trained for volume and intensity each week, with the other lift done for a light workout. Below is how the overall structure of the program will look:

Monday	Tuesday	Thursday	Friday
Volume Bench	Volume Squat	Intensity Bench	Intensity Squat
Volume Press	Volume Pulling	Intensity Press	Intensity Pulling

At this point in a career, many trainees will choose either the press as the priority – or more likely the bench press, as would be the case for a competitive powerlifter – and achieving precise balance between the two lifts will be of less importance. However, many athletes and general strength trainees want to put equal focus on both lifts. In this case, the trainee should switch the priority of the lifts week-to-week. To avoid stagnation, it is a good idea to vary the way each lift is trained when the press and bench are trained heavy in the same session.

A useful tool to add to the program at this stage is the 8-rep set. Sets of 8 do a good job of accumulating volume on the basic barbell exercises, and the slightly reduced load will give the trainee a good break from the monotony of sets of 5. The eight-rep set best fits the secondary lift on Monday.

Example Training Program

Phase I: Squat/Deadlift work to 5RM
Phase II: Squat/Deadlift work up to singles or doubles

Week	Monday	Tuesday	Thursday	Friday
1	Bench Press 5×5	Squat 5×5	Bench 5×1	Squat 5RM/5×1
	Press 3×8	Power Clean 5×3	Press 3–5RM	Deadlift 5RM/1×2
	LTE 3×10–12	GHR/Chins 3×10	Dips 3×15	BB Row 3×10
2	Press 5×5	Squat 5×5	Press 5×1	Squat 5RM/5×1
	Bench 3×8	Power Snatch 6×2	Bench 3–5RM	Deadlift 5RM/1×2
	LTE 3×10–12	GHR/Chins 3×10	Dips 3×15	BB Row 3×10

(5RM/5×1 = means work up to 5RM on phase 1, and work up to 5 singles on phase 2)

This is an extremely simple and flexible program. Many trainees enjoy it because it offers a little bit of everything – strength, power, and hypertrophy. The focus is primarily on singles and sets of 5. As a second volume day exercise, higher rep sets of 8 are introduced for the press and the bench press. This keeps volume high but the reduced load gives the lifter a break from the monotony of sets of 5.

On this program, the first "phase" would basically end when the lifter stopped making progress on Squat and Deadlift 5RMs and switched to singles and/or doubles. For the Press and the Bench, the lifter doesn't really work in phases. Instead, he would switch from a bench emphasis to a press emphasis on a weekly basis. If the lifter was competing in powerlifting, he would keep the bench press as the emphasis in his program on a year-round basis. A conservative starting place for this program (using percentages) would be: Singles = 90%   5RM = 80%   5×5 = 70%   3×8 = 60%

Program for Powerlifting or Power Sports

Phase I: 5×5 sets for volume, DE sets for Intensity
Phase II: DE sets for volume, 1–5RMs for Intensity

The intermediate lifter could run either phase for as long as he is making progress. The goal of phase I is to set new PRs on the 5×5 work for as long as possible while he fine-tunes his DE training on the intensity day. When progress runs out the trainee can switch his volume day stressor to DE with slightly higher percentages. Intensity day will use heavy singles across for as many weeks of progress as possible, ultimately culminating in new 1RMs. In phase II, DE volume deadlifts are dropped and the lifter will work up to a heavy double or single for as many weeks as possible.

Because this is a powerlifting program, there is less concern with equal treatment for the press, although it still should be trained regularly. All other assistance work is geared towards the lifter's individual weaknesses on the primary exercises.

The following is a 6-week snapshot of a lifter using this program. The sample program will illustrate the final 3 weeks of a lifter pushing towards limit attempts on his 5×5 max, and then transitioning into phase II.

Phase I

Week	Monday	Tuesday	Thursday	Friday
1	Bench Press 315×5×5 Weighted Dips 2×10–12 Triceps Pressdowns 3×10–15	Squat 425×5×5 Goodmornings 3×5 Lat Pulldowns 4×10	Bench Press 225×3×10 Press 3×5 Lying Triceps Extensions 3×8–10	Squat 300×2×10 Deadlift 385×1×10, 455×1, 515×1 Barbell Rows 4×10
2	Bench 320×5×5 Weighted Dips 2×10–12 Triceps Pressdowns 3×10–15	Squat 430×5×5 Goodmornings 3×5 Lat Pulldowns 4×10	Bench 245×3×10 Press 3×5 Lying Triceps Extensions 3×8–10	Squat 325×2×10 Deadlift 405×1×10, 475×1, 525×1 Barbell Rows 4×10
3	Bench 325×5,5,5,4,4 Weighted Dips 2×10–12 Triceps Pressdowns 3×10–15	Squat 435×5,5,5,4,3 Goodmornings 3×5 Lat Pulldowns 4×10	Bench 265×3×10 Press 3×5 Lying Triceps Extensions 3×8–10	Squats 350×2×10 Deadlift 425×1×10, 485×1, 535×1 Barbell Rows 4×10

Phase II

Week	Monday	Tuesday	Thursday	Friday
4	Bench 235×3×10 Press 3×5 Triceps Pressdowns 3×10–15	Squat 315×2×10 SLDL 3×5 Lat Pulldowns 4×10	Bench 355×1×5 DB Bench Press 3×6–8 Lying Triceps Extensions 3×8–10	Squat 475×1×5 Deadlift 550×1–2 Barbell Rows 4×10
5	Bench 255×3×10 Press 3×5 Triceps Pressdowns 3×10–15	Squat 340×2×10 SLDL 3×5 Lat Pulldowns 4×10	Bench 365×1×5 DB Bench Press 3×6–8 Lying Triceps Extensions 3×8–10	Squat 485×1×5 Deadlift 555×1–2 Barbell Rows 4×10
6	Bench 275×3×10 Press 3×5 Triceps Pressdowns 3×10–15	Squat 365×2×10 SLDL 3×5 Lat Pulldowns 4×10	Bench 375×1×5 DB Bench Press 3×6–8 Lying Triceps Extensions 3×8–10	Squat 495×1×5 Deadlift 560×1–2 Barbell Rows 4×10

High Volume/Low Intensity – Low Volume/High Intensity Training Pattern. A third method is illustrated here:

Monday	Tuesday	Thursday	Friday
Intensity Bench	Intensity Squat	Intensity Press	Intensity Deadlift
Volume Press	Volume Pulls	Volume Bench	Volume Squat

An advantage to this organization is that every week each lift is trained heavy in a completely recovered state. This allows the trainee the opportunity to handle max loads on every lift, every week. The disadvantage is that there is less systemic fluctuation in the stress. There is a benefit to placing the majority of the stressors together at the beginning of the weekly schedule. Using this method, every workout is heavy, and every workout is high volume. In general, this method will be more difficult for most trainees.

Below are several example overviews of how one might structure a training program based on this concept:

Monday	Tuesday	Thursday	Friday
Bench 5RM	Squat 5RM	Press 5RM	Deadlift 5RM
Press 5×5	Power Clean 5×3	Bench 5×5	Squat 5×5

Using this setup, the trainee would simply "run out" progress on each of the intensity lifts while trying to sustain sets across for the volume work. Once the 5RM ran out, he would begin the descent through triples, double, and singles.

Instead of running out progress on the intensity work, the same method could employ a cycling approach to the intensity day work:

		Week 1	Week 2	Week 3
Monday	Bench Press	2×3	3×2	5×1
	Press	5×5	5×5	5×5
	Triceps Ext	3×10–12	3×10–12	3×10–12
Tuesday	Squat	2×3	3×2	5×1
	Stiff-Leg Deadlift	3×5	3×5	3×5
	BB Rows	3×10	3×10	3×10
Thursday	Press	5×1	2×3	3×2
	Bench Press	5×5	5×5	5×5
	Dips	3×8–10	3×8–10	3×8–10
Friday	Deadlift	1RM	3RM	2RM
	Squat	5×5	5×5	5×5
	GHR/Chins	3×10	3×10	3×10

The Monday and Tuesday lifts (Bench and Squat) have been set up on a slightly different schedule than the Thursday and Friday lifts (Press and Deadlift). Bench presses and squats follow the pattern of 3, 2, 1. Presses and Deadlifts follow the pattern of 1, 3, 2. This is not a necessity, but the fluctuation avoids forcing the lifter to attempt heavy singles on all four lifts within the same week. The fluctuation in workload will help to keep the lifter from burning out and stagnating too early in the training cycle.

Lifters should keep volume high when using this type of program. The weight is important, but volume day work should not be so heavy that the lifter misses reps. In order to continue to hold sets of 5 across, the lifter may have to initiate several resets.

Below is another example program that also uses alternating days of volume and intensity. In this example the lifter will use a combination of dynamic effort work, heavy singles across, and 5×5. Rack Pulls and Snatch-Grip Deadlifts are worked into a rotation with regular deadlifts in order to keep the lifter from getting stuck. Also, in order to avoid asking the trainee to work with heavy singles on every training day, the program will operate in two different cycles. The first cycle will use singles for the squat and bench press and sets of 5 for the press and deadlift. After a few weeks the lifter can switch to 5s for the bench and squat and singles for the press and deadlift.

Phase I

		Week 1	Week 2	Week 3
Monday	Bench Press	5×1	5×1	5×1
	Press	60% ×3×10	65% ×3×10	70% ×3×10
Tuesday	Squat	5×1	5×1	5×1
	Deadlift	70% ×1×10	75% ×1×10	80% ×1×10
Thursday	Press	5×5	5×5	5×5
	Bench Press	60% ×3×10	65% ×3×10	70% ×3×10
Friday	Squat	60% ×2×10	65% ×2×10	70% ×2×10
	Rack Pull	5RM	5RM	5RM

Phase II

		Week 4	Week 5	Week 6
Monday	Bench Press	5×5	5×5	5×5
	Press	60% ×3×10	65% ×3×10	70% ×3×10
Tuesday	Squat	5×5	5×5	5×5
	Power Clean	5×3	5×3	5×3
Thursday	Press	5×1	5×1	5×1
	Bench Press	60% ×3×10	65% ×3×10	70% ×3×10
Friday	Deadlift alternated w/ Snatch-Grip Deadlift	1×1–2	1×1–2	1×1–2
	Squat	60% ×2×10	65% ×2×10	70% ×2×10

The length of time for each cycle can vary. The 3-week cycles in the program below are simply to illustrate how the lifter might set things up. The bigger point is that fluctuation in loading within the training week is important when the lifter plans to do high-intensity work 4 days per week. Working up to heavy singles in all 4 lifts every week will likely end progress very quickly. However, this extremely simple alternation between heavy singles and heavy sets of 5 can yield progress for a very long time.

THE NEBRASKA MODEL

The following program is based on a model that was made popular by Boyd Epley at the University of Nebraska, one of the first strength and conditioning programs in the country to place emphasis on the Olympic lifts as a tool for strength training for sports. This adaptation of the model also follows a high-volume to high-intensity weekly organization, but all four workouts each week are full body training sessions. The workouts are organized in terms of "fast & slow."

Monday
Power Snatch 6×2
Power Clean 6×3
Rack Jerk 3×2

Thursday
Power Snatch 5×1
Power Clean 5×1
Rack Jerk 3×1

Tuesday
Squat 5×5
Bench Press / Press 5×5
Barbell Rows 4×8 / Chins 3–5×8+

Friday or Saturday
Squat 5RM
Bench Press / Press 5RM
Deadlift 5RM

(Bench Press and Press alternated week to week)
(Barbell Rows and Chins alternated week to week)

SPLIT ROUTINES – HEAVY & LIGHT DAY

As the trainee grows and gets stronger, he may benefit from a slightly less stressful weekly program that does not include a volume and intensity workout in the same week. This is especially true for slightly older lifters who may have a more difficult time with recovery. A solution to this is to train each lift heavy and each lift light during the week. It is important to understand that the light day is not the same thing as a volume day in this scenario. It is true that volume days are lighter than intensity days, but they are still not considered light for the given rep range. The purpose of the light day is to facilitate recovery and to maintain the efficiency of the neuromuscular pathways used on each lift. The light squat day tends to be the most useful addition, especially with older lifters.

Many lifters and coaches do not really appreciate the utility of doing a light day at this stage in training, and it is true that many lifters experience roughly the same results with or without the addition of a light day of training. The decision to use a light day exercise is generally highly individual.

Example program:

Monday	Tuesday	Thursday	Friday
Bench	Squat	Press	Light Squat
Light Press	Light Pull	Light Bench	Deadlift

What is "heavy"? Heavy can easily be thought of as "stressful." The heavy day must be disruptive enough so that adaptation occurs and performance improves the following week. This generally means that the heavy day must have a volume component to it. Generally, sets of 5 across work very well. When the lifter ceases to make progress on the 5-rep set, a short taper into lower rep ranges is useful before starting back over with 5s. A short cycling of reps from 5 to 1 can also work.

What is "light?" A light exercise can essentially mean two things. The basic exercise can simply be repeated for a few moderately-loaded sets (65% ×5×3) or a less stressful variant of the parent exercise can be substituted. This approach works fine as long as volume is controlled. For instance, close-grip bench presses could be considered a light bench substitute when loaded appropriately and trained for about 3×5. Power cleans or Power snatches can be an excellent light day substitute for deadlifts.

Split Routine – Heavy/Light on Alternating Days

Monday	Tuesday	Thursday	Friday
Bench Press 6×3	Squat 6×3	Press 6×3	Light Squat 6×2
Light Press 6×2	Power Snatch 6×2	CG Bench 6×2	Power Clean 6×3
Dips 3×10–15	GHR/Chins 3×10	Dips 3×10–15	Deadlift 1×3

The above program is a split routine that would be appropriate for a well-conditioned general strength trainee. It is not an easy program, but it only requires that the lifter do one "hard" lift per day. The "6 sets" program is a derivative of an old Russian squat program, but it has been tailored for intermediate training. This program is a good change of pace for the trainee who has been training with sets of 5 for a long period of time. This is a good short term program to put in between programs built on the 5-rep set. It puts equal focus on squatting, pressing/benching, and pulling, and includes exercises for strength, power, and mass. Each exercise is trained twice per week, once heavy, and once light. In the case of the squat and the press, the light day exercise is 80% of the heavy 3s ×2×6. The light day exercise should not increase in weight throughout the training cycle. The lifter should seek to move it faster each time, as his 6×3 lift increases week to week. For bench pressing and deadlifts the program uses a lighter and less stressful variant of the parent exercise – light close-grip bench presses and power snatches in this particular example.

In this case, the program does not call for a heavy volume day and a heavy intensity day within the same week. The light day later in the week is there to keep motor pathways fresh for each lift, not to create additional stress. For the heavy days, this program uses a very simple system: progress on each lift for 6×3 will be made for as many weeks as possible, and then volume will be greatly reduced to just 3×3 (and 3×2 on the light day). The lifter will continue to add weight to the bar each week for 3×3, taking advantage of the tapering effect provided by the offload. The cycle will end when the lifter ceases to make progress for 3×3 and ends the cycle with a max triple or double. At that point, he could start the exact cycle over again – starting again with 6×3 but at a higher weight than the previous training cycle or move on to another intermediate program.

ONE LIFT PER DAY

The most bare-bones version of any split routine is to simply train one lift per day, and only do each lift once per week with no light day and no separate volume/intensity workouts. Again, a lifter is an intermediate because of his ability to set PRs on a weekly basis. If the lifter is only training each major exercise once per week, he must be creating enough stress during the session that adaptation occurs and performance increases the following week.

If the lifter is unable to do this with just one weekly session, it is likely that he needs to shift his programming to one of the more stressful programs that were presented earlier in the chapter. Many lifters who are training just one lift per day are doing a high volume of assistance work along with the main lift, which adds sufficient stress to result in progress the following week.

Reasons for this decision are often logistical. People's lives are busy and many trainees can't dedicate more than about an hour per day to training. After a trainee reaches a certain level of strength, it is not uncommon for the warm up sets, work sets, and rest between sets take 30–60 minutes just for a single heavy barbell exercise. Doing all-out 5×5 on squats with 10 minutes between sets will take up 40 minutes in rest time alone. For this reason, it is often more feasible for lifters to only schedule one hard exercise each day with perhaps a handful of less stressful and less time-consuming assistance exercises following the work sets. This type of program may also be reasonable for high-level athletes who are spending enormous amounts of time training and conditioning for their sport. MMA fighters for example, often have two practices per day (one grappling, one sparring) and also have to find time for high-threshold conditioning work prior to competition. This doesn't leave much time or energy for lengthy strength-training sessions.

It is better to do one thing right, than to try and rush 2 or 3 things into too short a time window. In powerlifting, competitors have been using splits like this for many years:

Monday – Squat + Assistance

Wednesday – Bench + Assistance

Friday – Deadlift + Assistance

The following is an example that might be appropriate for the general strength trainee who is also looking to add muscle mass and improve his physique. The focus should be on completion of the primary barbell exercise each day, and if the lifter has time and energy he can complete the assistance work.

Monday – Bench Day + Assistance (shoulders and triceps)

Tuesday – Squat Day + Assistance (hamstrings and back)

Thursday – Press Day + Assistance (chest and tricep)

Friday – Light Squat* + Deadlift + Assistance (back)

*Since deadlifts are generally performed for less volume than the other three major barbell lifts, it is a good idea to add a second squatting session (if possible) into the schedule. This will be a light squat day with shorter rest intervals that should fit into the trainee's schedule.

		Week 1	Week 2	Week 3
Monday	Bench Press	5×5	5×3	5×1
	Seated DB Press	3–5×10–12	3–5×10–12	3–5×10–12
	Seated Triceps Extensions (French Press)	3–5×10–12	3–5×10–12	3–5×10–12
Tuesday	Squat	5×5	5×3	5×1
	Stiff-Leg Deadlift	2–3×8–10	2–3×8–10	2–3×8–10
	Lat Pulldowns	3–5×10–12	3–5×10–12	3–5×10–12
Thursday	Press	5×1	5×5	5×3
	Weighted Dips or DB Bench Press	3–5×10–12	3–5×10–12	3–5×10–12
	Lying Triceps Extensions	3–5×10–12	3–5×10–12	3–5×10–12
Friday	Light Squat (80% of 5s)	3×5	3×5	3×5
	Deadlift	1RM or heavy singles	5RM	3RM
	Barbell Rows	3–5×10–12	3–5×10–12	3–5×10–12

In the above program, the rep range for the primary lift fluctuates from the beginning to the end of the week. This avoids having a week where the lifter must do heavy singles on all four training days. On week one, bench and squat are done for 5s and presses and deadlifts are done for singles. On week two, bench and squat are done for triples, and presses and deadlifts are done for 5s. On week three, bench and squat are done for singles, while press and deadlift are done for triples.

The Starr Model

A different model of weekly periodization described by Mark Berry in 1933 called for three training days per week and variation in workload among those days. In this model, the whole body is worked every day using many of the same exercises, but the amount of weight varies each day: a Heavy day, a Light day, a Medium day – the HLM model. Various permutations of this model have been used for several decades, one of the most popular being the version presented by Bill Starr in his 1976 book *The Strongest Shall Survive*. Starr's was a similar three-day-per week model, with the loads ordered from heavy to medium to light, a slightly different application of the load/rest relationship than in the Texas method described earlier in this chapter.

THE STARR 5×5

The most familiar version of the HLM system comes from *The Strongest Shall Survive*. Starr's text was essentially a tutorial on his system of training large groups of collegiate athletes, particularly football players. Starr found that his athletes responded best to high-frequency and high-volume squatting, but performance was best when athletes were *not* handling maximum poundages at each session.

Although Starr's trainees may have been great athletes, most of them were probably not great lifters. And all of them were trying to balance the demands of their strength program with the demands of their sport, their academic requirements, and the typical social life of a male in his late teens/early twenties. This situation has much in common with most recreational lifters or sport athletes. For the seasoned competitive lifter in his physical prime, frequent handling of maximum poundages is both doable and necessary for optimum progress. But the majority of those training with barbells will be doing so for a purpose other than competition in one of the strength sports. Family, careers, travel, age, injury, and quite frankly a lack of discipline and motivation will prevent most trainees from doing all that is necessary to prepare for a schedule that calls for a maximum output at every session. The trainee simply can't "get it up" to go all out 3–4 days per week, either physically or psychologically.

Starr's solution to this problem was the Heavy-Light-Medium training system. This gave the trainee the volume and frequency they needed to drive progress, but only called for *one* heavy day each week for each lift. The routine Starr outlined in *The Strongest Shall Survive* was based on the Squat, Bench Press, and Power Clean. Again, all exercises were done for 5×5 with the weight fluctuating throughout the week. This is not really the best way to organize training, but Starr had to deal with training large groups of athletes in a small space. You need a simple system to do this, and this was probably the best solution available.

In this context, "heavy" could be defined as the point where technique begins to break down, or the point where the more experienced trainee says it is. "Medium" could mean that technique is well maintained and the trainee feels like he's working hard but lots of "room" is left. "Light" should always mean that form is perfect and several sets across at that weight would not amount to a significant training stress. It takes an experienced coach to be able to apply this method effectively. But in the absence of an experienced coach, the starting point for a new program will have to be titrated up from warm-up weight to a point determined by the starting point objectives of the specific program.

An example week under Starr's system may have looked like this (using the squat as an example):

Monday:
  Squat 5 reps at 135, 165, 195, 225, 255

Wednesday:
  Squat 5 reps at 95, 125, 155, 185, 215

Friday:
  Squat 5 reps at 115, 145, 175, 205, 235

The same concept was applied to the Bench Press and the Power Clean.

Again, there were some flaws in the program, namely the narrow selection of exercises and the absence of deadlifts. Certainly, all athletes should be squatting, benching, and cleaning, while most athletes, and certainly most average gym-goers, would benefit from a wider variety of exercises for long-term progress. And it is perfectly acceptable to venture outside the original 5×5 protocol – because of the popularity of Starr's work in *SSS*, many have come to associate the Heavy-Light-Medium scheme strictly with his version of the 5×5 protocol, but this is a rather superficial understanding of the model.

The heavy/medium/light concept seems simple enough. More complex, though, is its correct application. Doing one set of 3 with 70% is light work and will facilitate recovery as "active rest" if used as part of a light-day workout. But what happens with 5 sets of 10 at 70%? Each trainee at the intermediate level has a specific training goal: strength, power, or mass, and each of these goals has a specific repetition range associated with it. Each range also has an intensity (%1RM) associated with it that is a maximal stress. For example, a trainee should be able to do three sets of 10 with about 75% of 1RM. This would be difficult, so its relative intensity is high for the repetitions. Knowing this, offload or recovery days can be planned for by reducing the intensity without changing the reps. If 3 sets of 10 reps with 70% constitutes the heavy day, offload would be 50–60% of 1RM for three sets of 10. But if 80% for sets of 5 is the work, 70% for sets of 10 is not offloading, and it will not facilitate recovery. It is important to understand the relationship between repetitions and intensity, how to manage that relationship correctly, and how trainees respond to it (see Table 7-1, p111).

Remember, the goal of any model of weekly periodized training is to produce a disruption in homeostasis through the cumulative stress of training days, and then allow adaptation to occur with the inclusion of the light day and the rest it provides. The light day is an absolutely essential component of the program; it is a recovery day. A light training load should not be enough to induce an overload and disrupt homeostasis, and it is not really a part of the overload event. It should be light enough to allow for recovery while at the same time providing enough work through the movement pattern to keep it fresh. Failure to include the light day indicates a lack of understanding of the actual workings of the program. A 70% day may seem too easy and appear to be wasted time, but the offloading it provides is necessary for progress. The average "Exercising" gym member focuses on how he feels during and after each workout – "I caught a most excellent pump today, my man!" – while the athlete "Trains" for long-term improvement. Do not yield to the temptation to push up the percentages on light days. Remember this, again: you don't get strong by lifting weights. You get strong by *recovering* from lifting weights.

Recovery begins immediately after each workout, as the body begins to repair the damage done by the stress so that adaptation can occur, and all the significant damage is done during the heavy workouts. Light days do not add to the damage. They aid recovery from it by increasing blood flow to the sore areas, working the joints through the ROM, and helping with fatigue the way nature has been dealing with it for hundreds of millions of years – by forcing recovery during unavoidable continuing activity. The light workout is therefore embedded in the part of the week in which recovery takes place. In this model, it does not matter what day of the week the light day falls on. A light day on Friday means that by Monday a trainee should be recovered and ready for more. If the light day is on Monday, the trainee should be recovered and ready for a larger load on Wednesday or Thursday.

PUTTING IT INTO PRACTICE

In general, the best way to operate an HLM training program is with 3 full-body workouts on a Monday/Wednesday/Friday type schedule. Each training session would consist of a Squat, a Pressing exercise, and a Pulling exercise. The exact exercises will be selected to fit the individual, based on his goals and level of advancement.

Squatting. For the general strength trainee, three squat sessions are best. This has a positive hormonal impact on the system as a whole, and will accelerate gains in both strength and muscle mass. Additionally, many do not give the squat its due regarding the technical nature of the lift. Like any other physical skill, squats need practice. Doing the lift 3 times per week (twice with moderate or heavier weights) gives the trainee the opportunity to hone perfect form and technique. This can be exceptionally beneficial for older trainees who tend to lose the "feel" of an exercise without some degree of frequency, but cannot manage multiple heavy sessions in the same week. This is also good for those who are particularly nonathletic and may have a hard time sustaining proper mechanics without regular practice. This type of trainee is often referred to as a "motor moron," and will benefit greatly from repeated exposure to this very technical movement.

One area of this program which lacks some precision is the offset from the heavy day to light day to medium. As with many things in strength training, there is no one answer that will work for everyone. But it is important to note that the degree of offset will grow based on the absolute strength of the trainee – a 500-lb squatter will probably need a higher percentage offset than a 200-lb squatter.

As a start, set the light day 10–20% lower than the heavy day, and set the medium day 5–10% lower than the heavy day. Stronger lifters will use the higher percentage offset, and weaker lifters (older trainees, women, etc) will probably use the lower percentage offset. Once a lifter has his estimate, it is permissible to use intelligence and experience to adjust the numbers accordingly. Recent training history always produces better data than percentages.

Pressing. In Starr's text, the basic pressing program was laid out much like the squatting program – a single exercise, constant volume, and fluctuating intensity over the course of a week. In Starr's program, the bench press was the exercise of choice for all 3 days. The benefit of this set up was that it was simple in concept and logistically feasible in a busy weight room with lots of athletes already occupying the squat racks. The squat is unique in that it has no rivals when it comes to leg exercises. Front squats, box squats, overhead squats, etc, are all decent exercises, but none of them match up to the transformative power of the basic back squat. Even in its light and medium versions, it could be argued that the squat is still a more effective tool than any other variant of the lift. With pressing it isn't quite so clear-cut. Both the bench press and the press should be included and given equal attention in almost any basic strength program. It is hard to say which is better – the press is certainly more functional from an athletic standpoint, but the bench is equally valuable since it allows for much heavier loads. Even those who discount the functionality of the bench press should realize that regularly training the lift will help to drive steady improvement of the press.

The basic recommendation is that the heavy-day exercise in the program should always be the bench press. In almost every situation the bench press will allow the trainee to use the most amount of weight relative to all other pressing exercises. For the light day exercise it makes sense to default to presses. Relative to just about any type of barbell pressing variant, the press will utilize the least amount of weight. For the medium day, there are a number of exercises to choose from. Here are a few examples:

Close-Grip Bench Press. This option would be for those who want to focus on the bench press as their primary exercise. This is a good option when using the HLM system for powerlifting. Close-grip benching has been utilized by competitive powerlifters for years as a primary assistance movement, and can be done with weights almost as heavy as the standard grip. The close-grip bench obviously stresses the triceps more than most competition style bench presses do, and because of this, it also serves as a powerful assistance exercise for the press as well. Especially from the midpoint on up, the press is largely dependent on triceps strength. Any exercise that allows the lifter to overload the triceps with heavy weights will have tremendous carryover to the press or the bench press.

Push Press. The push press is a potential medium day exercise. It would be a possible choice for many sport athletes, strongman competitors, or anyone who wanted to make overhead lockout strength the top priority, and still implement as much full-body exercise as possible. Push presses can be hard on the patellar and quadriceps tendons if they are already irritated, inexperienced trainees will find that they interfere with the timing of the press, and lockouts in the rack are probably a better option for most people in need of top-end lockout strength. But for the right lifter, they are an option.

Incline Press. The incline press moves the bar at an angle that is directly in-between the press and the bench press. Because of this, the incline could be considered the closest thing to a "hybrid" of the two exercises, and will have carryover to both the press and the bench press. Of the two, the incline will probably have more carryover to the bench press simply because the lifter is lying down against a bench, and the pecs are stressed slightly more than the delts. However, those that regularly take limit attempts on the press know that a significant amount of "upper chest" is utilized during reps that require a lot of layback to complete. Angles vary on incline benches, but lower inclines of 25–45 degrees will be much more helpful to bench presses, and steeper inclines of around 60 degrees will be of greater benefit to presses.

For a trainee who wants to focus mainly on mass and physique, inclines are better. Most successful bodybuilders will tell you that inclines are the staple of their chest training workouts as opposed to flat bench presses. The look that comes with a full and developed "upper chest" will greatly improve the aesthetics in a bodybuilder, and go a long way toward making the shoulder girdle appear bigger and wider.

An important point to make is that the trainee does not have to pick just one exercise and stick with it for any length of time. It is perfectly acceptable to focus on one for a period of a few weeks or months and then switch. It might even be a good idea to rotate the three movements on a weekly basis. This is an area where a lifter can permissibly sneak some variety into the routine to keep things mentally and physically fresh.

Pulling. As with the squatting and pressing program, Starr's basic program in *The Strongest Shall Survive* called for just one pulling exercise to be done each week – the power clean. Like squats and bench presses, power cleans were to be done for 5×5 arranged in a heavy-light-medium sequence throughout the week. If you had to choose just one pulling exercise to do 3 days per week for a group of athletes, power cleans would probably be the exercise of choice. Deadlifts are the better strength builder, but doing them three days per week would be difficult for most athletes to recover from. Similar to the pressing program, most athletes will receive greater benefit from a more diverse pulling program.

A fantastic general pulling program is to deadlift on heavy day, power snatch on light day, and power clean on the medium day. To build a strong pull off the floor, heavier weights must be handled than the Olympic lifts permit; deadlifts allow us to do this. By default, snatches are lighter than cleans and so the two Olympic variants fall neatly into the organization of this system. Here is an example of a basic pulling program:

Monday: Deadlift 1×5

Wednesday: Power Snatch 5–8 doubles

Friday: Power Clean 5 triples

There are, however, reasons to follow a different set up. A few options are presented below.

Eliminate one Olympic variant from the program and do the other one twice. As an example, many trainees may be cursed with an anthropometry – long forearms/short upper arms – that makes effectively racking a clean difficult. Many lifters cannot properly receive the bar on the shoulders, and are forced to catch it in their hands, either in the air over the delts or with the elbows down in a terrible position to support the load. This may be fine with lighter weights, but as the athlete's strength grows, racking a heavy clean in this manner can lead to serious aggravation in the wrists and elbows. Or it may simply result in a lot of frustration due to frequently missing reps. In this scenario, the trainee may simply choose to deadlift once per week, and snatch twice – once heavy, and once light.

The same scenario could present itself with the snatch. Older trainees in particular may find that the proper racking of the snatch is difficult due to a lack of flexibility in the shoulders. Sometimes this can be remedied with stretching and practice, and sometimes it cannot. An example would be a lifter with a history of rotator cuff surgeries or arthritis. In this scenario the trainee may decide that it is more prudent to eliminate the snatch from his program and clean twice per week, once heavy, once lighter, and continue to deadlift heavy once per week.

The benefit to this schedule is that the lifter will get very good at the lift being trained twice per week. For this reason alone, some trainees who are capable of doing both lifts may still only choose to concentrate on one so as to focus on its technical perfection. In this instance, it is recommended that the trainee select the clean over the snatch, simply because you can clean more weight, and heavier is generally better.

On a programming note, the Olympic variants don't need as much offset to be considered a "light day" because cleans and snatches are not limited by absolute strength, and a limit clean is not the same bone-on-bone effort that a limit deadlift represents. Taking 20 lbs off of a 400-lb squat doesn't really make it a "light day." The lifter is still going to be exerting a tremendous amount of effort to squat 380 lbs. This isn't necessarily true with the Olympic exercises. The lifter who can clean 225 for triples will generally find 205 lbs fairly easy. So when selecting light day weights, a 5–10% offset should be sufficient. As always, percentages are just guidelines. Always use your own experience and common sense to select the appropriate amount of weight.

Two slow pulls per week, one dynamic pull. In this instance, the lifter may decide that cleaning and snatching isn't doing much to drive his deadlift up. This is often the case when a lifter has a very strong deadlift, and is just not very good at cleaning or snatching. If the Olympic lifts are stuck in the high 100s for the snatch and low 200s for the power clean, those lifts probably aren't going to do much to drive a 600 lb deadlift. In order to get his deadlift unstuck, the trainee may decide to implement another "slow" pull such as a stiff-legged deadlift, Romanian deadlift, or even a goodmorning. If the lifter decides to use these in his program, they fit neatly into the medium day.

Example model:

Monday: Deadlift – work up to a heavy set of 5

Wednesday: Power Clean – 6 doubles

Friday: Stiff-Leg Deadlift 3×5

Many lifters will find that their low backs simply cannot recover from two "slow" pulling days per week. Others will do just fine, but may only be able to do so for short periods of time, say 6–12 weeks.

As a final note on the pulling program, there is a common issue for a few very strong deadlifters. Assume that our hypothetical lifter is doing the standard program of pulling heavy on Monday, snatching on Wednesday, and cleaning on Friday. In this scenario the lifter is getting mentally and physically fatigued from doing standard conventional deadlifts every single week, and progress is beginning to stall. It may be in this trainee's best interest to start rotating in other heavy deadlift variants. This will keep the heavy day "heavy" but will begin to introduce some fluctuation in loading each week, and may break the lifter out of his rut. A common rotation is to alternate week to week between a heavy 5-rep set of rack pulls and an 8-rep set of halting deadlifts. These are done in place of the regular deadlift workout. Or the lifter could select a maximum of 4 heavy pulling movements, including standard deadlifts. An example heavy day rotation might be:

Week 1: Standard Deadlift 1–5RM

Week 2: Snatch-Grip Deadlift 1–5RM

Week 3: Rack Pull 1–5RM

Week 4: Stiff-Leg Deadlift 3–5RM

In this scenario, the trainee would continue to snatch on his light day, and clean on his medium day.

Below are a handful of programs based on a HLM system. Remember: these are snapshots taken within the intermediate progression, and do not represent a recycling to a lighter start weight, as would occur with an advanced trainee.

Heavy-Light-Medium – General Strength Training or Powerlifting (Program #1)

Basic Overview

Monday – Heavy Day	Wednesday – Light Day	Friday – Medium Day
Squat 5×1–5	Squat 3×5 (20% of Mon)	Squat 3×5 (10% Mon)
Bench Press 5×1–5	Press 3×5	Close-Grip Bench 3×5
Deadlift 1×1–5	Power Clean 3×3	SLDL 3×5

12 week sample progression

Week	Monday	Wednesday	Friday
1	Squat 350×5×5	Squat 280×5×3	Squat 315×5×3
	Bench 275×5×5	Press 155×5×3	Close-Grip Bench 225×5×3
	Deadlift 415×5	Power Clean 205×3×3	SLDL 325×5×3
2	Squat 355×5×5	Squat 285×5×3	Squat 320×5×3
	Bench 280×5×5	Press 160×5×3	Close-Grip Bench 230×5×3
	Deadlift 420×5	Power Clean 210×3×3	SLDL 330×5×3
3	Squat 360×5×5	Squat 290×5×3	Squat 325×5×3
	Bench 285×5×5	Press 165×5×3	Close-Grip Bench 235×5×3
	Deadlift 425×5	Power Clean 215×3×3	SLDL 335×5×3
4	Squat 365×5×5	Squat 295×5×3	Squat 330×5×3
	Bench 290×5×5	Press 170×5×3	Close-Grip Bench 240×5×3
	Deadlift 430×5	Power Clean 220×3×3	SLDL 340×5×3

Week	Monday	Wednesday	Friday
5	Squat 370×3×5	Squat 300×5×3	Squat 335×5×3
	Bench 295×3×5	Press 175×5×3	Close-Grip Bench 245×5×3
	Deadlift 435×5	Power Clean 225×3×3	SLDL 345×5×3
6	Squat 375×3×5	Squat 305×5×3	Squat 340×5×3
	Bench 300×3×5	Press 177.5×5×3	Close-Grip Bench 247.5×5×3
	Deadlift 440×5	Power Clean 227.5×3×3	SLDL 350×5×3
7	Squat 380×3×5	Squat 310×5×3	Squat 345×5×3
	Bench 305×3×5	Press 180×5×3	Close-Grip Bench 250×5×3
	Deadlift 445×5	Power Clean 230×3×3	SLDL 355×5×3
8	Squat 385×3×5	Squat 315×5×3	Squat 350×5×3
	Bench 310×3×5	Press 182.5×5×3	Close-Grip Bench 252.5×5×3
	Deadlift 450×5	Power Clean 232.5×3×3	SLDL 360×5×3
9	Squat 390×3×5	Squat 320×5×3	Squat 355×5×3
	Bench 315×3×5	Press 185×5×3	Close-Grip Bench 255×5×3
	Deadlift 455×5	Power Clean 235×3×3	SLDL 365×5×3
10	Squat 395×1×5	Squat 325×3×3	Squat 360×5
	Bench 320×1×5	Press 187.5×3×3	Close-Grip Bench 257.5×5×3
	Deadlift 460×5	Power Clean 237.5×2×4	SLDL 370×5×3
11	Squat 400×1×5	Squat 330×3×3	Squat 365×5
	Bench 325×1×5	Press 190×3×3	Close-Grip Bench 260×5×3
	Deadlift 465×5	Power Clean 240×2×4	SLDL 375×5×3
12	Squat 405×1×5	Squat 335×3×3	Squat 370×5
	Bench 330×1×5	Press 192.5×3×3	Close-Grip Bench 262.5×5×3
	Deadlift 470×5	Power Clean 242.5×2×4	SLDL 380×5×3

Notes: The trainee begins the program with sets of 5 across on all exercises, except the clean. As the weight on the bar increases over time, the heavy day will change from 5×5 to 5×3, to accommodate the heavier weight. Eventually the 5×3 drops down to 5×1. The light and medium days stay at 3×5 until doing so makes those days no longer light or medium. In this case, the light day was dropped to 3×3 and the medium day was done for just 1×5. Additionally, the press and the power clean were reduced to 3×3 and 4×2 respectively, in order to keep putting weight on the bar week after week.

HLM – General Strength Training or Powerlifting (Program #2)

This is a 6 week snap shot of a slight variation of the same routine:

Week	Monday	Wednesday	Friday
1	Squat 350×5×5	Squat 280×5×3	Squat 315×5×3
	Bench 275×5×5	Press 155×5×3	Close-Grip Bench 225×5×3
	Deadlift 415×5	Power Clean 205×3×3	SLDL 325×5×3
2	Squat 355×5×5	Squat 285×5×3	Squat 320×5×3
	Bench 280×5×5	Press 160×5×3	Rack Bench 260×1×10
	Rack Pull 465×5	Power Clean 210×3×3	SLDL 330×5×3
3	Squat 360×5×5	Squat 290×5×3	Squat 325×5×3
	Bench 285×5×5	Press 165×5×3	Close-Grip Bench 235×5×3
	Deadlift 425×5	Power Clean 215×3×3	SLDL 335×5×3
4	Squat 365×5×5	Squat 295×5×3	Squat 330×5×3
	Bench 290×5×5	Press 170×5×3	Rack Bench 265×1×10
	Rack Pull 475×5	Power Clean 220×3×3	SLDL 340×5×3
5	Squat 370×3×5	Squat 300×5×3	Squat 335×5×3
	Bench 295×3×5	Press 175×5×3	Close-Grip Bench 245×5×3
	Deadlift 435×5	Power Clean 225×3×3	SLDL 345×5×3
6	Squat 375×3×5	Squat 305×5×3	Squat 340×5×3
	Bench 300×3×5	Press 177.5×5×3	Rack Bench 270×1×10
	Rack Pull 485×5	Power Clean 227.5×3×3	SLDL 350×5×3

This program offers a little bit more variety with the addition of rack pulls to the pulling program and dead-stop rack bench presses to the pressing program. Rack pulls for sets of 5 are alternated week-to-week with deadlifts, also for a set of 5. Rack presses are alternated week-to-week with close-grip bench presses. Ten singles with 30–60 second rest periods are used for the rack presses, since this particular exercise is best done for singles only.

HLM Program for Explosive Sports

Actual Program for collegiate volleyball player – 1 month snap shot:

1	Squat 155×5×5	Power Snatch 90×2×6	Power Clean 120×3×5
	Push Press 105×3×5	Squat 125×5×3	Box Squat 140×2×8
	Deadlift 205×5	Bench Press 115×5×3	Press 85×5×3
2	Squat 157.5×5×5	Power Snatch 92.5×2×6	Power Clean 122.5×3×5
	Push Press 107.5×3×5	Squat 127.5×5×3	Box Squat 142.5×2×8
	Deadlift 210×5	Bench Press 117.5×5×3	Press 87.5×5×3
3	Squat 160×5×5	Power Snatch 95×2×6	Power Clean 125×3×5
	Push Press 110×3×5	Squat 130×5×3	Box Squat 145×2×8
	Deadlift 215×5	Bench Press 120×5×3	Press 90×5×3
4	Squat 162.5×5×5	Power Snatch 97.5×2×6	Power Clean 127.5×3×5
	Push Press 112.5×3×5	Squat 132.5×5×3	Box Squat 147.5×2×8
	Deadlift 220×5	Bench Press 122.5×5×3	Press 92.5×5×3

Major differences in this program from the powerlifting program is the emphasis on the Olympic lifts. Because of this, they are moved to the first exercise on light and medium day so that they can be trained fresh. Medium day squats were changed from 3×5 to 8×2 and trained on a parallel box with an emphasis on speed. The pressing program was arranged in terms of Medium-Heavy-Light. This was done to put the bench press in between the two overhead movements.

General Heavy-Light-Medium. This program excludes the use of the Olympic lifts. Because of this, it is a good program for those trainees who may be a little older, or those who are mostly focused on training for physique.

Monday	Wednesday	Friday
Squat 5×5	Squat 3×5	Squat 3×5
Bench Press 4×5	Press 4×5	Incline Press 4×5
Barbell Row 4×8	Deadlift 1×5	Chins/Pull-ups 3–5×5–8

ADDING TRAINING DAYS

Another version of the HLM program was used by Dr. Mike Stone as early as 1976 and outlined in a number of his publications from the National Strength Research Laboratory at Auburn University in the early 1980s. Stone's method uses a simple load variation among 4 workouts per week (rather than

	Monday	Tuesday	Wednesday	Thursday	Friday	Saturday	Sunday
3	Medium		**Heavy**		*Light*		
	Heavy		**Heavy**		*Light*		
4	**Heavy**	Medium		**Heavy**	*Light*		
	Heavy	**Heavy**		**Heavy**	*Light*		
5	**Heavy**	Medium	**Heavy**		**Heavy**	*Light*	
	Heavy	**Heavy**	**Heavy**		**Heavy**	*Light*	
6	**Heavy**	**Heavy**	Medium	**Heavy**	**Heavy**	*Light*	

Table 7-2. Progression of the variations of training frequency and intensities. Note that each time a day is added, it is medium in intensity. Each schedule is used for a few weeks or months unti progress stalls, before attempting the next, more demanding, level. Notice that there is only one "light day" included in each weekly series and there is at least one complete day off each week. The 5- and 6-day versions of the program assume an Olympic weightlifting emphasis. If a 3 month adaptation period is given for each new frequency/load, this table would represent about two years of training and progression in both volume and intensity.

the 3 of previous incarnations). Both the Starr and Stone models call for varying the exercises between days in addition to varying the load. It works very well in its early 3 and 4-day stages for most strength and power athletes. Other coaches have adapted this program for Olympic weightlifters, adding a fifth and a sixth day as the athlete advances and adapts to an ever-increasing training load (Table 7-2). For general strength development and powerlifting, a 5-to-6 day program is excessive, but due to the nature of weightlifting training – most importantly the marked reduction in the amount of eccentric work provided by an emphasis on the snatch and the clean and jerk, as well as the emphasis on singles – the extra days do not provide the type of stress that more absolute strength work would, and thus the longer schedule can actually be recovered from.

Adding a day for the purpose of increasing training volume is actually different than doing a 4-day split routine as described above, where the four days are essentially two workouts that have been divided into four. When increasing training volume from a three-day schedule, another complete day is added and the entire body is trained, as on the other 3 days, but at a different intensity.

It is extremely important to understand that the addition of training volume in the form of extra training days works *only as long as recovery is being carefully managed*. Adding an additional day to a program that is already producing overtraining would obviously be a bad idea, so the Starr model must be carefully applied to the right situation. If it can be determined that overtraining is not the cause of an athlete's plateau, the careful addition of the fourth workout can prompt progress to resume. If it does not, a review of the recovery status of the lifter should reveal the problem, and the program should be adjusted accordingly.

INTENSITY VARIATION

It is imperative in the Starr model to vary training stress during the week in some form or another. Varying the intensity – the percentage of 1RM lifted – is only one way to do so. Doing the same heavy-day workout in a weekly schedule that calls for 2 heavy days per week will not work very long. When a week contains multiple heavy days, different ways to train heavy must be used each time or staleness will result. In the example above, 5 sets of 5 across on Monday with one heavier set of 5 reps on Wednesday is an excellent way to vary the quality of the heavy day and keep the intensity high. Using different numbers of reps at the same high relative intensity works well: for a week with 3 heavy days, a good organization would be 5 heavy sets of 5 across on Monday, one heavy triple on Tuesday, and 5 heavy singles on Thursday. The critical factor is the variation among the heavy workouts, keeping the overall training stress high while changing up the quality of the work done.

Rest between sets is a variable that lends itself to manipulation quite readily. In the earlier discussion of dynamic effort sets, we noted that control of the rest time is an important variable. All training facilities should have an analog clock with a sweep second hand for this purpose. Sets that would otherwise be easy can be made very hard by limiting recovery between sets to a minute or less, such that only partial recovery is possible and each following set is done in a climate of accumulating fatigue.

Some exercises are by their nature more demanding than others, in terms of their effects on recovery. Heavy, limit-level deadlifts are very stressful on the entire physiological system, making sets across at a high percentage of 1RM a bad choice for the deadlift because of their effects on the rest of the training week. One heavy set of deadlifts usually produces sufficient stress without the need for more sets. Conversely, the stress produced by even very heavy power cleans is of a different quality, since the factors that limit the amount of weight in the power clean do not involve absolute strength and therefore do not stress the contractile components of muscle, the ligaments and tendons, and the nervous system at the level the deadlift does. Heavy cleans produce their own unique type of stress, related to the impact involved in racking the bar, but it is quite different from that produced by a heavy deadlift. As a general rule, exercises strictly dependent on absolute strength for their execution at heavy weights are harder to recover from than technique-dependent exercises that are limited by skill of execution and power production and that are typically done without a significant eccentric component. This is why the Olympic lifts can be trained with a higher frequency than the primary strength exercises, and why training programs for athletes must take into consideration the relative intensities of the primary components of the program.

Whatever the method used, higher intensity work must be varied if it is to be used for long periods of time in the context of weekly programming. If variation does not occur, and good choices are not made about how to approach training stress variation, progress will slow prematurely.

FREQUENCY VARIATION

The obvious way to increase volume during the training week in the Starr model is to add workouts. Add training sessions one at a time and hold the volume constant for several weeks or months, until progress slows at that volume, at which point you can add another day. The tremendous number of possible combinations of workouts per week and light-medium-heavy loading make this model of training useful for 2 to 3 years, possibly longer than either of the other 2 models, especially for Olympic weightlifting. When introducing an additional workout, initially add it as a medium-intensity day. Later, as the trainee adapts to the load, the relative intensity of the additional day can be increased.

Progression through the number of workouts per week requires close observation of how the trainee tolerates each addition. Some trainees initially appear to handle a fourth training day with ease, but then crash 2 to 4 weeks later: work tolerance goes down, performance decreases, nagging injuries or pain become evident. This point may be the upper limit of the trainee's work capacity, the point beyond which overtraining will occur. Some offloading must happen for a short time, either by changing a heavy day to a light day or by eliminating a single workout (not the light one) for 2 weeks or until the trainee feels normal again. Failure to do so could easily result in a first exposure to overtraining, costing valuable training time and producing frustration and possible chronic injuries that could interfere with long-term progress. The way this first exposure to excessive overload is handled is crucial to later dealings with overtraining issues. Correct offloading and recovery now teaches the importance of recovery in the grand scheme of training and establishes a precedent for an intelligent approach to handling overtraining.

3-Day Model

Heavy	Light	Medium
Squat 5×5	Snatch – max	Clean & Jerk – max
Press 5×5	Front Squat 3×3	Box Squat 3–4×5
Deadlift 1×5	Bench Press 5×5	Push Press 5×3

The 3-day model is the introductory model for an aspiring Olympic weightlifter. Day 1 seeks to increase the lifter's base of general strength with a high volume of heavy squats, presses, and deadlifts. Although, these lifts are non-specific to the sport, strength is still the most important factor for the competitive lifter. Volume is high to build work capacity and muscle mass. Although bench pressing is technically the heaviest pressing exercise, it is placed on the light day, between the 2 overhead exercises. Because of this change, pressing is organized along the lines of Light-Heavy-Medium. This is a minor and relatively unimportant deviation from the overall organization of the training plan.

When working up to a max on the snatch and the C&J, the lifter will progress using singles only at 2.5 kg per attempt until he reaches his first missed attempt. He will then back the weight down approximately 10 kg and work up to another miss. He may make the number he missed the first time through, in which case he goes up another 2.5 and tries it. After the next miss, he is done with that lift. For the duration of this program, the term "max" in this context will mean this protocol.

Because this is intermediate-level programming, all other lifts will be PRed on a weekly basis for as long as possible.

Three Day Model – Phase II

Heavy	Light	Medium
Snatch – max	Snatch 75% ×1×5	Snatch 85% ×1×5
C&J – max	C&J 75% ×1×5	C&J 85% ×1×5
Squat 5×5	Front Squat 3×3	Box Squat 3–4×5
*Deadlift 1×5 / Snatch-Grip Deadlift 1×5	Press 5×5	*Push Press 5×3 / Bench Press 3×5

*Alternated weekly

In Phase II, pulling volume is greatly increased and the max-effort attempts are necessarily moved to the heavy day as the lifter's strength has increased. Due to increased volume of the competitive lifts some minor alterations have been made to the rest of the schedule. Deadlifts for a 5RM are a necessary part of developing a strong pull, but are very taxing to do every week. For this reason, deadlifts can be alternated on a weekly basis with the snatch-grip deadlift, also for a 5RM. On Friday, push presses and bench presses will also be rotated on a weekly basis.

Four Day Model (adds extra medium day)

Heavy-Mon	Medium-Tues	Light-Thur	Medium-Fri/Sat
Snatch – max	Snatch 85% ×1×5	Snatch 75% ×1×5	Power Snatch 4×2
C&J – max	C&J 85% ×1×5	C&J 75% ×1×5	Power Clean 4×2
Rack Jerk 2–3×1	Front Squat 85% ×1×3	Front Squat 75% ×3	Front Squat 80% ×2×2
Squat 3×5	Push Press 4×3	Press 3×5	Deadlift / Bench Press 5RM/3×5

In the first phase of the 4-Day Model, a medium day is added that includes the power versions of the lifts, along with the standard Heavy-Light-Medium days that have been used thus far on the competition lifts. On the heavy day, rack jerks may be added for a handful of singles after clean and jerks.

Squatting frequency will be increased to 4 days per week with 3 sessions being devoted to the front squat and the box squat being dropped as a medium day exercise. Because squat frequency is increased, some alterations must be made to the set-and-rep scheme. Back squats will be done first in the week, when the legs are the most fresh, so that PRs can be consistently attained. Sets will be dropped from 5 to 3 to accommodate the increased frequency. Front squats will primarily use singles and doubles at this point, to avoid creating excessive soreness or fatigue.

Deadlifts and bench presses are alternated on a weekly basis. These lifts are placed as the last lift of the training week so that they do not interfere with the performance of the other lifts in the program. Deadlifts and bench presses are necessary for strength development, but because of the stress they both create, it is wise to program them when the athlete has the most recovery time available, and it may be necessary to adjust Monday's training accordingly.

Four Day Model – Phase II (extra medium day becomes heavy day)

Heavy –Mon	Light – Tues	*Heavy –Thurs*	Medium Fri/Sat
Snatch – max	Snatch 75% ×1×5	*Front Squat – 1×1*	Power Snatch 4×2
C&J – max	C&J 75% ×1×5	C&J – max	Power Clean 4×2
Rack Jerk 2–3×1	Front Squat 75% ×3	Snatch – max	Front Squat 85% ×1×5
Squat 3×5	Press 3×5	Push Press 4×3	Deadlift 5RM / Bench Press 3×5
		Front Squat 1×1	

*On the second heavy session of the week, the lifter can institute a method borrowed from coach Jim Moser. The method entails working up to a heavy single front squat prior to testing the competition lifts. This has the effect of overloading the rack-version of the clean recovery, making the lighter clean feel more solid.

At this time, the lifter will have his first exposure to "maxing out" multiple times per week. It is not expected that the lifter actually set PRs on the second session of the week, although if he can, he should.

5-Day Model

Mon - Heavy	*Tues - Medium*	Wed - Light	Fri - Heavy	Sat - Medium
Snatch – max	Snatch 85% ×1×5	Snatch 75% ×1×5	Front Squat 1×1	Power Snatch 4×2
C&J – max	C&J 85% ×1×5	C&J 75% ×1×5	C&J – max	Power Clean 4×2
Rack Jerk 2–3×1	Front Squat	Front Squat	Snatch – max	Front Squat
Squat 3×5	85% ×1×3	75% ×3	Deadlift 1×5 /	85% ×2×2
		Press 3 × 5	Snatch-Grip	Push Press 4×3 /
			Deadlift 1×5	Bench Press 3×5

Most lifters will have spent the vast majority of their training career on 3 and 4-day strength programs up to this point. The addition of the fifth training day is likely much more work than the lifter has ever been exposed to. For this reason, the fifth medium day on Tuesday is strictly limited to a moderate number of singles in the competition lifts and the front squat.

With the additional day also comes more flexibility to manipulate the way some of the assistance exercises are trained. In this example, the lifter has chosen to slightly increase the amount of heavy pulling he does, and therefore deadlifts and snatch-grip deadlifts are alternated weekly on Friday's heavy day. In the 4-day model, the lifter was only pulling heavy once every 2 weeks. This means that push presses and bench presses will be alternated on Saturday if the lifter wishes to continue training both of these lifts.

Five Day Model – Phase II (extra medium day becomes heavy day)

Mon - Heavy	Tues - Heavy	Wed - Light	Friday - Heavy	Sat - Medium
Snatch – max	Front Squat 1×1	Snatch 75% ×1×6	Front Squat 1×1	Power Snatch 4×2
C&J – max	C&J – max	C&J 75%	C&J – max	Power Clean 4×2
Rack Jerk	Snatch – max	×1×6	Snatch – max	Front Squat
2–3×1		Front Squat	Deadlift 1×5 /	Push Press 4×3 /
Squat 3×5		75% ×3	Snatch-Grip	Bench Press 3×5
		Press 3×5	Deadlift 1×5	

Six Day Model (adds extra medium day)

Once the trainee makes the switch to training 6 days per week, special attention should be paid to maximizing recovery when possible. In this particular program the trainee will take advantage of the mid-week medium day offload and limit exercises to just 3. The same concept will be applied to the end-of-the-week light day.

Heavy	Heavy	Medium	Heavy	Medium	Light
Snatch – max	Front Squat 1×1	Snatch 85%×1×5	Front Squat 1×1	Power Snatch 4×2	Snatch 75%×1×5
C&J – max	C&J – max	C&J 85% ×1×5	C&J – max	Power Clean 4×2	C&J 75%×1×5
Rack Jerk 2–3×1	Snatch – max	Front Squat 85 ×1×5	Snatch – max	Front Squat 80% ×2×2	Front Squat 75%×3
Squat 3×5	Press 3×5		Push Press 4×3/	Deadlift 1×5 / Snatch-Grip Deadlift 1×5	
			Bench Press 3×5		

Six Day Model – Phase II (extra medium day becomes heavy day)

Heavy	Heavy	Medium	Heavy	Heavy	Light
Snatch – max	Front Squat 1×1	Power Snatch 4×2	Front Squat 1×1	Front Squat 1×1	Snatch 75% ×1×3
C&J – max	C&J – max	Power Clean 4×2	C&J – max	C&J – max	C&J 75% ×1×3
Rack Jerk 2–3×1	Snatch – max	Front Squat 85%×1×3	Snatch – max	Snatch – max	Front Squat 75% ×3
Squat 3×5	Press 3×5		Push Press 4×3	Front Squat 1×1	Bench Press 3×5 / Deadlift 1×5
	Front Squat 1×1		Front Squat 1×1		

In this example schedule the lifter has made the decision to return to just a semi-weekly deadlift schedule in order to accommodate the addition of a fourth heavy day for cleans and snatches. A decision such as this does not necessarily have to be permanent. After a period of time, the lifter may decide to go back to alternating deadlifts and snatch grip deadlifts on Saturday, and alternating push presses and bench presses on Thursday.

Most athletes will not need to even attempt training schedules of more than four days per week. There are few sports that benefit from more than four days of training outside their specific practice requirements. Powerlifting, as it has been traditionally trained, does not typically use more than four days per week, although some more progressive lifters have gotten good results by doing so and the paradigm may be changing. But field sports, Highland games, strongman competition, and team sports that use barbell training will not normally need any more gym time than a four-day program provides. So anyone interested in five or six days of training is probably a competitor in one of the barbell sports – weightlifting or powerlifting – or is a physique competitor.

For these athletes, each increase in training volume must be carefully gauged. As training progress slows each time volume is added, the cause of the plateau must be correctly evaluated to make sure that the slowdown is not caused by a non-volume-related training variable. It might be that the intensity is too high on one or more of the heavy days or too low on more than one of the heavy days, or that proper recovery is not being attended to. If the cause of the plateau is determined to be other than training volume, progress should be restored by fixing these problems before volume is increased again.

Very fit trainees who tolerate the five- and six-days-per-week schedules may further benefit from doing two workouts on one or more days per week. Dr. Keijo Hakkinen has shown that strength gains may be more efficiently produced by dividing up a day's training volume into two workouts instead of one. This system is used in many national team training situations where the athlete's schedule is completely free of outside constraints on time and recovery. Instead of spending two to three hours in the gym at one time, an hour or so two or more times a day allows the body to experience additional recuperation between training stresses. In collegiate programs and in professional sports situations, it is the strength coach's job to be there to help, and the athletes' responsibility to do everything they can to improve. But most athletes will not be able to conform to a schedule like this due to obvious conflicts with school, work, and family. In high school programs, the schedule is determined by the available time, not by what would be ideal for training.

The intermediate trainee can use this programming schedule for quite some time. There is a great deal of room for progression, with variations in both sets/reps and workout intensities as strength improves and the number of training sessions increases systematically. The limit on the number of workouts per week for this model of periodization is highly individual. Personal schedules, family commitments, work, and the ability to physiologically and psychologically adapt to high training volumes all play a role. At some level, the ability to increase training volume to the maximum tolerable level may determine the ultimate success of the athlete. Five heavy training days and one light day repeated every week for three months is something from which very few people can recover adequately; most will be overtrained on such a demanding schedule. The vast majority will not get even this far before overtraining becomes a major problem. Only the most genetically gifted athletes who are also able to devote all necessary time to training and recovery can function at this high level of loading without gigantic problems. The ability to do so indicates that the athlete can function and progress at the extremes of human ability, the very quality necessary for elite-level performance.

If it is determined that the trainee has reached the end of the usefulness of weekly training organization, advanced programming methods are warranted.

8

The Advanced

The advanced trainee has adapted to strength training to the point where a weekly training organization is no longer working. At this level of advancement, an overload event and subsequent recovery from it may take a month or more. Most lifters and strength athletes will never advance to this level unless they are active competitors in the barbell sports or strongman competitions. It represents the results of years of work under the bar and most of the journey along the curve of adaptation potential.

Again, the advanced lifter is a *competitor* in a strength sport. Athletes in other sports that use strength training – football, baseball, rugby, throwers in the field events – may be very strong, may have gotten that way over a long period of time in high school and college strength training, and much of this strength may be the result of more than just good genetics. But it is a rare individual who has managed to exhaust the complexity of all the potential intermediate programs discussed in chapter 7, especially in the context of a time-consuming field schedule. The overwhelming majority of advanced lifters are just that: competitors in powerlifting, Olympic weightlifting, or strongman. The field schedule usually interferes with the strength-training progression effectively enough to prevent the need for post-Chapter-7-style programming. And a guy training in his basement who never competes is never sufficiently motivated to have done so either.

Anyone who actually must use advanced-level post-weekly training *periodization* is someone who has dedicated himself to the strength sports, has sacrificed other aspects of life in the pursuit of competitive success, and will likely always – from now on, for better or worse – identify himself as "a lifter."

The History of Periodization

Periodization is the term most frequently used when referring to the organization of weight training programming into periods of time longer than the interval between two workouts. Its central organizing principle is the variation of volume and intensity in order to obtain a training objective. One of the most commonly referenced models of periodization is attributed to Leonid Matveyev of the Soviet Union, and is so entrenched in the literature that it is often referred to as "classical" periodization. The conventional wisdom is the assumption that Matveyev's model is the only way to program resistance training for everyone, regardless of their level of training advancement – test for a 1RM, apply Matveyev, and you're doing cutting-edge highly technical and highly-effective strength training. As we have seen, this is an oversimplification, no matter how satisfyingly complex it may appear to be.

The concept of periodic variation in training volume and intensity has been around for quite some time. It is quite probable that the training of ancient Greek athletes involved the use of periods of heavier and lighter training, especially considering the fact that the scheduling of games was dependent on the cycles of war and agriculture. At the turn of the last century, the term "photoperiod" was used to describe the phenomenon observed among athletes performing better in late summer and early fall. It was assumed that the amount of sunlight exposure contributed to the improved performance, and so the most stressful training was done in spring and summer.

As early as 1933, Mark Berry was using weekly variations in programming for his bodybuilders and weightlifters, and wrote about it in several publications. In the 1950s, Lazlo Nadori, a sports scientist and coach in Hungary, developed a model of periodization for his athletes. The development of this particular model was unique to Hungary and was separate from the evolution of Soviet block periodization, since no translations of his work into Russian were done. Translations from the Russian by Dr. Michael Yessis beginning in the 1960s made available the ideas of Yuri Verkhoshansky, Anatoliy Bondarchuk, and Vladimir Issurin to an already confused American audience. At about the same time, Russian weightlifting coach Leonid Matveyev developed his concepts of periodization, and his 1971 book provides several different models. Later in the 70s, Matveyev's book was translated into German and English. Having written the first "periodization" book available in the West, he became known as the father of periodization by default.

Also in the 1960s Matveyev's hated rival Yuri Verkhoshansky developed his system of "conjugated loading," openly stating that periodization was crap. But since his conjugated loading system was also periodized, it must be assumed that he really just thought Matveyev's approach to periodization was crap. In 1982, East German sports scientist Dr. Dietrich Harre edited *Principles of Sport Training*, which is essentially a fusion of the works of Nadori and Matveyev. A couple of years later, Frank Dick, the head of British track and field, "liberally recreated" Harre's book in English. Tudor Bompa, the Romanian author of the famous text *Periodization*, was trained in the East German system, and his first and subsequent texts are essentially reiterations and adaptations of Harre's adaptation of Nadori and Matveyev. And here we are today with no new thoughts, no new systems, and no real explanations of periodization since the last century. What we do have is a large misunderstanding about what periodization is and how to use it.

An Introduction to Advanced Programming

As we have previously observed, **novice trainees** have no use for complex programming. They are capable of adaptation so rapid that it permits them to merely add a little weight to the same basic exercises every time they train, and since they *can* do this, they *should* do this, because anything else wastes time. Once this capacity to adapt is exceeded by the level of adaptation – the stress necessary for causing homeostatic disruption exceeds the capacity to recover from it and adapt within the novice-response timeframe – the length of time for an overload event stretches to the period of a week's worth of training, and programming becomes a little more complex because of the need to manage recovery within a continuing application of workload. And then, after a much longer period of training and if the athlete continues on up the adaptation curve, the timeframe expands to the point where many weeks of carefully managed overloading and recovery are necessary for continued progress.

We have seen a glimpse of the complexity with which advanced training must be approached. In chapter 7 we saw training programs presented in multi-week snapshots that illustrated some variations

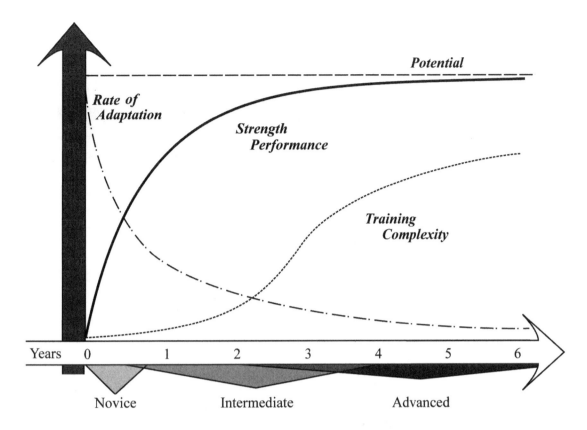

Figure 8-1. The generalized relationship between performance improvement and training complexity relative to time. Note the high level of program complexity required to drive progress of the advanced lifter.

within the week's loading. The fundamental differences in programming complexity between the intermediate and advanced levels are best illustrated by a side-by-side comparison of the two approaches. The following example is a comparison of how an intermediate and an advanced lifter might progress towards the same goal weight of 430 lbs for 5 singles across.

The intermediate lifter uses a volume workout on Monday that, once recovered from, will yield a PR by Friday. The advanced lifter uses an entire month (4 weeks) as a stress period, and hopefully culminates with at least one PR volume workout at the end of the 4-week cycle.

The advanced lifter will then apply a period of deloading and peaking that will last anywhere from 1–3 weeks. For the intermediate lifter, the deloading period is just 3 days and includes just one lighter, low-volume workout, and allows for a new "peak" to be hit on Friday. The advanced trainee will have multiple low-volume and submaximal workouts in weeks 5 and 6, the deloading phase, but as fatigue dissipates, the final week or two of the deloading period will yield one or more PR-setting workouts.

Texas Method (Intermediate)

     Accumulation = Monday (one high volume workout, at PR levels)

     Deload = Tues–Thurs. Includes one light, low volume workout on Wednesday

     Peaking = Friday. PR attempt at low volume, high intensity

Pyramid Model (Advanced)

Accumulation = 4 weeks. Multiple high volume workouts

Deload/Taper = 3 weeks. Mulitiple low-volume workouts building towards a peak

Peaking = 1 week. One or more PR-setting workouts at low volume, high intensity

A Comparison of an Intermediate and an Advanced 8-Week Progression

Week	Day	Intermediate Squat Progression	Advanced Squat Progression
1	Mon	*315×5×5*	315×5×5
	Wed	255×5×2	255×5×5
	Fri	*395×3*	320×5×5
2	Mon	*320×5×5*	325×5×5
	Wed	260×5×2	260×5×5
	Fri	*400×3*	330×5×5
3	Mon	*325×5×5*	335×5×5
	Wed	265×5×2	265×5×5
	Fri	*405×3*	340×5×5
4	Mon	*330×5×5*	*345×5×5*
	Wed	270×5×2	270×5×5
	Fri	*410×2×2*	*350×5×5*
5	Mon	*335×5×5*	350×3×3
	Wed	275×5×2	275×5×2
	Fri	*415×2×2*	395×1×5
6	Mon	*340×5×5*	355×3×3
	Wed	280×5×2	280×5×2
	Fri	*420×1×5*	410×1×5
7	Mon	*345×5×5*	360×3×3
	Wed	285×5×2	285×5×2
	Fri	*425×1×5*	420×1×5
8	Mon	*350×5×5*	365×3×3
	Wed	290×5×2	290×5×2
	Fri	*430×1×5*	*430×1×5*

Bold Italic = Personal Record

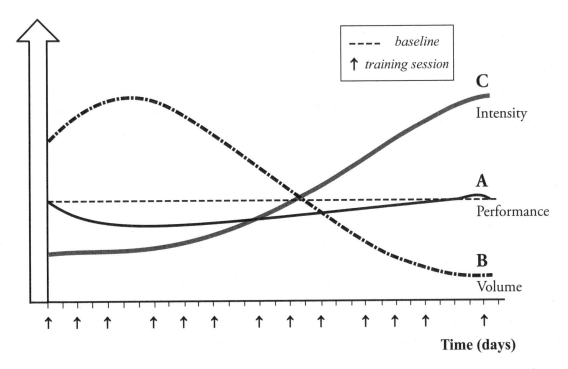

Figure 8-2. Thing 1. The advanced trainee responds to periodized programming over several weeks, a longer period of time than either the beginner or intermediate trainee (A). Thing 2. There is an inverse relationship between volume (B) and intensity (C) during a single training cycle for the advanced trainee.

In this example, the intermediate lifter would weigh perhaps 220, while the advanced lifter would weigh 181 – the bigger guy will still be an intermediate at weights the more advanced lighter man can only handle after longer under the bar. The point is that the intermediate lifter PRs every week, while the advanced lifter makes only 3 PRs during the whole 8-week period. For the intermediate, the "cycle" is the week, while for the advanced lifter the "cycle" is the 8-week period. The advanced lifter is stronger at the end of the 4-week volume period because 1) he got stronger by the end of the *previous* 8-week cycle and was able to return to volume-condition in 4 weeks to demonstrate that increased strength for 5×5, and 2) the cumulative effects of the 7 weeks of the *current* cycle produced the higher strength level on week 8.

Advanced programming therefore can – and must – utilize variations in volume and intensity over longer timeframes, because advanced adaptation takes place over longer timeframes. But even at this level of necessary complexity it is possible to succinctly summarize the general framework of advanced strength training. From Mark Berry's observations in the 1930s forward, the basic features of training for advanced athletes preparing for a competition have always been these two things:

Thing 1 – The closer an athlete is to his individual physical potential, the more important the cumulative effects of a series of workouts become (Figure 8-2, A).

Thing 2 – Training for more advanced athletes must be organized into longer periods of time, and those periods progress from higher volume and lower intensity toward lower volume and higher intensity (Figure 8-2, B, C).

As simple linear progression directs the novice's workout-to-workout training, and as simple weekly variation directs the intermediate's training, Thing 1 applies to athletes whose response to training has advanced to the point that several weeks at a time must be considered in their programming. Thing 2 is a function of the fact that advanced athletes compete, they do so at specific times, and their training has to allow all aspects of performance to peak at those particular times. A novice is not a competitive athlete, at least not in any serious sense. An intermediate may compete, but performance at the intermediate level is still progressing quickly enough that each weekend represents a peak anyway. Advanced athletes produce a peak by appointment only, and that peak must be scheduled in advance and trained for precisely and accurately.

PEAKING

Regardless of the type of cycle used to prepare for competition, for the advanced lifter the final two to four weeks prior to the event must include a reduction in both volume and intensity. Intensity is reduced by decreasing the percent of maximum load used in training. A limited number of near-maximal attempts are retained in the program during this period but are carefully distributed and separated by one or two workouts (only one to three heavy lifts once or twice per week in taper weeks). These heavier attempts maintain neuromuscular readiness and prevent detraining. Volume is reduced by limiting the number of reps performed, using singles and doubles only, and by decreasing both the number of sets and number of exercises included in a workout. The intent of these last weeks of training is to allow the body to recuperate so that it can respond with maximum effort and efficiency when challenged to do so. A good rule of thumb is a very light workout two days between the last workout and the competition, with the last heavy workout occurring five to seven days previous. Individual differences play a huge part in this decision, and personal experience will ultimately be the deciding factor for the advanced athlete.

With this in mind, two basic versions will be presented here. First, a very simple Pyramid Model that illustrates the general principles involved in longer programming models, and second, the Two-Steps-Forward-One-Step-Back model.

The Pyramid Model

The best way to jump into longer training cycles is with a very simple plan, similar to the example above, with a structure that consists of nothing more than a pyramid that lasts for a two-month period. This example uses the squat, and a lifter whose 1RM is 400 pounds, 5RM is 365, and 5 sets of 5 max is 340.

Week	1	2	3	4
Monday	300×5×5	315×5×5	325×5×5	335×5×5
Wednesday	250×5×5	250×5×5	250×5×5	225×5×5
Friday	305×5×5	320×5×5	330×5×5	345×5×5

These first four weeks make up the "loading" phase of the cycle. The total weekly training volume is much higher than the trainee has previously done, with five sets of five across for two heavy days per week rather than just one, and one offloading day. This volume is such that the trainee should experience some residual fatigue and may not make a PR for 5 sets of 5 by the end of week four. In fact, by Friday of week three the trainee might have trouble completing the prescribed sets and reps. But if fatigue has not accumulated, if recovery is occurring well, and all the reps of the fourth week's sets are finished, it would be useful to milk this process for another week, establishing significant new PRs for 5×5, before entering a peaking phase.

The four weeks that follow – the peaking phase – are dramatically different:

Week	5	6	7	8
Monday	340×3×3	360×3×3	380×3	350×3
Wednesday	250×5	250×5	250×5	250×5
Friday	350×3×3	370×3×3	390×3	400×3

As in the loading phase, another week can be added if warranted by recovery and progress in order to get the most out of the cycle.

Reducing the volume and total training stress in this second phase allows gradual recovery from the previously high training volume. During weeks 5 through 8, the trainee is actually "resting" from the previous high-volume work, and as fatigue dissipates and adaptation occurs, improved performance is attained. Weeks 1 through 4 are, in essence, doing the same job as the Monday high-volume workout in the Texas Method intermediate program, placing enough stress on the body to force adaptation, and weeks 5 through 8 function like the Texas Wednesday and Friday workouts, allowing for rest and adaptation and the demonstration of increased performance. But for the advanced trainee the process is stretched out over a much longer timeframe.

It is possible to successfully repeat a simple pyramid cycle like this several times, with virtually no changes other than an increased load. A trainee who completes this cycle might start the next cycle on week one, with Monday's workout weight set at 315×5×5, and end up with 415×3 at the end of week eight. This process could carry forward for many months, possibly longer.

Usually, a week or two of "active rest" or less-frequent training with moderate weights is a good idea between cycles to assure that the trainee is rested and ready to undergo another period of stressful training. After finishing the above cycle, squatting twice per week for 2 weeks with 2 or 3 sets of 5 at 300 pounds would be appropriate.

The effectiveness of the pyramid cycle is not limited to sets of 5 and 3. Loading could be 3 sets of 10. Peaking could be one set of 5. The important thing is to do sufficient volume during the loading phase so that fatigue is accumulated, enough to make performance at or near PR levels difficult but not impossible. A good rule of thumb is that if levels of 90% or more of 5RM cannot be performed during week three before any reduction in training volume occurs, the workload is probably too high. If the trainee is at or above PR levels at the end of the loading period, an increase in loading for the next cycle will probably work.

This simple example of the basics of longer programming can obviously be applied to all the lifts, not just the squat. There are also more complicated plans, each useful in its own particular set of circumstances.

POWERLIFTING FOCUS: 11-WEEK MEET PREP

The following is an example program using the Pyramid Model in preparation for a powerlifting meet. This program reduces volume and frequency, dropping from 3 times per week to just twice per week during the deloading and peaking phase. During the loading phase power cleans are done twice per week to keep pulling volume high. Deadlifts are easy to overtrain, so volume is accumulated with a slightly less-strenuous variant, the stiff-leg deadlift, done for 3 back-off sets. Presses and close-grip bench presses are used to fill in pressing volume, and strengthen the triceps for the heavier phase to come. When frequency is reduced in the peaking phase, the lifter will work to get to a Wednesday/Saturday schedule. This is done because powerlifting meets are done on Saturdays, and it is a good idea to condition the body and mind to train heavy on Saturday morning. The first part of the taper will use Mon-Thurs-Sun-Weds-Sat. After that, the lifter will stick with just Wednesday and Saturday until meet time.

This simple introduction to pre-meet planning illustrates the interplay of all the lifts, their loading phase, and the taper prior to competition.

Loading

Week	Monday	Wednesday	Friday
1	Squat 405×5×5 Bench 300×5×5 Power Clean 205×3×5	Squat 315×5×5 Press 175×5×5 Deadlift 455×5 SLDL 365×5×3	Squat 410×5×5 Close-Grip Bench 265×5×5 Power Clean 210×3×5
2	Squat 415×5×5 Bench 305×5×5 Power Clean 215×3×5	Squat 325×5×5 Press 180×5×5 Deadlift 465×5 SLDL 375×5×3	Squat 420×5×5 Close-Grip Bench 270×5×5 Power Clean 220×3×5
3	Squat 425×5×5 Bench 310×5×5 Power Clean 225×3×5	Squat 335×5×5 Press 185×5×5 Deadlift 475×5 SLDL 385×5×3	Squat 430×5×5 Close-Grip Bench 275×5×5 Power Clean 230×3×5
4	Squat 435×5×5 Bench 315×5×5 Power Clean 235×3×5	Squat 345×5×5 Press 190×5×5 Deadlift 485×5 SLDL 395×5×3	Squat 440×5×5 Close-Grip Bench 280×5×5 Power Clean 240×3×5
5	Squat 445×5×5 *Bench 320×5×5* Power Clean 245×3×5	Squat 355×5×5 *Press 195×5×5* *Deadlift 495×5* *SLDL 405×5×3*	*Squat 450×5×5* *Close-Grip Bench 285×5×5* *Power Clean 247×3×5*
6	*Squat 455×5×5* *Bench 325×5×5* *Power Clean 250×3×5*	Squat 365×5×5 *Press 200×5×5* *Deadlift 500×5* *SLDL 410×5×3*	*Squat 460×5×3,* 440×5×2* *Close-Grip Bench 290×5×5* *Power Clean 252×3×5*

New PRs = **bold italic**

*An illustration of what happens if a lifter cannot complete 5×5. Volume must be kept high, but weight on the bar can be reduced so that the lifter is not missing reps.

Deload/Peak, reduce frequency

Week	Monday	Thursday	Sunday
7	Squat 460×3×3	Squat 470×3×3	Squat 480×3×3
	Bench 325×3×3	Bench 335×3×3	Bench 340×3×3
	Deadlift 505×3	Power Clean 252×2×4	Deadlift 510×3
	SLDL 415×5		SLDL 420×5

Notice that the weight on the squat and bench for Monday's workout is the same as the heaviest sets from the previous week, but everything is done for significantly lower volume. After the low-volume Monday workout and two full days of rest, the trainee should be able to add weight to the bar on Thursday's workout.

Peaking

Week	Wednesday	Saturday
8	Squat 490×3×3	Squat 495×3×3
	Bench 345×3×3	Bench 350×3×3
	Power Clean 255×2×4	Deadlift 515×3
		SLDL 425×5
9	Squat 500×3×3	Squat 505×3×3
	Bench 355×3×3	Bench 360×2×3
	Power Clean 257×2×4	Deadlift 520×3
		SLDL 425×5
10	Squat 510×3×3	Squat 520×1×5
	Bench 365×2×3	Bench 370×1×5
	Power Clean 260×2×4	Deadlift 530–540×1
11	Light Day	Meet
	Squat 365×3×3	Squat 550
	Bench 295×3×3	Bench 380
	Power Clean 225×2×3	Deadlift 565

Most non-barbell sport competitors will not reach the advanced stage of training where monthly progression is necessary. Frequent interruptions to the training schedule and injuries will likely keep most sport athletes at the intermediate level, oscillating between different types of programs for the course of their competitive career. However, some serious competitors will reach the advanced stage, and it is critical for them to know how to structure their strength program around their sports training.

PYRAMID MODEL FOR POWER SPORTS

Below is an example of how the above program could be slightly altered and used as preparation for athletic competition. In this example, the focus shifts from bench pressing to overhead pressing movements. Push presses are added and sets and reps are changed to best suit the movement. Additionally, the third squat day is changed to dynamic effort (this could also be done for powerlifting). The pulling program is slightly diversified with the addition of the power snatch in place of one of the power clean days, and deadlift volume is accumulated through the dynamic effort followed by one heavy single.

Day 1	Day 2	Day 3
Squat 5×5	Squat 5×5	DE Box Squat
Push Press 6×3	Bench Press 5×5	70–75% 2×12
Power Snatch 6×2	Deadlift 70–80% ×1×10	Press 5×5
	90%+ ×1×1	Power Clean 5×3

The above outline would be "loaded" for 4–6 weeks with PRs being planned for the final week or two. This program could be tapered by splitting up the workload into 4 training sessions of much shorter duration than the full-body workouts used in the loading phase. Volume is still greatly reduced, even though frequency is increased. This may be a good idea when the frequency of sports practice and conditioning sessions increases and the trainee must lift and practice the same day. It is helpful to have only one or two things to get done in the gym under these circumstances. For the power athlete, it is also helpful to be able to train the Olympic lifts without excessive fatigue. Below is an example of the peaking phase:

Monday	Tuesday	Thursday	Friday
Squat 3×3	Power Snatch 8×1	DE Box Squat	Power Clean 4×2
Press 3×3	Bench Press 3×3	75% ×2×8	Push Press 2×2
		Deadlift 1×5	

PYRAMID MODEL FOR MMA

The following is a more detailed example of implementing a Pyramid Model on top of a rigorous sports practice and conditioning schedule. Mixed Martial Arts (MMA) is a weight-class sport heavily dependent on practice and conditioning. Because of this, an MMA fighter would never need quite the volume and frequency under the bar as a barbell sport competitor, although he may still reach levels of advancement where monthly progression is necessary. The fighter may use a split routine in both the loading and deloading phases of training, in order to keep his sessions as short as possible. The Pyramid Model works particularly well in conjunction with sports where practice and conditioning increase prior to competition. During training phases where practice and conditioning work are at moderate levels, the athlete can use a loading phase for strength. When practice and conditioning ramp up, the athlete simultaneously tapers his strength work.

A 12-week camp leading up to a fight might include 2 different 6-weeks phases of training.

Phase 1: Heavy Loading for Strength × 4 days per week (accumulation), 6 practices per week + 2 conditioning sessions per week

	Monday	Tuesday	Wednesday	Thursday	Friday	Saturday
AM	Upperbody Strength	Lower Body Strength	Strength Recovery/ Restoration	Upperbody Strength	Lower Body Strength	MMA Practice
PM	MMA Practice	MMA Practice + Prowler Conditioning	MMA Practice	MMA Practice	MMA practice	Conditioning 400 m repeats on incomplete rest

(Sunday: Off, Recovery/restoration)

Phase 2: Peaking strength × 3 days per week (intensification), 9 practices per week + 3 conditioning sessions per week

Week		Monday	Tuesday	Wednesday	Thursday	Friday	Saturday
1	AM	Upper Strength	Recovery/ Restoration	Lower Strength	Recovery/ Restoration	Upper Strength	MMA Practice
	Noon	MMA Practice	Conditioning 400m sprints	MMA Practice	300yd Shuttle run repeats	MMA Practice	Prowler Conditioning
	PM	MMA Practice	MMA Practice	MMA Practice	MMA Practice	MMA practice	
2	AM	Lower Strength	Recovery/ Restoration	Upper Strength	Recovery/ Restoration	Lower Strength	MMA Practice
	Noon	MMA Practice	Conditioning 400m sprints	MMA Practice	300yd Shuttle run repeats	MMA Practice	Prowler Conditioning
	PM	MMA Practice	MMA Practice	MMA Practice	MMA Practice	MMA practice	

(Sunday: Off, Recovery/restoration)

In the intensification phase of this particular program, the trainee reduces the frequency of his upper and lower workouts so that each workout is being hit once every 3–4 days instead of twice every week.

So the accumulation phase was this:

Mon – Upper   Tues – Lower   Thurs – Upper   Fri – Lower

Intensification is this:

Mon – Upper   Weds – Lower   Fri – Upper
Mon – Lower   Weds – Upper   Fri – Lower

Strength Program for an MMA Competitor

Accumulation

Monday	Tuesday	Thursday	Friday
DE Press 70% ×3×10	Weighted Chins 10×2	Press 5×5	Weighted Pull-up 5×5
Bench Press 5×5	DE Squat*	Push Press 2×3	Squat 5×5
Floor Press (w/ pause) 2×5	60–70% ×2×12	Weighted Dips 3×6–8	Paused Goodmornings 3×5
	DE Deadlift 70–80% ×1×20		

*(chins and squats can be done in alternating sets)

Intensification (rotated Mon/Wed/Fri)

Upper I	Lower I
DE Press 75% ×3×8	Weighted Chins 5×1, 1×5–8 (back off)
Bench Press 3×3	DE Squat 80% ×2×8, then 90% ×2, 95%×1–2, 100%+×1
Floor Press (w/ Pause) 3RM	Deadlift 90% ×2, 95% ×1–2, 100%+ ×1

Upper II	Lower II
Press 3×3	Pull-ups for max reps × 5 sets
Push Press 1–3RM	Squat 5RM
Dips for max reps × 3 sets	Goodmornings (GMs) 5RM

Sample of Hypothetical MMA fighter (6 weeks loading, 6 weeks deload/peaking)

Phase 1: Loading

Week	Monday	Tuesday	Thursday	Friday
1	DE Press 175×3×10 Bench Press 285×5×5 Floor Press (w/ pause) 300×5×2	Weighted Chins 35×2×10 S/S DE Squat 285×2×12* DE Deadlift 350×1×20	Press 190×5×5 Push Press 220×3×2 Weighted Dips 3×6–8	Weighted Pull-up 15×5×5 Squat 365×5×5 Paused GMs 200×5×3
2	DE Press 175×3×10 Bench Press 290×5×5 Floor Press (w/ pause) 305×5×2	Weighted Chins 35×2×10 DE Squat 310×2×12* DE Deadlift 375×1×15	Press 195×5×5 Push Press 225×3×2 Weighted Dips 3×6–8	Weighted Pull-up 15×5×5 Squat 375×5×5 Paused GMs 205×5×3

Week	Monday	Tuesday	Thursday	Friday
3	DE Press 175×3×10 Bench Press 295×5×5 Floor Press (w/ pause) 310×5×2	Weighted Chins 40×2×10 DE Squat 335×2×12* DE Deadlift 400×1×10	Press 200×5×5 Push Press 230×3×2 Weighted Dips 3×6–8	Weighted Pull-up 17.5×5×5 Squat 385×5×5 Paused GMs 210×5×3
4	DE Press 175×3×10 Bench Press 300×5×5 Floor Press (w/ pause) 315×5×2	Weighted Chins 40×2×10 DE Squat 285×2×12* DE Deadlift 350×1×20	Press 205×5×5 Push Press 235×3×2 Weighted Dips 3×6–8	Weighted Pull-up 20×5×5 Squat 395×5×5 Paused GMs 215×5×3

Volume PRs

Week	Monday	Tuesday	Thursday	Friday
5	DE Press 175×3×10 **Bench Press 305×5×5** Floor Press (w/ pause) 320×5×2	Weighted Chins 45×2×10 DE Squat 310×2×12* DE Deadlift 375×1×15	**Press 207×5×5** Push Press 240×3×2 Weighted Dips 3×6–8	Weighted Pull-up 22.5×5×5 **Squat 400×5×5** **Paused GMs 220×5×3**

Loading-Set Volume PRs

Week	Monday	Tuesday	Thursday	Friday
6	DE Press 175×3×10 **Bench Press 310×5×5** Floor Press (w/ pause) 325×5×2	Weighted Chins 45×2×10 DE Squat 335×2×12* DE Deadlift 400×1×10	**Press 210×5×5** **Push Press 245×3×2** Weighted Dips 3×6–8	Weighted Pull-up 25×5×5 **Squat 405×5×5** **Paused GMs 225×5×3**

* chins & squats done as supersets (S/S)
PR = **bold italic**

Phase 2: Intensification

Week	Monday	Wednesday	Friday
1	Press 185×3×8 Bench Press 315×3×3 Floor Press 335×3	Weighted Chins 55×1×5, 25×6 DE Squat 355×2×8, 385×2, 425×2 Deadlift 450×2–3	Press 215×3×3 Push Press 255×3 Dips 3 sets to failure

Week	Monday	Wednesday	Friday
2	Pull-up 5 sets to failure Squat 415×5 GMs 235×5	Press 185×3×8 Bench Press 320×3×3 Floor Press 345×3	Weighted Chins 　60×1×5, 25×7 Squat 355×2×8, 385×2 　425×2,450×2 Deadlift 475×2
3	Press 220×3×3 Push Press 260×3 Dips for max reps – 3 sets	Pull-up 5 sets to failure Squat 420×5 GMs 235×5	Press 185×3×8 Bench 325×3×3 Floor Press 350×3
4	Weighted Chins 　65×1×5, 25×8 DE Squat 355×2×8, 　425×2, 475×2 Deadlift 500×2	Press 225×3×3 Push Press 265×3 Dips 3 sets to failure	Pull-ups 5 sets to failure Squat 425×5 GMs 240×5
5	Press 185×3×8 Bench Press 330×3×3 Floor Press 355×3	Weighted Chins 70×1×5, 　35×5 Squat 485×1×5 Deadlift 515–520×1	Press 235×1×5 Push Press 275×1–2 Dips 1 set to failure

Week 6 – Fight week. Light squats and presses on Tuesday

In the intensification phase, several changes are made aside from the reduction in frequency. First, all DE work volume is reduced by 2–4 sets and the weight on the bar is increased about 5% as long as speed can be maintained. Each week, after DE squats, the trainee will work up to a heavy double or single above 90%. Dynamic effort deadlifts are dropped from the program as a means of volume accumulation. Instead, the trainee will pull all warm-up sets as "speed sets" and will work up to heavy doubles and singles above 90%. Most of the volume sets of 5 work is dropped for either triples across or a single heavy set of 5. Both will allow fatigue to dissipate while allowing the trainee to add weight to the bar each week. Dips and pull-ups will be done for bodyweight only (or very light weights in the case of a very strong trainee) to failure for multiple sets. This will allow a little endurance work for the upper body just prior to fight time. After spending several weeks doing the weighted versions of the lifts, the lifter should be able to crank out some very high-rep sets. Weighted chins will stay very heavy and will be done for singles across with maximum poundages, followed by one lighter back-off set of 5–8.

It is rather unusual for chins and pull-ups to be done as the first exercise of the day, prior to squats. In an MMA-focused program, this is done for a specific reason. In grappling sports like Judo, BJJ, and MMA, forearm, biceps, and lat strength is incredibly important. Many of the techniques rely heavily on pulling and squeezing strength in the hands and arms. For this reason, priority has been given here to what is generally just an assistance movement for competitive lifters. Even though chins and pull-ups are upper body exercises, it works well to put them before squats, since squats aren't affected too much by this fatigue. Putting them before pressing exercises would negatively impact the presses, while putting them after presses negatively impacts the chins and pull-ups.

CLASSIC POWERLIFTING TAPER

This version of the Pyramid Model is a classic tapering method that was popular among powerlifters in the 80s and 90s, and it is experiencing resurgence today, in large part because of the simplicity of the methodology. The classic taper is flexible enough to be used for anywhere from 8–16 weeks. It starts with high volume (often sets of 8) and goes down to doubles and singles over the course of the program. Sets and reps can vary from lifter to lifter, but it was common to train sets of 8 for 3–4 weeks, followed by sets of 5 for 3–4 weeks and then 3–4 weeks of triples, doubles, and singles. PRs are targeted for the last week of each 3–4 week phase: the old PR for each rep-range would be scheduled in the next-to-last week of each phase, with a new PR in the final week.

For example, our lifter's previous bench press PR was 300×8×3. When setting up his training plan he might do 300×8×3 in week 3 of the 4-week block of 8s. Based on how 300×8×3 goes, he may attempt anywhere from 302×8×3 to 310×8×3 in week 4. An experienced lifter will be able to make the proper choice. For Week 1 and Week 2, the lifter will simply work backwards by 5–10 lbs. So the whole 4-week block of 8s training might look like this:

Week 1: 280×8×3
Week 2: 290×8×3
Week 3: 300×8×3 (old PR)
Week 4: 302–310×8×3 PR

This same process should be applied to all other phases as well.

When setting up these types of programs, it is acceptable to make minor adjustments to the way the exercises are performed during the "easy" weeks leading up to the PR. For bench presses, all of the reps might be paused or done with a closer grip. Some of the reps could also be paused for squats. For deadlifts, the easier weeks could be done with a wider grip, progressing from a snatch grip back to a normal width. Once the lifter reaches his PR weeks, standard competition technique is used to complete all the sets and reps.

Targeted assistance work is generally necessary in this type of program. Advanced lifters will have determined which exercises are most appropriate at this stage of their careers, and the choice of assistance movements is thus highly individual. The use of various assistance exercises is explored below.

Below is an example 12-week program that has been used in many different versions. The hypothetical lifter using this program has a 550 Squat, 400 Bench, and 625 deadlift.

Example 12 week Classic Powerlifting Taper

Week	Monday	Wednesday	Friday
1	Squat 385×8×3, paused Glute Ham Raise 3×10 Weighted Sit-up 3×10	Bench Press 280×8×3, close grip, paused Incline Press 2×8–10 Bodyweight Dips 2 sets × failure	Snatch-Grip Deadlift 435×8 SLDL 365×10×2 Barbell Rows 225×10×2 Lat Pulldowns 3×10–12

Week	Monday	Wednesday	Friday
2	Squat 400×8×3, set 3 paused Weighted Glute/Ham 3×10 Weighted Sit-up 3×10	Bench Press 290×8×3 (closer grip) Incline Press 2×8–10 Bodyweight Dips 2 sets × failure	Snatch-Grip Deadlift 455×8 SLDL 2×10 Barbell Rows 2×10 Lat Pulldowns 3×10–12
3	Squat 415×8×3 Glute/Ham 3×10 Weighted Sit-up 3×10	Bench Press 300×8×3 Incline Press 2×8–10 Bodyweight Dips 2 sets × failure	Snatch-Grip Deadlift 475×8 SLDL 2×10 Barbell Rows 2×10 Lat Pulldowns 3×10–12
4	Squat ***430×8***, 405×8×2 back-off Weighted Glute/Ham 3×10 Weighted Sit-up 3×10	Bench Press ***310×8×3*** Incline Press 2×8–10 Bodyweight Dips 2 sets × failure	Deadlift, comp. grip ***495×8*** SLDL 2×8–10 Barbell Rows 2×10 Lat Pulldowns 3×10–12

This 4 week block ends with PR sets of 8.
PR = ***bold italic***

Week	Monday	Wednesday	Friday
5	Squat 450×5×3 Glute/Ham Raise 3×10 Weighted Sit-up 3×10	Bench Press 330×5×3 Weighted Dips 2×8–10 Lying Triceps Extension 2×10–15	Deadlift 515×5 SLDL 2×8 Barbell Rows 2×8–10 Lat Pulldowns 3×10–12
6	Squat 465×5×3 Weighted Glute/Ham 3×10 Weighted Sit-up 3×10	Bench Press 340×5×3 Weighted Dips 2×8–10 Lying Triceps Extension 2×10–15	Deadlift 530×5 SLDL 2×8 Barbell Rows 2×8–10 Lat Pulldowns 3×10–12

PR sets of 5

Week	Monday	Wednesday	Friday
7	Squat ***480×5×3*** Glute/Ham Raise 3×10 Weighted Sit-up 3×10	Bench Press ***350×5×3*** Weighted Dips 2×8–10 Lying Tricep Extension 2×10–15	Deadlift ***545×5*** SLDL 2×8 Barbell Rows 2×8–10 Lat Pulldowns 3×10–12

Drop one work set from squats and bench and transition to triples

Week	Monday	Wednesday	Friday
8	Squat 500×3×2 Weighted Glute/Ham 3×10 Weighted Sit-up 3×10	Bench Press 365×3×2 Close-Grip Bench 2×5 Weighted Dips 2×6–8	Deadlift 565×3 SLDL 2×5 Barbell Rows 2×8–10 Lat Pulldowns 3×10–12
9	Squat 515×3×2 Glute/Ham Raise 3×10 Weighted Sit-up 3×10	Bench Press 375×3×2 Close-Grip Bench 2×5 Weighted Dips 2×6–8	Deadlift 585×3 SLDL 2×5 Barbell Rows 2×8–10 Lat Pulldowns 3×10–12
10	Squat 530×2×2 Weighted Glute/Ham 3×10 Weighted Sit-up 3×10	Bench Press 385×2×2 Close-Grip Bench 2×5 Weighted Dips 2×6–8	Deadlift **605×3** SLDL 2×5 Barbell Rows 2×8–10 Lat Pulldowns 3×10–12

Final Training Week; one top set on squat and bench

Week	Monday	Wednesday	Friday
11	Squat **550×2** (doubled old 1RM) Glute/Ham Raise 3×10 Weighted Sit-up 3×10	Bench Press **400×2** (doubled old 1RM) Close-Grip Bench 2×5 Weighted Dips 2×6-8	Deadlift 455×5 SLDL – drop this exercise for recovery purposes Barbell Rows 2×8–10 Lat Pulldowns 3×10–12

Meet Week – Light squat and bench press

Week	Tuesday or Wednesday	Saturday
12	Squat 80% ×3×2–3×3 Bench Press 80% ×3×2–3	Squat 575 Bench Press 415 Deadlift 655

ADVANCED STRONGMAN TRAINING PROGRAM – CLASSIC TAPER

The basic organization of this program includes 2 gym days (Monday and Tuesday) that focus primarily on the standard barbell exercises and assistance work specific to the athlete's weaknesses.

Monday – Press Day
Tuesday – Squat Day
Thursday – Event-Specific Pressing
Saturday – Other Events

Monday will generally focus on pressing, push pressing, bench pressing, and accessory triceps work to improve lockout strength. Tuesday will always be based on squats. Depending on the athlete and the specifics of the upcoming competition, deadlifts can be done either before or after squats on Tuesday or reserved for Saturday's event day. The lighter pulls such as power cleans, RDLs, or goodmornings would also be done on Tuesday.

Thursday is another pressing day, but will focus on working with the implements specific to the upcoming competition. These will vary from one training cycle to the next. Viking Presses, logs, axles, and thick-handled dumbbells are all potential events at a contest. There is also variation in how the contest lifts might be performed. The event could be done for maximum repetitions or could be done for 1RMs. Sometimes every pressing rep is preceded by a clean, and sometimes the implement is only cleaned once. The athlete should train for the specific events in the upcoming meet, and should do his homework about what they are.

Saturday is scheduled for all the other events, most of which will be lower-body focused. Most competitions have some form of deadlifting, for reps, max weight, or as part of a medley, and all will have one or multiple carrying events for distance – yoke runs, farmer's walk, and keg or stone carries. Other potential events include things like stone loading and tire flipping. Many strongmen choose Saturday as "event day" for logistical reasons. Competitors often have to drive to a warehouse or storage facility separate from their gym, and it takes time to get everything out and put back up, to get access to empty parking lots, or to coordinate training time with partners. However, training all the events together conditions the lifter's body for a contest where multiple events will be performed consecutively on the same day. Ideally, Saturday's training should be arranged in the same order as the upcoming contest.

In any case, it makes sense to put some distance between squat day and event day just for recovery purposes. This type of training is very demanding, and exceptionally careful attention must be paid to planning for recovery from these two murderous workouts.

In the sample program below, training will be arranged in 3 different 3–4 week cycles that work from high to low volume in preparation for the meet. In our hypothetical scenario the upcoming competition will consist of:

Log Press /Push Press for Reps (225 lbs)
Tire Deadlift for 1RM, equivalent to knee-height rack pull
Farmer's Walk – 200 ft
Yoke Run – 200 ft
Tire Flip – 100 ft

The lifter will train the Tire Deadlift with standard deadlifts and rack pulls from 3 different pin positions in the power rack. The positions will be set with the plates 2 inches (pos. 1), 4 inches (pos. 2), and 6 inches (pos. 3) off the ground. Position 3 will place the bar at roughly the same height the bar will be during the tire deadlift.

Overview:

    Phase I – 4 weeks of 8s + Event Specifics; 1 week deload

    Phase II – 4 weeks of 5s + Event Specifics; 1 week deload

    Phase III – 4 weeks peaking; competition

Phase 1: 4 weeks of 8s + Event Specifics

Week	*Press Day* Monday	*Squat Day* Tuesday	*Event Presses* Thursday	*Other Events* Saturday
1	Press 185×8×3 Bench 3×8–10 Lying Triceps Extension (LTE) 2–3×10–12	Squat 385×8×3 RDL 3×8 Prowler or Sled Conditioning Work	Strict Log Press 3×8 Rack Lockouts (with log) 2×8–10 Weighted Dips 3×10–15	Deadlift 8RM Farmer's Walk 2×200 ft Yoke Run 2×200 ft Tire Flip 2×100 ft
2	Press 195×8×3 Incline Press 3×8–10 LTE 2–3×10–12	Squat 405×8×3 RDL 3×8 Prowler or Sled Conditioning Work	Log Press 3×8 Rack Lockouts (with log) 2×8–10 Weighted Dips 3×10–15	Rack Pull (pos. 1) 8RM Farmer's Walk 2×200 ft Yoke Run 2×200 ft Tire Flip 2×100 ft
3	Press 205×8×3 Bench 3×8–10 LTE 2–3×10–12	Squat 425×8×3 RDL 3×8 Prowler or Sled Conditioning Work	Strict Log Press 3×8 Rack Lockouts (with log) 2×8-10 Weighted Dips 3×10–15	Rack Pull (pos. 2) 8RM Farmer's Walk 2×200 ft Yoke Run 2×200 ft Tire Flip 2×100 ft

PR attempts

Week	Press Day Monday	Squat Day Tuesday	Event Presses Thursday	Other Events Saturday
4	Press **215×8×3** Incline Press 3×8–10 LTE 2–3×10–12	Squat **445×8×3** RDL 3×8 Prowler or Sled Conditioning Work	Strict Log Press 3×8 Rack Lockouts (with log) 2×8–10 Weighted Dips 3×10–15	Rack Pull (pos. 3) 8RM Farmer's Walk 2×200 ft Yoke Run 2×200 ft Tire Flip 2×100 ft

Deloading week

Week	Press Day Monday	Squat Day Tuesday	Event Presses Thursday	Other Events Saturday
5	Press 185×5×2 Bench 2×5	Squat 385×5×2 Prowler or Sled Conditioning Work – lowered volume	Log Press 2×5 (use a medium weight) Dips 2×10–15	(No Pulling) Farmer's Walk 1×200 ft Yoke Run 1×200ft Tire Flip 1×100 ft

Phase 2: 4 weeks of 5s + Event specific

Week	*Press Day* Monday	*Squat Day* Tuesday	*Event Presses* Thursday	*Other Events* Saturday
1	Press 225×5×5 Bench 3×5 LTE 2–3×10–12	Squat 465×5×5 RDL 3×5 Prowler or Sled Conditioning Work	Strict Log Press 3×5 Log Push-Press 2×5 Weighted Dips 3×10–15	Deadlift 5RM Farmer's Walk 4×100 ft (overloaded) Yoke Run 4×100 ft (overloaded) Tire Flip 4×50 ft (overloaded)
2	Press 235×5×5 Incline Press 3×5 LTE 2–3×10–12	Squat 475×5×5 RDL 3×5 Prowler or Sled Conditioning Work	Strict Log Press 3×5 Log Push-Press 2×5 Weighted Dips 3×10–15	Rack Pull (pos. 1) 5RM Farmer's Walk 4×100 ft Yoke Run 4×100 ft Tire Flip 4×50 ft
3	Press 245×5×5 Bench 3×5 LTE 2–3×10–12	Squat 485×5×5 RDL 3×5 Prowler or Sled Conditioning Work	Strict Log Press 3×5 Log Push-Press 2×5 Weighted Dips 3×10x-15	Rack Pull (pos. 2) 5RM Farmer's Walk 4×100 ft Yoke Run 4×100 ft Tire Flip 4×50 ft

***PR* attempts**

Week	Monday	Tuesday	Thursday	Saturday
4	Press **255×5×5** Incline Press 3×5 LTE 2–3×10–12	Squat **495×5×5** RDL 3×5 Prowler or Sled Conditioning Work	Strict Log Press 3×5 Log Push Press 2×5 Weighted Dips 3×10–15	Rack Pull (pos. 3) 5RM Farmer's Walk 4×100 ft Yoke Run 4×100 ft Tire Flip 4×50 ft

Deloading Week

Week	Monday	Tuesday	Thursday	Saturday
5	Press 3×3×225 Bench 2×5	Squat 3×3×455 Prowler or Sled Conditioning – reduce volume	Log Press 3×5 (use medium weight)	(No Pulling) Farmer's Walk 1×200 ft Yoke Run 1×200 ft Tire Flip 1×100 ft

Phase 3: Peaking

Week	Press Day Monday	Squat Day Tuesday	Event Presses Thursday	Other Events Saturday
1	Press 265×5 Bench 2×5 (5RM regular grip, 5RM close grip) LTE 2–3×10–12	Squat 525×5 RDL 2×5 Prowler or Sled Conditioning Work	Log Push Press 3–5RM Strict Log Press 2×12–15 Weighted Dips 2×10–15	Deadlift 2–3RM Farmer's Walk 2×200 ft Yoke Run 2×200 ft Tire Flip 2×100 ft
2	Press 270×5 Incline Press 2×5 LTE 2–3×10–12	Squat 535×3–5 RDL 2×5 Prowler or Sled Conditioning Work	Log Push Press 3–5RM Strict Log Press 2×12–15 Weighted Dips 2×10–15	Rack Pull (pos.1) 3RM Farmer's Walk 2×200 ft Yoke Run 2×200 ft Tire Flip 2×100 ft
3	Press 275×5 Bench 2×5 LTE 2–3×10–12	Squat 545 × 3–5 RDL 2×5 Prowler or Sled Conditioning Work	Log Push Press 3-5RM Strict Log Press 1×12–15 Weighted Dips 2×10–15	Rack Pull (pos. 2) 3RM (or no heavy pulling) Farmer's Walk 1×200 ft Yoke Run 1×200 ft Tire Flip 1×50 ft

Meet Week; Complete Deload

Week	Tuesday or Wednesday	Saturday
4	Squat 80% ×2×3 Press 80% ×2×3 Light/Low Volume Sled Conditioning	**Meet**

The Two Steps Forward, One Step Back Model

A second model, a variation on one formerly taught in USA Weightlifting's coaching development program, manipulates the workload in four-week blocks, with progress made by connecting a series of these blocks using progressively higher loads. Each block starts with a week at a baseline load of moderate intensity. The second week moves average intensity up about 10%. The third week is an offload or recovery week where average intensity is reduced. This lighter week enables a fourth-week increase, resulting in a PR of some sort. The next four-week cycle begins at an intensity greater than the previous cycle's starting point. Each of the series of four-week blocks prepares the lifter for the next progressively heavier block. Each four-week cycle is slightly different in sets and rep-range, but they flow seamlessly toward the contest date with the object of improving the specific aspects of performance required that day.

As with all our previous references to the use of percentages in programming, they are again used here to represent the relative variations in load between the weeks within the training block. An advanced lifter knows where to start the cycle if he understands the relationships between the loads that make up the schedule; that starting point *may* be predictably relevant to his 1RM, and it *may not* be. Age, sex, injuries, and recent training history always exert more control over where we start our programs *this time* than a concrete relationship to a previous contest performance. Very long term progress is demonstrated by the trend in 1RM, and as data points 1RMs are useful, but even a recent 1RM is not fine-enough a marker to determine where we will start a 12 or 16-week block of training. The 1RM for an exercise can indicate a ballpark starting point, but recent 5RM activity – from, say, *last week's* 5RM workout – is a much more accurate way to determine workloads that need to be done *this* week. The data is fresh and relevant because the work is being done within the same overload event and rep-range. For the first workout in the cycle, the advanced lifter will rely on his experience to help him decide what weights to use, based on what he knows must happen in the following weeks.

Block 1: Base work, run 2 to 3 times.

Week 1: 5×5 @ 90 percent of 5×5-across PR
Week 2: 5×5 @ PR
Week 3: 2×5 @ 80 percent of 5×5 PR
Week 4: 5RM

Block 2: Transition, run once before peak

Week 1: 5×3 @ 93% of 5×5-across PR
Week 2: 5×3 @ 5RM, deload after set 3 if necessary to maintain 3 reps
Week 3: 3×3 @ 80% of 5RM
Week 4: 3RM

Block 3: Peaking

Week 1: 3×3 @ 90% of 3RM
Week 2: 5 singles across @ 3RM + 3%
Week 3: 2×2 @ 85% of 3RM
Week 4: Meet Week

This 12 to 16-week block could be run twice before a meet. Four-week blocks are strung together into a longer period during which volume decreases and intensity increases, so it is necessary to identify the target date in advance and count back from there (this is a common feature of all contest-oriented programming). The number of weeks between the starting date and the contest date determines the number of Block-1 segments, although an advanced lifter can probably never use more than 3 of these – a 12-week period of Block 1 training – before a taper is necessary. Using a Block-1/Block-2/Block-3 progression without repeating Block 1, four cycles with one week's active rest after each would fill out a year's training schedule. But things usually do not work out this way, and shorter or longer programs can be designed using the same principles.

A SAMPLE TSFOSB POWERLIFTING MEET CYCLE

The following program includes two cycles through Block 1, and one cycle each through Block 2 and 3. Lower stress assistance exercises are not shown, and power clean and dips numbers are not stipulated due to the highly individual nature of their expression.

Training Week
Monday – Heavy Bench + Bench Assistance
Tuesday – Light Squat + Heavy Pulling
Thursday – Light Bench + Press
Friday – Heavy Squat + Light Pulling

In this program, the lifter is using a strategy of not directly training the deadlift. Instead he is using a combination of rack pulls, halting deadlifts, and power shrugs. Power cleans are kept as a light day pulling exercise throughout each week of the program. Power shrugs are used in week 3 (the deload week) as the heavy pulling exercise. Even though power shrugs are trained very heavy, they are limited to one set of 5 except for the first workout, and the range of motion is very short. This produces less relative stress than haltings and rack pulls, while at the same time allowing the lifter to load the traps and get used to very heavy weight on the arms. This makes it a good exercise for the deloading week.

In this scenario, our lifter is weak at the top of his deadlifts and has chosen to train the rack pull twice within each cycle (week 2 and week 4), and the halting deadlift only on week 1. If the lifter is weak off of the floor, he might decide to reverse this priority, doing haltings on week 2 and 4, and rack pulls only on week 1.

Block 1, 2 cycles

Week	Monday	Tuesday	Thursday	Friday
1	Bench Press 300×5×5 Weighted Dips 4× 8–10	Squat 365×5×3 Halting Deadlift 465×8	Close-Grip Bench Press 270×5×3 Press 185×8×3	Squat 405×5×5 Power Clean 4×3
2	Bench Press 335×5×5 Weighted Dips 5 × 8–10	Squat 365×5×3 Rack Pull 455×5×2	Close-Grip Bench 305×5×4 Press 185×8×4	Squat 450×5×5 Power Clean 5×3
3	Bench Press 265×5×3 Weighted Dips 2×8–10	Squat 365×5×3 Power Shrug 545×5×2	Close-Grip Bench 255×5×2 Press 175×8×2	Squat 365×5×3 Power Clean 2×3
4	Bench Press 350×5 Weighted Dips 3×8–10	Squat 365×5×3 Rack Pull 495×5	Close-Grip Bench 320×5 Press 200×8	Squat 475×5 Power Clean 3×3

Week	Monday	Tuesday	Thursday	Friday
5	Bench Press 305×5×3 Weighted Dips 4×8–10	Squat 365×5×3 Halting Deadlift 485×8	Close-Grip Bench 280×5×3 Press 190×8×3	Squat 410×5×3 Power Clean 4×3
6	Bench Press 340×5×5 Weighted Dips 5×8–10	Squat 365×5×3 Rack Pull 505×5	Close-Grip Bench 310×5×4 Press 190×8×4	Squat 455×5×5 Power Clean 5×3
7	Bench Press 270×5×2 Weighted Dips 2×8–10	Squat 365×5×3 Power Shrug 595×5	Close-Grip Bench 265×5×2 Press 180×8×2	Squat 365×5×2 Power Clean 2×3
8	Bench Press 355×5 Weighted Dips 3×8–10	Squat 365×5×3 Rack Pull 515×5	Close-Grip Bench Press 325×5 Press 205×8	Squat 480×5 Power Clean 3×3
Block 2				
9	Bench Press 315×3×3 Weighted Dips 4×5–7	Squat 365×5×3 Halting Deadlift 505×5	Close-Grip Bench 285×5×3 Press 200×6×3	Squat 425×3×3 Power Clean 4×3
10	Bench Press 355×3×5 Weighted Dips 5×5–7	Squat 365×5×3 Rack Pull 525×5	Close-Grip Bench 310×5×4 Press 200×6×4	Squat 480×3×5 Power Clean 5×3
11	Bench Press 285×3×2 Weighted Dips 2×5–7	Squat 365×5×3 Power Shrug 625×5	Close-Grip Bench 265×5×2 Press 190×6×2	Squat 385×3×2 Power Clean 2×3
12	Bench Press 370×3 Weighted Dips 3×5–7	Squat 365×5×3 Rack Pull 540×5	Close-Grip Bench 330×5 Press 220×6	Squat 500×3 Power Clean 3×3
Block 3				
13	Bench Press 335×3×3 Weighted Dips 4×4–6	Squat 365×5×2 Halting Deadlift 515×5	Close-Grip Bench 305×3×3 Press 205×4×3	Squat 450×3×3 Power Clean 4×3
14	Bench Press 380x1x5 paused Weighted Dips 4x4–6	Squat 365x5x2 Rack Pull 555x5	Close-Grip Bench 340x2x4 Press 205x4x4	Squat 515x1x5 Power Clean 5x3

Week	Monday	Tuesday	Thursday	Friday
15	Bench Press 315×2×2 Weighted Dips 2×4–6	Squat 365×5×2 Power Shrug 655×5	Close-Grip Bench 300×3×2 Press 200×2×2	Squat 425×2×2 Power Clean 2×3

Meet Week

Week	Monday	Thursday	Saturday
16	Squat – work up to opener, 495 Bench Press – work up to opener, 385 Deadlift – work up to last warm up, 475. Perfect set up and technique	Squat 135×5×3/Bench 135×5×3/Power Clean 135×5×3 as a Superset	Meet Day Squat 540 Bench Press 395 Deadlift 560

Arguably the most important step in the stress/recovery/adaptation cycle is the recovery – without it, adaptation does not occur. For the novice, a simple day off between workouts is sufficient. For the intermediate, several days are required, during which a lower-stress workout or two are performed to preserve skill and conditioning. For the advanced trainee, the recovery phase can be one or two weeks of decreased training load, comprising several workouts that are low enough in volume to allow fatigue to dissipate but high enough in intensity to maintain the adaptations needed to demonstrate peak performance.

Not infrequently, an athlete can perform a new PR following a week off. This occurs despite the fact that the meet performance was also a PR the previous week. If this occurs, the athlete has mistimed or misloaded training, the taper, or both, since additional adaptation took place after it was anticipated. This indicates that the performance PR was not what it could have been had programming been more precise. These mistakes will happen to every athlete and coach, and they are opportunities to learn.

OFF-SEASON POWERLIFTING ROUTINE

The following routine is meant for gains in both strength and muscle mass. The volume of assistance work is very high. The lifter should attempt to make all sets and reps for each lift, but weight can be adjusted set-to-set to make sure that all the volume is completed.

In this example, Dynamic Effort work is done on the squat and bench press. On the base, loading, and peaking weeks, the volume is the same. Loading weeks will use the heaviest weights of any week in the cycle. Deloading weeks will use the same weight as the base week but for less volume. Peaking weeks will use a weight somewhere between the weights used for the base/deload and the loading weeks. Remember: DE work is designed to train explosive power. The idea is that the peaking weeks will use the optimal amount of both weight and speed, so that power is maximized during the peak, even with a lighter weight.

For the DE Bench, a 4-week cycle might look like this:

Base: 60% ×3×10
Loading: 66% ×3×10
Deloading: 60% ×3×6
Peaking: *63% ×3×10 very fast*

As always, Dynamic Effort weights should be based upon bar speed and not strictly on percentages. Adjust as necessary.

Example Split:

Monday	Tuesday	Thursday	Friday
Bench Press	Squat	DE Bench Press	DE Squat
Weighted Dips	Romanian Deadlift	Press	Deadlift
Lying Triceps	(RDL)	Triceps Pressdowns	Barbell Rows
Extensions (LTE)	Pulldowns or Chins		

Sample 4-week cycle

Base (20 reps @ 70% for squat/bench, 10 reps for deadlift, 40 reps for assistance)

Week	Monday	Tuesday	Thursday	Friday
1	Close-Grip Bench Press 280×5×4	Squat 385×5×4 RDL 4×10	DE Bench Press 240×3×10	DE Squat 330×2×12 Deadlift 435×5×2
	Weighted Dips 4×10	Lat Pulldowns 4×10	Press 4×10	Barbell Rows 4×10
	LTE 4×10		Triceps Pressdowns 4×10	

Loading (25 reps @ 80% for squat/bench, 15 reps for deadlift, 50 reps for assistance)

2	Bench Press 320×5×5	Squat 440×5×5	DE Bench Press 260×3×10	DE Squat 360×2×12 Deadlift 500×5×3
	Weighted Dips 5×10	RDL 5×10	Press 5×10 (or 6×8)	Barbell Rows 5×10 (or 6×8)
	LTE 5×10	Lat Pulldowns 5×10	Triceps Pressdowns 5×10	

Deloading (10 reps @ 75% for squat/bench, 5 reps for deadlift, 20 reps for assistance)

3	Close-Grip Bench Press 300×5×2	Squat 415×5×2 RDL 2×10	DE Bench Press 240×3×6	DE Squat 330×2×8 Deadlift 470×5
	Weighted Dips 2×10	Lat Pulldowns 2×10	Press 2×10	Barbell Rows 2×10
	LTE 2×10		Triceps Pressdowns 2×10	

Peaking (15 reps @ 85% for squat/bench, 5 reps for deadlift, 30 reps for assistance – PR on top-set assistance work)

Week	Monday	Tuesday	Thursday	Friday
4	Bench Press 340×5×3	Squat 465×5×3	DE Bench Press	DE Squat 345×2×10
	Weighted Dips 4×8	RDL 3×10	250×3×10	Deadlift 530×5
	LTE 3×10	Lat Pulldowns	Press 4×8	Barbell Rows 4×8
		4×8	Triceps Pressdowns	
			3×10	

Descending sets are a good idea on extremely high volume days like 5×10 so that the lifter is not missing reps. This is especially true for triceps-dependent exercises like Dips and Presses. These movements tend to fail rather suddenly during the set when utilized for high reps. It is very difficult to hold sets across. A 5×10 Dip workout might look like this:

Bodyweight ×10
Bodyweight + 50 lbs × 10
Bodyweight + 25 lbs × 10
Bodyweight + 25 lbs × 10 (8 reps, then 2 reps)
Bodyweight × 10

On peaking weeks, the lifter should attempt to set a PR for the specified rep range for one top set. For example, if the Press is prescribed for 4×8, then the workout might look like this:

185×8 (PR)
175×8
165×8×2

POWER SPORTS PROGRAM

The following program has been used with competitive throwers, but would be applicable to any advanced athlete for emphasizing both strength and power.

Phase 1

Olympic Lifts	*Strength*	*Olympic Lifts* (~5% less than Mon)	*Strength*
Monday	Tuesday	Thursday	Friday
Power Snatch	Squat	Power Snatch	Box Squat (DE)
Power Clean	Push Press	Power Clean	Press
	Bench Press		Deadlift

Phase 1 Example

	Olympic Lifts	Strength	Olympic Lifts	Strength
Base	Monday	Tuesday	Thursday	Friday
1	Power Snatch 230×2×3	Squat 465×5×3	Power Snatch 220×2×3	DE Squat 385×2×10
	Power Clean 285×3×3	Push Press 255×3×3	Power Clean 275×3×3	Press 235×5×3
		Bench Press 325×5×3		Deadlift 540×5

Loading

2	Power Snatch 245×2×5	Squat 515×5×5	Power Snatch 235×2×5	DE Squat 450×2×12
	Power Clean 300×3×5	Push Press 285×3×5	Power Clean 290×3×5	Press 260×5×5
		Bench Press 360×5×5		Deadlift 570×5

Deloading

3	Power Snatch 215×2×2	Squat 415×5×2	Power Snatch 205×2×2	DE Squat 385×2×8
	Power Clean 255×3×2	Push Press 225×3×2	Power Clean 245×3×2	Press 210×5×2
		Bench Press 290×5×2		Deadlift 510×3

Peaking

4	Power Snatch 260×2	Squat 550×5	Power Snatch 250×2	DE Squat 420×2×10
	Power Clean 315×3	Push Press 305×3	Power Clean 305×3	Press 275×5
		Bench Press 375×5		Deadlift 600×5

The athlete should run through Phase 1 several times as a training block, each time increasing loads (especially on loading and peaking weeks) and making necessary adjustments on both volume and intensity in each phase. Advanced programming at this level is highly individual and it is nearly impossible to ensure that every set, rep, and load is absolutely optimal. Examples of this adjustment might be shaving off a set or two on a loading week if volume becomes excessive. For a very strong squatter, 3 or 4 sets of 5 might be better than 5 sets for loading. Or perhaps the intensity in the deloading week is a little too low to maintain optimal performance in the peaking week, and the lifter decides to increase percentages by 5%.

After progressing through the Phase 1 block, volume is lowered and intensity is raised for the Phase 2 block prior to competition. Training frequency will also be reduced to three days per week, not only to allow for extra recovery, but also to allow for extra practices and technique work prior to meet day. Run the Phase 2 program only once before the contest.

Phase 2 Example

Base	Monday	Wednesday	Friday
1	Power Snatch 235×2×3	Power Clean 290×3×3	Press 240×3×3
	Rack Jerk 325×1×3	Deadlift 550×3 (reduced to triple for recovery)	Push Press 265×2×3
	Squat 480×3×3		DE Squat 385×2×10
		Bench Press 335×3×3	

Loading			
2	Power Snatch 250×2×5	Power Clean 305×3×5	Press 275×3×5
	Rack Jerk 350×1×5	Deadlift 580×5	Push Press 305×2×5
	Squat 550×3×5	Bench Press 375×3×5	DE Squat 450×2×12

Deloading			
3	Power Snatch 220×2×2	Power Clean 260×3×2	Press 220×3×2
	Rack Jerk 300×1×2	Deadlift 520×3	Push Press 245×2×2
	Squat 440×3×2	Bench Press 300×3×2	DE Squat 385×2×8

Peaking			
4	Power Snatch 265×2	Power Clean 320×3	Press 290×3
	Rack Jerk 375×1	Deadlift 610×5	Push Press 320×2
	Squat 580×3	Bench Press 390×3	DE Squat 420×2×10

THE KSC ADVANCED POWERLIFFTING PROGRAM

The following is an advanced program that operates in a series of 4-week blocks of training. Each training block follows the pattern of 3 weeks of loading, followed by a 1-week deload.

This program has proven to be effective on a 3-day-per-week schedule, training heavy once per week. An additional fourth day can be added on the weekend for an increased volume of bench press-specific assistance work.

Generally, the program is arranged:

Monday – Squat and Squat Assistance

Wednesday – Bench Press and Bench Press Assistance

Friday – Deadlift and Deadlift Assistance

Saturday or Sunday – Bench Press Assistance (optional)

There is a 4-part structure to every training session. First, the lifter will perform a single high-intensity effort set of 1–3 reps in the competition lift for that day. In general, each three week loading block follows a pattern of a triple in week one, a double in week 2, and a single in week 3. As an advanced lifter, these are not intended to be a maximal effort every week. It is important for the coach and the lifter to distinguish between a 3RM and a Heavy Triple – they may not always be the same thing. Using the suggested percentages to start this program, it will likely take several blocks of training to establish new 3RMs, 2RMs, and 1RMs on a weekly basis – ideally, in the 1–3 cycles leading up into a competition. However, the first 2–3 blocks of training it is preferred that the lifter not perform the high-intensity work at PR levels. Instead the focus will be making improvements in other areas of the program.

The second portion of the workout will be volume work with the competition lifts. Here, we have borrowed from legendary powerlifter Fred Hatfield and his CAT principles. CAT, or Compensatory Acceleration Training, is essentially identical to the Dynamic Effort Method. In short, we will be using submaximal weights moved with maximal speed and acceleration. The bulk of the work will be in the 70–80% range for sets of 2–3 reps – submaximal in that these loads could typically be performed for sets of 5–10 reps. However, by keeping reps low and bar speed high, the lifter can maximize force production and minimize accumulating fatigue over the course of weeks and months.

Typically, each 3-week loading block will not focus on increasing loads week to week. Instead, loads will often be held static while volume is increased. The intensity is elevated every training block or every couple of blocks rather than every week. For squats and deadlifts, use between 4 and 6 total sets of 2–3 reps. Some may do better by lowering the deadlift volume to between 3–5 total sets. Some may find that for bench presses, a slightly higher volume of 6–8 total sets can be used. Rest time is generally limited to about 2 minutes between sets.

The third portion of each workout is an assistance exercise for the competition lift. These will generally be barbell-based exercises that resemble the parent lift in performance and in load, but the range of motion is manipulated to address a particular weakness in the ROM. For squats, good assistance exercises include variations of the squat such as high-bar squats, box squats, or pause squats. For the bench press, good choices include close-grip benches or incline presses. Deadlift variations might include deficit deadlifts, stiff-leg deadlifts, or rack pulls.

Assistance exercises are generally trained in the 5–8 rep range with maximal or near-maximal intensity. A common practice is to begin a 3-week block of training with a weight that can be performed for sets of about 8 reps and then add load and reduce reps over the course of 3 weeks so that each block terminates with heavy limit sets of 5 reps. Alternatively, the lifter may be able to sustain a given rep range for 3 weeks, while adding weight each week. In general, as long as improvement is being made week-to-week or block-to-block the finer details are not terribly critical. Subsequent blocks can either repeat this movement again, following a similar rep scheme with added load, or the lifter may choose to rotate to a different exercise for the following block.

The fourth part of each training session is higher-rep assistance work, usually 1–2 exercises that address individual weaknesses. These movements should be lower-stress non-barbell exercises performed for several sets of higher repetitions in the 8–20 range.

Below is a breakdown of an entire week of training:

Monday – Squat and Squat Assistance

> Competition Squat – work up to a top set of 3 @ 85% of 1RM*
>
> Volume/Speed Squat – 4–6 sets of 2–3 reps @ 70-80% of 1RM
>
> Assistance Squat – 1–3 sets of 5–8 reps
>
> Belt Squat – 2–3 sets of 15–20
>
> Glute Ham Raise or Leg Curl 2–3 × 8–10

Wednesday – Bench Press and Bench Assistance

> Competition Bench Press – work up to a top set of 3 @ 85% of 1RM
>
> Volume/Speed Bench – 4–8 sets of 2–3 reps @ 70–80% of 1RM
>
> Assistance Bench Press – 3 sets of 5–8 reps
>
> DB Bench Press or Dips – 3 sets of 10–15 reps
>
> Lying Tricep Extensions – 3 sets of 10–15 reps

Friday – Deadlift and Deadlift Assistance

> Competition Deadlift – work up to a top set of 3 @ 85% of 1RM
>
> Volume/Speed Deadlift – 3–6 sets of 2–3 reps @ 70–80% of 1RM
>
> Assistance Deadlift – 1 set of 5–8 reps
>
> Barbell Rows – 3 sets of 8 reps
>
> Lat Pulldowns – 3 sets of 10–12 reps

Deadlift and squat frequency can be once a week, or it can be increased by adding a lighter squat session or squat variation to Friday's deadlift-focused workout, and a lighter deadlift or deadlift variation to Monday's squat-focused workout.

In the program outlined below, the trainee would have the option of swapping the assistance squat and deadlift exercises on Monday and Friday in order to increase the frequency of the lifts during the week. This is largely a matter of preference as total volume would remain the same. The frequency of each lift will be an individual consideration based on preference and personal experience.

Depending on how close the lifter is to a meet, each block of training can be biased towards volume or intensity. The further out the lifter is from competition the more benefit there may be from increasing training volume with a given load versus raising intensity prematurely. As with the Dynamic Effort Method, the goal of the CAT-style volume sets is not to push the weight up every week. Instead the goal may be to move the same loads with greater bar speeds, greater volumes, or even greater training density (i.e. more work with less rest between sets).

Below is an example of 16 weeks of training (4 blocks) leading towards a competition.

Week	Monday	Wednesday	Friday
1	Squat 85% × 3	Bench Press 85% × 3	Deadlift 85% × 3
	Squat 70% × 3 × 4	Bench Press 70% × 3 × 6	Deadlift 70% × 3 × 4
	High-Bar Squat 3 × 8	Close-Grip Bench 3 × 8	SLDL 1 × 8
	Leg Curl 3 × 8–10	Incline DB Press 2 × 12–15	Barbell Rows 3 × 8–10
	Heavy Abs 3 × 10	LTE 3 × 10–15	Lat Pulldown 3 × 10–12
2	Squat 90% × 2	Bench Press 90% × 2	Deadlift 90% × 2
	Squat 70% × 3 × 5	Bench Press 70% × 3 × 7	Deadlift 70% × 3 × 5
	High-Bar Squat 3 × 6	Close-Grip Bench 3 × 6	SLDL 1 × 8
	Leg Curl 3 × 8–10	Incline DB Press 2 × 12–15	Barbell Rows 3 × 8–10
	Heavy Abs 3 × 10	LTE 3 × 10–15	Lat Pulldown 3 × 10–12
3	Squat 95% × 1	Bench Press 95% × 1	Deadlift 95% × 1
	Squat 70% × 3 × 6	Bench Press 70% × 3 × 8	Deadlift 70% × 3 × 6
	High-Bar Squat 3 × 5	Close-Grip Bench 3 × 5	SLDL 1 × 8
	Leg Curl 3 × 8–10	Incline DB Press 2 × 12–15	Barbell Rows 3 × 8–10
	Heavy Abs 3 × 10	LTE 3 × 10–15	Lat Pulldown 3 × 10–12
4 (Deload)	Squat 85% × 1	Bench Press 85% × 1	Deadlift 85% × 1
	Squat 70% × 2 × 4	Bench Press 70% × 2 × 6	Deadlift 70% × 2 × 4
	Leg Curl 3 × 8–10	Incline DB Press 2 × 12–15	Barbell Rows 3 × 8–10
	Heavy Abs 3 × 10	LTE 3 × 10–15	Lat Pulldown 3 × 10–12
5*	Squat 87% × 3	Bench Press 87% × 3	Deadlift 87% × 3
	Squat 75% × 3 × 4	Bench Press 75% × 3 × 6	Deadlift 75% × 3 × 4
	High-Bar Squat 3 × 8	Incline Bench Press 3 × 8	SLDL 1 × 6
	Leg Curl 3 × 8–10	Dips 3 × 10–15	Barbell Rows 3 × 8–10
	Heavy Abs 3 × 10	LTE 3 × 10–15	Lat Pulldown 3 × 10–12
6	Squat 92% × 2	Bench Press 92% × 2	Deadlift 92% × 2
	Squat 75% × 3 × 5	Bench Press 75% × 3 × 7	Deadlift 75% × 3 × 5
	High-Bar Squat 3 × 6	Incline Bench Press 3 × 6	SLDL 1 × 6
	Leg Curl 3 × 8–10	Dips 3 × 10–15	Barbell Rows 3 × 8–10
	Heavy Abs 3 × 10	LTE 3 × 10–15	Lat Pulldown 3 × 10–12

*Beginning in Week 5, it is not necessary to use percentages for the single top set. It is better to use the training data from the previous training cycle to guide load selection for the heavier attempts. Percentages are used here for illustration purposes only.

Week	Monday	Wednesday	Friday
7	Squat 97% × 1	Bench Press 97% × 1	Deadlift 97% × 1
	Squat 75% × 3 × 6	Bench Press 75% × 3 × 8	Deadlift 75% × 3 × 6
	High-Bar Squat 3 × 5	Incline Bench Press 3 × 5	SLDL 1 × 5
	Leg Curl 3 × 8–10	Dips 3 × 10–15	Barbell Rows 3 × 8–10
	Heavy Abs 3 × 10	LTE 3 × 10–15	Lat Pulldown 3 × 10–12
8 (Deload)	Squat 85% × 1	Bench Press 85% × 1	Deadlift 85% × 1
	Squat 75% × 2 × 4	Bench Press 75% × 2 × 6	Deadlift 75% × 2 × 4
	Leg Curl 3 × 8–10	Dips 3 × 10–15	Barbell Rows 3 × 8–10
	Heavy Abs 3 × 10	LTE 3 × 10–15	Lat Pulldown 3 × 10–12
9	Squat 89% × 3	Bench Press 89% × 3	Deadlift 89% × 3
	Squat 80% × 2 × 4	Bench Press 80% × 2 × 6	Deadlift 80% × 2 × 4
	Pause Squat 3 × 5	Close-Grip Bench 3 × 8	Deficit Deadlift 1 × 8
	Glute/Ham Raise 3 × 8	Incline DB Press 2 × 12–15	Pull-ups 3 × 8–10
	Heavy Abs 3 × 10	Cable Pressdowns 3 × 15–20	DB Rows 2 × 12–15
10	Squat 94% × 2	Bench Press 94% × 2	Deadlift 94% × 2
	Squat 80% × 2 × 5	Bench Press 80% × 2 × 7	Deadlift 80% × 2 × 5
	Pause Squat 3 × 5	Close-Grip Bench 3 × 6	Deficit Deadlift 1 × 6
	Glute/Ham Raise 3 × 8	Incline DB Press 2 × 12–15	Pull-ups 3 × 8–10
	Heavy Abs 3 × 10	Cable Pressdowns 3 × 15–20	DB Rows 2 × 12–15
11	Squat 99% × 1	Bench Press 99% × 1	Deadlift 99% × 3
	Squat 80% × 2 × 6	Bench Press 80% × 2 × 8	Deadlift 80% × 2 × 6
	Pause Squat 3 × 5	Close-Grip Bench 3 × 5	Deficit Deadlift 1 × 5
	Glute/Ham Raise 3 × 8	Incline DB Press 2 × 12–15	Pull-ups 3 × 8–10
	Heavy Abs 3 × 10	Cable Pressdowns 3 × 15–20	DB Rows 2 × 12–15
12 (Deload)	Squat 85% × 1	Bench Press 85% × 1	Deadlift 85% × 1
	Squat 75% × 2 × 4	Bench Press 75% × 2 × 6	Deadlift 75% × 2 × 4
	Glute/Ham Raise 3 × 8	Incline DB Press 2 × 12–15	Pull-ups 3 × 8–10
	Heavy Abs 3 × 10	Cable Pressdowns 3 × 15–20	DB Rows 2 × 12–15
13	Squat 91% × 3	Bench Press 91% × 3	Deadlift 91% × 3
	Squat 80% × 3 × 4	Bench Press 80% × 3 × 6	Deadlift 80% × 3 × 4
	Pause Squat 1 × 5	Floor Press 3 × 5	Rack Pulls 1 × 5
	Glute/Ham Raise 3 × 8	Dips 3 × 10–15	Barbell Rows 3 × 5
	Heavy Abs 3 × 10	LTE 3 × 10–15	Lat Pulldown 3 × 10–12

Week	Monday	Wednesday	Friday
14	Squat 96% × 2	Bench Press 96% × 2	Deadlift 96% × 2
	Squat 80% × 3 × 5	Bench Press 80% × 3 × 7	Deadlift 80% × 3 × 5
	Pause Squat 1 × 5	Floor Press 3 × 5	Rack Pulls 1 × 5
	Glute/Ham Raise 3 × 8	Dips 3 × 10–15	Barbell Rows 3 × 5
	Heavy Abs 3 × 10	LTE 3 × 10–15	Lat Pulldown 3 × 10–12
15	Squat 101% × 1	Bench Press 101% × 1	Deadlift 101% × 1
	Squat 80% × 3 × 6	Bench Press 80% × 3 × 8	Deadlift 80% × 3 × 6
	Pause Squat 1 × 5	Floor Press 3 × 5	Rack Pulls 1 × 5
	Glute/Ham Raise 3 × 8	Dips 3 × 10–15	Barbell Rows 3 × 5
	Heavy Abs 3 × 10	LTE 3 × 10–15	Lat Pulldown 3 × 10–12

Week	Tuesday	Thursday	Saturday
16	Squat 80% × 2 × 4	Squat 60% × 2 × 4	Meet
	Bench Press 80% × 3 × 4	Bench Press 60% × 2 × 4	

For pre-meet purposes, some lifters may prefer Monday as the Deadlift focused session, with the Squat session performed on Friday. This would allow more time for recovery between the last heavy deadlift session prior to the meet, and a smaller gap between the meet and the last heavy squat session.

Additionally, the week before a meet can be somewhat individual in terms of how much or how little volume and intensity a trainee prefers to do. Many lifters prefer just one light session instead of two.

AN ADVANCED OLYMPIC WEIGHTLIFTING PROGRAM

The following 12-week program is a strength-based approach to the problem of advanced Olympic weightlifting programming. It is an adaptation of the principles of the famous Bulgarian coach Ivan Abadjiev that come to us through our good friend Jim Moser who adapted the program using some of the philosophies of the Starting Strength program. Moser and his sons worked with Abadjiev extensively.

The snatch and the clean & jerk are excellent ways to display the aspect of strength we call "power," but they are not very good at building or maintaining it. The Olympic lifts are not limited by absolute strength, but rather showcase the ability to convert that strength into explosive force using efficient technique. Since the ability to explode is largely controlled by the genetic capacity for neuromuscular efficiency, the snatch, clean, and jerk are limited thereby, and these lifts lack the capacity to *train* absolute strength. The nature of Olympic lifting – technique-dependent singles at weights light enough to be accelerated – precludes the use of the snatch and the clean & jerk for strength development for any post-novice lifter. For all but a handful of lifters gifted with amazing explosive ability – and therefore the capacity to recruit enough motor units in an explosive lift to adequately *train* their contraction in the *practice* of explosive movements – Olympic lifters must do the same thing to get strong and stay strong that the rest of us do: they must squat, press, and deadlift heavy weights.

This program integrates the two types of training. It assumes a lifter in his mid-20s at a bodyweight of 115 (all weights are in kilos in this program), with a snatch of 165, C&J 200, squat 300, press 150, deadlift 320, bench press 200, and front squat 230 – strong, but not strong enough to succeed at the international level. This program is designed for a lifter who is already accustomed to a high volume of training, *and cannot be used for an unadapted lifter.*

Notes:

1) The sequence "front squat/snatch/clean&jerk/front squat" indicates a warm-up to a fairly heavy front squat single, followed by a progression of snatch singles to a heavy snatch or a missed attempt depending on where in the schedule it is, a progression of singles to a heavy C&J or a miss, and another run up to a heavy single front squat. The weights used are determined by the lifter each day, based on his subjective assessment of his condition. The initial front squat single prepares the lifter's brain for the heavy explosive efforts that follow without tapping-in too deeply, and the last front squat teaches the lifter's body the continued application of strength under conditions of fatigue – like that always encountered in a 3rd attempt on the meet platform. If a miss is called for, the first missed attempt at work weight (not during the run-up) stops the progression. If "-10 back to 1 miss" is called for, the load is lowered 10 kg and then a second run-up is performed in 2.5–3 kg jumps up to the missed weight. If the miss is made, stop and go to the next lift.

2) Rack jerks are dropped to the platform and reloaded. Do not lower and re-rack these. Eccentric shoulder work is important, and is adequately trained during the press, and isometric work is trained at the end of the cycle with jerk supports.

3) This program is designed to expose the lifter to a very high volume of heavy snatch and C&J singles, so that the lifter gets used to performing the contest lifts with a high degree of technical proficiency at the weights encountered at the contest. The technique used for light snatches and C&Js *do not carry over* to heavy attempts, so heavy singles must be done. The driver behind the ability to handle the heavy explosive load is the strength base, which increases along the guidelines of the TSFOSB method.

4) The taper at the end of the program is critical to the success of the program, and cannot be omitted to continue the cycle. It cannot be emphasized enough that **this program is a brutal exposure to loads that will overtrain any lifter** if not used properly, and proper use entails an appreciation of the purpose of the taper for the peaking effect at the contest. The combination of the use of high numbers of heavy snatch/C&J singles with periodized absolute-strength components makes this a potent dose of physical stress for the advanced competitive lifter, and this must be understood and respected. Some days will probably entail the use of 2 workouts per day, if not more. If multiple workouts are used, the FS/Sn/C&J/FS sequence should be done in one session.

Week	Monday	Tuesday	Wednesday
1	Front Squat Snatch to 1 miss, -10 back to 1 miss C&J to 1 miss, -10 back to 1 miss Front Squat	Snatch 130×1×15, 1min Rack Jerk 200, 205, 210, 215 Press 112.5×5×3 Squat 230×5×3	Front Squat Snatch to 1 miss C&J to 1 miss Front Squat
2	Front Squat Snatch to 1 miss, -10 back to 1 miss C&J to 1 miss, -10 back to 1 miss Front Squat	Snatch 133×1×15, 1min Rack Jerk 200, 210, 215, 215 Press 125×5×5 Squat 255×5×5	Front Squat Snatch to 1 miss C&J to 1 miss Front Squat
3	Front Squat Snatch to 1 miss, -10 back to 1 miss C&J to 1 miss, -10 back to 1 miss Front Squat	Snatch 135×1×15, 1min Rack Jerk 200×1×4 Press 100×5×2 Squat 205×5×5	Front Squat Snatch to 1 miss C&J to 1 miss Front Squat
4	Front Squat Snatch to 1 miss, -10 back to 1 miss C&J to 1 miss, -10 back to 1 miss Front Squat	Snatch 137×1×15, 1min Rack Jerk 205, 210, 215, 220 Press 135×5 Squat 275×5	Front Squat Snatch to 1 miss C&J to 1 miss Front Squat
5	Front Squat Snatch to 1 miss, -10 back to 1 miss C&J to 1 miss, -10 back to 1 miss Front Squat	Snatch 139×1×15, 1min Rack Jerk 200, 205, 210×1×2 Press 117.5×3×3 Squat 240×3×3	Front Squat Snatch to 1 miss C&J to 1 miss Front Squat
6	Front Squat Snatch to 1 miss, -10 back to 1 miss C&J to 1 miss, -10 back to 1 miss Front Squat	Snatch 141×1×15, 1min Rack Jerk 208, 213, 218, 222 Press 135×3×3 Squat 275×3×3	Front Squat Snatch to 1 miss C&J to 1 miss Front Squat

Week	Thursday	Friday	Saturday
1	C&J 162×1×10, 2min Power Clean 165×2×3 Front Squat 190×3×3	Front Squat Snatch to 1 miss, -10 back to 1 miss C&J to 1 miss, -10 back to 1 miss Front Squat	Front Squat Snatch to 1 miss C&J to 1 miss Bench Press 190×5×3
2	C&J 164×1×10, 2min Power Snatch 133×2×3 Front Squat 210×3×3	Front Squat Snatch to 1 miss, -10 back to 1 miss C&J to 1 miss, -10 back to 1 miss Front Squat	Front Squat Snatch to 1 miss C&J to 1 miss Deadlift 320×5
3	C&J 166×1×10, 2min Power Clean 166×2×2 Front Squat 170×2×2	Front Squat Snatch to 1 miss, -10 back to 1 miss C&J to 1 miss, -10 back to 1 miss Front Squat	Front Squat Snatch to 1 miss C&J to 1 miss Front Squat Bench Press 195×5×3
4	C&J 168×1×10, 2min Power Snatch 137×2×2 Front Squat 218×3	Front Squat Snatch to 1 miss, -10 back to 1 miss C&J to 1 miss, -10 back to 1 miss Front Squat	Front Squat Snatch to 1 miss C&J to 1 miss Deadlift 305×5
5	C&J 170×1×10, 2.5min Power Clean 170×2×2 Front Squat 177×2×3	Front Squat Snatch to 1 miss, -10 back to 1 miss C&J to 1 miss, -10 back to 1 miss Front Squat	Front Squat Snatch to 1 miss C&J to 1 miss Front Squat Bench Press 200×5×2
6	C&J 172×1×10, 2.5min Power Snatch 140×2×2 Front Squat 218×2×4	Front Squat Snatch to 1 miss, -10 back to 1 miss C&J to 1 miss, -10 back to 1 miss Front Squat	Front Squat Snatch to 1 miss C&J to 1 miss Deadlift 315×3

Week	Monday	Tuesday	Wednesday
7	Front Squat Snatch to 1 miss, -10 back to 1 miss C&J to 1 miss, -10 back to 1 miss Front Squat	Snatch 143×1×10, 1min Rack Jerk 205×1×2, 210×1×2 Press 108×3×2 Squat 220×2×3	Front Squat Snatch to 1 miss C&J to 1 miss Front Squat
8	Front Squat Snatch to 1 miss, -10 back to 1 miss C&J to 1 miss, -10 back to 1 miss Front Squat	Snatch 146×1×10, 1min Rack Jerk 200, 210, 218, 225 Press 157×3 Squat 285×3	Front Squat Snatch to 1 miss C&J to 1 miss Front Squat
9	Front Squat Snatch to 1 miss, -10 back to 1 miss C&J to 1 miss, -10 back to 1 miss Front Squat	Snatch 149×1×10, 2min Rack Jerk 210, 215, 220×1×2 Press 141×3×3 Squat 260×3×3	Front Squat Snatch to 1 miss C&J to 1 miss Front Squat
10	Front Squat Snatch to 1 miss, -10 back to 1 miss C&J to 1 miss, -10 back to 1 miss Front Squat	Snatch 152×1×8, 2min Rack Jerk 220, 225, 230 Press 160 ×1×5 Squat 295×1×5	Front Squat Snatch to 1 miss C&J to 1 miss Front Squat
11	Front Squat Snatch to 1 miss, -10 back to 1 miss C&J to 1 miss, -10 back to 1 miss Front Squat	Snatch 155×1×5, 3min Rack Jerk 230, 240 Press 135×2×2 Squat 245×2×2	
12	Front Squat Snatch C&J Front Squat		Front Squat Snatch to opener C&J to opener

Week	Thursday	Friday	Saturday
7	C&J 175×1×8, 3min Power Clean 175×1×2 Front Squat 165×2×3	Front Squat Snatch to 1 miss, -10 back to 1 miss C&J to 1 miss, -10 back to 1 miss Front Squat	Front Squat Snatch to 1 miss C&J to 1 miss Front Squat Bench Press 205×3×2
8	C&J 178×1×7, 3min Power Snatch 145×1×2 Front Squat 225×2	Front Squat Snatch to 1 miss, -10 back to 1 miss C&J to 1 miss, -10 back to 1 miss Front Squat Jerk Support 235×5×2	Front Squat Snatch to 1 miss C&J to 1 miss Deadlift 320×3
9	C&J 181×1×6, 3min Power Clean 181×1 Front Squat 200×2×3	Front Squat Snatch to 1 miss, -10 back to 1 miss C&J to 1 miss, -10 back to 1 miss Jerk Support 250×5	Front Squat Snatch to 1 miss C&J to 1 miss Front Squat Bench Press 210×3×2
10	C&J 183×1×5, 3min Power Snatch 150×1 Front Squat 230×1×5	Front Squat Snatch to 1 miss, -10 back to 1 miss C&J to 1 miss, -10 back to 1 miss Jerk Support 265×5	Front Squat Snatch C&J (no misses) Deadlift 325×2
11	C&J 185×1×5, 3min Front Squat 185×2×2	Front Squat Snatch C&J Jerk Support 275×3	Front Squat Snatch C&J Front Squat
12	Snatch C&J		**MEET**

It is likely that the most advanced athletes in the world will not require programming beyond the complexity presented here. If they do, their experiences in having reached that point will have equipped them for this adventure. Athletics at the elite level is a highly individual thing, and all who have the ability to perform at this level have also acquired the ability to exercise judgment commensurate with the physical capacities they possess. Experiment, learn, and, above all, teach those of us who want to know.

9

Special Populations

We have argued that highly individualized training is necessary to reach close to full physical potential, and that the closer the trainee gets to his potential performance, the more important this specificity becomes. But this raises a very important question: Do the training models presented here, when applied at the appropriate level – novice, intermediate, and advanced – work for all populations? Do they work for women, children, older people, and injured people? And the answer is: Yes, they pretty much do.

Women

It is very important to understand the following exceptionally true thing: women are not a special population. They are half of the population. With a few exceptions regarding sets and reps, they are trained in the same way as men of the same age and level of training advancement. By virtue of a different hormonal profile – and the chronic and acute effects of that hormonal profile, from her date of conception until she competes in her last meet – the rate and the magnitude of change in strength, power, and mass will differ, but the biological processes that bring about those changes are otherwise the same as those in men. Since the processes are the same, the methods used to affect progress are also the same. And the response to the method depends on the effectiveness of the method, not the sex of the individual using it. Many excuses have been made over the centuries that exercise has been practiced, sometimes by women, but usually *for* them. The bottom line is that everyone, regardless of sex, gets out of a correctly designed training program exactly what they put into it. Ineffective "firming and toning" routines have no basis in physiology, and the results obtained from them demonstrate this rather conclusively.

That said, there are several important differences between the performances of men and women, both in the weight room and on the field. As a general rule, women do not have the same level of neuromuscular efficiency as men. There will be overlap between the top 30% of women and the bottom 30% of men, but men are, on average, stronger and more explosive than women. This is probably due to the differences in hormonal profile, specifically the acute and chronic effects of the much lower levels of testosterone they have been exposed to since before birth, and it is evident across the spectrum of performance.

Volume (reps)

Intensity (%1RM)	Light	Medium	Heavy
100	—	—	1
90	—	2	5
80	5	8	10
70	8	10	12
60	10	12	15
50	15	25	25+

Relative Intensity

Table 9-1. The women's version of Table 7-1, illustrating the difficulty of a rep scheme as it varies with volume and intensity. The numbers in the table represent reps.

Women can use a higher percentage of their 1RM for more reps than men can, because of their inability to recruit maximum numbers of motor units into contraction. Women can do more reps closer to 1RM because they don't use as many of their motor units for each rep, and fewer of the available pool used per rep means more unfatigued motor units to use in the next rep. More reserve capacity means more reps per set at any submaximal intensity. A female's 1RM performance is therefore not as efficient in demonstrating what in a male would be his true *absolute strength*. Women's performances in the standing vertical jump, throws, snatches, cleans, jerks, and other explosive movements that involve high levels of motor unit recruitment are also performed at lower levels than those by men of the same size and level of training advancement. And women's upper-body strength suffers from the large relative difference in local muscle mass distribution. All these things explain why there are women's divisions in essentially all sports. Even golf, tennis, table tennis, and billiards have separate women's divisions.

As a practical matter, if daily, weekly, or monthly programming models are used to increase strength or power, some modifications are required for women since the intensities used are based on the individual 1RM, and women can work with a higher percentage of this 1RM for reps. For example, Table 7-1 indicates that 70% for 10 reps would constitute a heavy set with a high adaptive stimulus, when, for women, this is only a medium set with a moderate adaptive stimulus. By the same token, if increased mass is the goal, a relatively larger amount of high-volume work over a longer time at a slightly higher intensity would be needed. Table 9-1 adapts the data in Table 7-1 for female populations.

The menstrual cycle may introduce a scheduling factor. The variability of discomfort and the associated effects of menses requires close cooperation between trainee and coach, especially at higher levels of training advancement where a competitive schedule will demand attention to all performance and training parameters. For novice women, it will present no greater an obstacle to training than it does for anything else in the monthly schedule.

One other consideration: the average American female is protein, iron, and calcium deficient. All of these deficiencies may affect health and performance. Most American women, in a misguided attempt to reduce fat intake, have managed to also reduce their protein intake to levels below that which will support training and recovery. Protein intake for female athletes should follow the same guidelines used for men – 1 gram per pound of bodyweight per day. Low iron stores can affect metabolism and

Figure 9-1. Women are more likely to believe that weight training is unimportant to health and sports performance than men. There is also a social and media-driven misconception that all weight training produces big, masculine, muscle-bound physiques. This generally does not occur in women without anabolic steroids. The strongest women in the United States perform at their best and look healthy and athletic through the use of correctly designed weight training programs.

oxygen transport, leading to a perception of chronic low energy or fatigue. Altering the diet to include more iron-rich foods, cooking with cast iron cookware, and dietary iron supplementation are good ideas. Low calcium intakes predispose every age group to lower bone density and degeneration (osteopenia). Virtually every study examining weight training with osteoporotic women shows dramatic improvement in bone density. Adequate calcium is needed to allow this adapation to occur.

So, there are differences in the physical characteristics of the two sexes, but they still are trained the same way. The mechanisms of stress/recovery/adaptation may be constrained at different levels by the hormonal milieu, but they operate the same way. Vertebrate physiology is much older than the human species; with very few exceptions, the rules are the same for all of us. Tissues adapt to stress by getting stronger, and the physiological response to the stress is a function of the stress, not the sex of the organism to which the tissue belongs.

Novice & Intermediate Training

For a novice woman, 5-lb jumps on the squat and deadlift will be used, and will normally continue for as many weeks as any normal novice progression. Perhaps on the 2nd or 3rd workout a 10-lb jump may be taken – this is sometimes the case when the initial weights have to be kept artificially low due to the inability to grasp some technical aspect of a lift. Such a breakthrough can happen on squats and deadlifts, while this seldom occurs with upper-body movements. Bench Presses, Presses, and Power Cleans may allow 5-lb jumps over the first few workouts, but will begin microloading – the use of plates smaller than 2.5 lb/1.25 kg to allow smaller than 5-lb incremental increases – by the 2nd or 3rd week, and sometimes as soon as the second workout for very petite women.

Typically women will start training with sets of 5 just like men – 3 sets across for squats, benches, and presses. Women typically can do sets across for deadlifts as well, for the neuromuscular reasons already discussed. But after about 6–8 weeks, experience has shown that the novice progression lasts longer if the reps switch from 3 sets of 5 to 5 sets of 3 after the first sign of a slowdown. Given the neuromuscular inefficiency inherent in women's physiology, the stress produced by the slightly heavier triple at the same 15-rep volume more closely simulates the effect males get from 3 sets of 5.

Example novice progression, 1-month snapshot. In this example, we assume that the basic novice linear progression has been followed for 6–8 weeks and steady progress has been made for sets of 5 on the squat, press, bench press, and deadlift.

Week	Monday	Wednesday	Friday
7	Squat 115×5×3	Squat 120×5×3	Squat 125×5×3
	Bench Press 80×5×3	Press 60×5×3	Bench Press 82×5×3
	Deadlift 145×5×3	Power Clean 70×3×5	Deadlift 150×5×3
8	Squat 130×5×3	Squat 135×5×3	Squat 140×4, 4, 3
	Press 62×5×3	Bench Press 84×5×3	Press 64×4, 4, 3
	Power Clean 72×3×5	Deadlift 155×5×2, 155×4	Power Clean 74×3×5

Switch to triples across

Week	Monday	Wednesday	Friday
9	Squat 140×3×5	Squat 145×3×5	Squats 150×3×5
	Bench Press 86×3×5	Press 64×3×5	Bench Press 88×3×5
	Deadlift 160×3×4	Power Clean 76×3×5	Deadlift 165×3×4
10	Squat 152×3×5	Squat 154×3×5	Squat 156×3×5
	Press 66×3×5	Bench Press 90×3×5	Press 68×3×5
	Power Clean 78×3×5	Deadlift 170×3×4	Power Clean 80×3×5

The lifter will sustain this simple progression for as long as possible, perhaps undergoing just one reset when progress comes to a halt and she starts missing reps. This typically adds 3–4 months to the length of time the novice progression can work for a female. Once she stagnates for a second time, she will move on to intermediate training.

Intermediate training will be set up along the same modified guideline as the novice program. Volume will be accumulated through 5–6 sets of triples, and the first few weeks of intensity day training will attempt 3RMs. After just a few weeks of trying for 3RMs, she will switch her intensity-day focus to singles and doubles, while maintaining progress for triples across on volume day.

For an early intermediate or novice male lifter the deadlift and power clean are mutually beneficial. The absolute strength developed on a deadlift helps to improve power cleans, while the volume and speed of power clean training help to improve the deadlift. Often, as the male grows in strength the power clean becomes less help to the deadlift, due to either technical inefficiency or the genetic inability to produce high levels of power. For women, very few have the innate ability to express a high degree of power anyway. So, for a female trainee it is highly unlikely that volume on the Olympic lifts will drive progress on the deadlift, and that a strong deadlift is a big help to her snatch and clean pull. (This one-sided relationship – with the deadlift and squat driving all progress on all pulling exercises – is an important thing for women's Olympic weightlifting to realize.) For women, it might be best to keep the deadlift as a volume-day stressor.

Women's Texas Method Example. Phase 1 will use 6 triples across as the volume day load, set at about 90–95% of the 3RM on Friday. Typically, women will use a larger percentage of their repetition maximum for volume day work. But, as with men, it may take a few workouts to determine the optimum percentage offset between volume and intensity days. As the trainee gets stronger, her percentage offset may increase and she may also switch from 6 sets across to just 5.

Bench Presses and Presses will alternate in priority every other week. On bench-focused weeks, presses will be trained for 3×3 at about 90%–95% of volume day weights. On press-focused weeks, bench presses will be trained for 3×3 at about 90–95% of volume day weights.

Power Cleans and Power Snatches will also alternate priority from week to week. On Friday, the heavy day will use 6 sets of doubles for a PR, and the Wednesday light day will use 3 sets of doubles for about 90–95% of the 6×2 PR.

Program Overview:

Phase 1

Week	Monday	Wednesday	Friday
1	Squat 6×3 (90%–95% of 3RM) Bench Press 6×3 (90%–95% of 3RM) Deadlift 3RM, back off 5 lb ×3×2	Squat 3×3 (90% of Monday) Press 3×3 (90%–95% of volume day presses) Power Snatch 3×2 (90–95% of volume day snatch)	Squat 3RM Bench Press 3RM Power Clean 6×2 (PR)
2	Squat 6×3 Press 6×3 Deadlift 3RM, back off 5lb ×3×2	Squat 3×3 Bench 3×3 (90%–95% of volume day bench presses) Power Clean 3×2 (90%–95% of volume day power cleans)	Squat 3RM Press 3RM Power Snatch 6×2 (PR)

Phase 2

The primary adjustment will be a drop from strictly 3RMs on Friday to a rotation of doubles and singles. If Power Snatches and Power Cleans cease to progress for doubles, then the trainee may benefit from adding heavier singles on Friday. Timed singles on a 1–2 minute clock are a good way to accumulate volume at a high percentage of 1RM.

Example 1 Month Progression in Phase 1:

Week	Monday	Wednesday	Friday
1	Squat 160×3×6 Bench Press 100×3×6 Deadlift 205×3, 200×3×2	Squat 145×3×3 Press 75×3×3 Power Snatch 110×2×3	Squat 175×3 Bench Press 115×3 Power Clean 150×2×6
2	Squat 162.5×3×6 Press 80×3×6 Deadlift 210×3, 205×3×2	Squat 147.5×3×3 Bench 90×3×3 Power Clean 135×2×3	Squat 177.5×3 Press 90×3 Power Snatch 120×2×6
3	Squat 165×3×6 Bench Press 102.5×3×6 Deadlift 215×3, 210×3×2	Squat 150×3×3 Press 77×3×3 Power Snatch 112×2×3	Squat 180×3 Bench Press 117.5×3 Power Clean 152×2×6
4	Squat 167.5×3×6 Press 82×3×6 Deadlift 220×3, 215×3×2	Squat 152.5×3×3 Bench 92.5×3×3 Power Clean 137×2×3	Squat 182.5×3 Press 92×3 Power Snatch 122×2×6

Example 1 Month Progression in Phase 2:

Week	Monday	Wednesday	Friday
1	Squat 170×3×6 Bench Press 105×3×6 Deadlift 225×3×4	Squat 155×3×3 Press 79×3×3 Power Snatch 115×2×3	Squat 185×2×3 Bench Press 120×2×3 Power Clean 155×1×10
2	Squat 172.5×3×6 Press 84×3×6 Deadlift 230×3×4	Squat 157.5×3×3 Bench Press 95×3×3 Power Clean 140×2×3	Squat 195×1×5 Press 94×2×3 Power Snatch 125×1×10
3	Squat 175×3×6 Bench Press 107.5×3×6 Deadlift 235×3×4	Squat 160×3×3 Press 82×3×3 Power Snatch 117×2×3	Squat 187.5×2×3 Bench Press 125×1×5 Power Clean 157×1×10
4	Squat 177.5×3×6 Press 86×3×6 Deadlift 240×3×4	Squat 162.5×3×3 Bench Press 97.5×3×3 Power Clean 142×2×3	Squat 200×1×5 Press 98×1×5 Power Snatch 127×1×10

Youth

The long history of the human race demonstrates conclusively that the children and young people of our species are quite capable of handling loads while remaining uninjured, and indeed reach their physical potential despite – or perhaps because of – work that is often regarded as heavy by modern society. Every big, strong, healthy farm kid who grew up hauling hay attests to this obvious fact. What are the chances that the human race evolved in the absence of the need for the young of the species to occasionally lift heavy things? The population-wide paucity of adults stunted or otherwise irreparably damaged by the handling of heavy loads – barbell or otherwise – attests to the ability of humans of all ages to successfully adapt to the stresses of work and growing up with vigorous physical interaction with their environments.

Although the ACSM's standards of care and resource manual now considers youth weight training to be safe and healthy, there remains in the medical community a strong bias against using physically taxing methods of strength training on teenage and younger populations. One professional association of pediatricians recommends that only moderate weights with moderate repetitions be used. They strongly discourage high-volume work (enough sets and reps to increase muscle mass) and high-intensity work, the kind necessary to develop strength and power. They provide a variety of reasons for training youth using only machines with predetermined movement pathways, thus limiting the development of balance and coordination. This group of medical professionals actually recommends that all high-intensity and high-volume training be postponed until full sexual maturity. This would effectively remove the vast majority of high school athletes from weight rooms, soccer fields, and swimming pools, and compromise an athlete's safety and performance during full-contact sporting events (which, interestingly enough, are not discouraged).

When the scientific and medical literature is evaluated objectively, a different picture emerges. Training loads (relative to 1RM), frequencies, and durations similar to those commonly used in the training of competitive weightlifters are effective in increasing strength in children, and a significant body of scientific evidence and practical experience supports this fact. Strength increases in youth are closely related to the intensity of training; higher-intensity programs can and do increase strength in preadolescents in six weeks or less. This is because the mechanisms of adaptation are functioning the same way they do in adults, albeit without the benefit of the adult hormonal milieu.

The safety of this type of training for kids is well documented. Programs supervised by qualified coaches, in which training loads are prescribed and monitored by professionals, have proven to be safer than typical physical education classes. Several studies since the 1970s have reported extremely low to zero rates of injury during training programs of from several weeks to a year in duration and have suggested that weight training prevents injury rather than causes it. Even the handling of maximum weights by children has been scrutinized for safety. Avery Faigenbaum showed that properly supervised maximal lifting in 6- to 12-year-olds resulted in no injuries, providing further evidence that even high-intensity training, properly supervised, can be a safe and healthy undertaking for children. The AAU Junior Olympic Games has long featured Olympic weightlifting, and has somehow weathered the scrutiny of the pediatric medical community.

Properly conducted weight training programs are safe for children for the same reason they are safe for everyone else: they are normal human movements that are scalable. The loads used can be precisely adjusted to the ability of the child to use them with correct technique. Correct technical execution prevents injury, since by definition "correct" means controlled, even for explosive movements. The load on a 5-kg bar can be increased one kilogram at a time, allowing very fine control over the stress that a child experiences in the weight room. Contrast this with team sports that involve ballistic skills, a speeding ball, and other kids moving rapidly under varying degrees of control. Uncontrolled

Injury Rate	Sport or Activity	Injury Rate	Sport or Activity
6.2	Soccer	0.1	Squash
1.92	Rugby	0.07	Tennis
1.03	Basketball	0.05	Badminton
0.57	U.S. Track-and-Field	0.044	Gymnastics
0.37	Cross-country	0.0012	Weight Training
0.26	U.K. Track-and-Field	0.0008	Powerlifting (competitive)
0.18	Physical Education	0.0006	Weightlifting (competitive)
0.1	Football		

Table 9-2. Injury rates per 100 participation hours in various sports. From Hamill, B. "Relative safety of weight lifting and weight training." *Journal of Strength Conditioning Research* 8(1):53–57, 1994.

impact and rapid deceleration are inherent in such sports and the forces they apply to a child's body are unpredictable, completely unscalable, and therefore unsafe, as injury rates in the world's most dangerous sport, soccer, conclusively demonstrate. If you add American football pads to this scenario, which blunt the perception of the effects of impact between the players, you are bound to get the types of injuries that occur when kids run into each other thinking it won't hurt very badly.

RECOMMENDATIONS

Based on the available medical and scientific data and the decades of experience of the authors, we strongly recommend the following guidelines for youth weight training:

1) Weight training programs for youth should be conducted by well-trained adults. In the current absence of educational opportunities at the collegiate level, adults become well-trained through personal experience, coaching experience, study, and association with other competent professionals. *It is imperative that parents evaluate the qualifications of those potentially charged with coaching their children.*

2) To effectively and safely coach youth weight training in a group setting, a coach/trainee ratio of 1:10 or better is recommended. Every weight room is a teaching environment, not just a fitness facility where kids exercise. Any facility – private, commercial, or educational – that allows children and adolescents to train without instruction and active supervision at an adequate coach/kid ratio is inviting problems.

3) Weight training should take place in facilities properly equipped to support safe training practices.

4) Properly supervised skill-based weightlifting programs (and gymnastics, dance, soccer, martial arts, and all other physical programs) are appropriate for children and can commence as early as 6 years of age.

5) The use of maximum training loads has been alleged to place the young athlete at risk of injury. No data exists that substantiates this claim. The use of maximal and near-maximal loads is encouraged, under the proper supervision *using proper warm-up and proper technique.* These loads should be used cautiously and applied only as part of a regimented training program for technically proficient trainees.

6) The primary problem encountered when training younger children and adolescents is the inability to effectively control the eccentric portion of a weighted movement. The descent in a squat or the lowering of the bar in other exercises is a skill that many young trainees will have to be taught as a specific part of the instruction.

7) The use of novice programming with kids must be based upon the maturity of the kid, and the ability to recover from progressively heavier loads will depend largely upon maturity and hormonal status. It is recommended that no attempt be made to apply the full novice linear progression until Tanner Stage 4 has been reached.

8) Training should be fun. Kids are motivated by fun. When training is no longer fun, kids will no longer want to train, *and should not be forced to.*

Older Lifters

Masters athletes, usually defined as individuals 35–40 years of age and over, depending on the sport, are a growing population. As the U.S. population ages, masters competitions are increasing in popularity across the spectrum of sports. Depending on the sport, it is not uncommon to see younger masters-age-group athletes do quite well in national and international events competing against much younger athletes. Powerlifting has a long tradition of masters athletes winning in open competition. The only thing preventing a middle-aged trainee from getting stronger, bigger, and more powerful is his own attitude about training and age.

As humans advance beyond middle-age, some significant changes generally occur. Sarcopenia (loss of muscle cells), increased body fat, performance loss, and reduced flexibility are common effects of aging. This is largely because the average adult has a greatly reduced activity level and becomes increasingly sedentary, which leads to a loss in muscle mass (atrophy); in the totally inactive older adult, this loss is compounded by sarcopenia. The loss of functional muscle causes a loss of performance. It has been demonstrated that about 15% of performance capacity can be lost per decade with inactivity, and even when activity is maintained at a relatively high level the loss of performance proceeds with age. The logical extension of this accumulating loss in performance is ultimately the loss of functional mobility, unless steps are taken to prevent this as much as possible.

A significant aspect of the loss of muscle mass is the unfortunate fact that the loss seems to be selective for the higher-threshold motor units that contribute to power production. Coupled with the changing quality of the connective tissues comprising the tendons and ligaments, the practical result of this aging-related effect on the program is the diminished capacity to use the clean and snatch productively and the increased likelihood of tendon and joint injury during any explosive or dynamic movements. Sports such as basketball, racquetball, tennis, and soccer that active older people often enjoy begin to pose a risk – one that is fortunately mitigated by getting and staying stronger.

The loss of muscle also means the loss of metabolic machinery; muscles account for most of the calories a healthy person burns daily, and smaller muscles burn fewer calories. Most people don't reduce the amount of food they consume as activity diminishes, and the result is an average increase in body fat of 2.5 to 3% per decade.

The loss of muscle mass has another insidious effect that becomes more perceptible at an advanced age: a loss of proprioception and balance, as well as the obvious loss of strength. The ability to process information the body receives about its position in space is important to performance for an athlete, and in an older adult it is crucial for safety. And the ability to handle the weight of one's own body mass – keeping it in a position over the feet and handling the leverage created between its center of mass and the balance point when its position is changed – is an obvious function of strength. Both these capacities are developed and maintained with exercise that requires balance, coordination, and strength, and barbell training fits this description perfectly.

In fact, barbell training is the best prescription for the prevention of all of these age-related problems. Staying in (or getting into) the gym slows the decay in muscle mass and pushes the onset of pathological atrophy back for decades. Even in the 60- to 90-year-old range, training reduces the loss of muscle mass to less than 5% per decade. Several studies have shown that 80-year-olds who were inactive but began training with weights actually gained muscle mass and improved their strength, proprioception, and balance. This effect was directly related to the amount of leg work included in the program and the resulting improvements in leg strength. Leg strength was also responsible for improving the ability to walk faster in older people. In one study, twelve weeks of strength training was shown to increase walking endurance by 38%, something walking by itself fails to do.

Less obvious to those unfamiliar with weight training is the fact that lifting weights alone will improve flexibility. The majority of apparent flexibility problems in older people are probably strength-related – the body will not use a range of motion it cannot support itself in. Strengthening a complete range of motion returns that ROM to a usable status, while also serving as a very effective dynamic stretch. Osteoarthritis is a clinical condition caused by degenerative changes in joints and a loss of joint function. Patients with arthritis typically reduce their activity level to eliminate discomfort, which results in a continually decreasing activity level and subsequently reduced physical capacity, which eventually results in their not doing anything much at all. Several studies have shown that increasing the strength of the musculature around an affected joint decreases pain and improves function significantly. A number of these studies used squats to reduce knee pain.

In fact, Barbell Training is Big Medicine, to quote Jonathon Sullivan MD PhD from his article for StartingStrength.com:

> "There is much talk in the aging studies community about "compression of morbidity," a shortening of the dysfunctional phase of the death process. Instead of slowly getting weaker and sicker and circling the drain in a protracted, painful descent that can take hellish years or even decades, we can squeeze our dying into a tiny sliver of our life cycle. Instead of slowly dwindling into an atrophic puddle of sick fat, our death can be like a failed last rep at the end of a final set of heavy squats. We can remain strong and vital well into our last years, before succumbing rapidly to whatever kills us. Strong to the end."

A significant consideration for the masters athlete is the reduction in recovery capacity. Attention to recovery factors and avoiding overtraining are particularly important for this population.

When novice masters trainees start a program, the process is the same for that of a younger novice; all the same rules apply, within the context of reduced recovery ability and the initial physical condition of the trainee. Masters athletes may find that intermediate-level programming such as the Texas method works better when adopted sooner than a younger novice would; for a person with age-compromised recovery ability, a weekly increase in load is easier to adapt to than the workout-to-workout progress required by linear progression, and will provide for longer continued improvement. The principles of stress and adaptation still apply, and they always will as long as basic health remains intact.

The bottom line is that unless a person has significant pathology (is terribly sick) or is post-geriatric (no longer living), that person can benefit from a weight training program similar to those used with younger populations at the same level of training advancement.

Figure 9-2. Older adults are not necessarily weak adults. Regular training can lead to a lifetime of strength. Jack Levavi (*left*) and Greg Harper (*right*) demonstrate.

THE NOVICE AND POST NOVICE PROGRAM: ADAPTATIONS FOR OLDER POPULATIONS IN THEIR 50S, 60S, 70S, AND 80S

For the novice trainee under fifty, it is unlikely that much adjustment to the basic program is needed for at least a few months. For the trainee over 50, some adjustments must be made to compensate for the loss of physical strength that occurs as humans age. The two primary differences between old and young trainees are the rate at which recovery and adaptation occur (much slower for older adults), and the inability to perform certain exercises correctly. Sometimes the inability to perform an exercise is due to a pronounced lack of strength, but sometimes it is due to structural limitations or deformities that have been created over time through injury, surgery, neglect, or disease.

We understand that 50 is an arbitrary number, and that classifying everybody as "over 50" or "under 50" is an oversimplification. Most 50-year-old trainees will not need the same level of remediation as a 75-year-old trainee. And it may be true that some trainees in their late 30s or 40s may benefit from these concepts. The point is that older trainees adapt more slowly to training stress, and often start from a much deeper strength and fitness deficit than a novice at 22. This means that most over-50 trainees will require some intelligent age-adjusted programming in order to get stronger on a barbell-based strength program.

When designing a training program for an older trainee, it is useful to start with the basic novice program as the model, and strip things down from there.

Basic Novice Model:

A	B
Squat 3×5	Squat 3×5
Bench Press 3×5	Press 3×5
Deadlift 1×5	Power Clean 5×3

The basic novice program calls for an A/B rotation spread out over a 3-day weekly schedule, i.e. Monday/Wednesday/Friday. For older novices, reducing the frequency of training will be the first and most important adjustment to the program. The standard 48–72 hour window of recovery provided by a 3-day-per-week program is not enough time to recover from a difficult full-body strength training session. Many older novices (generally 40s and early 50s) can tolerate a 3-day-per-week schedule for a few weeks, provided the program starts with fairly conservative weights – and it is definitely recommended that older novices begin with conservative weights. As loads increase and recovery becomes difficult, training frequency must be reduced from the standard 3-days-per-week model to one of the 4 suggested models below. They are listed in order of most aggressive to most conservative.

Model 1. Model 1 is a "1-on-2-off" schedule. Here the lifter trains a day, then takes 2 days off, and then trains again. He trains 3 days per week some weeks, but always has 2 days off after each workout. A sample schedule looks like this:

> Mon – Workout A
> Thurs – Workout B
> Sun – Workout A
> Weds – Workout B
> Sat – Workout A
> Tues – Workout B
> Friday – Workout A

This simple adjustment to normal novice programming has worked wonders for many older trainees. Most novice trainees – young and old – recognize that the Monday workout after the 2-day rest is when they feel the freshest and strongest, so the 2-day rest is used after every workout instead of just Fridays. The downside is that this schedule doesn't fit into some people's lifestyle because of work, family, social commitments, and gym availability.

Model 2. The solution to scheduling difficulties with Model 1 is Model 2. Train twice per week on a fixed schedule. Any 2 non-consecutive days can work, but it is wise to spread these days evenly over the course of the week: Mon/Thurs, Tues/Fri, Weds/Sat evenly spreads the workload out over the course of the week. This allows 2 days off after one session and 3 days off after the second session. Training Tues/Thurs, for instance, is less than ideal. It is likely that one day off is not enough recovery time, and it is possible that 4 days off allows some detraining to occur.

Example:

> Mon – Workout A
> Thurs – Workout B

The choice between Model 1 over Model 2 will be determined by external circumstances, rather than anything about the training itself – there will be little difference in the results from either program.

Model 3. This is an even more conservative approach: the "3 in 2" schedule. The lifter will train Monday & Friday one week, and Wednesday the next. This results in 3 training sessions every 2 weeks, with either 3 or 4 days of recovery after each workout. This model works well for trainees in their late 60s or 70s.

Example:

> Monday – Workout A
> Friday – Workout B
> Wednesday – Workout A
> Monday – Workout B
> Friday – Workout A
> Wednesday – Workout B

Model 4. This is the most conservative approach of all: training once per week. This yields slow progress, but progress nonetheless, and there is virtually no danger of overtraining. Rank novices will benefit from a higher-frequency program because they need more exposure to the lifts, to become more proficient and because it is unlikely that an entire week of recovery is necessary for any trainee who is completely new to strength training. The once-per-week option is best suited to the older lifter in his late 70s or 80s who has been training for several months, who has plateaued his progress, and has decided to concentrate on strength maintenance.

CONSIDERATIONS IN EXERCISE SELECTION

Squats. The most common problem encountered in the older trainee is the initial lack of strength required to reach proper depth. Many trainers and coaches mistakenly attribute the inability of a trainee to squat to depth as lack of flexibility or mobility. This is rarely the case, especially with older populations. It is certainly true that an older trainee *may* be less flexible and mobile than his younger counterpart, since the bottom position of the squat is likely one that doesn't get used more than a couple of times a day, and then with help from the arms. But with the proper stance and leg alignment, it is exceptionally rare for someone to be so inflexible that a parallel squat cannot be attained. Many older novices are simply not strong enough to squat to parallel and then return to the standing position. This situation is compounded by a heavy bodyweight. So how do you start a strength program built around the barbell squat if you cannot do one correct *bodyweight* squat to depth?

There are two methods that work. The first method involves making the difficult part of the ROM easier. ROM not used is ROM not strengthened. This can be done by replacing the squat with the leg press machine until the whole ROM is strong enough to be done with the lifter's bodyweight and a 15-pound training bar. The leg press is not perfect – it completely lacks the balance component of squats, the hips stay in flexion even at lockout, and the squat stance cannot usually be perfectly duplicated. But it does allow the bottom of the squat's ROM to be progressively loaded effectively enough that it will eventually yield the strength to perform a passable bodyweight squat, thus setting the stage for effective barbell training. The leg press is a very good choice if the equipment is available. The empty carriage is warmed up with in normal fashion and the load titrated up to work sets of 10. When the work sets are about equal to the lifter's bodyweight – usually after a month or so – try the squat again, and it should be strong enough to train it effectively. Even extremely weak detrained people can use this method to build sufficient strength through the ROM with whatever increments are necessary to do so. Any gym that deals with geriatric trainees should invest in a good 45-degree leg press. It uses up some floor space, but its function for older and overweight people cannot be duplicated with any other equipment.

A less-than-perfect approach to this problem in the absence of the leg press is the use of the power rack and resistance bands stretched across the pins to provide assistance through the bottom of the ROM. Resistance bands – of the type used to change the effective load on a barbell during the rep – can also be used to deload the trainee's bodyweight during the rep. The bands are stretched across the inside of the rack between the rack pins at whatever height and combination of multiple bands is necessary to intercept the trainee's hips on the way into the bottom of the squat. The elastic stretch of the band assists the lifter in the bottom while allowing the ROM to be moved through for the necessary reps. The resistance is controlled by the height of the bands in the rack and the band tension, again using sets of 10 at work-set-level resistance. The bands are gradually lowered and the tension reduced until the trainee is doing a squat unassisted. This is not nearly as precise a method as plates on a leg press, but it can be made to work if necessary.

The second method uses a bodyweight squat at partial depth that progressively deepens. Over the course of multiple workouts, the depth of the bodyweight squat is lowered until the trainee can hit 3×5 repetitions below parallel with good form. Once this is achieved, a light bar can be used on the back and actual training of the squat can begin.

The best way to set this up is with a bungee cord horizontally strapped across the power rack. The cord should be set to the limit of the trainee's range of motion – often the "quarter squat" position on the first day, about the middle of the hamstring as he stands in front of the rack. The trainee squats down and touches the cord with his glutes and come back up.

This is obviously different from the previous method, where the bands provided assistance with the trainee's bodyweight through the complete ROM. Here, the much-lighter cord only functions as a depth gauge, telling the trainee when the depth target has been reached and serving as a signal to come back up. Each training session the cord is lowered a small amount, until over time the trainee can do 3×5 below parallel. If the power rack has fine hole spacing (1 inch apart) the cord can be set 1 hole lower each training session as a way to drive progress. Anyone experienced with box squatting knows that every inch of increased depth makes a large difference; so it is with this method as well. If the power rack has more typical 3-inch hole spacing, moving down a hole each training session will be too aggressive, so the floor of the rack will have to be shimmed with mats to control the increase in depth to the 1-inch standard.

The older, overweight, or very weak trainee cannot be expected to add more than about 1 inch of depth per training session. Be patient with the process and the full squat will come. It is also important that squat mechanics are correct, even at partial depth. Hips back, knees out, and driving up with the hips are what make any squat work, so this progression must ensure that everything necessary for a full-depth squat has been used correctly, and thus strengthened enough to make full depth possible.

The bungee cord is the preferred method for a progressively deeper partial squat progression, as opposed to having the trainee squat to a box or bench. The box allows the trainee to relax at the bottom of the movement, rock backwards and forwards, wallow around, and gather momentum to come back up. Even for advanced competitive lifters, the ability to "stay tight" at the bottom of a box squat requires a tremendous amount of hamstring strength and focus, neither of which an older novice lifter possesses. Novices taught to squat to a box can very easily become dependent on it, and never learn how to rebound off their hamstrings and drive up with their hips. Since the bungee cord acts only as a marker for depth and is not strong enough to provide any assistance at the bottom, tightness is learned from the beginning and the transition to regular squats is much more fluid.

It must be noted that light barbells are of the utmost importance for the older novice. Going from bodyweight squats to a 45-lb barbell is much too aggressive an increase for an overweight or deconditioned trainee of any age. The best way to discourage this demographic is to fail to invest in the equipment necessary to train them, and then assuming it's their problem and not the coach's.

Shoulder flexibility is another common problem associated with the squat in older trainees. The inability to properly hold the bar in place for a low-bar position squat is almost universal in this age group. For those with arthritis, an extreme kyphosis, or surgically-repaired shoulders, the range of motion necessary for this exercise may not ever be achievable. In this case, the coach must carefully experiment with a high-bar position back squat. If the high-bar squat is the primary exercise, the very important differences in the two exercises will affect programming. High-bar squats place significantly more stress on the knees than low-bar squats, due to the differences in their mechanics. Knees, being weaker and smaller than hips, are very sensitive in older trainees. Coaches should be careful to progress very conservatively on high-bar squats, and if squats are being done multiple times per week, it is a good idea to limit the heavy day to just once per week.

Deadlifts. This very important exercise should be done by every trainee that can, and this includes almost everybody. Many people who cannot squat because of knee pathology can still quite successfully deadlift significant weights, and the use of very light bars and 5–10 lb bumper plates make the movement accessible to nearly anyone. For those novice trainees who are using one of the remedial squat programs, deadlifts are an essential component of the progression to full range of motion loaded squats. The two remedial methods (the assisted ROM and progressive partials) do not adequately stress the hamstrings, glutes, and low back the way full depth loaded squats do. So deadlifts become the primary stressor of the posterior chain for these trainees, and it is especially critical to master and progress the deadlift as rapidly as possible.

As mentioned before, deadlifts can normally be done every session for the first few weeks of the novice program. But as strength increases on the lift, so does the stress it places on the lower back. For an older trainee especially, chronic inflammation in the lower back or SI joints can become a problem if the stress is not properly managed. For many older trainees, doing 1–2 sets of deadlifts once per week is all the stress that is needed to drive progress, and is all the stress than can be recovered from on a weekly basis. And back extensions and situps done later in the week may do more harm than good for an older lifter with a "glass back."

A light barbell with light "training" plates can be loaded to as little as 25 lbs. In almost all cases, even the most deconditioned trainees can deadlift 25 lbs for a set of 5 reps. It is actually quite common for people unable to squat their own bodyweight to be able to deadlift 40 kg the first week of training, and for most people unable to do so, the reason is not physical capacity, but fear of the weight. For severely compromised and perhaps apprehensive elderly people, it is possible to deadlift as little as 10 –15 lbs using a kettlebell. The reasons for using kettlebells would be based on the availability of equipment – a 45-lb bar and 10-lb bumper plates weighs 65 lbs, and this may indeed be a little too heavy for some very old people. Light kettlebells in the 10–50 lb range are now widely available at most commercial sporting goods stores, and may be faster and easier to access than light training bars and training plates. The kettlebell allows the weight to be easily placed at the mid-foot position and the lift to be performed with approximately the same mechanics as with a barbell. The stance may be slightly wider with the kettlebell deadlift, but it is *not* pulled with a wide stance like a sumo-style deadlift.

The Press. The two primary problems associated with the press are the lack of appropriate equipment and the lack of adequate shoulder flexibility, as mentioned earlier. The vast majority of older trainees of both sexes cannot start the press with a 45-pound bar, and access to bars light enough to accommodate the strength of the trainee is obviously very important. For older lifters, especially older females, the gym must be furnished with 10-kg or perhaps even 5-kg bars that allow for proper instruction, warm-up, and work set selection. These must be accompanied by plates that allow the loading of 1 lb/0.5 kg increments, so that steady progress is still possible in the absence of a teen-age male's adaptation capacity. If proper equipment to press is not available, its acquisition should be made a priority.

If the trainee is actually not strong enough to press an 11-lb bar, the simplest solution is to omit the exercise at first and focus solely on the bench press for upper body strength. Training the bench press every workout for a short time is a good way to get the chest, shoulders, and triceps strong enough to put an actual barbell overhead; 2–4 weeks of bench pressing every workout should be enough time for most people to build enough upper body strength to press a light bar overhead 5 times. Once 5 reps can be performed, the regular AB rotation of pressing and benching can begin.

A severe lack of mobility in the shoulders is really a very typical problem for novices in their 60s and up. Life seems to take a heavy toll on shoulders and knees, and knees are easily replaced with perfectly functional prostheses these days – shoulders, not so much. Shoulder osteoarthritis often prevents a functional lockout position from being reached, and if the problem is true bony arthritis, the situation cannot be corrected. The bar cannot be completely locked out at the top of the lift and the final position will be well forward of the balance point vertical to the glenohumeral joint, a very stressful position that should not be used by anyone to press. If the problem is soft-tissue extensibility, it can be cleared up with a few workouts, practicing the lifts, and some stretching. But if the problems are structural, practice and stretching aren't going to help, and it may be quite harmful to keep trying. If the ROM reduction is minor, then the best advice is to "do the best you can" – press as much weight as possible within the confines of the joints' limited mobility, if it doesn't hurt. It is important to understand that the limit weight of a press that cannot be properly locked out in balance will be much lower than for a full-ROM press. The weights will become too heavy to hold at a point forward of the shoulder joint, and pain in the shoulders, traps, and even the low back are likely consequences. If the ROM limitations are severe, it may be that pressing cannot be done with a weight significant enough to be of any value, and the lift must be excluded from the program.

The Bench Press. This valuable weight room staple provides the older trainee an opportunity to handle the most significant weight of all the upper body exercises. If the press is for some reason not possible, the bench press becomes even more important as the primary movement for upper-body strength. But aging shoulders are often aggravated by bench presses too; it is not uncommon for the bench to cause shoulder pain in some trainees, or to irritate preexisting shoulder injuries. These problems can sometimes be remedied by altering the grip width – narrower is usually better for the sensitive shoulder.

Power Cleans. One of the most common questions concerning the application of the basic novice program to older populations is about whether or not to include power cleans. There are reasons to exclude the power clean from the program, some of which have already been discussed. For the older novice trainee, development of explosive power is not a realistic expectation of the training program. More specifically, cleans and snatches may present technical problems in properly racking the bar for older trainees with poor flexibility. Wrists, elbows, shoulders, and knees can take an unnecessary amount of abuse when stubbornly trying to master these exercises. The decision to clean or snatch will ultimately be left up to the lifter and coach. For the 50-year-old male lifter with good fitness, decent strength, and no injuries, the Olympic lifts are a perfectly acceptable part of his program. For the 50-year-old overweight and completely deconditioned female, it is unlikely that cleans or snatches will provide enough value to offset the risk of doing them. In general, it can be assumed that the older the trainee, the less benefit the Olympic lifts contribute, and for trainees that are late 60s and older, there is no reason whatsoever to include them in a novice strength program.

Chin-Ups/Pull-Ups. Chins are an extremely useful assistance exercise. They provide a complete workout for the lats, arms, and grip. But for many older novices, particularly those who are also overweight, full-bodyweight chin-ups and pull-ups are not possible, and working up to them is not a realistic goal. The most suitable alternative is the lat pulldown machine. If the trainee can do chin-ups, then he should do them, and there is no reason to use the lat machine. If he can't, lat pulls are done for 3 sets of 8–10 repetitions at the end of the workout. Various handles are available for most lat machines, but the most comprehensive grip is the supine chin grip, about shoulder width, palms facing the lifter. This allows the greatest range of motion for the lats and incorporates the biceps to a greater degree than any other version of the exercise. This grip can potentially cause some wrist or elbow pain, especially for those who have had an injury, and an alternative grip should be used in this case.

If the gym does not have a lat pulldown machine (this would be an unusual commercial gym), hanging rows can be used to get some work on the upper back and arms. A bar set inside the rack at squat height can accommodate this exercise, and 3 to 4 sets of 10–12 reps are appropriate.

SETS AND REPS

Older novices will benefit from sets of five reps just like trainees of any other age as their base rep range. The potential for severe muscle soreness and inflammation is much *much* higher for an over-50 trainee, these people do not tolerate soreness as well as younger lifters, and higher-rep training (8–12) tends to cause more soreness and more inflammation than lower-rep training due to the greater volume of eccentric work. For the basic barbell exercises, especially for squats and deadlifts, there is little need for older trainees to use more than 5 reps per set. Three sets across for squats, presses, and bench presses, and 1 work set of 5 for deadlifts will work well for older novices. The standard novice program for a beginning trainee looks like this:

Example 1: Deconditioned 55 year old male

Phase 1: Rotate A/B workout on Mon-Wed-Fri schedule

Workout A	Workout B
Squat 3×5	Squat 3×5
Bench Press 3×5	Press 3×5
Deadlift 1×5	Lat Pulldowns 3×10*

*Deadlift 1×5 on workout A and B until progress slows, then introduce lat pulldowns after 2–4 weeks.

Phase 2: Reduce Frequency to twice per week (Monday/Thursday)

Monday	Thursday
Squat 3×5	Squat 3×5 (20% reduction from Monday)
Bench Press 3×5	Press 3×5
Lat Pulldowns 3×10	Deadlift 1×5

Example 2: Overweight 65 year old female

Phase 1: Trainee too weak to squat or press overhead

Monday	Thursday
Leg Press 3×10	Leg Press 3×10
Bench Press 3×5	Bench Press 3×5
Deadlift 1×5	Deadlift 1×5

Phase 2: Trainee progresses to squat and press, reduces deadlift frequency

Monday	Thursday
Squat 3×5	Light Squat 3×5
Bench Press 3×5	Press 3×5
Lat Pulldowns 3×10	Deadlift 1×5

Example 3: Underweight 78-year-old male, severe arthritis in shoulders

Perform the following every 4–5 days (follow the "3 in 2" schedule):

> Deadlift 1×5 (begin program with light 3×5)
> Bench Press 3×5
> DB Front Squat* 3×5 or Leg Press 3×10
> Lat Pulldowns 3×10

*Dumbbell front squats are a squat variant that can be performed with trainees who cannot effectively squat with a barbell. Dumbbells are held on the shoulders in the "front squat" position. Because this exercise is limited to relatively light weights only, it is relegated to assistance-exercise status and placed after the deadlifts. The deadlift becomes the primary strength exercise in the program and should be done prior to squatting, when legs are the least fatigued. Before dumbbells are added to this exercise, the trainee should be able to do 3×5 on a below-parallel bodyweight squat.

As trainees progress and grow stronger, the 3-sets-across method may become more difficult to recover from, both throughout the week and within the workout itself. There will come a point where there is a need for an alternative method to add weight to the bar, while keeping enough volume in the program to drive continued adaptation.

Post-Novice Programming. There are a few very important points to keep in mind when structuring a post-novice program for an older adult:

1) Older adults need frequent breaks from very hard training.

2) Older adults do not benefit from high-volume workouts.

3) Older adults detrain very quickly when intensity is reduced.

4) Weights must be progressed very conservatively.

Keeping these points in mind, post-novice programs for older adults must fluctuate between "hard" and "easy" workouts, volume must be moderate, and intensity must be kept high.

Phase 3: Introduce post-novice sets and reps

Monday	Thursday
Squat 5×5 (ascending sets)	Light Squat 4×5 (ascending sets)
Bench Press 1×3–5 + 2×5 back off	Press 1×3–5 + 2×5 back off
Lat Pulldown 3×10	Deadlift 1×3–5 + 1×5 back off

Ascending Sets of 5 (The Starr 5x5). There are 2 methods which fit these criteria and have proven to work well for this population. The first method is to work up to single working set, using ascending sets of 5 repetitions. Once the trainee achieves a new 5RM, he will add weight to the bar, but the reps for the top set at the new weight will drop to a double or triple. The following week, he keeps the same weight on the bar, and assuming he got a triple the previous week, does 4 reps. On the third week, the weight again stays the same, but for 5 reps. The second workout of the week takes each lift up to the last warm-up set and stops there. The following example is for a 55-year-old male trainee who ends his novice progression at 225×5×3. The following week he would do these heavy-day numbers:

Week 1	Week 2	Week 3	Week 4
45×5×2	45×5×2	45×5×2	45×5×2
135×5	135×5	135×5	135×5
165×5	165×5	165×5	165×5
190×5	190×5	190×5	195×5
210×5	210×5	210×5	215×5
230×3	230×4	230×5	235×3

The light-day workout stops at the last warm-up set for heavy day.

Back-off Method. A second method is to warm up to the work set for the day, followed by 2–3 back-off sets with a 5–10% reduction in load.

Using the same hypothetical trainee, the progression looks like this:

Week 1	Week 2	Week 3	Week 4
45×5×2	45×5×2	45×5×2	45×5×2
135×5	135×5	135×5	135×5
165×2	165×2	165×2	165×2
190×1	190×1	190×1	195×1
210×1	210×1	210×1	215×1
230×3	230×4	230×5	235×3
205×5×2	205×5×2	205×5×2	210×5×2

Both methods fulfill the criteria laid out previously – heavy/light workouts, moderate volume, sustained high intensity, and a conservative pace.

When a trainee drops from a work set of 5 at 225 to a double or triple at 230, intensity has been increased, but the physical and mental stress has been eased a bit by the volume reduction. The first week or two at the new weight should be perceived as "easier" than the last week's set of 5. At this pace, the older trainee has 3–4 weeks to adapt to the new load before moving up in weight again, but performance is still increasing with the rep added each week.

The primary difference between these two methods is the placement of the volume work. The Starr Method places the volume in the warm-ups, prior to the work set, and is the easier of the two methods. It works well for squatting with older trainees – the ascending sets of 5 provide an excellent warm up for stiff legs and low backs, and provide plenty of opportunity for practice and coaching. The back-off method places the volume after the primary work set of the day. This is the more stressful of the two methods since it involves more sets; the lifter still has to do a number of warm-up sets to get to his work set, and then do additional back-off sets. The back-off method works well for bench presses and presses, and even deadlifts. If back-off work is done for deadlifts, it should be limited to just one set. And the two methods can obviously be combined, Starr for squats and back-off for presses and pulls.

An important similarity in the two methods is that both accomplish all the volume and intensity work in the same session for each lift. In a program such as the Texas Method, there is a day for high volume, and a day for high intensity. Although one day is lighter than the other, neither day is light – the lifter has two very stressful workouts in the same week. Older trainees cannot recover from a workload this aggressive. If the older trainee is to perform the same lift multiple times per week, it should be arranged in terms of heavy/light or hard/easy, never volume/intensity.

Post-Rehabilitation Trainees

All athletes who train hard enough to compete will get injured. This is the sorry truth of the matter, and anyone dissuaded from competition by this fact would not have made a good competitor anyway. Progress involves hard training, and hard training involves pushing past previous barriers to new levels of performance. To the extent that this can cause injury, successful competitive athletics is dangerous. It is a danger that can and must be managed, but it is important to recognize the fact that athletes get hurt. If they want to continue to be athletes afterwards, it is equally important to understand how to manage and rehabilitate injuries successfully so that they don't end a career. Also, accidents happen, both related and unrelated to training.

Severely damaged tissue cannot be repaired through rehabilitation. Rather, the surrounding healthy tissue is strengthened in order to take over the load once carried by the now non-functional tissue. If someone has a survivable heart attack, such as a myocardial infarction, part of the heart muscle dies. The dead tissue no longer contributes to the contraction of the heart, but the heart continues to beat and deliver blood. Immediately after the infarction, the efficiency with which the heart delivers blood is low, but without missing a beat, the remaining healthy, functional heart muscle begins to adapt because it continues to be loaded, provided that you fail to die. In order to adapt to the missing force generation capacity of the damaged tissue, the remaining muscle contracts more forcefully and rapidly increases in mass for weeks and months until the force of contraction is counterbalanced by the tensile strength of the collagen scar, completing the remodeling process. The end result is the recovery of the heart's ability to generate contractile force even having lost some of its original muscle irrecoverably. The change in contractile geometry of the ventricle will not actually allow the return to 100% of normal function. This altered geometry, even with thicker walls after hypertrophy, is inherently less efficient than the original ventricle, but it functions well enough that normal activities can eventually be resumed. And in fact, the resumption of normal activities is what drives the *ability* to resume normal activities.

Severe muscle damage in other parts of the body constitutes a similar but less dire situation. If a muscle is severely damaged to the point of necrosis, not only will the remaining tissue adapt to the loss of function of the damaged tissue by increasing its functional capacity, but the surrounding muscles that normally aid the damaged muscle in its biomechanical role will assume part of the workload. This is classically illustrated in the scientific and medical literature in "ablation" experiments, where the gastrocnemius muscle (major calf muscle) is removed (usually in frogs, not people) and the underlying soleus and plantaris muscles rapidly adapt and assume the load once carried by the gastrocnemius. It is well documented that these newly stressed muscles change dramatically, both chemically and structurally, after ablation in order to return the whole mechanical system to "normal" function. The recovered structures are not as good as the original equipment, but they function at a high percentage of the original capacity.

In both the previous scenarios, recovery of function occurred after only a short period of reduced loading, essentially the duration of time needed for the resolution of inflammation and any other blatant pathology. A rapid return to an increasing functional load is required to induce adaptation and recovery. Even in the infarcted heart, a return to normal load represents a functional overload of the remaining tissue: the same amount of force must initially be generated by a smaller muscle mass, so it is under a higher relative load. The adaptation that facilitates the return to normal function is a response to the stress to the system produced by the injured area's decrease in function. The injury that necessitates the compensation is the source of the stress to the surrounding tissues, and they respond by adapting to the new demands placed on them. Without the injury, the adaptation would not occur, just as no adaptation ever occurs in the absence of stress.

While caution is necessary to avoid further injury, the belief that rehabilitation can occur in the absence of overload represents a failure to comprehend the basic tenets of the physiology and mechanics of the living human body. Again, we have evolved over time to be able to remodel damaged tissue while it is being utilized – heart, liver, kidney, bone, and muscle are necessary for sustained existence, and had we not been able to heal it without bed rest, hospitals, and doctors, we would have been eaten by the hyenas a long time ago.

Most injuries experienced in the weight room, on the field, and in daily life do not rise to the severity of necrosis. They are inconvenient, painful, aggravating, and potentially expensive to deal with, but they do not alter the quality of life for a significant period of time. But the same principles apply to healing them that apply to more severe injuries, because the mechanisms that cause them to heal are the same. The concept of "letting" an injury heal beyond an initial few days reflects a lack of understanding of the actual processes that cause the return to function. A less severe injury that does not involve tissue necrosis nonetheless involves an overload of the immediate ability of the compromised tissue, thus stimulating the processes that cause repair. In this particular instance, care must be taken to ensure that the structure that is healing receives its normal proportion of the load, because the object is to return this particular structure to full function, not to allow the adjacent structures to assume the load and thus preventing the injured tissue from healing fully. This is accomplished by the enforcement of very strict technique during exercise of the injured area. It hurts more this way, but the long-term return to full function depends on the correct amount of stress to the injured area.

During supervised rehabilitation, the workloads used should be light enough to allow recovery of function locally, within the injured tissue, but this load will not be stressful enough systemically to maintain advanced fitness levels. When the athlete is released to unrestricted activity, enough detraining has occurred that a change in programming will be required. Six to eight weeks in rehabilitation can result in the loss of enough overall performance to warrant return to a program of simple progression, even for an advanced athlete. Once pre-injury or pre-disease performance levels have been regained, a return to normal training at that level can follow. As discussed earlier, strength is a resilient quality, and strength lost through detraining can be recovered much more rapidly than it was initially gained.

Remember our definition of the stress/recovery/adaptation process from chapter 1:

> **Stress** *is an event that produces a significant change in the environment of an organism, sufficient to disrupt the physiological state that exists within an organism in equilibrium with its current environmental conditions.* **Adaptation** *to the stress event is the organism's modification of its physiology to compensate for the new environmental conditions as it* **recovers** *from the stress.*

This definition provides an insight into effective rehab: it must be sufficiently *stressful* to cause an *adaptation* if it is to yield a return to a state that is better than before, the process of which facilitates a return to the previously high level of performance. The state of the injured athlete is lower than before he was injured, so the current/injured level of performance must be challenged if improvement upon it is to occur. This is the same *training* process that yielded the heightened performance before the injury, and it must be undertaken again, as unpleasant a prospect as that may be for the injured athlete.

The biggest mistake made by therapists is the incorrect application of this concept. Many of them seem to regard the injury itself as the stressor, and fail to realize that 1) the stress of injury has already been adapted to, that 2) the subsequent lack of training (detraining) stimulus is a stress that has likewise been adapted to, and 3) that the rehab they provide must be sufficiently intense to produce the stress/recovery/adaptation response that took the athlete to his previous level of performance. "Rehab" – in the sense an athlete uses the term – cannot do its job unless it provides sufficient stress to cause the adaptation to that stress, just like it did the first time, and mistaking the stress of the injury that occurred days, weeks, or months in the past for something that must be allowed to rest more or heal a little bit longer is a failure to understand the fundamental processes that govern performance.

Authors

Mark Rippetoe is the author of *Starting Strength: Basic Barbell Training, Practical Programming for Strength Training, Strong Enough?, Mean Ol' Mr. Gravity*, and numerous journal, magazine and internet articles. He has worked in the fitness industry since 1978, and has been the owner of the Wichita Falls Athletic Club since 1984. He was in the first group certified by the National Strength and Conditioning Association as a CSCS in 1985, and the first to formally relinquish that credential in 2009. Rip was a competitive powerlifter for ten years, and has coached many lifters and athletes, and many thousands of people interested in improving their strength and performance. He conducts seminars on this method of barbell training around the country.

Andy Baker is the owner of Kingwood Strength and Conditioning in Kingwood, Texas. He has a degree in Sport and Health Science from American Military University. Andy attended Texas A&M University before joining the Marine Corps in 2003. He saw two combat deployments in Iraq before finishing his degree in 2007. Shortly afterward he opened KSC, a private training facility near Houston that offers barbell training to competitive athletes and the general public, as well as program consultation for competitive lifters. Andy is a competitive powerlifter. He lives in Kingwood with his wife Laura and two kids, and spends the tiny amount of spare time he has fishing and hunting.

Stef Bradford, PhD is the operations manager of The Aasgaard Company and Community Organizer for StartingStrength.com. She received her doctorate in pharmacology from Duke University in 2004. She has been strength training most of her life and a competitive Olympic weightlifter for several years. She teaches barbell training throughout the country.

Credits

PHOTOGRAPHS

by Thomas Campitelli: Figures 3-1, 9-1, 9-2

ILLUSTRATIONS

by Stef Bradford unless otherwise noted.

by Jason Kelly Figure 4-2

EMG and force diagrams used in Figure 5-2 courtesy of Jaqueline Limberg and Alexander Ng of Marquette University

Index

C

D

Olympic lifters and, 70
partial movements, 70
partial squat for, 70-71
purpose of, 72-73
synergy and, 70
variables in, 70
Exercises (intermediate)
ancillary or assistance, 70
lower-back-specific, 109
training for powerlifting and, 107
Exercises, large-scale multi-joint, 69
Explosive sports, HLM program (intermediate), **167-168**

F

Fascia described, 45
"Fast-twitch" muscle fiber, (Type II A & B), 47, *T 4-1, 47*
Fatigue, **19-20**
Fatty acids, essential, **26**
inflammatory process and, 26
Field sports, training needs for, 174
"Fitness" franchises, 3-4
Flexibility
defined, 76
how much?, 77
maintained, 77-78
training through full ROM and, 77-78
Flexibility from warm-up, 77-78
hip and knee, 77
range-of-motion and, 77
Football, endurance and, 64, 66
Football lineman
power output calculated for, 36
strength application for, 34
stronger/bigger, 39
Football play, work to rest ratios and, 43
Football players, advanced programming and, 72
"Football-specific" programs, performance and, 72
Force production/high-rep set EMG, *Fig 5-2, 74*
Front squats, Olympic trainee (intermediate), 109
"Functional Training" facilities, 3-4
"Functional Training specialists"
ipsilateral/contralateral movements and, 42
lunge derived exercises and, 42
unilateral exercises for sports and, 42

G

General adaptation syndrome, **13-19**
General considerations (intermediate), **107-115**
exercises for, 109-110
variation for, 114-115
Genetic potential defined, 59

Genetic traits, expression of, 59
Genetics
elite designation and, 9
stress adaptation and, 6
variations in training due to, 9
Genotype
defined relative to phenotype, 59
functional phenotypic expression of, 6
optimum expression of, 6
successful marathon competitor and, 60
unfulfilled, 15
Glycogen stores
fuel from, 25
hydration and, 26
hypertrophy and, 52
Glycolysis, 48
ATP produced by, 50
Glute/ham raises, 89
Goodmornings, 142, 143, 145, 164, 194
"Go-heavy-or-go-home" approach, 31
Going backward: detraining, **61-62**
Growth hormone, 56

H

Health clubs, staff, equipment, training in, 3
Healing from an injury, 236-238
Heart attack, survivable (myocardial infarction), 237
your hearts rehabilitation after a, 237
"Heavy" & "light" defined, 157
High-intensity glycolytic-type work, 58
Hockey, endurance and, 64
HLM (heavy-light-medium) powerlifting program #1, **165-166**
HLM powerlifting program #2, **167**
HLM program for explosive sports, **168**
HLM & adding training days, 168-169
frequency variation for the, **170-175**
intensity variation for the, 170
Hockey, endurance and, 64
Homeostasis
caloric intake & output balance for, 25
overtraining & reestablishing, 21
Homeostasis disruption
advanced trainees and, 8-9
advanced trainee's recovery from, 20
already-adapted-to load and, 15
elite athlete's and, 67
exercise, caloric need and, 25
force adaptation and, 7
glycolytic intensity and, 59
maximum technical performance and, 44
musculoskeletal discomfort and, 14
novice trainees and, 14

N

O

R